THE DENVER PRESS CLUB

150 Years of Printer's Devils, Bohemians, and Ghosts

Alan J. Kania

Alan J. Kania

To order additional copies of this book, contact:
Xlibris
1-888-795-4274
www.Xlibris.com
Orders@Xlibris.com
547160

Dedicated to fellow Club Historians
Thomas F. Dawson (1880)
and
Robert G. Seymour (1922)

and Carmen Green, Joe Diner, Jimmy Wong, James "The Gracious Greek" Fillas, Tom Foutch and all the other eccentric club managers, stewards, and bartenders who held the Denver Press Club emotionally sane and properly hydrated for 150 years.

With gratitude to my wife, Terry; David Primus of the Gunnison (Colorado) Pioneer Museum, Colorado film historian Howie Movshovitz, the library staffs of the Denver Public Library Western History Collection and History Colorado; Bill York-Feirn, Tom Foutch, Ken Johnson, Judith DeLorca, Jane C. Harper, Barb Head, and Mike McClanahan for all their advice, support, and researched-contributions to the development of this story.

COVER PHOTO: The president of the United States tried his hand behind a hand-crank newsreel motion-picture camera in Denver, Colorado while visiting with the Denver Press Club. "Warren G. Harding, movie operator," 1920, photograph, https://www.loc.ov/item2016828310/.

BACK COVER PHOTOS: Author Alan J. Kania; 2001 caricature by Jean Tool; photograph by permission of Platinum Studio.

CONTENTS

FOREWORD

"Eccentrics"

The beloved Denver radio and newspaper journalist, and long-time press club regular Gene Amole, may have introduced the history of the oldest press club in the country with his signatory one-word lede that opened each of his *Rocky Mountain News* columns.   *lead*

"News is only the first rough draft of history," has been attributed to many different sources. Alan Barth, an editorial writer for the *Washington Post,* used the phrase in a review of Harold L. Ickes' *Autobiography of a Curmudgeon,* an exposé published in a 1943 edition of the *New Republic.* Not only is this story of the Denver Press Club a rough draft of Colorado history, it is also a biography of Rocky Mountain curmudgeons, eccentrics, and purveyors of political policy.

I have intentionally relied upon the journalistic talents of Denver's pioneers of the Fourth Estate to provide the foundation for this story. Since 1867, a limited number of official Denver Press Club records and board minutes have survived archival disasters. Much of the history of the Denver Press Club had to be re-constructed by viewing most of Denver's unindexed newspapers preserved on microfilm at the Denver Public Library. When I began staring at the microfilm readers, I didn't need reading glasses; today I do. During the latter years of this research, I have been relieved from optical tedium by numerous digital newspaper databases that are available and searchable through online subscription services. As the number of digital newspapers grow for the benefit of researchers, so will the anecdotal stories of the Denver Press Club.

The information for this story was culled from local and national newspapers, a handful of authors who found our story interesting enough to publish in books that included references to the press club, and through the few surviving board minutes and reports that have been preserved. The stalwarts of the club added their recollections to these pages even when some of their stories became more colorful with each passing version of the events. While some aspects of the history of the Denver Press Club are fluid with supportive information from newspaper accounts, personal anecdotes, and official board minutes; other stories may look like bullet-points with little context. Omitting these random pearls-and-perils may appeal to the more literary wordsmiths among us, but it would miss a hodgepodge of historical information that shouldn't be left on the cutting-room editorial floor.

Philosopher, essayist, poet, and novelist Jorge Agustín Nicolás Ruiz de Santayana y Borrá (or George Santayana as his American friends knew him) wrote, "Those who cannot remember the past are condemned to repeat it."[1] The story of the Denver Press Club will continue to grow as more archival documentation is found and will provide lessons for future press-club members and boards. With this book as a starting point, the next editions will hopefully nullify Sr. Santayana's concern.

Newspaper stories and official board minutes provide semi-formal and formal accounts of past press-club events. But since this is also a story of the eccentric characters whose finger-tips carried the indelible tell-tale mark of printers' ink; their anecdotes and reputations must also be preserved in this tale. Sometimes the language of the era is cringe-worthy with its racist overtones. As enlightenment very slowly catches up to us, I've retained the racist language as a historical reminder of the progress we have made and the long journey that still lies ahead of us. I've also provided long quotes that were often originally written in the passive voice. This is a style frowned upon by many modern editors, and journalists; but provides the flavor of a flamboyant writing style instead of contemporary brevity of ideas. The soliloquies of O. J. Goldrick's rambling run-on sentences are far more fascinating than a 140-character Tweet or the minimal participation of a "Like" icon on a Facebook page.

"A press club is an organization for journalists and others professionally engaged in the production and dissemination of news. A press club whose membership is defined by the press of a given country may be known as a National Press Club of that country,"[2] the all-wise Wikipedia resource explained.

The Denver Press Club successfully rode the changes from an informal fraternal-type organization that morphed into a national organization that sought to meet the economic and social needs of its members during turbulent times. Established just a few years after the first cabins were built along the Cherry Creek, "A" press club (as it was described in a November 1867 newspaper) was formed in the basement of a Denver grocery store. What was described as rot-gut, or walapite wheat whisky was served in a below-ground escape where newspapermen, who were often expatriate pressmen from the United States print shops, gathered. If they couldn't carve out a niche as communicators in the fledgling frontier communities, they sometimes tried their hand panning for gold along nearby mountain streams, much like their California brothers did a decade earlier. They all followed a long line of writers who emigrated from Eastern smog-laden cities to Colorado to recover from life-shortening respiratory diseases.

Despite the fierce competition among the newspapermen, the creation of a press club in Denver provided a sense of familiar conviviality in a frontier town outside the boundaries of the thirty-seven states that comprised the so-called civilized portion of the country.

With the admission of Colorado into statehood in 1876, greater attention fell upon the official mouthpieces of the community. If Denver was to gain respectability as more than a wild-west supply town, community and business leaders had to rely on how their enterprises were portrayed. Few eastern establishments wanted to do business around the image of gunfights, saucy ladies, and spittoons perpetuated by novelists Edward S. Ellis, Bret Harte, Karl May, Joaquin Miller (Cincinnatus Heine Miller) and others who were popular for their exaggerated portrayals of the wild West.

The Denver Press Club was known for many things, depending on the public image of the press at the time. It was an escape for editors and publishers to get a few hours of peace from irate advertisers, subscribers, and readers. It was a place of good-natured camaraderie among competing local newspapers. It was a place where presidents, who came from journalistic backgrounds, could shed the constant en garde politician vs. reporter relationship and enjoy off-the-record discourse away from the public eye. It was a place where national and international experts came together with the public and engaged in productive social and political discourse on current events without meaningless blather. And it was a safety net for notoriously underpaid and under-appreciated journalists looking for a cheap meal to support themselves and their families when times were tough.

One occasional visitor to Denver was the colorful Oscar Wilde. "There is much to be said in favor of modern journalism," he wrote in *The Critic as Artist,* Part II, in 1891. "By giving us the opinions of the uneducated, it keeps us in touch with the ignorance of the community. By carefully chronicling the current events of contemporary life, it shows us of what very little importance such events are. By invariably discussing the unnecessary, it makes us understand what things are requisite for culture, and what are not." When the *Colorado Daily Tribune* learned that Wilde would come to Denver in 1892, the newspaper implored the city to treat him with the civility due a stranger and guest. "It is perhaps a good thing that Denver has no university or college to turn out a mob of fresh young asses to insult a gentleman who has probably forgotten more than they could possibly be capable of learning."[3]

Several articles written by William Newton Byers, who served both as Denver's first editor/publisher and as the first president of the Denver Press Club, were compiled for the Introduction of this book. The articles have been editorially consolidated by this author.

The Denver Press Club was established in 1867 as a men-only press organization. The Denver Woman's Press Club was founded in 1898 as one of the oldest women's press clubs in the country. Using many newspapers from the Denver area as primary sources of information, I found references to the "Denver Press Club" that mentioned women members. Because the articles were written at a time when women were not members of the Denver Press Club, I can only surmise that the articles should have clarified that it was the Denver WOMAN'S Press Club that was being portrayed. But things became complicated when the appearance of the "Writers' Club" began to appear in the newspaper reports years after the actual Denver Woman's Press Club was incorporated. The issue is further complicated with references to the "Denver Women's Writers' Club" (and other combinations of names) that could have been a name-combination of two possible organizations for female writers. The same occurred with reference to the Colorado Press Club as a combination of the Colorado Press Association and the Denver Press Club``.

The Writers' Club was a group of women working in the press world, but there was no association that this was a different name for the Denver Woman's Press Club. Without available documentation to combine the two organizations of women writers, I had to go the path that documented research led me in describing the Writers' Club was a separate group that may have morphed back into the Denver Woman's Press Club. It is my job to report the history of the Denver Press Club with minimal re-writing of primary-source research; readers can provide their own interpretation of history.

The story of the Denver Press Club crosses several cultural transformations in American life where minorities were sometimes described in less than humanistic terms. While some readers may respond to some semantics used in this book with some disdain, I prefer to remain faithful to the language of the day as a teachable experience.

For retired editors, grab a fistful of red-and-blue pencils, pour yourself a glass of Taos Lightning, and immerse yourselves in what is either the story of the oldest press club in the country, or what some may describe as the longest running poker game, peppered with anecdotes and a semi-edited collection of editorial faux-pas from this city's celebrated journalistic storytellers.

1   Wikipedia
2   Wikipedia
3   *Colorado Daily Tribune*, February 13, 1892, p. 4

INTRODUCTION

Early Journalism in Colorado[1]
Wm. N. Byers
First editor of the *Rocky Mountain News* and early president of the Denver Press Club

In common with the fortune of all other pioneer undertakings and enterprises, the press met with great trials, difficulties and misfortunes. The *Rocky Mountain News,* as is well known, was the first newspaper established in this region of [the] country. It was my fortune to inaugurate that enterprise, though others were temporarily associated with me in the undertaking.

The pioneer newspapers of Denver were the *Rocky Mountain News* and the *Cherry Creek Pioneer.* Both went to press first upon the evening of April 22, 1859. The question as to which came from the press first—that is, the first printed sheet—has been often discussed and disputed, but our information at the time was that the *News* had priority by about twenty minutes.

In February 1859, Dr. George C. Monell of Omaha; Thomas Gibson of Fontanelle, Nebraska; and myself agreed to purchase a press and material to start a paper in the new mines. At Belleview [Bellevue], a few miles below Omaha, on the Missouri River, there was such a printing office as we wanted lying idle—the relic of a starved-to-death newspaper. Such things are not common, but that was one. The plant for the *News* was purchased at Bellview [Bellevue], Nebraska for Dr. Monell, Thomas Gibson and myself, under the firm name of William N. Byers & Co. Mr. Gibson and myself came with it to Denver. Dr. Monell started from

Omaha a couple of months later to join us, but at the crossing of the South Platte, now Julesburg, he joined the great, bright army of "go-backs" and returned home, carrying our new and much needed supply of paper with him. John Dailey came out with the office as its foreman. He was frequently "all hands."

On the 8th day of March the outfit left Omaha. The wagon carrying the press mired down in one of the main streets of that city so that it had to be dug out, and finally partially unloaded before the train got out of town. Eight miles was made the first day.

On the third day, after crossing Elkhorn River on a military bridge, we broke the ice and traversed for two miles [on] a sheet of water from one to four feet deep. Streams were all flood[ed], the mud bottomless, snow and rain storms frequent, and it was the last day of March when the caravan reached Fort Kearney, 185 miles from Omaha.

At Fort Kearney we learned that another printing office had passed west a few days before from St. Joseph, Missouri, bound for Pikes Peak. Our informant said the proprietor had "a bee gum" [a container used for bee colonies] pretty near full of types. From there the road was better and progress much faster. At Fort St. Vrain I left the train and reached Denver on horseback on the 17th of April, on the night before the celebrated stampede began which carried back, or turned back on the plains, four-fifths of all the people who that year set out for the promised land.

On April 20 the train arrived as day was fading into night. The wagon bearing the press stuck fast in Cherry Creek at the point where Blake Street Bridge now is, but everybody was ready to put a shoulder to the wheel and it was soon boosted out. The printing material was unloaded, carried to its attic office and work began that night. Forty-eight hours later the first number of the paper was printed. Another snow storm was raging, the roof leaked like a sieve, and we had to put up a tent over the press to keep the forms dry whilst the sheets were being printed.

The press from St. Joseph, Missouri, had reached the Cherry Creek Camp several days before. It belonged to Jack Merrick, a jolly, wide-awake printer who was yet busy getting acquainted with the people. It was a small concern, consisting of a lever press capable only of printing a page of cap-size, and a box of type in "p's"—that is, all mixed together. [NOTE: It was a nightmare for a typesetter to mix together similar-looking type. As a result, the expression "minding your p's and q's" became a command for orderliness in the print shop.]

Jack reached Denver a week or more ahead of us, and to him is entitled the credit of bringing the first printing press to the region of country now embraced in Colorado. Jack set up his office in a cabin, not far from the crossing of Larimer and Sixteenth Streets, on the natural prairie floor and under a dirt roof. His material remained just as it had been unloaded from the wagon, but when we began work he did the same and there was a close and spirited race as to who should get to press first. Both papers were printed the same evening, but a self-constituted committee that vibrated actively between the two offices decided that the *News* was victorious by about twenty minutes. Merrick's paper was named *Cherry Creek Pioneer* and only one number was ever printed. That ended the *Pioneer* and marked the first newspaper death in Colorado.

After getting that out, the publisher rested a few days and then caught the gold fever and started for the new diggings in what is now Gilpin County. To procure an outfit, he traded his office to Mr. Gibson of the *News* for about thirty dollars' worth of provisions. Jack shouldered his grub and started for the mountains whilst Gibson gathered the *Pioneer* establishment into his arms and carried it to the *News* office.

Merrick mined until he got broke and then came down and worked at the case on the *News* for a "raise" and so charged off from one to the other during that year and the next. For nearly two years he worked alternately at setting type in the *News* office and at prospecting or mining in Gilpin county.

At the first alarm of war, he hurried to the states and enlisted in one of the earliest volunteer regiments organized in Illinois. He served his term with credit and gained promotion. When mustered out, he returned to his former home, Leavenworth, Kansas; and secured a commission in a Kansas veteran regiment. About the close of the war, he was provost marshal in Leavenworth where, whilst in the active discharge of his duty, he was killed in a street riot. Poor Jack, he was one of the most generous, big-hearted men that ever lived, and the real pioneer of our craft in Colorado.

The weekly publication of the *News* was continued with tolerable regularity. I think only one or two numbers were missed that summer, though several may have been only half sheets, and others were on brown paper.

The *News* was located near the corner of the streets now known as Eleventh and Holladay [now called Market Street in Lower Downtown Denver]—then Ferry and Fourth—under the shadow of a large cottonwood tree that yet stands in the first named street. It was in an attic over Uncle Dick Wootton's saloon. Uncle Dick had arrived a few months earlier from Mexico with a small stock of miscellaneous merchandise and a good supply of walapite whiskey. He built a log cabin a little more than a story in height, and roofed it with clapboards, or "shakes." The ground floor was the ground and here Uncle Dick opened his store. Upon the joists above was laid a loose floor of boards cut out with a whip saw. There was a rough stairway outside and an entrance to this attic room through a door in the north gable. It had probably been used for storing goods in or for a sleeping apartment, but when we came it was empty, and Uncle Dick kindly offered its use for a printing office.

Work soon settled into a regular routine. We lived, ate and slept in the same room with the office. Our camp outfit, whilst crossing the plains, was our furniture and kitchen fixtures now, and our blankets were spread on the floor. Uncle Dick's dry goods and groceries had long since run out and his stock was now reduced to "hardware" as the boys called the remnants of Mexican wheat whiskey—possibly it held out because of the proximity of the Platte [River where Wootton may have watered down his stock of whiskey] or he may have been thoughtful about that article than anything else when he bought goods. At any rate, "Walapite" represented the business and the "store" had become a saloon. Naturally it saw a good deal of roughness, and many of its frequenters were "mighty handy with their pistols." Stray shots were frequent, and we of the printing office overhead, soon learned that an inch pine board wouldn't stop a Colt's dragoon or navy bullet, so we got more boards and doubled the floor under our beds. None of us were [sic] killed in that campaign.

I came a little in advance of the wagons and outfit, having left them at Fort St. Vrain, forty-two miles down the river, and when quarters had been secured, the first duty was to clear the snow out of the room and make it ready for use. Then I went prospecting with Andy Sagendorf up along the banks of the Platte, first upon one side and then upon the other. The Georgia boys were taking out gold directly opposite where the Exposition building now stands, making from nothing up to two dollars or so per day to the man. This was all the mining that was going on. They kindly allowed me to wash a couple of pans from the bedrock in a pit they had just stripped from which I obtained forty-two cents.

The nearest post office was at Fort Laramie, two hundred and twenty miles north, and the mail reached there from the States but once or twice a month. About the first of May a messenger was induced to go to the post office. His route was through a wilderness without a house or a civilized human being in the entire distance. He made the trip in two or three weeks and brought back a mule-load of letters and papers which were delivered upon the payment of twenty-five cents each for the former, and fifty cents each for the latter; meantime a reaction had followed the great excitement, men who came to Cherry Creek expecting to scoop gold dust out of its bed by the shovelful, or gather nuggets in gunny bags, returned to the States and swore that there was no gold at Pikes Peak that the reports were all humbug, and the men who circulated them had been hanged as they deserved.

The newspapers accepted the new reports, and it became the general belief that the bubble had bursted [sic]. The *News* was denounced in savage terms. In the latter part of May the pioneer coach of the overland line came in, and after a few weeks their daily arrival and departure became almost as regular as the railway trains of to-day. These carried the mails as express matter, but newspapers enjoyed the usual free privileges. In one of the first coaches came Horace Greeley, and a few days later he, with A. D. Richardson of the *New York Tribune,* and Henry Villard, of the *New York Herald,* visited the Gregory Mines. After a careful examination, they united in a report of what they had seen, which was published June 11, in an extra of the *News* over their signature.

Its reception East excited downright newspaper howls. The edition was printed on wrapping paper, and many charged that it was a forgery. Mr. Greeley's visit West was not generally known, and the other gentlemen were not then famous, as they afterwards became; hence it was pronounced a villainous device to entice emigrants upon the great American desert where they were liable to die of starvation. One Eastern paper stated that "Byers, having lied his paper black in the face, is now using the name of a celebrated journalist to give credit to his false reports," or words to that effect. But the Greeley report was the turning point, and although met with derision at first, it soon gained credit, and nobody has since doubted the wonderful richness of Colorado.

The *Pioneer* press, which was a "cap" size lever machine, remained idle in the *News* office until the first of July 1859, when Mr. Gibson took it to Mountain City, between where are now the cities of Black Hawk and Central, in Gilpin county, and established the *Rocky Mountain Gold Reporter.* The office reached there on the 4th of July and was greeted by an enthusiastic reception. This was the first paper published in the mountains. The *Reporter* lived four or five months until the beginning of winter. At that time, it was believed that the mountains were not habitable during the winter, and nearly everybody left there or prepared to leave upon short notice.

About the first of November 1859, Mr. Gibson discontinued the *Gold Reporter,* and hired his press to the Boston Company, who were then starting Golden City. Upon it they established the *Western Mountaineer,* the fourth paper attempted, which a few months later was enlarged, printed upon new type with a new press, and became a very creditable publication. Among its editors that winter were A. D. Richardson and Thos. W. Knox, both of whom afterwards gained national reputations.

The next newspaper venture came from Chicago early in the spring of 1860. It was owned by H. Rounds and Edward Bliss. The four proprietors became jointly and equally The News Printing Company. Following immediately after, Thomas Gibson returned from the States with another office, and on the first of May published the first number of the *Rocky Mountain Herald,* which was the first daily paper published in the country. A few weeks later *The News* began publishing a daily edition, and soon after a second, called the *Bulletin.* In 1863 Messrs. Rounds & Bliss were bought out by Byers & Daily, the material removed to the *News* office and the paper discontinued. I believe there were no other newspaper changes in Denver until in 1864, when the *News* office having been destroyed by the Cherry Creek flood.

The *Herald* was published for circulation among the incoming emigrants and was continued long. Competition between the *News* and *Herald* grew very warm, and personalities indulged in were exceedingly bitter. Both offices established pony express lines to the principal mining camps in the mountains, and their daily editions were delivered to subscribers in Black Hawk, Central Nevada, Missouri City, and along many miles of the gulches in that neighborhood in from three to four hours from the time they were printed. Each paper had an office, an agent, and a corps of carriers at Central City.

The subscription price for the daily edition was twenty-four dollars per year, the retail price twenty-five cents per copy. Payment was generally made in gold dust, nor were the means for obtaining news from the states any better or less exacting in enterprise. For more than two years nearly all mails were sent and received by express at a charge of twenty-five cents for each letter, and ten cents for each newspaper; ordinary freights averaged ten cents, and frequently ran up to twenty-five cents per pound. Express freight was one dollar per pound.

The rebellion was raging in the states and a general Indian war in progress on the plains, occasioning long delays and frequent losses, many a hundred pounds of paper cost a hundred dollars for carriage alone. In 1861 the telegraph was extended to Fort Kearney, where it rested nearly two years. The Denver papers immediately began taking news dispatches which were forwarded from Kearney by express on the regular daily coaches, but upon important occasions they came by pony express and at heavy cost.

The *Herald* discontinued, and the *News* thereafter printed upon the *Herald* material until further additions and removals were made to the office. For several years following the *News* had the field entirely to itself in Denver.

My memories in connection with the business are varied, generally pleasant, and always interesting. There were sore trials and many disappointments. There were times when I found it prudent to disguise myself, or to vary my route homeward, when I left the office after night, because of threats against my life. The office was often threatened. Once only was it attacked. For years it was the rule to keep arms always in reach and ready for use. The editor sat at his table with a pistol in reach; the compositor stood at his case with a gun leaning against his stand. The cause for such precaution was the outspoken tone of the paper against lawlessness and disorder.

The years of 1862, 1863 and 1864 were trying ones for the two daily newspapers that remained in Denver; Messrs. Rounds and Bliss retired from the *News* in 1863, the *Herald* underwent a number of changes in name and management. A harassing Indian war on the plains prostrated business and cut off the mails and interrupted all commerce. Trains laden with merchandise were robbed or burned; teams driven off and men killed.

During the summer of 1864, when the trouble culminated, Denver and the immediate vicinity lost about fifty citizens who were murdered by Indians; most of them were killed whilst en route to or from the States. The daily mail route along the Platte was broken up and nearly all the stations burned.

As misfortunes never come singly, that season was exceptional for its disasters. On the 20th of May occurred the celebrated Cherry Creek flood, known by that name only because it occasioned more destruction of property and loss of life at Denver than in any other one locality. It was no less terrible and proportionately more destructive along Plum Creek, the Fontaine qui Bouille, and other streams than along Cherry Creek. By it Denver lost a large amount of property. The *News* office and its contents were destroyed, leaving not a vestige.

Three or four weeks after its proprietors bought the *Herald* office and resumed the publication of the *News*. The Indian war thickened until practically all of Colorado was cut off from the Eastern States. For weeks at a time there were no mails, and finally they were sent around by Panama and San Francisco, reaching Denver in from seven to ten weeks; of course, newspapers suffered with everybody and everything else. All supplies were used up; wrapping paper, tissue paper and even writing paper were used to keep up the daily issues of the *News,* now the only one remaining in Denver, if not in the Territory.

In August martial law was proclaimed, and the Third Regiment of Colorado Volunteers raised in less than a week in order to chastise the Indians. The regiment was equipped and provisioned by the people but was subsequently accepted and mustered into the United States service for one hundred days.

The Sand Creek campaign followed, and the great battle of the same name, for which the people of Colorado are yet condemned and execrated by self-righteous philanthropists of the East. The *News* office furnished fourteen recruits for that regiment, and thereafter for a time the paper was printed by a detail of soldiers. It was very small and contained little besides military orders and notices.

The campaign lasted about ninety days, and then followed peace. For two or three years the *News* had the field in Denver almost entirely alone, then new enterprises were started, and the number of newspapers has since multiplied rapidly—some to become permanent, as the *Tribune, Herald, Times,* and others, and many others to flourish for a brief period and then die. The same has been the case all over the Territory, now State. Newspapers have been among the first enterprises in all new towns of any importance.

Colorado may be justly proud of her newspaper press. It has always been creditable and enterprising. It is emphatically so to-day. Upon the average it is infinitely superior to the newspapers of equal communities in other parts of the United States, as those of the United States in proportionate number, enterprise and average ability, lead the world. This would not be, except for the intelligence of our people and their encouragement of newspapers. As the State may be proud of her papers, so the papers may thank the people of the State who support them. No other like number of people pay for and read so many.

1   Consolidated from two exposés by William Newton Byers: "The Days of '58: A History of Early Journalism and Pioneer Journalists Who Are Now Famous," *Denver Republican*, September 13, 1883, pp. 1-2; and "Early Journalism in Colorado," William Newton Byers, *Magazine of Western History*, Vol. IX, No. 6, April 1889; pp. 692-697.

CHAPTER 1

Occasionally some rather absurd errors get into the newspaper itself, by failing to secure correction in type. When it so happens, unless they involve misstatements of facts, or affect interests which should not suffer thereby, editors generally find it best to let them pass, trusting to the intelligence of their readers to remedy the matter.[1]

Walking the news beat in early Denver was an aromatic and auditory experience. The dust from the adobe dirt streets provided a slightly, musty hint of a fresh-cut hay field, a whiff of a sweating horse against leather chaps, the pungent redolence of fresh droppings from a passing horse or a stray dog, and whatever was left over in the alley adjacent to the myriad of saloons that dotted Denver. Against the sound of creaking buckboards passing through town, the bark of a nearby dog, and the boisterous rants of competing businessmen—there was the metallic clacking of flywheels on printing presses and the distinct fragrance of printers' ink in the fresh mountain air.

Early in the 19th Century, members of the United States Congress debated the value of expanding the western border of the United States to the Rocky Mountains and beyond. Massachusetts Senator Daniel Webster, scoffed at any consideration of public funds expounded upon the savage and desolate West.

"What do we want with this vast, worthless area?" Senator Webster expressed with frustration. "This region of savages and wild beasts, of deserts, shifting sands and whirlwinds of dust, of cactus and prairie dogs? To what use could we ever hope to put these great deserts, or those endless mountain ranges, impregnable and covered to their very base with eternal snow? What can we ever hope to do with the western coast, a coast of three thousand miles, rock-bound, cheerless, uninviting, and not a harbor on it? What use have we for such a country? Mr. President [Thomas Jefferson], I will never vote one cent from the public treasury to place the Pacific coast one inch nearer to Boston than it now is."[2]

The Fremont expedition to the Great American Desert brought back tales that helped dispel the prevailing false impression about the American West, but pre-existing opinions about the Wild Savage West affected the politicians in the more civilized American East. Five years after Senator Webster's speech, Senator George McDuffie of South Carolina bristled at the thought of running a railroad through the western foreboding land. He described the 700 miles east of the Rocky Mountains as uninhabitable, and unsuitable for agriculture because of the arid climate. "I would not give a pinch of snuff for the whole territory," Senator McDuffie told his peers in Washington. "I wish the Rocky Mountains were an impassable barrier. If there was an embankment of five feet to be removed I would not consent to expend five dollars to remove it and enable our population to go there. I thank God for his mercy in placing the Rocky Mountains at that place."[3]

It wasn't until the cry of "gold" in 1849 brought eastern adventurers across the mid-west, across the impassable Rocky Mountains and on to California. As the success of finding gold subsided, most returned east, some pausing to try their hand at panning for gold near the eastern Front Range of the Rocky Mountains. In May 1854, the Territories of Kansas and Nebraska were created by Congress, but dissension arose among those who considered the rest of the West as a wasteland on one side, and recognition of the Rocky Mountain West's potential for economic development on the other side.

Colorado became a haven for adventurous colorful characters — and a magnet for writers who thrived on telling their stories to the rest of the civilized country.

Of all the editors and other newspapermen working the typography establishments of Denver Colorado, the most eccentric was O. J. Goldrick. He arrived in Denver wearing a glossy plug hat, a broadcloth Prince Albert, and boiled shirt. In lavender gloved hands, Goldrick held a bull whip to drive his team of oxen forward. He was born in Ireland and emigrated to America where he sold books in Ohio, raised pigs, and wrote poetry; and when gold fever spread throughout the country in 1859, Goldrick headed

West. When the townspeople in Denver saw this dapper dandy swearing at his oxen in Latin, they considered him to be the most educated person in town, and immediately hired him as a school teacher. Goldrick also became an editor of several newspapers and was a colorful chronicler of events that became important to Colorado's history.

Any time the news was scarce, reporters like O. J. Goldrick were able to bring their intellect, literary prowess, and language to their readers. In an 1864 edition of the *Rocky Mountain Daily News,* Goldrick explained what it was like to wake up one morning: "Twas Wednesday morning. The steam whistle of Moyn & Rice's mill and the shrill short sound of the Planter's second bell burst on the circumambient air and blew the atmospheric bellows against our auricular tympanum, sounding the melodies of morn, and telling us 'twas time to desert our couch, don our unmentionables, get some spiritual and physical strength, and start per Cottrell & Co.'s swift and comfortable stage line for the South and intermediate settlements. We did so, just as Phoebus, fresh from his Atlantic bath, bolted out of his orient gate and glistened the gloomy, grey-eyed morning air with golden beams of beauty."[4]

There was an image of Denver merely as a cow-town composed of ignorant cowboys, cattle rustlers, gamblers, con artists, and other transient roustabouts. It's interesting to compare the reputation of uneducated early residents with the sophisticated language of Denver's fledgling journalists.

Byers' newspaper, the *Rocky Mountain News,* was printed on the second floor of Richens Lacey Wootton's log-constructed business block. Born in Mecklenburg County, Virginia in 1836, Wootton moved West to work as a hunter at Bent's Fort on the Arkansas River. He traded with the Sioux Indians for buffalo hides, buckskins, and Indian ponies. His supply train was laden with Indian trinkets, hunting supplies, and household staples.

In 1858 Wootton packed his supply wagon for a family visit, but only got as far as the fledgling Denver City and Auraria. He broke out a couple of barrels of "Taos Lightning" (rot-gut wheat whiskey) and offered free samples while supply-hungry settlers perused his wagon. His popularity among the imbibing westward immigrants was so great that they began calling him "Uncle Dick." With his immediate success and trading connections, his family chose Denver City to open a general store. He parlayed his good business management with a welcoming invitation to the growing number of newspaper publishers and editors to use his "cyclone cellar" where he stored his liquor as their sanctuary away from irate news readers, subscribers, and advertisers.

*My first trading on the site of the present "Queen City of the West"
was carried on in a style about as primitive as Indian trading …
I moved into a log cabin and without waiting for any such thing as shelving
or counters to be put in I commenced business. I had several barrels
with me which I rolled alongside of each other and used as a counter.
What was in the barrels doesn't matter, but it was something that
every well-regulated store kept on hand in those days. I think
there are a few highly respected old gentlemen still living in Denver
who will remember what it was and would be willing to testify
that it was a good article, if it did come high.*

UNCLE DICK WOOTTON

*"Uncle Dick" Wootton: The Pioneer Frontiersman of the Rocky Mountain
Region,* Howard Louis Conard, W. E. Dibble & Co., Chicago, 1890

Because supplies grew scarce when supply trains failed to reach Denver, editions of the newspaper varied in size and frequency. Wootton explained that supplies weren't the only threat to the new publishers; "I remember one time, when they had been carrying on something of a warfare against the lawless element in the town, that two desperate characters made their appearance in the neighborhood of the building one morning and shot all the windows out of the printing office. The [gun]fire was returned from the inside and before the shooting ceased [and] one of the desperadoes was killed. About the first question, Byers asked of employees in those days was whether he could handle a gun to good advantage, and a printer who was handy in this respect stood well with the proprietors of the paper, even though he had a multitude of shortcomings as a compositor."[5]

As more print shops opened with their versions of the daily or weekly papers, newspapermen began bickering among themselves about each other's publication quality and editorial biases. "Some of these hyper-critics here can't themselves spell six consecutive monosyllables without making 'much' the most miserable mistakes, yet to hear 'em talk, they flatter themselves that they are 'some' and qualified to judge of unscrewing the tomcat's tail as well as the surgeon that performs the operation. There are a great many fellows, old and young, in office and out of business, putting a heavy swathe and cavorting in the shade, who, comparing themselves with themselves, pass here for some pumpkins, while, if the truth would be told, have no more body nor brains than the peeling of a persimmon! Those parvenu boors to define newspaper writing is absurd, although occasionally amusing!"[6]

The dry climate of Denver made sidewalks an unnecessary inconvenience, suitable only as an ornamental luxury, much like a storekeeper who wasted his inventory on umbrellas, despite the "delusive fiction and a discomforting fraud," according to an article in the Denver *Republican*. A heavy rain or the melting snow in springtime made walking through the muddy streets "a painful and grotesque tiptoeing, a bewildering and picturesque zigzagging, or a grim, desperate wading." The sale of foot rubbers was considered an abomination by most people. Ladies seeking to go shopping for the upcoming opera season prompted them to venture onto the slick muddy streets as though they were going to an execution. Men wore out door mats by incessantly scraping their soles. Only the bootblack was joyous at this time of year.

"The loyal Coloradan still clings to his traditions," the *Republican* reported. "He will pull his foot out of six inches of mud and tell how delightful it is to live in a country where the climate is so dry that you can always go safely upon the streets in satin slippers."[7]

Denver residents, living outside the United States in the territorial county of Jefferson, wanted news from the States. The War Between the States was underway, and the fate of President Abraham Lincoln was soon etched into the history of the entire country. With no other form of communication with the outside world, townspeople gathered when they heard the rattle of the presses. The editors asked subscribers not to loiter around the print office to grab one of the newspapers saved for sale by newsboys on the street.[8] For readers who wanted to preserve their papers and protect them from "bummers" who stole delivered copies of the latest edition, newspaper editor "Professor" Goldrick suggested business offices, hotels, saloons, and public resorts have the town carpenter build a wooden file with a clasp.[9]

A few years later, Publisher/Editor William N. Byers proposed that readers preserve their editions of the newspaper by binding them in leather-binders for the edification of future generations instead of just discarding each edition.[10]

*****

By the end of 1879, there were fifteen daily and fifty weekly newspapers in Colorado. Denver had four large dailies that challenged the admiration of everyone who appreciated "pluck and perseverance."[11]

"Newspaper subscriptions are infallible tests of men's honesty," explained Byers. "If a man is dishonest he will cheat the printer in some way—say that he has paid when he has not—or sent money, and it was least by mail—or will take the paper and will not pay for it, on the plea that he did not subscribe for it—or will move off, leaving it to come to the office he left. Thousands of professed Christians are dishonest, and the printer's book will tell fearfully on the final settlement of the judgment day."[12]

Delivery of newsprint was at the mercy of the wagon trains from the East. Printers published "half-sheet" editions to stretch their supply of newsprint and even resorted to wallpaper or wrapping paper on occasion. The abbreviated editions published military orders, local and legal notices, short advertisements, but most advertisers had to wait until the regular newsprint shipments reached Denver.[13] Publishers dropped any "dead" advertisers not current with their payments. "It is unjust to actual advertisers to crowd their notices in with non-paying ones, and we make it a rule not to do it to any considerable extent,"[14] explained the *Rocky Mountain News.*

Newsmen received their regional and national copy via the telegraph or post office. Serious local news occasionally graced the pages of the Denver newspapers. In 1863, a drunken patron knocked over a wood-burning stove in the lower downtown business district of Denver; the resulting fire destroyed most of the wooden pioneer buildings. The following year, the buildings and homes along the normal trickle of Cherry Creek were swept away in a flash flood following a torrential downpour in the southern Douglas County hillsides. The *Rocky Mountain News'* creek-side press office washed into the mud. O. J. Goldrick, writing for a competing newspaper, wrote in his rambling but colorful style from his position on the banks of the creek as the muddy water rushed past him:

On May 19, 1864, a torrential rainstorm south of Denver sent floodwaters flowing through the normally peaceful Cherry Creek. Homes and businesses (including *The Rocky Mountain News*) were buried under the floodwater mud.

Courtesy of the Library of Congress, The Great Flood, Denver, Colorado Territory / George D. Wakely, Cherry Creek Colorado Denver. 1864 photograph. https://www.loc.gov/item/2012646013

About the midnight hour of Thursday the 19th instant, while almost all in town were knotted in the peace of sleep, deaf to all noise and blind to all danger, snoring in calm security and seeing visions of remoteness radiant with the rainbow hues of past associations, or roseate light he gilded hopes of the fanciful future—while the full faced queen of night shed showers of silver from her starry throne down o'er fields of freshness and fertility, garnishing and suffusing sleeping nature with her filmy brightness, fringing the fatherly cottonwoods with lustre, enameling the housetops with coats of pearl, bridging the erst placid Platte with beams of radiance and bathing the dry sands of Cherry Creek with dewy beauty—a frightful phenomenon sounded in the distance, and a shocking calamity presently charged upon us. The few who had not retired to bed, broke from their buildings to see what was coming. Hark! What and where is this? A torrent or a tornado? And where can it be coming from, and whither going? These were the questions soliloquized and spoken, one to the other. Has creation's God forsaken us, and has chaos come again? Our eyes might bewilder, and our ears deceive but our hearts, all trembling and our scared souls soon whispered what it was—the thunders of Omnipotence warning us "there's danger on the wing," with Death himself seeming to prompt our preparation for the terrible alternative of destruction or defense! Presently, the great noise of mighty waters, like the roaring of Niagara or the rumbling of an enraged Etna burst upon us, distinctively and regularly in its sounding steps as the approach of a tremendous train of locomotives. There was soon a hurry to and fro in terror, trying to wake up one's relatives and neighbors, while some favored few who were already dressed darted out of doors and clamorously called their friends to climb the adjacent bluffs and see with certainty for themselves. Alas, and wonderful to behold! It was the water engine of death dragging its destroying train of maddened waves, that defied the eye to number them, which was rushing down upon us, now following its former channel and now tunneling direct through banks and bottoms a new channel of its own. Alarm flew around, and all alike were ignorant of what to think, or say, or do, much less of knowing where to go with safety, to save others. A thousand thoughts flitted o'er us, and a thousand terrors thrilled us through. What does this mean? Where has this tremendous flood or freshet, this terrific torrent come from? Has the Platte switched off from its time-worn track and turned its treasures down to deluge us? Have the wild water-spouts from all the clouds at once conspired to drain their upper cisterns, and thus drench us here in death? Have the fluid foundations of the Almighty's earth given way, and the fountains of the great deep burst forth on fallen men, regardless of that rainbow covenant which spanned in splendor yon are of sky last evening? Is the world coming to an end, or a special wreck of matter impending? These, and thoughts like these, troubled the most fearless souls . . .[15]

With the *Rocky Mountain News* office washed away by the flood, the newspaper thanked past subscribers for their support, and the competing newspapers for picking up the slack for the two weeks the newspaper was without a press. Because the *Rocky Mountain News* had one of the largest circulation figures for the principal towns and rural communities throughout the Civil War Union states, the New York and Philadelphia centers shipped an additional 200 copies of their weekly editions to the news-hungry Denver readers. The business interests of the Territory, returning soldiers from the War Between the States, and increase of government employees were among the newsworthy stories the paper would include in their Denver editions.[16]

Byers noted that some misguided eastern "capitalists" admired the growth of the newspaper publishing businesses in Denver and attempted to enter the fray with their own poorly funded publications. He believed many of these well-intentioned entrepreneurs thought a handsome profit could be realized immediately after the first edition. "There never was a greater error," wrote Byers, "as there is not one daily paper out of a thousand that has not been a struggling starving [enterprise] during the first year or years of its existence."

With each newspaper that attempted to compete in Denver, most quickly ended their run, leaving the *Rocky Mountain News* as the only stable publication in the 1860s. Byers attributed the longevity of the *News* to the obstinacy of the proprietors "and perfect faith in the growth and improvement of the country."[17] The cost of running a paper in 1866-dollars was approximately $1200 per week to address a voting population of an estimated 1200 voters in Denver; two-thirds actually purchased copies of the daily newspaper. There were less than 100 potential advertisers in the county and it was necessary for them to pay an average of $6.50 each week in advertisements to help underwrite the newspaper.

When newspaper circulation and advertising was flush, the proprietors made a fair profit, but when either revenue source was weak, the profit line immediately felt the impact. If several newspapers in a community created an image that each was successful, more entrepreneurs attempted to add new publications to the market. "Since Denver has settled, there never has been two newspaper offices in the city between whom the patronage of the public was equally divided, that could pay expenses," wrote Byers. "These are the facts in the case, and if you think that we write of it merely to deter them from attempting the enterprise of adding another newspaper office to the city, they are perfectly welcome to try it for themselves."[18]

During the next few months, more newspapers joined the list of Denver publications, and a new joke began to circulate on the streets of Denver. After throwing down one of the Denver dailies, a chap asked,

> "What's the matter, Mr. —?"
> "They're four things they call *news*-papers, in Denver," he replied. "And there's not half as many 'editors' in the city!"
> "Oh! That's a mistake, Mr. —. The trouble is that they've too many 'editors' such as they are! A *journalist* is what nearly all of 'em need!"[19]

Each wannabe-editor added their publications to the support of the competing discussions that dominated the political discourse in the community. To visiting newsmen from other parts of the country, the bickering among local publications was symbolic of the wild west. A correspondent from the St. Louis *Democrat* reported, "They shoot at each other terrible salvoes of satire, often raking one another fore and aft. The people are divided, like the rest of American humanity, into two distinct classes, republican and democrat, the former being largely in the majority."

The correspondent noted the Republican-sided *Rocky Mountain News* was the most factual and demonstrated a love of the territory. The daily *Mountaineer* (1860-1861) maintained a secessionist editorial policy before the Civil War between the States. Colorado's statehood had to wait until 1876.[20] The *Golden City Register* wrote and published newspaper versions of geological and other abstruse studies. The *Central City Register* was an unorthodox mountain paper, full of idiosyncrasies appropriate to the mountain communities, radical politics, and developments in Colorado. The *Colorado Times* (formerly the *Black Hawk Mining Journal*) was fiercely Democrat-sided in its editorial views.

Even the Methodist-Episcopal Sunday Schools of Colorado began publishing its own newspaper, the *Sunday School Casket*,[21] through the auspices of the *Rocky Mountain News* office. By mid-May, the *Weekly Colorado Tribune*[22] was added to newsstands with the pretentious motto "Industry, Virtue, and Truth." With the advent of John Walker as the editor,[23] it didn't take long for him to begin apologizing for his inexperience.

> "To the Public—It is with considerable diffidence that I make my bow to the readers of the *Tribune* as its local editor, although I have had some little experience on other journals, in the same capacity. It is not because I have any doubts of my ability (I'm not over modest) to make an acceptable column of local reading, but because just at this time, while business of every kind is so nearly at a dead lock, I am fearful that I shall not be able to create sufficient interest to make the *Tribune's* local column an interesting feature. Hoping, however, that my fears may prove groundless, and that the public will overlook small errors and aid me by full and early information in all matters that interest the public, I'll continue for a time to be the public's faithful reporter."[24]

The newspaper further defended itself with a reprint from the London *Times*. "A good editor, a competent newspaper conductor, is like a general or poet born, not made. Exercise and experience give facility, but the qualification is innate, or it is never manifested. On the London daily papers, all the great historians, novelists, poets, essayists and writers of travels have been tried, and nearly everyone has failed. 'I can,' said the late editor of the London *Times,* 'find any number of men of genius to write for me, but very seldom a man of common sense.' Nearly all successful editors are of this description. A good editor seldom writes very much for his paper. He reads, judges, selects, dictates, alters, and combines; and to do all this well, he has but little time for composition. To write for a paper is one thing—to edit a paper another."[25]

The power of the press continued to spark discussions among Denver's young publishers as they forged their identity in the growing community. The *Weekly Denver Tribune* published remarks from the Pittsburgh *Commercial* about the influence of the New York police papers. The papers claimed to serve as censors of morals by collecting publications from around the country that reported scandals. The resulting exposé was more successful in spreading the corruption of the scandals instead of resolving them. "For the purposes they have in view, they are under the necessity of organizing a corps of caves droppers, gossips, libelers, ramifying through all parts of the land, who are expected to discover, invent or manufacture scandal in proportion to the pay they get for it. The convergent streams of vileness and lies are poured into one or another of these police papers, and thence are issued for the people's reading."[26] The *Tribune* remarked it was impossible to escape "some pollution of mind or damage of conscience, or some loss of self-respect"[27] from reading polluted publications.

The *Colorado Weekly Tribune* continued the discussion on the role of journalism by re-publishing comments made in *Wilkes' Spirit.* "Thirty years ago, the orators ruled America; today it is ruled by the editors. There is a class of men among bankers and merchants and lawyers who affect a condescension towards the journalist which is intensely amusing. The writer for the newspaper appears to their blinking eyes a kind of literary adventurer, who is to be tolerated for his genius, but not to be trusted in business. They are ignorant that it is the newspaper that sells their goods, furnishes all their facts, and presents them gratuitously with their opinions. They do not know . . . That the newspapers of America sold millions of national bonds. They do not know . . . That the newspapers of America sent five hundred thousand men to the war. They do not know that the newspapers will nominate the candidates for the Presidency, determine the election, dictate the legislation of Congress, and decide whether Andrew Johnson is to be impeached. Newspapers lead them by the nose wherever they go, but they do not feel the pressure, which is the particular reason why we give this especial tweak."[28]

As new publications opened in Denver, Byers offered a few requirements needed by a good "local editor." According to the premier Denver publisher, a good local editor "must be young, polite, affable and good looking; adoring old maids, unprotected females, pug-nosed babies and poodles—a defender of guilty rascals and staff and support of neglected wives, always on hand to chaperone dilapidated spinsters or lisping affectatious[sic] misses—ever ready in wit, wisdom and folly—prepared to unfold to questioning bores the news by telegraph ere they arrive—smoke vile cigars and pronounce their stench a heavenly aroma—drink strychnine whisky and puff it as umbrosial[sic] nectar—praise shoddy clothing under the name of purple and fine linen—attend all gatherings, from an Orthodox communion down to a gambling hall dance, and stay with any of them all night, and yet be prepared to grind out fun, sentiment and gravity during next day—imbibe gin-cocktails, brandy-smashes and champagne with high officials, and pray or talk through his nose with the parson—teach a class at Sabbath school and the latest stroke at billiards—a connoisseur on the turf or at the prize ring, and must attend all bull baite[sic], dog-fights, and boxing matches, and always bet his bottom dollar at the race-course—must make a note of every Indian, nigger, beggar, or bob-tail dog that is on the street, and be cognizant of all filth, dead carcasses and garbage that may accumulate in the highways and alleys, bearing meekly the meledictious[sic] of the city fathers, who vote him a nuisance therefore. He must not complain if his exchanges are stolen, cost out at elbows, last dollar gone, or his washer-woman clamors for her pay; and finally, must be the willing victim of every ruffian that wants to thrash the editor, and bear without murmuring the clamorous importunity of the 'imp' for 'more copy.'"[29]

While Byers may have begun the passage with a sense of humor, the concluding phrases were a veiled challenge to Frank J. Stanton of the *Gazette*. Byers believed the *Rocky Mountain News* post-office box was being pilfered of news dispatches intended for the *News;* Byers suspected the culprit was his arch-rival Stanton, stating that the post-office theft was conducted "by children, under direction of an older head."[30] The military commission investigating the Sand Creek affair (where an Indian encampment was horrifically overrun by Colonel John Chivington and 675 soldiers, killing all the Cheyenne and Arapaho Indians camped nearby in

Kiowa County near Eads, Colorado)[31], sent a copy of the testimony to the *News*, but the dispatch appeared on the pages of the *Gazette*. After Byers published his allegations of theft against Stanton, the retribution was swift and physical.

Byers told readers that two men stalked him one night, but he escaped unscathed. The relationship between Byers and Stanton had been contentious with Stanton threatening canings and "physical chastisement" upon Byers. Byers rarely called attention to his handicapped leg, unless he could generate public sympathy in an affray with a disgruntled reader. Or the erudite publisher could use his impressive cane with a swagger to emphasize his professional stature in the town.

On another occasion, Byers was standing near the stage office, bidding farewell to a party leaving to return to the States, Stanton allegedly made a surprise attack, bludgeoning the left temple of Byers' skull with his own heavy cane. "The coward nerved himself up to the task of assaulting a disabled man unaware," reported Byers in his newspaper, "but the presence of one who is capable of self-defense, and who will exercise that capacity if called upon, is too much for him. Such a thing in humanity's shape is utterly beneath our contempt, and we now forever abjure all further notice of so disgusting an object, with the full understanding, however, that if the snake attempts to bite us, we will kill it if we can."[32]

Once tempers subsided, Byers admitted that his public notoriety attracted enemies; even among friends, as differences of opinion developed. "My course in such cases," Byers humbly wrote, "has always been honest and I have respected the like opinions of my opponents. Such differences are no good cause for personal estrangements or animosities, and I have striven not to entertain them. At the same time, I am fully aware that I have my faults, 'To err is human.'"[33]

The atonement between the two newspapers was short-lived. Byers continued to gore his nemesis by publishing a "Prospectus" that he claimed was written during a time of the *Gazette* editor's spiritual disability. "The course of the *Gazette* for the coming year will be consistent with the want of character which it has maintained in the past. Aspiring to be the organ of bushwhackers, draft-skedaddlers and slanders generally, no pains will be spared to store its columns with the choicest morceaux of abuse and detraction, that shall come to the knowledge of its editor . . . In order to keep our self to the proper mood for the great work before us, any of our friends who may know a cripple, incapable of defending himself, will please have one such placed in our way occasionally so that we can amuse our self by knock[ing] his brains out with a cane. No cripple who can raise a hand in self-defense shall be entitled to the honor of a castigation at our hand, neither must the victim know of our intended onslaught."[34]

Despite Byers' propensity to write searing editorials against elected officials and competing newspapers, he also oddly published a front-page account defining the roles of "Journals, Journalists, and Readers:"

It is high time that western journals should take a higher tone and cease to resound to the use of the vulgar and can't phrases that disgrace their columns. The publication of articles that verge upon the obscene, simply because of their pot-house wit should be discontinued. Such things charm only the vulgar who, it is well known, are not the most profitable class of readers. They serve to give an insight to the young into the vulgar and profane pleasures of the world, that they otherwise might never obtain, and pander only to the taste of the depraved and vicious. The tone of the press should be such as will elevate, educate and refine society, bringing it continually to a higher state of intelligence and moral worth. When its efforts are directed in an opposite direction, we need not look for any other than the most disastrous moral deformity, especially if the journals so acting, should have a sufficient paying support, to enable them to continue to their hellish work.

Under the best support, however, such Journals are constantly lessening their influence for the public good, and the community that sustains them, and finds pleasure in their perusal, rapidly retrogrades from bad to worse, until the roading does not satisfy their depraved appetites, which must be satiated by acts of vice, either of lewdness or dissipation. The Journal then loses its hold upon the popular favor, and is justly deprived of a support, which, on its first departure from the path of moral rectitude should have been withdrawn.

The art of journalism to be practiced in its best sense, is one of infinite labor. None but those who have tried it may be aware of the trials and mental work of an editor of a popular daily paper. Everything to its columns, from the clippings from exchanges, down to the wording of a marriage or funeral notice, is expected to pass under his eye. All sorts of tastes are to be ministered-to but let him beware who among these chooses to make the taste of the vile paramount to the others. Never should this taste of the vicious for vulgar wit be allowed to find a morsel for their entertainment in the paper, or like the horse-leech's daughter [Proverb 30:15], they will be continually crying, "give, give," until the support of the good, true, and upright is withdrawn, and the panderer to vice left to the wreck of his fortune, brought about by his own folly. We do not mean by this that real wit, fun and sentiment should find no place in our public journals; but we do mean that it should be of a cheery refined character, such as a man would not be ashamed to repeat before his wife or daughter in the home circle, and would be elevating as well as amusing, that would make keener and brighter the power of human enjoyment, and not tend to lessen and blunt the salute by teachings of scurrility and wickedness.

Of readers, there are many, and various classes, among these are the stupid, the miserly, the melancholy, the grumbling, the gay-and-festive, the literary epicure, and the appreciative. The first of these reads without understanding, the mental man not following the thought or plan of the writer, but merely lumbering along mechanically without sense or reason. This class of readers do not read much. They find no pleasure in knowledge, and it is too laborious work for them to try to obtain it.

The second class are those who like the man who took all medicines left in his house himself, after his wife's convalescence from a long illness, lest they might be wasted, reads the whole paper through with exactness, commencing with the title and ending with the printer's mark at the close of the last advertisement on the fourth page. He pays for his paper, is anxious to get the worth of his money, and knows about as much as a parrot of what he has read after one of his perusals. This class of readers usually get their education by accident.

The melancholy reader, solemn as a starved owl, seeks his pleasure in death notices, obituaries, etc., and usually remembers enough of what he has read to bore others with the repetition of the same, with elongated, bilious countenance, and slowly wagging lantern jaws. The gay and festive reader seeks only the accounts of balls, parties, marriages, bon mots, etc. And relishes exceedingly a good joke, no matter at whose expense the same is perpetrated. He is generally a good fellow. If not given to taproom witticisms.

The grumblers are of that class who only seek for faults and overlook all virtues in the search. These readers find fault with everything, either in the material, menial or mechanical makeup of the paper. Their sole business is fault finding. We don't like them and neither does anyone else, for the reason that their mission, if they have one, is to make everything appear unlovely, and in as bad a light as possible.

The literary epicure is a careful reader. He understands what he reads, and carefully stores away in the recesses of memory any real choice rid-bit he may find for future reference. He is sometimes disposed to censure a journal as insipid but should recollect that all tastes are not like his own, and that most minds are content with coarser food than he chooses.

The appreciative reader has a knowledge of the labor requisite in making a readable paper. He understands and enters fully into the feelings expressed in every article. He likes his newspaper and will not do without it. No matter whether an article favors his particular theories or not he will read it, and if possible, gain instruction therefrom. This class composes the readers that journalists like best and are the real bone and sinew of society.[35]

When Byers turned his vitriolic editorial pen against Governor William Gilpin in 1866, Representative B. R. Golvin proposed a resolution to denounce the editorial columns of the *Rocky Mountain News* that described the governor's January speech as "dealing in ambiguous and hifaluting[sic] language as undignified and unworthy the columns of any respectable newspaper of Colorado."[36]

As soon as it was introduced, the proposal was immediately tabled, but not before Byers published one more editorial salvo toward the governor's office. "The *Rocky Mountain News* is no venal readying [sic] press, and even when we assist in placing men in positions of power and influence, we know of no law compelling us to pronounce the braying of an ass, the roaring of a lion. The wording of Gov. Gilpin's message may be very fine, but for practical purposes, a chapter from Humboldt's Cosmos, or a tale of Baron Munchausen, has as much bearing upon the interests of the State of Colorado. When we sink to that depth of flunkyism [sic] that will make us praise where we should censure, then it will be time for denunciatory resolutions against us to be adopted."[37]

Instead of relying on the rumors spread by other editors from more-established journalism communities, the St. Louis *Democrat* determined that a first-hand visit to meet the eclectic editors of the Denver community was a better way to ascertain the value of the community's burgeoning journalistic fraternity. "Some people," reported the *Democrat's* unnamed correspondent, "insisted that the editors were savage fellows ever ready with pistol and Bowie knife to fight those who differed with them, but that was a foul slander for I have a distinct recollection of the gentlemanly appearance and politeness of Messrs. Byers and Hollister. Next time I visit Colorado territory I propose making a visit to the editors a specialty."[38]

Editorial visitations to Denver began in October 1867 as Colonel G. P. Smith[39] of the *Jacksonville Journal* suggested bringing 150 "knights of the goose-quill" to Denver. The idea spread to organizations that included Captain Richard Sopris, president of the Agricultural Society in Colorado.[40] He encouraged an editorial excursion among eastern farmers to see the potential of growing crops in the West through the use of irrigation canals. The visitors were greeted and entertained by the mayor, city-council members, officials and members of the press from Denver newspapers and others from neighboring towns. Raising a champagne glass to the visiting newspapers, a grand toast was made:

To the Press of our Country
To the Press of Denver
To the Ladies, though absent, in memory dear, and
To the City of Denver.[41]

When the guests returned to their seats, a dinner of local wild-and-raised food was followed by speeches on current-event issues and a brass-band concert that completed the gala evening. Denver had a reputation for fine hospitality when greeting visitors from the East who were eager to learn of the mineral and agricultural resources in the new territory.

As the 1867 "editorial excursion" departed Denver, they left their fellow journalists with a tribute published in the *Rocky Mountain News.* "[T]o each and all of you we feel greatly indebted for the active part you have taken in contributing to our comfort and pleasure during our sojourn among you. We assure you that we bid you farewell with many regrets, that we cannot remain longer with a people so generous and hospitable, and that when we can contribute in any way to the advantage of Colorado we shall heartily do so, never forgetting our obligations to you. Hoping that your most sanguine hopes in reference to the future of your city and territory may be fully realized, we bid you adieu."

From most of the eighteen newspapermen who were part of the first press excursion, the reviews published in Eastern newspapers were complimentary[42] and were expected to draw even more visitors in the future. One anonymous "leaker," however, sent a misinformed report of Denver's railroad plans and prospects to *The Denver Times.* The Denver paper responded that the "scribbler" was "guilty of libel, as is also the paper that publishes his letter, and but for the fact that neither is worthy of attention we think that an example would be made in this particular case. A prosecution for the offense would be too much like 'casing a beggar to catch a louse.'"[43]

The role of "a press club in Denver" began to develop as a cosmopolitan representative of the West. McClure's post office news store kept eastern dailies, weeklies and monthly newspapers, stationery supplies, and copies of Richardson's newly published *Beyond the Mississippi.*[44] But the role of the newspaper editor was portrayed as one of the most challenging professions in the West. A judge may adjourn his court, schools and houses of worship may close their shutters, but "the journalist must forget before to-morrow the sorrows of to-day, must write gayly and freshly, as a newsmonger, on the trifle of the hour, whatever burden has been laid upon the same hour, by Providence or his brains as a man."[45]

Another editorial excursion of 150 editors from Chicago found their way to the Rocky Mountains in October, accompanied by Mr. George Pullman of the Chicago-based Pullman Palace [Railroad] Car Company.

During the previous year, the U. S. Senate amended the Pacific Railroad Bill, proposing an opportunity for the Kansas Pacific Railroad to connect with the Union Pacific at a point against the foothills west of Denver.[46] This rail route was to replace the financially ailing horse-drawn Butterfield Stagecoach line to protect the supply-line to the Denver and Rocky Mountain area. The proposed railroad would provide Front-Range farmers with an opportunity to send 100,000 acres of cultivated crops to Eastern markets. The bill did not pass, but an amendment to the original allowed the Union Pacific to build a connector-spur to the western line of the Territory providing that the Colorado Central would use the government subsidy for track-building and provide their proportionate share for track up-keep.[47]

"Denver was but a feeble, struggling, inchoate frontier metropolis then," Frank Hall of *The Denver Times* wrote, "with great aspirations based upon rather insecure foundations, but it had some strong men who, as the sequel proved, were equal to the emergency of building and fortifying a great prestige. It possessed the same spirit in 1867-to-1868 which in later times made it famous throughout the country, and those who were foremost in promoting railway enterprises when the Union Pacific was rushing along the continent at the rate of three or four miles a day, are still among the leaders of the present epoch. They had very little money, it is true, but they possessed the energy and fertility of resource which, rightly applied, brings mighty consequences."[48]

The success of the press excursion and the proposed railroad spur into Denver produced interest in several new programs that developed in November of that year. The first was the development of the Board of Trade [later called the Chamber of Commerce] to help promote business to the rest of the country.[49] The second founding was much subtler. Just as the transformation of Uncle Dick Wootton's general store became an oasis for Walapite wheat whiskey that embodied the pistols of inebriated patrons to challenge the safety of the proprietors of the *Rocky Mountain News* office in the attic. Another general store owned by the Londoner family united and embodied members of the press to shoot off quills of printers' ink after partaking in a rot-gut whiskey marketed as "Taos Lightning."

It was said that Londoner arrived in the area when Pikes Peak was merely a hole in the ground and Denver was dirt. He began a wholesale/retail grocery business by himself, but was later joined by his brother, Julius Londoner. Together they added wines and liquors; particularly sherry and El Paso. He maintained two large store rooms with basements—one facing Fifteenth just below the corner of Blake, and the other on Blake near the corner of Fifteenth Street. The wholesale side of his business extended from Old Mexico, west to Utah, north to the Black Hills, and east to Kansas.[50]

Wolfe Londoner often extended his hospitality by opening his "Cyclone Cellar" to the camaraderie of the Fourth Estate. Londoner fancied himself to be a writer and enjoyed the vibrant friendship offered by Denver's diverse scribes. His supply trains brought food stuffs from the southwest along with barrels of "Taos Lightning." The whiskey became a drawing card to hydrate a lively game of poker among competing editors while the freshly published newspapers were being distributed.

Studio portrait of Wolfe Londoner; grocer, friend of the Denver Press Club, and Mayor of Denver (1889-1891).

Courtesy of the Denver Public Library, Western History Collection, Call #Z-4976

As the *Denver Post* reported, "Everybody knows the secrets of the 'cyclone cellar,' so there is no secret about it at all. It is a place of refuge, where one meets with boundless hospitality and is invited to rest while the storms of life blow over."[51] As one of the earliest suppliers of goods to the young town, Wolfe was often beset by irate customers and negotiated inconsistent financial arrangements with others. "Whatever adverse criticism was made of him, he endeared himself forever to the newspapermen," Ida Libert Uchill wrote in *Pioneers, Peddlers, and Tsadikim.* "In the basement of his fancy food store, he founded his 'Cyclone Cellar' where reporters sought relief from the pressure of the outside world above them and were regaled with Londoner's stories and plenty of 'ink,' which was sold under a different label upstairs."

Another Colorado newspaper described, Londoner's Cyclone Cellar was not a place where people escaped cyclones, but "it will be a point from which cyclones will be manufactured and started on their career. The storms will be those of mirth, and the subscriber will get his money's worth." Others believed the cyclones actually originated when journalists returned home as the sun rose, and their wives discovered most of their husbands' paychecks were lost to a few losing poker hands.

A simple, untitled, local 1867 news item merely reported that "a press club" was established in the bowels of Londoner's Cyclone Cellar among Denver newsmen in time for Thanksgiving libations that year. Since Colorado had yet to become a state, no incorporation papers were filed, not even with the territorial government. For his generosity, the press boys made Londoner a lifelong honorary officer of the press club. William N. Byers later claimed he was elected the first president of the Denver Press Club and anecdotally provided a second source attributing the origins of the club as November 1867, but two other press accounts in the 1890s provided a different account of the club's origin as three years earlier.

"In 1864, I think it was," related Wolfe Londoner, contradicting Byers; "we organized the Denver Press Club. I believe I was the first president of it — either president, or vice president — and that organization proved a great success. We used to meet in my rooms over my store at Fifteenth and Blake streets, and we certainly did have great times. W. B. Vickers, W. E. Pabor, M. J. Gavisk and a number of others, all able men and prominent in the profession, used to gather with us there, and later, in the days of Gene Field, O. H. Rothacker, Will Visscher and others of that bright eccentric coteries of good fellows . . . I was, in fact, a sort of god-father to them all and loved them all most warmly."[52]

In a different newspaper account, Londoner again identified the origin of the press club to be in 1864 at the same location, in the rooms of Constitution Hall before the flood of the same year wiped out much of Lower Downtown. When Major J. B. Thompson, special agent of the Indian bureau, vacated his offices in the building after the Sand Creek Massacre, Mr. Londoner organized the first press club with a half-dozen newspapermen from the three newspapers that covered the town.[53]

The first formal rooms of the Denver Press Club were located above Wolfe Londoner's grocery store (located on the far left side of the picture) at 15th and Blake Streets.

Courtesy of the author

As press club legends and fleeting memories influenced by liberal draws of libations are wont to occur, the origins of "THE" Denver Press Club were probably established in 1867 in the rooms of Constitution Hall in Lower Downtown. "A" press club of camaraderie among Denver's early chroniclers of the news, probably began in 1864 over unlimited tappings of Taos Lightning, many losing hands of poker, and free-flowing fraternal, yet often adversarial, friendships. The lack of formal records indicates the structure of the press club was purely social. We may never definitively learn whether the club began in 1864 or more likely in 1867; nor whether that organizational birth was in the Cyclone Cellar or in more comfortable quarters in a Londoner grocery building.

Londoner's profession was in mercantile sales, but his love of the press earned him a newspaper beat on his résumé. He accompanied the National Editorial Association to Mexico City where he interviewed President

Porfirio Díaz—a journalistic scoop that annoyed his professional editorial friends.[54] Several loving cups, gifts from the National and Colorado Editorial associations, were proudly displayed on Mr. Londoner's mantel at home. "The newspaper boys have been good to me," he explained, "they have honored me for more than I deserve, and I am grateful."[55]

"The spirit of the American game," the *Colorado Sun* described, "seemed to linger about the old building for on the occasion of the regular weekly meeting the usual glass of pale sherry or burgundy customary upon entering the room would hardly disappear before the question, 'Where are the chips?' would be answered by the production of the tools and the commencement of a poker game lasting away into the 'wee small hours.' The game was not a heavy one. The building in which it was played was never lost, but 5-cents ante and 50-cents limit was heavy enough to make many a scribe go back to his work minus a week's salary and plug a bad headache."[56]

At the turn of the next century, the State Editorial Association chose to immortalize Londoner's basement by making the *Cyclone Cellar* the name of a proposed monthly publication. Wolfe Londoner was the publisher and Colorado poet and writer Willie E. Pabor served as editor and manager.[57] Subscriptions included admission to the infamous cellar.[58] In describing both namesakes, the *Littleton Independent* announced, "The editors of Colorado now have a 'sure buff' place of refuge. When the man or woman filled with wrath and armed with a meat-ax or broom-stick, comes to the editorial sanctum to raise one cyclone for the hapless editor, he can fly to Wolfe Londoner's 'Cyclone cellar' and there breathe out his woe in safety and seclusion."[59] When questioned about the future of Denver's editorial sanctuary and Londoner's other business enterprises, he responded, "No sir, I shall not allow a mere trifle like my grocery house, nor any other branch of my private business, to interfere with the success of the 'Cyclone Cellar.' It has come to stay — so long as it can — and I shall stay with it."[60]

The publication lasted a month; W. E. Pabor moved on to publish "Drops of Ink" as a successor to Wolfe Londoner's literary "Cyclone Cellar."[61] The heritage of the libatious "Cyclone Cellar" lives on.

1   *Daily News,* August 3,1867, p. 4
2   Daniel Webster, 1838; (Smiley, 164)
3   Senator George McDuffie; January 25, 1843 (Smiley, 128)
4   "The Himmalaya [sic] of Style," *Rocky Mountain News,* April 12, 1864, p. 4

5 *Uncle Dick Wootton: The Pioneer Frontiersman of the Rocky Mountain Region,* Howard Louis Conard, Lakeside Press, Chicago, Christmas 1957

6 *Rocky Mountain News,* July 7, 1864, p. 7

7 "Denver Sidewalks," *Denver Republican,* January 17, 18XX, p. 4

8 "Bear in Mind," *Rocky Mountain News,* May 17, 1864

9 "File your papers," O. J. Goldrick, associate editor; *Rocky Mountain News,* June 29, 1864

10 Ibid

11 *History of the City of Denver, Arapahoe County and Colorado,* W. B. Vickers, O. L. Baskin & Co., Historical Publishers, Chicago, 1880, p. 20

12 *Rocky Mountain News,* July 7, 1864, p. 4

13 "Out of Paper," *Rocky Mountain News,* September 13, 1864, p. 1

14 "The Reason Why," *Rocky Mountain News,* December 1, 1864, p. 4

15 Colorado Prospector, April 1994, p. 3-4

16 "Important to Subscribers," *Rocky Mountain News,* June 7, 1865

17 "Publishing a Newspaper," *Rocky Mountain News,* October 25, 1866, p. 1

18 Ibid

19 *Rocky Mountain News,* as originally published in *The Denver Times,* March 7, 1867, p. 4

20 *Colorado Newspaper: A History & Inventory, 1859-2000;* Jane C. Harper, Craig W. Leavitt and Thomas J. Noel; Colorado Press Association, 2014, p. 121

21 "Sunday School Casket," *Denver Daily News,* January 19, 1867, p. 2

22 "Introductory," *Colorado Tribune,* May 15, 1867, p. 4

23 "The Colorado Tribune," *Weekly Denver Tribune,* June 12, 1867, p.2

24 "To the Public," *Weekly Denver Tribune,* June 12, 1867, p. 3

25 "Editors," *Weekly Denver Tribune,* June 26, 1867

26 "Corrupting Newspapers," *Weekly Denver Tribune,* November 6, 1867, p. 8

27 Ibid

28 "Newspapers," *Colorado Weekly Tribune,* December 18, 1867, p. 5

29 *Rocky Mountain News,* May 16, 1865

30 "The Cowardly Attack," *Rocky Mountain News,* April 16, 1865, p. 1

31 U. S. National Park Service website, https://www.nps.gov/sand/learn/management/upload/site-location-study_volume-1-2.pdf

32 "The Cowardly Attack," *Rocky Mountain News,* April 16, 1865, p. 1

33 "To the Public, *Rocky Mountain News,* April 16, 1865, p. 1

34 "Prospectus," *Rocky Mountain News,* December 12, 1865, p. 2

35 "Journalism, Journalists, and Readers," *Rocky Mountain News,* January 4, 1866, p. 1

36 "Denouncing the News," *Rocky Mountain News,* 10 January 1866, p. 1

37 "Denouncing the News," *Rocky Mountain News,* January 10, 1866, p. 1

38 *Rocky Mountain News,* September 10, 1867, p. 4

39 "Retrospective," *Weekly Denver Tribune,* September 25, 1867

40 "The Fair and the Editorial Excursion," *Weekly Denver Tribune,* September 25, 1867, p. 5

41 "Our Editorial Guests," *Rocky Mountain News,* October 19, 1867, p. 1

42 "Cities Courtesies," *Rocky Mountain News,* October 28, 1867, p. 1

43 *Rocky Mountain News,* November 30, 1867, p. 4

44 *Daily News,* November 23, 1867, p. 4

45 "Editorial Labor," *Weekly Denver Tribune,* August 28, 1867, p. 6

46 *History of the State of Colorado,* Frank Hall, the Blakely Printing Company, Chicago, 1889, p. 393

47 Ibid, p. 394, 395

48 Ibid, p. 41

49 "Organization of a Board of Trade," *Weekly Colorado Tribune,* November 20, 1867, p. 2

50 "Wolfe Londoner," *Denver Tribune,* January 1, 1878, p. 7

51 "Oldest Merchant in Denver and No Fires or Failures," *Denver Post,* January 23, 1910, p. 35

52 "Editor Wolfe Londoner Expresses His Opinion of a Few New-Fangled Things in Journalism," *Denver Post,* 21 August 1898, p. 21

53 "Oldest Merchant in Denver and No Fires or Failures," *Denver Post,* January 23, 1910, p. 35

54 Ibid

55 Ibid

56 "Stiff Game of 'Hanky Panky,'", *Colorado Sun,* July 10, 1892, p. 24

57 *Summit County Journal* (Breckenridge, CO), February 4, 1900, p. 3

58 *Colorado Transcript* (Golden, CO), February 21, 1900, p. 4

59 "The 'Cyclone Cellar,'" *Littleton Independent,* February 23, 1900, p. 1

60 Ibid

61 *Daily Journal* (Telluride, CO), May 12, 1900, p. 2

CHAPTER 2

No gentleman that is a man, or man that is a gentleman will persist in pilfering the good of his neighbor's paper and cheating the printer out of what is his reasonable due. Yet, even in Denver City, Colorado Territory, U.S.A., there are classes of chaps that will run around each night and sponge their reading out of their neighbor's paper, rather than come to town like men and order the paper left at their own domiciles. Such men are miserly and mean enough to skin a flea for the hide and tallow, tho' they might spoil a six-bit jackknife in the attempt.[1]

The arrival of the railroad spurred jealousy among the competing sectional rivalries. Rail owners sought the editorial community support of individual newspapers. Fueled by additional competition among political interests, sparring editors took their contempt for the editorial adversaries to the pages of their respective publications.

"The *News* can see nothing but the interest of Denver," the *Miners' Register's* editor observed, "… while the *Transcript* is a veritable dog in the manger, neither able to eat hay nor willing the oxen should. And as the *Transcript* barks, the *Times* echoing answers back, and *visa versa* [sic]; like the little yelpers in the suburbs of great cities, who make night hideous till the people in hearing wish they had never been born."[2]

The incivility among Denver papers continued for years. The *Tribune* and the *News* (according to an editorial in the *Denver Daily Times*) were engaged in "harsh words and contemptible flings."[3] Partisan newspapers took umbrage at claims of corruption within the territorial government.

The *Fairplay Sentinel* was just one of many territorial newspapers that described the journalistic fracas: "The *Denver Tribune* is wading and reveling in the blood of its stolen thunder. This Robespierre of modern journalism, fighting as it is, for that which nine-tenths of the people believe to be just and right, so disgusts the general reader with its vain-glorious boastings, its sensationalism, and its want of sound logic, that they are almost compelled to believe that lying is one of the fine arts, and that the *Tribune* possesses this accomplishment to an eminent degree. Corruption should receive the condemnation of every honest man, but at the same time it were better for the press at large to discard flaunting scare-heads, vain boastings, etc., and in their stead produce evidence that can be proven by logical reasoning and argument."[4]

In 1868, O. J. Hollister took over the editorial responsibilities of the *News* and explained the paper's political style and physical appearance. "The prime object of both its editors," explained Hollister, "will be to give the freshest and fullest intelligence possible. . .. It will, of course, advocate the political ideas it always has, and in such spirit as to promote harmony and unity in the party of which it is the organ."[5] Likewise with his "brethren of the press," Hollister pledged to maintain "the cordial relations that now exist between us. Difference of opinion need not necessarily create ill feelings, difference as to facts can be settled one way or the other by reference to admitted authority."[6]

In 1872, *The Denver Daily Times* explained their publication was "the workingmen's organ of Denver," an independent advocate of "the greatest good to the greatest number" without adverse influence from "soulless corporations" and "more local intelligence than any other daily in Denver."[7]

Most Colorado newspapers were blatantly obvious about their editorial political support and readers expected to see the *Denver Republican* and the *Denver Democrat* editorialize their masthead. As Denver prepared for the 1876 national elections, another democratic-daily started publication. In response, the *Rocky Mountain Herald* editorialized on the prospects of another political newspaper competing for limited advertising revenue. "Two democratic papers cannot prosper here, any more than two republican, two German, or two agricultural ones. They may eke out a pittance for a little while, but nothing more. The town is too small, and the Territory too sparse of people, and too glutted with county papers, to patronize five *dailies* in Denver! Better begin to beg for a living at once and be done with it. . .. Talk is cheap, but it takes money to buy cider or to establish a newspaper. The *old established* Denver papers, which stood by the town through thick and thin, ought, in equity, to have all the support you can spare them now, instead of bestowing it on every new scheme which comes around to 'claim' your patronage."[8]

Instead of fighting the competition, the *Rocky Mountain Herald* published another editorial, a week later, to clarify that the role of the public press was to serve as the protector and conservator of the public. The newspaper must be faithful to the people and protect them from schemes, cheats or endangerment to their welfare, life, or morals. "The community's interests can be served by showing up frauds . . . [t]rying to thrive at the public's expense. The press which, for a matter of patronage, ignores an outrage or allows an injury on its community, ought to merit the contempt of mankind, if not deserve the damnation of God!"[9]

Despite the *Herald's* warning, three new newspapers began publication in May 1875—the Greeley *Horticulturist,* the *Alma News,* and the *Colorado Springs Free Press.* The *Herald* continued to insist there were three too many daily newspapers in Denver, and "thrice too many 'weeklies.'" Denver needed just one good morning daily paper, a good evening daily (of opposite or independent political views), one good agricultural newspaper, one good German-language paper, plus the reliability of the *Rocky Mountain Herald.* "All other are bound to become, if they are not already, mere impecunious, adventurous barnacles on the body politic. This is what 'everybody says,' and it 'must be true.'"[10]

Two days later, the daily *Transcript* and the daily *Democrat* ceased publication; allegedly due to an over-saturation of political newspapers funded by individuals and groups with their agenda for the community. "Blackmailers and blatherskites," wrote the *Herald,* "sap heads and swell heads, may hang along here for a year or two, but they don't do themselves or their too-confiding victims any good, in the long run. Denver is beginning to see through these latter-day schemers, and has, at last, begun to discriminate between modest merit, established industry, and independence of salary in any shape. The *Herald* has witnessed the death of a dozen catch-pennies here since '60 and shall see a couple more before '76. Serves 'em right. Denver demands only 'straight goods,' and don't like too large a supply of even that."[11]

Denver was not the only community that was dealing with an over-saturation of newspapers and a churn from papers that failed in the competition for limited readership. During 1874-1875, approximately

1,000 newspapers failed throughout the country. It was calculated that eight-million dollars (or $8,000 per newspaper) were invested in each defaulted newspaper. Among those investors in the newspaper business were "275 merchants and advertisers, 315 school teachers, 57 lawyers, 4 blacksmiths, 33 plasterers, 10 farmers, 200 fanatics of various classes afflicted with literary lesion, 100 ambitious but visionary young men who drew upon their fathers and thus suddenly exhausted large margins of the paternal capital, and 6 lottery men."[12]

As early as 1879, the *Daily Times* editorialized the demise of many newspapers that began in the first decade of Denver City.

Daily Times, July 7, 1879; courtesy of the author

For the first decade, the Denver Press Club remained an informal oasis for newspapermen to escape irate politicians, subscribers, advertisers and anyone else vital to the publishing business. Occasionally, the bleary-eyed and ink-stained denizens of the Cyclone Cellar ventured out, only to slip into a darkened theater of vaudevillian character. In 1877, writers for the various newspapers fell into the habit of having a late-Saturday-night brunch at the old "opera" house. Located in the old log building at what is now 16th and Lawrence Streets, it was said the theater closed if a sudden rain shower poured through the vast number of bullet holes in the roof. The press club boys and Forrester were close friends and the proprietor always reserved a twelve-to-fifteen front-row seats for their evening trysts. The *Greeley Tribune* reported about the appearance of the pressmen, "however grave in appearance and deportment, it was only on rare occasions any of them were taken for clergymen."[13]

During one November 1877 performance, a member of the Denver Press Club failed to arrive until half-way through the performance. When the latecomer finally appeared, the entire front-row gathering of his peers rose with the utmost gravity. The actors, aware of the late arrival, stopped the play and stood in silent honor of the tardy patron. The reporter was taken aback, but quickly regained his dignity and proceeded to his chair as the audience and actors roared in approval.[14]

After being admitted to the Union as the 38th state in 1876, Colorado welcomed the Denver Press Club's formal incorporation in 1877. In the rooms of Mr. Londoner on Fifteenth Street over the Exchange Bank, the gentlemen appointed a committee to prepare the organizational paperwork.[15] The formalized name remained as "The Denver Press Club" — "to promote fraternal feelings among the members and afford an inter-change of ideas regarding business. There will also be literary features, and project for a publication under the auspices of the club, is assuming shape."[16]

The men reconvened on Thanksgiving afternoon to approve the constitution and by-laws (written by club member "Professor" Dellenbaugh)[17] and elected officers: William N. Byers (president), Captain Frank Hall (vice president), Thomas F. Dawson (secretary), and W. B. Vickers (treasurer). Wolfe Londoner joined the four to fill out the executive committee of the organization. A committee on literature included Chairman Henry Ward, Captain J. T. Smith, R. G. Dill, William Whist, and J. Harrison Mills.[18] During a subsequent special meeting, Professor Nathan Shepard, Colonel Pickett (a sculptor), J. J. Lambert (business proprietor), and General Raymond M. Stevenson (editor of the Pueblo

Chieftain) were approved as honorary members. During the next decade, the membership outgrew Londoner's modest accommodations.

A suite of rooms in the opera-house block was sufficient to accommodate the forty newspapermen from Denver who immediately joined the revamped club in 1886. While the active membership was local newspapermen, the editors of the state were enrolled as non-active members. The initiation fee was $10, and dues were $1 per month; non-active members paid $5 per year.[19]

On Christmas Eve, the press club received its first Christmas present. Mrs. Eva Davidson donated a handsome wastebasket, lined on the inside with corded silk and the outside covered with dark-red Berlin wool decorated with white flowers. The exterior cover included the initials "D. P. C."[20]

The seventeen available members of the newly reformulated Denver Press Club proposed to receive their friends on New Year's Day during a reception[21] in the large private room of Wolfe Londoner. The *Colorado Weekly Chieftain* in Pueblo described their host as "the friend in need, who has been bilked oftener than any other man in Colorado by unworthy members of the newspaper fraternity."[22] The New Year's reception was determined to demonstrate that the Denver Press Club "should take the lead in setting a good example, worthy the emulation of the public."[23] The wives of the press-club members joined Miss Schleicher, a prominent Denver singer, and her mother to perform the musical entertainment for the reception.[24] The literary committee conducted a debate on the subject of "The Relation of the Press to Public Entertainers."[25]

Beginning at 9 a.m., more than 300 community leaders passed through the Denver Press Club room that was lavishly decorated with cedar, fresh plants and flowers to complement the refreshment tables full of turkey, cold meat, sandwiches, and a variety of cakes.[26] W. E. Pabor read a poem, "The Editor's Dream," and a dance band provided music until after midnight.[27] The governor was attending the press-club reception plus a second reception at the armory for the Governor's Guards. The refreshment committee served excellent coffee, and other spreads, but offered no wine at either event, "which was very thoughtful on the part of the receivers, for a fellow had to go somewhere to sober off occasionally," according to the *Colorado Weekly Chieftain*.[28]

Most newspapermen of that era embraced the reference of "being Bohemians," a popular term for artists and writers with informal and unconventional social habits. Likewise, it didn't take the club members long to forego the need for formal record-keeping for the Secretary of State and return to the casual games at the poker table. For various reasons, the membership gradually dwindled. The *Greeley Tribune* reported, "some of the brightest went to Riverside," acknowledging that the city cemetery was beginning to fill. "Of others who came in, some intended to make their fortune in a year or two and go home, and others were bohemians. Hence, they did not become members of the club, and in time it became an event of the past."[29] The club never ceased operation, but it did return to the level of a social club among a coterie of colorful Bohemian newspapermen.

Competition wasn't the only challenge faced by newspapers of that era. Alexander Graham Bell's invention of the telephone was thought to threaten any opportunity for people to gather together to receive information. The *New York Times* reported, "Thus the telephone, by bringing music and ministers into every home, will empty the concert-halls and the churches."[30] However, the phone became "an ingenious invention" within a year, enabling the transmission of news, information, and entertainment. Quickly it was eclipsed by another new invention—the phonograph allowing communication to be recorded and saved for future use.[31]

Captain W. H. Pierce was the first to introduce Alexander Graham Bell's new invention to Denver. He built a system that connected his coal office on Blake Street to the Denver & Rio Grande Railroad depot approximately 1600-feet away.[32] Two years after the invention of the phone, Mr. F. O. Vaille stepped forward to help Denver become inter-connected with other phone users throughout the country. Headquarters for Denver's first phone system was located on Larimer Street over Frick's shoe store.[33] It was activated on February 20, 1879 "and radiated thence to every point of the compass, covering the entire city like a monster cobweb" to 200 subscribers. Messengers were attached to the telephone office to deliver messages to people not yet connected to the new communication device. To help Denver residents adjust to the telephone, the phone company issued the following instructions to subscribers:

1. Always hang the telephone on its hook, as your circuit cannot be used by others until the telephone is so hung.
2. Never touch the instrument when the bell hammer stands away from the bell, as that indicates that the line is in use.

3. To signal—press the button on the right of the bell.
4. To communicate with the Central office—signal two bells, wait for their response, after which remove the telephone from its hook, and be careful to push the hook to the left; and then, holding the telephone firmly to the ear, you will hear the voice of the operator at the central office.
5. To converse with stations on your circuit—signal slowly the number of the station you desire to converse with. After receiving their response, sound your own signal, that they may know who is to talk with them.
6. To converse with stations not on your own circuit—notify the central office with whom you wished to be placed in communication, first giving your own name; then hang your telephone on its hook, and as soon as the desired connection is made the operator at the central office will tap your bell once, as a signal to go ahead; and prompt attention to these signals is desired, to save waiting on the part of either party.
7. When your signal is sounded, always answer by repeating it, when you will hear the station calling, sound their signal, that you may know with whom you are to talk.[34]

The *Tribune* had two telephones—one in the editorial room and the other in the business office. The *Times* sarcastically noted that if the editor wanted to talk to the business manager, he could wheel his stuffed chair to the telephone, signal the telephone switchboard at the phone company headquarters on Larimer Street, and ask to be switched to the newspaper's business manager located in the next room.[35] Superintendent Vaille explained he was not responsible for such laziness.

Three operators were on duty at headquarters during the day and one at night. As a "gift" to the community, Superintendent Vaille considered giving subscribers the exact time of day at high noon on each day. "To carry out this plan," the *Denver Daily Times* explained, "at one minute before twelve the wires will all be grounded, and the editor of the time department given control. Each bell will strike once a second for forty-five seconds. The patrons will know that it is fifteen seconds before twelve when these strokes cease, and they can consult their watches to get the exact time. The next stroke will be at twelve, followed by four other strokes, or one every second, when they will cease, and the business be conducted in its usual manner until one minute before twelve on the following day."[36]

By 1882 there were 605 telephones in daily use in Denver with an additional 25 being added every month. Five hundred miles of telephone cable crisscrossed throughout Denver. When a *Denver Times* reporter went to visit the central switching office, he noted a new development in the communications of information as a social network among people. "The scene is a curious one. A 'perfect Babel' prevails—not a Babel of confusion or noise—but a Babel of meaningless and semi-mechanical words and phrases. Every reader has heard the disconnected ejaculations of a party using a telephone. Imagine ten such people, the tones of their voices indicating a perfect lack of interest in their utterances, all talking together around an upright table of brass bands and little pegs. 'Hellos,' 'Wells,' and numbers being their sole responses, and an entire absence of the ringing or clattering which seems to be an inseparable characteristic of the telephone . . ."[37]

Next on Vaille's list was to introduce "a scheme which will be hailed with joy by numerous patrons" — the establishment of public telephones at various places throughout the city for the benefit of non-subscribers for 10-cents a call.

Editorial parties continued to travel to Denver. The 1877 Kansas party of 80 notables arrived via the new Kansas Pacific railroad.[38] Wolfe Londoner would have represented the Denver Press Club but was incapacitated. "That sucker," reported the *Daily Times*, "who stuck his foot through the demijohn [a large globular water bottle wrapped in wicker] the other day produced a permanent discouragement."[39] When the party reached Denver, the injured Londoner and C. H. McLaughlin showed the flat-landers the wonders of the Chinese wash houses (in the vicinity of Denver's opium dens and brothels). When Denver Press Club member Fred Salomon learned of the tour, he piously exclaimed, "May the Lord have mercy on their souls." The *Daily Times* questioned whether Salomon's blessing was intended for the two press-club guides, the Kansas editors, or the Chinese.[40]

The Kansas scribes, many of whom made earlier visits to the fledgling Colorado communities, were impressed with Londoner's representation of the Denver Press Club despite his foot wound. "He made the lemonade," *The Denver Times* reported, "cut the bread, and buttered it, comforted the sorrowing, nursed the sick, and in fact did everything that could be done for such a crowd, besides stuffing their note books full of jokes, and incidents and stories of the early days in the regions through which the train passed."[41] In return, the Kansas editors and the Denver Press Club members presented Londoner with a solid silver goblet inscribed to Londoner for his hospitality. "When the cup was produced," it was reported in the *Times*, "[Londoner] was so overcome by his emotions that, the present 'being what is termed among the medical fraternity as a 'dry cup'—he proceeded to fill it up with tears and in broken tones spoke of the astonishment and pleasure afforded him."[42] The newspapermen then adjourned to take a "wet cup."

The press excursion rose to approximately 200 people as the Union Pacific brought another party of editors, professors and capitalists from Boston and New York, to Boulder Falls.[43] The assistant superintendent of the Bobtail Mine guided some of the people 1,000 feet into the mine to take ore samples as souvenirs of their visit.[44] The return trip filled the baggage car with bushes, shrubs and trees from the mountains, and cactus and soap-weed from the plains; "Petrifactions" and topaz were collected along the Platte River. "The interest taken in whatever could be found relating to Colorado indicated a superior order of intelligence in the party," reported the *Daily Times*.[45]

Wolfe Londoner's exuberance during the Kansas press excursion was followed by deep mourning a few weeks later when his wife suddenly took ill, lost consciousness, and quickly passed away. Her attending physicians attributed the rapid onset to "congestion of the brain."[46] A large concourse of leading citizens, in a long line of carriages, accompanied Rabbi Samuel Weil of Congregation Emanuel to the Hebrew cemetery in Denver.[47]

The Denver Press Club was euphemistically considered the keeper of the cultural mores of the region because of the professions of most of its members. The club was more realistically a vessel for cultural booking press-agents to get the word out about traveling performers. Two groups of entertainers arrived in Denver at approximately the same time in 1878. The McGibney Family was performing to good audiences in the leading churches in Denver. Madame Rentz and her Female Minstrels were creating a sensation at the bawdier "opera" houses. Public opinion was divided on the morality of Madame Rentz' troupe. To settle the matter, the Sunday edition of the *Mirror* alerted the Denver Press Club and reported, ". . . the front seats would be reserved for graybeards and bald-headed sinners, who are supposed to be past all redemption."[48]

"Being a high moral and eminently respectable association," the newspaper continued, the Denver Press Club held a secret meeting and appointed Messrs. Henry Ward of the *Tribune,* W. B. Vickers of the *News,* R. G. Dill of the *Times* and Capt. Smith of the *Democrat* to join Wolfe Londoner and Halsey Rhoades of the *Town Talk* to fill those front-row seats and report on the morality of the performance. Rhoades was added to the list because he was well-acquainted with most of the blondes in the performance. Mr. M. B. Leavitt, the gentlemanly manager of the theater, invited the party into the green room (more appropriately renamed the wine room) at the end of the performance, where the ladies of the company were interviewed about the morals of their show. The *Chieftain* continued the story for their readers, complete with coded descriptions to make the article palatable to family readers:

> Smith was made spokesman of the committee, and approaching Miss Montague, the finest built one of the "Forty Thieves," he inquired after some hesitation.
>
> "Is this thing all on the square, or is it like some of the packages sent out to their dupes by the fellows who advertise counterfeit money, all saw-dust?"
>
> The troupe answered in chorus: "You came here to find out, satisfy yourselves, gentlemen."
>
> The committee immediately withdrew, declaring their willingness to take the word of the ladies. As the party bowed themselves out, Vickers remarked audibly to Dill and Ward—casting a bashful glance at Miss Santley— "But hasn't she got a fine pair of calves for a heifer?"[49]

"The committee on legs" (as the newspaper described them) reported to the full press club membership the next evening. In their opinion, there was no fraud connected to the show and nothing "necessarily immoral" any more than "The Black Crook" (the first book musical that became the prototype of the modern musical theater).

Things were quiet for the club in 1878, prompting the *Central Call* newspaper to ask if the "intellectual coterie" was still in operation. The *Rocky Mountain News* was quick to respond, implying club members were busy walking the streets of Denver searching for news stories. "The club is in an active, healthy state of preservation—rather, retired, though still compact, firm to its constitution and by-laws, and alive to the fact that—'these are the times that try men's soles [sic].'"[50]

To prove the club was still active, a special meeting was scheduled in mid-May to decide whether "a journalist is a gentleman or a vagabond."[51] Club leaders expected full attendance. The revived and re-awakened press club began accepting invitations from the railroads that connected Denver with the mountain communities who were encouraging tourists to visit the Rocky Mountain resorts.[52]

The Denver publishing industry also experienced considerable changes in their focus and ownership. In 1878, the *Sunshine Courier* moved to Boulder and became the *Boulder County Courier* before it merged with the *Boulder News*. The *Longmont Post* began publishing with William L. Condit as editor before retiring shortly afterward. W. E. Pabor began publishing the *Valley Home and Farm*. The *Colorado Springs Gazette* published a temporary daily during the elections but became a "bright and sparkling" permanent daily. In Lake City, C. L. Peyton retired from the *Silver World*, leaving H. C. Olney alone at the editor's desk. Sax Cramer acquired the *Cañon City Avalanche* and changed it to the *Cañon City Record*. Mathias Custer launched the *Alamosa News*, and the *Independent* was moved from Garland to Alamosa. Ouray's *San Juan Sentinel* ceased publication. The rapid growth of Leadville prompted R. S. Allen to establish the *Reveille* as a daily newspaper. William Hogan suspended the *Alma News* and added the *Eclipse* to compete with the *Reveille* in Leadville. The *Trinidad Enterprise and Chronicle* became a daily and took on upcomer the *Trinidad Daily News* published by Henry Sturgis. C. E. Parkinson took over the *Douglas County News* and changed it to become the *News-Letter*. Publisher Laird & Marlow of the *Central Call* acquired the *Daily Register* from H. M. Rhoads. The *Greenbacker* was born in Denver. Captain R. G. Dill and others bought the *Mirror*, and the *Rocky Mountain News* was purchased by W. A. H. Loveland who changed it from a Republican newspaper to a Democratic one.[53]

The first word that year from the press club wasn't about the journalistic members; it was about their esteemed friend, Wolfe Londoner. In *The First Hundred Years: An Informal History of Denver and the Rocky Mountain News*, Robert L. Perkin described Mr. Londoner as a proprietor who grew to become "a rotund grocer who later was elected mayor and who enjoyed great popularity among the newspapermen because of his well-stocked cellar."[54]

RESIDENCE OF WOLFE LONDONER, DENVER, COL.

The second floor of Wolfe Londoner's private residence at 600
Champa Street became the Denver Press Club in the late 1870s.

History of the City of Denver, Arapahoe County and Colorado; O. L.
Baskin & Co., Historical Publishers; Chicago, 1880, p. 418.

After the passing of his wife in 1877, Londoner was once again ready to
"commit matrimony" two years later and was building a handsome residence
on the north side of Denver at 600 Champa Street.[55] The *Colorado Weekly
Chieftain* learned that one large room on the top level of the new home
was being set aside ("by special agreement with his future better half")[56]
for future meetings of the Denver Press Club. The new press-club house
was handsomely finished in several kinds of ornamental wood. "Wolf[e]
is one of the best fellows living," the newspaper continued, "whose sunny
disposition and excellent social qualities are a fortune to him. The *Chieftain*
wishes him any amount of happiness."[57]

On Thursday evening, April 17, 1879; Wolfe Londoner and Fanny
Anthony were married in her parents' home at 793 Lawrence Street.[58]
Among the gifts sent by admirers of the couple, the Denver Press Club
provided a table setting of silver forks, knives, and other flatware.
Accompanying the gift was a note: "The Denver Press Club presents its
compliments and the accompanying present, wishing you all the happiness
that connubial bliss can bring. May these tokens of our affection correspond

in their sterling worth with the quality of your devotion to each other, and may your love be pure gold instead of merely solid silver. Your affectionate friends, The Denver Press Club."[59]

Soon it was back to normal for the club. During an Odd Fellows' anniversary reception on April 28, 1879, the Odd Fellows presented a tastefully frosted cake to the Denver Press Club. The members retreated to their new club-house room ". . . To discuss the manner of its disposal," related the *Denver Daily Times*. "Some time was occupied in arguing the question during which the present disappeared. Both the question and the cake were effectually disposed of at one-and-the-same time."[60] The second piece of press-club news to reach the newspapers was "an irresponsible report" that claimed the Denver Press Club would challenge the Medical Society to a baseball game. The *Denver Daily Times* explained there was no truth to the claim, "The Press Club bats with its head, not with a stick."[61]

Earlier in the year, Denver editors learned that Joseph P. Farmer, senior owner of the *Democrat* succumbed to heart disease on New Year's Eve in Galena, Illinois. He left Denver just a fortnight earlier to be with his family for the holidays. He was one of Colorado's wealthiest stockmen and senior proprietor of the *Democrat* since September 1876.[62] Together with the Cattle Growers' Association, the Denver Press Club met at Walhalla [one of Denver's theaters on Curtis Street] and proceeded together to the Catholic Cathedral for the January 3 requiem mass.[63]

By May, the *Daily Democrat* was for sale under a chattel mortgage. The newspaper office was crowded with gentlemen anxious to acquire a first-class newspaper. The *Denver Daily Times* reported, "the combined assets of the crowd were variously estimated at from a dollar-and-a-half to ten dollars, but each man kept his hand on his pocket and his mouth shut." The office was taken by the county treasurer to pay two years of back taxes, but the Farmer estate paid the taxes and turned the *Democrat* over to Henry Ward and his financial backers who converted the paper into the *Republican*, Denver's third newspaper supporting that political party.[64]

The *Denver Daily Times* acknowledged "it is simply an old form in a new dress." Editor Ward defined the policy of the paper as an "aggressive and unrelenting warfare upon the Democratic party, and the devotion of its power to the upbuilding of the Republican organization, and the maintenance of the principles it fought for in its wrestle with State's rights rebellion. This is our comprehension of the duty of every Republican newspaper in the land at the present time."[65]

Despite each major community in Colorado having their own press club, the State Press Association was formed in 1878 at what is now the intersection of 17th and Wazee in Lower Downtown Denver as a "press organization." Twenty-three gathered to create "an organization to take trips and drink booze."[66] The Colorado Press Association's contemporary website states a Colorado editor reported on the subsequent field trip that the organization members took to Central City. "Everything went smoothly until the train reached a defile known as Running Lode Gulch; here two coaches jumped the track and crashed into the ditch. Fortunately, no great damage was done, the editors suffered chiefly from injured dignity."[67]

Like the Denver Press Club, the statewide Colorado Press Association initially began as a fraternal organization, but later progressed to likewise being an advocate of freedom of speech, continuing education for journalists, and civil discourse on democratic issues. The organization began with fifty members in 1879, representing the fifty-nine newspapers in the state at the time. Many newspapermen were members of both organizations, blending similarities of the mutual advocates of the First Amendment, William N. Byers' hospitality, and Wolfe Londoner's elixir in oak barrels.

Meanwhile, the Denver Press Club maintained their appreciation of Colorado's extensively connected railroad system. Colonel C. W. Fisher, superintendent of the South Park Railroad, invited the club to have exclusive access to their new railcar. Holding down security and selectively blocking the aisles for the special event was none other than Wolfe Londoner. The *Denver Republican* reported "The stupendous form of Wolfe Londoner obstructed the entrance to the car—a vigilant guard, massive as the Cardiff giant, puffed up, and powerful as Hercules—preventing the entrance of all except those who displayed the insignia of the club—either as members or guests."[68]

Four baskets of lunch were prepared for each traveler plus two crates of strawberries and several cases of Alken & Rogers ice cream. As the *Republican* editor reported, the train pulled away from Union Station and headed up the Platte, "into the gorges through which it rushes into the cool cañon, and while you idled away your time in church, or sweltered and perspired in your limited nook of shade, we, with undamped linen, gazed on nature, clad in her bright green verdure, unsmirched by city soot or dust of highways, while we were fanned by snow-chilled winds, which, rushing from the wintry peaks, drop to the valleys and become gentle zephyrs with the refreshing touch of mighty altitudes yet upon them."[69]

As the train of journalists and friends approached the scenic canyons and gorges, a young Mr. Jingle decided to tempt the wordsmiths with an obvious pun— "This is gorge . . .." upon which "a wilderness of booted limbs" sudden thrust in the lad's direction, sending the punster sailing across the train car. The newspaper account continued, "A score of delicate journalistic handkerchiefs were seen in use brushing the toes of a score of small journalistic boots in silence, and the youthful Jingle was dismissed . . . without a word of censure, praise or hope of a better existence."[70]

Other press club members were pressed into service for other purposes. Frank Woodbury straddled the pilot [or cow catcher] at the front of the steam locomotive, successfully frightening cattle from the track. Once the train reached the town of Webster, it stopped for a twenty-minute lunch break before heading up the steeper grade to Kenosha Hill and eventually to the 10,200-foot marker; the greatest altitude reach by any railway in America; before heading down into South Park. Fellow wordsmith, Tom Dawson took advantage of a rest-stop for the train, filled his hat with peanuts and ventured outside to stretch his legs. He carelessly sat down on a large cactus plant, leaping up before he could say "dang" and count to one — although he did say "dang" according to the paper. He reportedly said that he was confident that no other journalist in the excursion was half full of so many good "points."

The Denver pressmen barely had time to resume their daily assignments at their respective newspapers when members of the State Press of Ohio arrived on the Kansas Pacific. Described in the newspaper as the "Knights of the Quill," the Ohio excursionists planned to stay a few days before returning home. A four-o'clock mini-excursion was arranged with twenty-five horse-drawn carriages that pulled up to the ladies' entrance of the American House (where the Ohio guests were staying). Mayor Richard Sopris and members of the city government helped load their guests into the carriages.

The first stop was in West Denver where the party paused at the Denver Brewery to judge between Denver and Ohio beer before viewing the network of irrigation ditches. A quick stop at the residence of Colonel James Archer, and then the party continued on to Wolfe Londoner's home where the Denver Press Club hosted a reception before returning to the American House at 7 p.m. A half hour later, most of the gentlemen went out onto 15th Street to witness the unscheduled skills of the Denver Fire Department. An alarm was turned in from Box 13 at George Tritch's store.

Within 90 seconds of sounding the alarm, the Denver Fire Department arrived, and water was pouring onto the building.[71]

Board meetings were held twice a year, and the Fourth of July 1879 meeting was hosted at Londoner's home.[72] Before business was conducted, Wolfe Londoner invited the members and guests to spend an hour burning $200 worth of fireworks "during which several bald heads were treated to blisters,"[73] according to the *Denver Daily Times*. Wolfe Londoner stood on the portico of his Champa Street mansion "with a blazing Roman candle in each hand, shedding brilliant sparks in fiery showers on the bald apex of his head, while fire crackers by the pack flashed and detonated about his feet—his herculean figure, thus brought out from the obscurity of night, looked amidst the flash and blaze of streaming fire, like Ajax defying the lightning."[74]

Once the supply of fireworks was exhausted, refreshments were "introduced and disposed of" by the partiers. "After all had eaten and imbibed till they found it more pleasurable to quit than to continue," the *Daily Republican* related, "and when the smell of powder and the odor of burning Havanas filled the house, the club retired to its rooms, and was called to order by the President. Club members excused themselves from the ladies, retired to a den at the top of the house and elected the incumbent officers:[75] A. J. Woodbury (president), Wolfe Londoner (vice president), B. F. Zallinger (secretary), M. J. Gavisk (assistant secretary), and F. J. V. Skiff (treasurer). The Executive Committee included the officers plus S. T. Armstrong.[76]

Little attention was paid in the newspapers about the Denver Press Club until Thanksgiving when Wolfe Londoner hosted one of his over-the-top dinner parties for the press club and their guests. Shortly before 5 o'clock, nearly every street car passing 600 Champa Street came to a stop to allow one or two attractive men with their ladies on their way up the steps to the home of Mr. and Mrs. Londoner. A warm fire in the elegant parlor provided an opportunity for the guests to mingle before the doors were flung open "revealing a dining room in every way adequate to a well-regulated family."[77]

The 1879 Thanksgiving fare included familiar luxury meals, some of which will sound completely foreign to 21st century culinary palates and got sillier as the menu expanded into references to several Denver newspapers and the publishing business in general — Soups (green turtle and bouillon), Fish (fresh mackerel, Rocky Mountain trout, Boulder shad, and railroad ties). Joists (turkey with oyster dressing), boiled leg of mutton, roast beef with stewed onions, and boiled tongue. Game (antelope with pioneer dressing, poker, snipe, mountain sheep, antelope with saw-dust stuffing, and black-tail deer), Entrees (poached eggs, larded quail, belle fritters, oyster patties, apricot charlotte, fillets of chicken with barnacle sauce, *Reveille* quads, *Banner* grouse, roller-moulds garnished with press rags, and commercial hash). Press board (South Park Salad, chicken salad, pickled cucumbers). Vegetables (small potatoes, cabbage, green corn, green peas, sweet potatoes, Fort Collins carrots, mashed turnips). Various puddings and Pastry (sponge cake, pound cake, roller cake, ink cake, puffs, dump-pile jelly, a la Vandemoer, Stimson Charlotte, oranges, apples, dates, figs, walnuts, hickory nuts and other hard nuts, confectionery, taffy). Fluids (Holly Water, Kentish cider, mocha coffee, tea, Bona Rye, and others).[78]

Denver Press Club events had a reputation of providing gatherings that were full of culinary delights, international entertainment, and western hospitality. For a community that was only two decades old, the local journalists reveled at every opportunity to correct their cow-town image when their eastern peers traveled to the wild west.

1 *Daily News,* March 17, 1864, p. 4
2 "The Railroad Interests of Colorado and the Newspapers," *Colorado Tribune,* December 11, 1867, p. 7
3 *Denver Daily Times,* May 9, 1872; p. 2, c. 1
4 "The *Denver Tribune:* What the Territorial Press Think of that Concern," (originally published in the *Fairplay Sentinel), Denver Mirror,* April 26, 1874, p. 1
5 *Rocky Mountain News,* O. J. Hollister, May 4, 1868
6 Ibid
7 *Denver Daily Times,* May 28, 1872, p. 1. c. 3
8 *Rocky Mountain Herald,* March 6, 1875, p. 2
9 *Rocky Mountain Herald,* March 27, 1876, p. 2
10 *Rocky Mountain Weekly Herald,* May 8, 1875, p. 3
11 *Rocky Mountain Herald,* May 29, 1875, p. 2
12 *Rocky Mountain Herald,* June 19, 1875, p. 2
13 "Letter from Denver," *Greeley Tribune,* January 13, 1892, p. 4
14 Ibid
15 *Rocky Mountain News,* November 6, 1877, p. 4
16 *Rocky Mountain News,* November 13, 1877, p. 4
17 *Colorado Weekly Chieftain* (Pueblo, CO), April 25, 1878, p. 2
18 "An Organization Perfected," *Rocky Mountain News,* December 1, 1877, p. 4

19 "Denver Press Club Adopts Constitution and By-Laws," *Western Gazette*, edited 75 years later by Jack Riddle, February 12, 1961, Vol. 2, No. 7

20 *Rocky Mountain News*, December 25, 1877, p. 4

21 *Denver Daily Times*, December 12, 1877, p. 4

22 *Colorado Weekly Chieftain* (Pueblo, CO), December 13, 1877, p. 1

23 "The Press Club," *rocky Mountain News*, December 12, 1877, p. 4

24 "State Items," *Colorado Weekly Chieftain* (Pueblo, CO), December 20, 1877, p. 2

25 "The Press Club," *Rocky Mountain News*, December 12, 1877, p. 4

26 *Colorado Weekly Chieftain* (Pueblo, CO), January 10, 1878, p. 2

27 "The Denver Press Club," *Rocky Mountain News*, January 3, 1878, p. 3

28 *Colorado Weekly Chieftain* (Pueblo, CO), January 10, 1878, p. 2

29 "Letter from Denver," *Greeley Tribune*, January 13, 1892, p. 4

30 *Rocky Mountain Weekly Herald*, June 17, 1876, p. 1

31 "The Phonograph," *New York Times*, November 7, 1877

32 *Colorado Weekly Chieftain*, January 10, 1878, p. 2

33 "The Telephone System," *Denver Daily Times*, February 1, 1879, p. 1

34 "Halloo There!" *Denver Daily Times*, February 28, 1879, p. 4

35 *Denver Daily Times*, March 1, 1879, p. 4

36 "By Telephone," *Denver Daily Times*, March 19, 1879, p. 4

37 "Local News, Telephonic: A Call on Manager Vaille and a Visit to the Operating Rooms—Public Telephones to be Erected in Denver," *Denver Times*, April 12, 1882, p. 3

38 "The Kansas Editors," *Daily Times*, June 18, 1877, p. 4

39 *Daily Times*, June 20, 1877, p. 4

40 *Daily Times*, June 22, 1877, p. 4

41 Cupped," *Denver Times*, June 27, 1877, p. 4

42 "Cupped," *Denver Times*, June 27, 1877, p. 4

43 *Daily Times*, June 30, 1877, p. 4

44 *Daily Times*, July 9, 1877, p. 4

45 *Daily Times*, July 10, 1877, p. 4

46 "Sudden Death," *Daily Times*, September 20, 1877, p. 4

47 "Mrs. Londoner's Funeral," *Daily Times*, September 22, 1877, p. 4

48 *Colorado Weekly Chieftain* (Pueblo, CO), January 24, 1878, p. 2

49 *Colorado Weekly Chieftain* (Pueblo, CO), January 24, 1878, p. 2

50 "A Pertinent Question," *Rocky Mountain News*, May 3,1878, p. 4

51 *Denver Daily Tribune*, May 16, 1878, p. 4

52 "From the Capital," *Colorado Miner* (Georgetown, CO), July 13, 1878, p. 2

53 "Colorado Newspaper Changes, 1878," *Denver Daily Times*, January 3, 1879, p. 4

54 *The First Hundred Years: An Informal History of Denver and the* Rocky Mountain News," Robert L. Perkin; Doubleday & Company, Inc., Garden City, New York, 1959

55 "The Editorial Excursion," *Denver Daily Times,* June 27, 1879, p. 4

56 *Colorado Weekly Chieftain* (Pueblo, CO), March 20, 1879, p. 3

57 *Colorado Weekly Chieftain* (Pueblo, CO), March 20, 1879, p. 3

58 "Wolfe Londoner's Marriage," *Denver Daily Times,* April 18, 1879, p. 4

59 "Society Gossip," *Daily Democrat,* April 19, 1879, p. 4

60 "Honors to the Press Club," *Denver Daily Times,* April 28, 1879, p. 4

61 *Denver Daily Times,* May 8, 1879, p. 4

62 "Death of Joseph P. Farmer," *Denver Daily Times,* January 2, 1879, p. 4

63 *Denver Daily Times,* January 3, 1879, p. 4

64 "Sale of the Democrat," *Denver Daily Times,* May 16, 1879, p. 1

65 *Denver Daily Times,* June 4, 1879, p. 2

66 Colorado Press Association, www.coloradopressassociation.com website, 2015.

67 Ibid.

68 "Sky High by Rail," *Denver Daily Republican,* June 16, 1879, p. 1

69 Ibid.

70 Ibid.

71 "The Editorial Excursion," *Denver Daily Times,* June 27, 1879, p. 4

72 *Denver Daily Times,* July 3, 1879, p. 4

73 "Denver Press Club," *Denver Daily Times,* July 5, 1879, p. 4

74 "Press Club: The Semi-Annual Meeting and Election of Officers," *Denver Daily Republican,* July 5, 1879, p. 1

75 Ibid

76 "Denver Press Club," *Denver Daily Times,* July 5, 1879, p. 4

77 "The Press Club: Enjoying a Thanksgiving Dinner," *Denver Times,* November 28, 1879, p. 4

78 Ibid

CHAPTER 3

The Tribune is learning that little newspapers, like small pistols, are capable of doing great execution in the hands of men who are loaded.[1]

The 1880 annual meeting of the Denver Press Club was reported as the "Second Annual" based on the 1878 revamped incorporation of the club. Officers included Ottomar H. Rothacker (president), J. E. Leet (vice-president), B. F. Zallinger (secretary), G. P. McArthur (assistant secretary), John J. Vandemoer (treasurer), Henry Ward (orator), H. B. Jeffries (librarian), W. E. Pabor (poet), and Thomas F. Dawson (historian).[2]

The March-first edition of the *Denver Daily Republican* referred to "an interesting meeting of the Colorado Press Club"—a possible editing error of combining the names of the Colorado Press Association and the Denver Press Club. The newspaper noted the club was rapidly increasing in membership and prosperity, and "Colorado is just that much in advance of many rival States laying claims to literary culture."[3]

Part of that culture arose during a regular meeting of the press club. After the normal business of the club and discussions of "absorbing topics," club members discussed giving a grand ball as a fund-raising benefit for Ireland and famine-stricken districts of Germany. Tickets for the March 31 event were fixed at $2.50 per couple at Walhalla Hall.[4] Unfortunately, the ball had to be "indefinitely" postponed because of the death of prominent journalist and press club past president, William B. Vickers.

William B. Vickers was the president during the 1878 reorganization of the Denver Press Club.[5] After a lengthy history with journalists and a law degree from Utica, New York; Vickers attempted several ill-fated forays into the newspaper business, a run for the New York state legislature, and as a bookkeeper/manager of a distillery. He moved to St. Joseph, Missouri to start another newspaper which rapidly increased in circulation due to his sharp paragraphs and terse editorials. His *Herald* newspaper helped get him elected to two terms in the Missouri State Legislature after which he "retired" and became the Collector of Internal Revenue under President Johnson. He also purchased two more newspapers, the *Monday Morning News* and the *Gazette* in St. Joseph.

Bone cancer struck, and he died of complications following the amputation of the diseased limb. The *Boulder News and Courier* eulogized Vickers in an article that was reprinted in the *Denver Daily Republican:* "The deceased was one of the most prominent and promising men of the State, an ornament to the profession of journalism, which he long led at Denver; a Republican as able as he was ardent, and—best of all—a good man, loved and respected by all who knew him. He died in the prime of life and will be mourned by the whole State of Colorado, and a host of friends all over the Union."[6]

President O. H. Rothacker and Secretary B. F. Zallinger called for a special meeting of the press club and requested the old associates of Mr. Vickers be present.[7] Pallbearers for their past-president's funeral included W. N. Byers, M. J. Gavisk, Prof. Aaron Gove, John R. Hanna, Dr. J. F. Foltz and C. W. Sanders. The rest of the club was encouraged to attend as a unified group.[8] The members formed a double line outside the funeral parlor to flank the casket as it was loaded into the horse-drawn hearse to be borne to Denver's oldest operating cemetery, Riverside Cemetery, in North Denver.[9]

*****

According to the U.S. Bureau of Census, Denver was the 50th largest city in the country in 1880. The 35,529 citizens were also extremely well-read. The number of eastern journals read in Denver included 46 copies of the *Chicago Times,* 30 of the *Chicago Tribune,* 24 of the *New York Herald,* 12 of the *New York Graphic,* 8 of the *New York Tribune,* 6 copies of *Kansas City Times,* 4 of the *Kansas City Journal,* 10 *Cincinnati Enquirer,* 28 *St. Louis Globe-Democrat,* 4 *St. Louis Republican,* 6 *Philadelphia Times,* 32 San Francisco weeklies, 218 *Harper's Weekly,* 91 *Frank Leslie's Illustrated Weekly,* 91 *Harper's Bazaar,* 320 *New York Ledger,* 287 *New York Weekly,* 313 *Police*

Gazette, 307 *Police News,* 137 *Waverley Magazine,* 123 *New York Clipper,* 121 *Fireside Companion,* 104 weekly varieties, 89 *Boys of New York,* 78 *Saturday Journal,* 76 *Chimney Corner,* 96 *Irish World,* 69 *Puck,* 230 *Frank Leslie's Popular Monthly,* 212 *Harper's,* 211 *Scribner's,* 30 *Harper's Young People,* 57 *Demorest's,* and 23 copies of *Ballou's.*[10]

While the intention that a free press is always on the sleeve of hardworking journalists, a free lunch and a napkin-like sleeve of Denver's 19th-Century journalism community was also at the forefront. As one unnamed poetic editor of the *Denver Republican* recited,

> We may live without poetry, music, and art,
> We may live without conscience, and live without heart,
> We may live without friends; we may live without books,
> But civilized man cannot live without cooks.
> We may live without books — what is knowledge but grieving?
> We may live without hope—what is hope but deceiving?
> We may live without love—what is passion but pining?
> But where is the man [who] can live without dining?[11]

During the three-day, Fourth of July 1880 holiday, most of the restaurants were closed and the free food at the hotels lured local journalists to forage for themselves. The newest hotel, the Windsor, attempted to "edifying the editor with elegant edibles" by sampling the hotel's cuisine. The *Republican* reported, "At the hour appointed, a full dozen of regular and honorary members of the press gang gathered in the office of the hotel, and feeling the responsibility of the occasion, did their best to look intellectual . . . The promiscuous company fled through the halls, inspected the parlors, tried the elevator (the liquid ones came later), and lounged down into the *tete-a-tetes.*"[12] The hotel manager noted the press corps was lingering near the dining-room doors. With theatric greatness, he flung them open to expose a feast laid out for the reporters and editors.

"Did they eat?" the *Republican* rhetorically questioned, "If you have ever seen an editor eat, you would not ask the question. There were only two well-fed men in the party, the rest being more of the cadaverous intellectual type. . .. After the wine came on the guests were so quiet and devoted themselves so assiduously to the 'liquid divine' that we were tempted to glance from the necks of the bottles to the necks of the editors to see if they were not also labeled 'Mumm, extra dry.'"

In a separate article, the *Republican* more-seriously reported that the opening of the Windsor Hotel was another step toward advancing the importance of Denver as a modern city. "Journalists," the newspaper reported, "should specially commend that spirit of courage, enterprise and daring that induces foreign capital to come here, anchor in this city of the plains, and blossom out into such splendid proportions . . . The press—which we believe is the lever that tips up the world—should encourage every great enterprise like this, encourage it by strengthening the hands of the men who have ventured so much in order to open to the public and keep open this grand hotel, so richly and amply furnished, so splendidly provided in every appointment craved by the outer and inner man. With mountains filled with gold and silver, and with a Queen City boasting such regal mansions as the Windsor, surely Colorado may well be entitled the Jupiter in the Federal galaxy. It is often charged that the press is moved by gas or wind. If the newspapers this morning indulge in extra puffing, we can reply, 'It is the wind, sir.'"[13]

The following week, the 1880 gathering of the State Press Association convened in Denver at the parlors of the American Hotel. Wolfe Londoner, once again on behalf of the Denver Press Club,[14] opened his home to the guests of the association. As guests arrived in their horse-drawn carriages, they paused to enjoy Londoner's front yard brilliantly illuminated by Japanese lanterns.[15] Mr. and Mrs. Londoner hosted a reception to entertain the editors from around the state before sending them off for several days of train excursions to tourist resorts in mountain communities.

The *Republican* and the *Rocky Mountain News* took the event as an opportunity to use the address made by Colonel Charles Brownell Wilkinson (editor of the *Denver Republican*) to reflect upon the value of newspapers. The colonel related that newspapers reflected the community; the character, condition of their readers, and the moral-and-physical stamina of the people. "We can realize something of the importance of the trust laid upon us when we reflect that every newspaper brings home to our firesides, imparts to any households, and impresses on our children; its sentiments of propriety or its tone of contamination."[16] Readers in foreign countries considered the newspaper as the "oracle of the community" as it spoke volumes on a community's prosperity or worldly decline.

With that ostentatious responsibility, journalists laughed about community responsibility. "Denver journalism is hard to beat," explained the *Denver Daily Times*. "The reporters killed a man a few days ago and then when he protested that he wasn't dead they charged him with fraud about it, and intimated that he ought to be."[17]

Early journalists were multi-taskers, responsible for nearly all aspects of gathering the news, reporting it, and distributing the publications to the people. By the 1880s, the labors of publishing provided an administrative level that opened opportunities of free time for the newspaperman. An unnamed *Republican* reporter spent his week writing three or four columns, revising twice as many written by others, and walking less than fifteen miles a week. His physician advised that he get more exercise than that, or he'll have the short life many Denver newspapermen experienced. A popular activity for elite newspapermen was to go horseback riding; the Republican newspaperman took up the sport for exercise. Not being a trained equestrian, he departed to the newly developing suburbs of Denver for his first riding lesson.

"The level roads and brown hill-sides of the plains beyond the fairgrounds proved a great allurement to him," the competing *Denver Daily Times* reported. "He rode, on and on at a swift gallop until he had gone ten miles out. Pony began to get tired and ceased its gallop to begin to buck. One jerk followed another until by one grand upheaval the journalist was sent whizzing throughout the air like Barnum's flying angel. As ill-luck would have it, he fell flat upon one of those beautiful beds of cactus which adorn our plains, to the delight of every aesthete in the state. The cactus is a nice thing to look at, but it doesn't answer very well as an easy chair. When he got out of his dilemma, he found his pony scampering off towards town. The sun had set, night was coming on, and Denver was ten miles away. Nothing was left but to walk into town. The *Republican* office was reached at midnight. The pony had come in safe but had lost its saddle, for which the unfortunate rider had to pay $37.50. His surgeon charged the other $12.50 for his search for the collection of cacti which he brought into town with him, so that the gentleman is out full half a week's salary. But, then, he has had a valuable experience, has obtained a good deal of exercise, and he can write learnedly of the soil east of Denver."[18]

Denver continued to prosper, and the transportation system grew to meet the needs of tourists and would-be journalists escaping the polluted eastern cities. In 1867 it took twelve days to travel from New York to Denver; by 1881, train travel on the Omaha & Denver Short-Line required only seventy-two hours.[19]

In 1882, the city was over-run with wheezing journalists. Eastern scribes, tired of writing a column a day and resting only on Sundays, deluged Denver newspaper managers with job applications for the sake of their broken health. The *Rocky Mountain News* reported after arriving at the newspaper office at 11 a.m. and working at "full strength" until 3 a.m. the next morning, "they would find the nipping, eager air on their homeward journey very bracing and pleasant. Keeping up this gait day after day and week after week, knowing no Sunday and only a mere suggestion of pay day, is both exhilarating and strengthening, and the sickly journalist that would not feel its beneficial effects in a year or two must be past praying for."[20] The *Tribune* likewise explained that unemployed newspapermen yet to leave the East, should stay clear of Denver, "The city is already full of gifted young literature on the hunt for work."[21]

Considering the hard lives of the Colorado pioneers, it was no coincidence that there were 323 retail liquor stores[22] within the city limits, providing fortitude to the 36,000 residents. Others sold alcohol "for medicinal purposes," prompting people to imbibe for more closeted purposes, often behind the doors of a journalistic sanctuary.

The Denver Press Club revamped their organization once again in 1882 and settled into a suite of five rooms in an unreported location that they purchased for $2,000. As the *Castle Rock Journal* reported, "This will be an organization of which the city may well be proud."[23] The next two decades provided the Denver Press Club with many opportunities to proudly display their esoteric style of journalism.

The Rev. DeWitt Talmage, an East-coast clergyman in the Reformed Church in America and Presbyterian Church, was a competitor of Henry Ward Beecher, an American Congregationalist and brother to Harriet Beecher Stowe, an American abolitionist and author of *Uncle Tom's Cabin*. In his later years, Rev. Talmage became a prolific lecturer, writer, and champion reformer against vice and corruption. A portion of one of his sermons was preached to a congregation of journalists and reprinted in the *Rocky Mountain Herald*:

> One of the great trials of the newspaper profession is
> that its members are compelled to see more of the shams
> of the world than any other profession. Through every
> newspaper office, day after day, go all the weakness of
> the world—all the vanities that want to be puffed, all

the revenges that want to be reaped, all the mistakes that want to be corrected, all the dull speakers who want to be thought eloquent, all the meanness that wants to get its wares noticed gratis in the editorial column, in order to save the tax of the advertising column, all the men who want to be set right who never were right, all the cracked-brained philosophers with stories as long as their hair, and as gloomy as their finger nails in mourning, because bereft of soap, and the bores who come to stay five minutes, but talk five hours. Through the editorial and reportorial rooms all the follies and shams of the world are seen day after day, and the temptation is to believe neither in God, man nor woman. It is no surprise to me that in your profession there are some skeptical men—I only wonder that you believe anything.[24]

Journalists were even defined by the way they held a newspaper, according to the *New York Herald*. Most people believed the broad-sheet paper should be held in both hands with their fists pointing in the direction of people facing the reader. As they turn the pages, each would brush the reader's face and ears. A skilled journalist can fold one page in half lengthwise, turning it from right to left as he wishes a new half.[25]

The club settled into several rooms at the St. James Hotel, accommodating the forty-to-sixty members who elected R. W. Woodbury as president of the Denver Press Club in 1884.[26] A new constitution and set of by-laws were drawn to allow the membership to include businessmen in addition to the editorial and news writers of the city. "The new club enters upon its existence with very bright prospects," wrote the *Rocky Mountain News,* "and will before long have a membership of not less than 100. It is the intention to keep open club rooms, run a library and give social receptions from time to time. Such an organization has been needed for some time, and newspapermen generally rejoice at its foundation."[27]

The recognition of the journalism club appeared in odd ways. A long article about the mines that honeycombed the Bare Hills Mining District in western Fremont county (ten miles southwest of the town of Cripple Creek), published a passing reference to "J. Y. Jacks of the Denver Press Club Gold Mining Company is doing some work out beyond this region."[28]

An examination of the Colorado mining records for this book failed to find any evidence of such a claim. Other odd references to members of the press club crept into print.

Police reporters lined up outside the old Denver City Hall located at 14th and Larimer Streets. Front row: George Flanagan and Mudge Ransom. Back row: George Minot, Walter Lovelace, unknown man, Johnny Day, and Joe Satterthwaite. The police reporters' room was the former morgue in the sub-basement of City Hall. Five newspapers were represented: *Denver Post, Rocky Mountain News, Denver Times, Denver Republican, and Denver Express.* (circa 1912).

At police headquarters, the eight-foot long, 700-pound desk used by police-reporter Farmer Baxter was reported stolen. The desk was built with 200 "pigeon-holes" that could hold 10,000 reports of burglaries and "undercover" notes of unpublished police stories. Even the police officers used the desk to store hundreds of "rogue gallery" photographs of potential suspects of other crimes. Detectives Emrich and Duffield suggested the thief was H, an alleged diamond-thief and burglar. The *Denver Daily Times* cast some doubt on Salter's role in the crime "for Plunk has only one arm at the present writing"[29] and lifting the 700-pound desk seemed unlikely.

Another filler piece in the *Denver Daily Times* indicated that "it is worth remembering, especially when staying at hotels, that if the bed clothing is not sufficiently warm, two or three newspapers spread between the blankets will insure a comfortable night."[30]

When a reporter was interviewing Bartender Steve Brodie of the Auditorium Hotel, the press-writer mentioned the bartender should mix "a genuine Bowery drink," something that may not be on the typical Denver Press Club bar menus. Brodie began to provide the reporter with such a concoction — two-thirds of a champagne glass of sparkling wine followed by a generous portion of tabasco sauce. "The newspaperman objected to the color, but under the stimulus of a unanimous cry of 'bottoms up,' he drained the glass, much to the dismay of his stomach lining. Yesterday, the reporter was scanning the registers with one hand on his head and the other near the fourth button of his vest."[31]

Another nationally prominent member of the Denver Press Club was Eugene Field, poet laureate for children. His self-effacing, irrepressible sense of frivolity was well known by all the press-club members. Field was managing editor of the *Denver Tribune* in 1881 and a popular Denver Press Club member before leaving in 1883 to capture his reputation as the "children's poet." His home at 315 W. Colfax fell into ruin until the Titanically famous Molly Brown purchased it and donated it to the City of Denver that designated it as a historical landmark. The ruins were moved, brick-by-brick, to 715 S. Franklin Street where the restored house is overseen by Field's poetic characters of Wynken, Blynken and Nod sculpted by Mabel Landrum Torrey.

During his memorial services in 1899, his peers gathered a legacy-roast in his memory. Among his orators was the Honorable Wolfe Londoner, now the ex-mayor of Denver as well as a long-time member of the Denver Press Club, who began his Shakespearean eulogy with "Alas, poor Gene; I knew him well, and like all others who ever came within the charming circle of his intimate acquaintance I became his fast friend, his loving slave and often, oh how often, his submissive victim."[32] As an early assistant editor of the *Tribune* in Denver, Field often had the opportunity to write about the leading characters of his day "as they circled within the sphere of his cognizance, and he did it in that happy, piquant, merry vein of his own in such manner as to cause his criticism (if such they can be called) to be copied, broadcast throughout the press of the country."[33]

Emma Abbott (1850-1891) made her operatic début in New York in 1877 but launched the Abbott English Opera Company the following year and immediately began a national tour to bring opera to communities that had limited access to the arts. When Eugene Field had the opportunity to meet the opera star during an appearance in Denver, he coolly invited her to accept a banquet sponsored by the Denver Press Club, "an aggregation of congenial souls ready for anything on earth with one exception—formality. Imagine the surprise and dismay of these doughty knights of the quill when confronted with a most tasty and refined note of invitation delivered by special messenger to meet the great Emma Abbott at a grand banquet under the auspices of the Denver Press Club."[34] As the banquet hour approached, every member of the Denver Press Club arrived wearing swallow-tailed coats and white ministerial-looking neckties; attire that required many to borrow from more cultured acquaintances.

Practical jokes were commonplace between Wolfe Londoner and Field. When Londoner was appointed chairman of the Republican county central committee, he was delegated to stir up enthusiasm for the Republican party among "the colored voters of the city." He chose to meet with as many community leaders as possible and was succeeding in his quest when a mysterious announcement was published in the newspapers: "Wanted! Every colored man in the city to call at Wolfe Londoner's store. A carload of Georgia watermelons just received for especial distribution among his colored friends. Call early and get your melon!"[35]

When the Londoner store opened, "an ever-increasing cloud of dusky humanity gathered about the entrance until business in the store and travel on the street came to a standstill. No explanations could appease the fast-gathering displeasure of the crowd, and expostulations were taken as only subterfuges to avoid fulfilling the tempting promises of the morning papers, for whose juicy suggestions numberless mouths were waveringly waiting."[36] Londoner only had a few melons on hand and had to use the new telephone system to order a full carload of melons at an exorbitant price and distributed them among the newly-signed-up members of the Republican party. Deacon Williams introduced Londoner to the brethren: "I now take great pleasure in introducing to you our friend and brother, Wolfe Londoner, who always advises us to do the right thing and stands ready, at all times, to help us in the good fight, and although he has a white skin, his heart is as black as any of ours."[37]

Londoner learned that Field was the instigator behind the watermelon advertisement and decided on a suitable plot of revenge. Another mysterious advertisement appeared in the newspapers: "Wanted—to buy a dog! Highest price paid for good watch dog! Apply to E. Field."[38] Field's building soon filled with stray dogs of every kind, color, shape, and disposition. Londoner continued. "The building was alive with dogs, the stairs were jammed with dogs, the hallways were running full with dogs and more were seeking admittance. Cries, howls, snapping, biting and fierce fighting ran riot among the canine conglomeration, and when the general tumult and battle had extended to the owners as well as the brutes themselves, the police department was called to quell the uproar and inform the vendors of dogs that Mr. Field had all the dogs he wanted. He certainly ought to have been satisfied with the assortment I sent him."[39]

A funicular was a mountainside railcar that was counter-balanced by a similar railcar moving in the opposite direction. Passengers could ride any of several funicular cars along the Front Range of Colorado's Rocky Mountains.

Courtesy of the author

During a Denver Press Club excursion to Manitou, members bunked at the local hostelry. A woman who lost her husband found an opportunity to captivate Field with her sad tale of trouble and sorrow. So-moved by the story, Field enlisted the assistance of his fellow scribes to promote a fund-raising benefit in Manitou for the poor woman. He had no performers in mind, but the near-impromptu event was scheduled that very evening. The hour arrived, the townspeople filled the seats; all that was missing were performers. Using his skills as a piano-player, Field attacked the piano, sang, recited poetry, and told amusing anecdotes in a surprisingly adept one-man show. Fellow club members were dispatched to pass through the audience with outstretched hats to collect funds for the woman in distress.

The press club members mingled with other hotel guests before heading to their appointed rooms for the night. Shoes were left outside the rooms, so the night porters could polish the day's dust from them and have them shiny when the men arose the following morning. "One glance was enough," Londoner continued. "Field marshaled his pals of the club. Every shoe in the house was quickly and silently gathered up and thrown out the near window which overlooked a precipitous ravine of sixty feet depth. This not being considered enough, the unruly gang proceeded to pound on each door until everyone in the house was aroused, and then ensued pandemonium—threats, expletives, oaths, shrieks and confusion on every side—which lasted until morning."

The following morning while hotel guests searched for their shoes, the press-club members — "demure, sedate, innocent, they descended to breakfast," Londoner continued. While sipping their coffee, the landlord, well known by the pressmen, approached Mr. Field with a paper which Eugene carefully perused before arising from his table to address his peers. He professed thanks for the magnanimity of the landlord's presentation of a receipt paid in full for all the expenses incurred at the hotel, providing that the club members agreed to one condition. The landlord asked that immediately after breakfast, the members of the Denver Press Club should leave his Manitou establishment and never return.

Less than two weeks later, another shout was heard when representatives of the Denver Press Club met a Minnesota contingent of 247 editors and other pressmen as they left their Union Pacific special train at Denver's Union Station. "Gopher, Gopher, Gopher state / Editors, Editors, wise and great! / Boom-a-lac-a, Boom-a-lac-a! / Rah! Rah! Rah! / Editors! Editors! Minneso-Ta!"[40] The high-decibel chant continued as the Gopher editors made their way toward Wolfe Londoner's store on Arapahoe Street. Amid the chants, the visiting editors got lost and huddled in geographic consultation. A delivery wagon lumbered by and one of the visitors questioned what name was written on the wagon. "Wolfe Londoner!" shouted a dozen voices. "Well, the only way to locate ourselves," said one editor, "is to follow that vehicle to Wolfe's store!"[41]

The wagon lumbered down the street at a brisk clip, with the contingent of editors keeping pace. Wolfe Londoner was standing outside his establishment as the wagon delivered the men to Londoner who graciously directed them to the basement for an "allopathic dose of medicine."[42] After a brief night of rest at the Windsor Hotel, representatives of the Denver newspapers took the guests on a tour of Denver from City Park to Elitch Gardens and points in between before migrating back to Wolfe Londoner's store. K. G. Cooper supervised entertainment for the ladies who accompanied the editors. An orchestra showed up and provided musical entertainment interrupted by welcoming speeches and additional Gopher chants.

Managers for the various railroad lines and other transportation companies flocked to provide service to the Minnesota editors; offering excursions to all sections of the state to show the guests the commercial, tourism, and other attributes of Colorado. The relationship between visiting editors and the Denver Press Club served as the primary source of marketing the value of the state to the rest of the country.

A Mexican editorial excursion, sponsored by the Chamber of Commerce and Mr. E. H. Talbott of the *Railway Age* publication, scheduled a visit to Denver on a national tour.[43] An eastern faction of editorial visitors from New York, Connecticut, New Jersey, Maine, Maryland, Massachusetts, Pennsylvania, Ontario, Nova Scotia, and Indiana spent twelve days on a "junket tour" covering 3,000 miles.[44] Unfortunately, not enough notice was given for the Denver Press Club to prepare a suitable celebration.

While the camaraderie among newspapers through the Denver Press Club was homogenous, the rivalry was palpable on the pages of competing newspapers. *The Aspen Times* disguised the names of the *Rocky Mountain News* and the *Republican,* but the mountain newspaper accurately reflected the editorial cat-fight between two of the Denver newspapers: "The superannuated imbecile of the *Morning Subsequent* calls us *Windy* and the incongruous incognito of the *Evening Apex Circular* charges us with endeavoring to mislead the readers of the *Times* in reference to the apex question. As to the first mentioned relic of fossilized journalism, we pause only to remark that if we could not raise more effective wind than he produces on topics of vital interest to the public we would emigrate to some rejuvenating springs like Glenwood, and there, soak something out and leave room for ideas. As to the other mentioned pinnacle of inequitable freshness, we have to say, etc."[45]

David G. Weems, an 1888 Baltimore inventor, began soliciting investors to organize an electric transit line between Baltimore and Washington, D.C. for the rapid delivery of newspapers and other time-sensitive information. The transport would be elevated twenty-feet from the ground so that it would not interfere with any farmer who needed to cultivate fields that were bisected by the electric transit line. Bundles of newspapers could be dispatched on the extended electric line, making the 801-mile trip to Chicago within two hours. The distance between San Francisco and New York would transport newspaper bundles within nine hours.[46]

A 400-mile-an-hour newspaper delivery system was a fantasy of Mr. Weems, but a faster way of writing news stories was spreading throughout the country approximately the same time. The typewriter added a clacking sound that remained an auditory staple of the newsroom for another century. "With the aid of this little machine," P. G. Hubert, Jr. observed, "an operator can accomplish more correspondence in a day than half-a-dozen clerks can with the pen and do better work."[47] The 1888 version of the typewriter replaced an all-capital-letter version of the mechanical printer. Compared to pen-and-paper, Hubert determined that a typewriter could save 40 minutes out of an hour. One major typewriter company, Remington, cashed in as 1,400 typewriters were sold in 1882 and 14,000 were sold five years later.

The new typewriters were made in the same factory that was responsible for forging many of the revolvers that were used during the Civil War. Hubert appreciated the symbolism when he wrote, "In the old days the sword was forged into the plough share; in our day the gun has given way to the typewriter."[48]

The transcontinental railroad brought newspapermen to Denver as a convenient rest stop between the industrial cities of the East and the deserts, mountains, and arid rangelands west of Denver. Between the established publishing enterprises of the eastern United States and the prospering West Coast, volumes of virgin newsprint pages waited for printers' ink to tell new stories. Eager to stretch their legs and breathe the crisp but oxygen-deprived air of Denver, some of the nation's prominent scribes walked from Union Station, through the downtown streets of Denver, to whatever location housed the Denver Press Club in the late 1800s. Bringing a sense of humor to the facts-and-figures of the newspaper pages, columnists began writing of current events and the quirks of human nature. Mark Twain (1835-1910) was followed by the lesser-known Western humorist, Edgar Wilson "Bill" Nye (1850-1896), a beloved frequent visitor to the Denver Press Club.

Bill Nye traveled across the country and settled in Wyoming in 1876 where he studied law but spent his leisure time writing humorous "letters" to the *Cheyenne Sun* for $1 a column. Utilizing his East-coast legal training, he moonlighted as justice of the peace for six years in Laramie. When a reporter asked if he ever married anyone during that time, Nye responded, "Oh yes, I married my wife, and after that, I used to marry others and then try them for other offenses."[49] For two years, Mr. Nye struggled as a country lawyer, still relying upon opportunities to write humor from his everyday experiences. When the *Denver Tribune* began publishing his comedic Wyoming newspaper columns; his $60 annual newspaper income dwarfed his more modest law-practice income. The publisher of the Democratic newspaper, *Laramie Sentinel*, hired him as their editor, the pressman, and babysitter for the owner's children until 1877. "If I hadn't had a red-hot political campaign, and measles among the children, at the same time," Nye explained after resigning from the paper, "You can't mix measles and politics."[50] After a few years of freelancing for the *Cheyenne Daily Sun, Denver Tribune,* and *Salt Lake Tribune,* Nye eventually took a job with the *Laramie Daily Times* for a few more years.

In 1881, he published his own newspaper in Laramie as an homage to his favorite mule, Boomerang—an oft-airborne equine that landed in unpredictable places. Nye published the *Boomerang* over a livery stable where he posted a sign on the ground level, advising visitors to "twist the tail of the gray mule and take the elevator"[51] to the newspaper office on the second floor.

Denver Press Club members Gene Fowler (left) and
Bill Nye (right) gained a national interest as literary
entertainers and traveled with James Whitcomb Riley
(center). Their performances brought homespun stories
and humor to theatrical stages throughout the country.

Photography Collection, Miriam and Ira D. Wallach
Division of Art, Prints and Photographs, The New York
Public Library, Astor, Lenox and Tilden Foundations.

Like most humorists, according to the *Indiana State Journal,* Bill
Nye had an "almost womanly gentleness . . . His amiability was never
clouded, and his good humor on more than one occasion was a boon to his
companions."[52] At the height of his career in the third quarter of the 19th
Century, Nye was commanding $30,000 a year for his writings and his
popularity on the lecture platform. He often traveled with fellow writers
James Whitcomb Riley and Denver Press Club prankster Eugene Field.
For seven years, he furnished editors with two columns a week, a feat that
couldn't be matched even by Mark Twain. Not all editors appreciated his
humor; one such boss described him as "an idiot and a crack-brained rattle-
snake editor from Moosehead Lake"[53] (his birthplace in Maine).

Nye's adaptation of western manipulation of the English language prompted a Boulder [Colorado] College professor of rational psychology to write to the *Boomerang* with a question, "What is literature?"

"What is literature?" Nye pontificated, half-contemptuously at his own columns, "Cast your eye over these logic-imbued columns, you sun-dried savant from the remote precincts. Drink at the never-failing *Boomerang* spring of forgotten lore, you dropsical wart of a false and erroneous civilization. Read our 'Address to Sitting Bull,' or our 'Ode of the Busted Snoot of a Shattered Venus de Milo. If you want to fill up your thirsty soul with high-priced literature. Don't go around hungering for literary pie while your eyes are closed, and your capacious ears are filled with bales of hay."[54]

When a reporter inanely asked why he chose the nom de plume of "Bill Nye" he explained that his first columns in the Rocky Mountain newspapers were supposed to be unsigned, but editors kept printing a byline but with the wrong given name. As a compromise, he used the byline "Bill Nye" instead of Edgar Wilson Nye. His explanation to the reporter continued with a nod to his legal training and his trademark tongue-in-cheek style—"I am not especially proud of the name, for it conveys the idea to strangers that I am a lawless, profane and dangerous man. People who judge me by the brief and bloody name alone instinctively shudder and examine their fire arms. It suggests daring, debauchery and defiance to the law. Little children are called in when I am known to be at large, and a day of fasting is announced by the governor of the state. Strangers seek to entertain me by showing me the choice iniquities of their town. Eminent criminals ask me to attend their execution and assist them in accepting their respective dooms. Amateur criminals ask me to revise their work and to suggest improvements."[55]

A "royal banquet" was held at the St. James Hotel on February 15, 1882. In a retrospective article published twenty-years later in the *Denver Times,* John E. Leet provided a detailed account of the "Famous Bill Nye Banquet," gleaned from newspaper extracts that were published at the time of the event and his own remembrances that evening.[56] Among the notable newspapermen of the Denver Press Club were General J. C. Wilson, Hon. Wolfe Londoner, F. J. V. Skiff, John E. Leet, C. O. Ziegenfuss, W. L. Visscher, Eugene Field, Charles A. Raymond, E. D. Cowen, Will E. Baker, Halsey M. Rhoads, A. P. Waite, General Raymond M. Stevenson,

H. L. Feldwisch, F. O. Dickensheets, James Treadway, Hamilton S. Wicks, and guest-of-honor E. W. Nye.

The program was delayed because the "thirteen superstition" was present. In the 1800s, "thirteen at a table" was considered unlucky because one of the people would die within the year. The origin of the superstition supposedly was based on thirteen people being at the table during the Last Supper; a similar explanation also existed with Norse mythology.

"Owing to the night work of the active journalists, many were not expected until late," wrote Leet. "I did not know that I increased the crowd to thirteen and could not understand why they waited an hour before starting. Finally, a hotel clerk was called to march in with us so as to make the number fourteen. A. P. Waite explained the superstition to me and expressed the opinion that the clerk could not break the hoodoo. He insisted that only thirteen journalists sat down to the banquet and that, as he understood it, my chance to die within a year was best because I was the thirteenth to arrive. I ridiculed the superstition and offered to bet him a round sum that he would, while I would not, die within a year. He had consumption, and it took much champagne to inspire him with glee. Before the year was out, I attended his funeral."[57]

The speakers' platform and each table were decorated with elaborate and exquisitely arranged floral displays. The dining fare was as varied as the men and women awaiting the introduction of the guest of honor. The celebrants feasted on raw oysters, consommé a la Royale, sherry, baked white fish a la Parisienne claret, roast turkey stuffed with oysters, asparagus, baked mashed potatoes, tenderloin of beef (larded), mushroom sauce, French peas, new potatoes, broiled quail on toast, omelet soufflé, vanilla ice cream, assorted cakes, tea, coffee, and brandy and Mumm's extra dry champagne.[58]

The feast cost $7 per plate with as much free champagne as the revelers could consume. Mr. Bailey, proprietor of the St. James Hotel, underestimated the hollow legs of the newspapermen and their guests and found himself to be a big loser. The press club banqueters made an ad hoc assessment of eight additional dollars per attendee to reimburse the proprietor for the excessive consumption of champagne.

A toast to Nye's home state of Wyoming was made before his ascent to the podium to give what the press club attendees expected to be a humorous speech. A solemn Nye rose and carefully unfolded several sheets of statistics of Wyoming's resources — the wheat yield for the previous year, the output of minerals, the number of livestock in the territory, and other tedious statistics. "He was as serious as a professor in an agricultural college lecture room," reported the newspaper, "and during the first ten minutes of the reading, his guests, thinking he was leading to something better, maintained a respectful silence."[59]

Field and others began to smirk and soon the banqueters were in an uproar of laughter despite Nye's continuing deadpan presentation of Wyoming statistics. Field and Nye began heckling each other, which prompted the press club members to sustain the laughter the entire night. It was noted that Nye was only drinking buttermilk and Field was partaking of nothing stronger than seltzer. The humor and camaraderie of the night began at 9 p.m. and lasted until nearly 8 a.m. the following morning. Instead of ordering a carriage to convey the two gentlemen to the Windsor Hotel where Nye was staying, the entire banquet hall emptied to form a procession to the St. James Hotel lobby.

Once Field suspected his friend was asleep, he requested the hotel staff send up his business card to announce his presence. At regular intervals, the other press club members did the same until Nye recognized that he was not going to be allowed any sleep that morning and he reappeared in the hotel lobby to spend the rest of the day with his hosts. Neither Field nor Nye forgot about the event and wrote about that night in Denver that launched both their careers as humorists outside the newsroom.

Years later after he recovered from early onset of spinal meningitis during an epidemic of the disease, Nye went to visit his brother in Wisconsin where he was caught outdoors when a cyclone almost killed him. He used to explain that his baldness was attributed to his hair being blown off by the cyclonic winds. Another explanation of his baldness was attributed to the fact his head was growing faster than his hair. Nye's kidney ailments and other medical problems ultimately left him paralyzed for the last ten days of his life when Bill Nye passed away on February 26, 1896, at his home in Asheville, North Carolina.

The over-the-top, knee-slapping anecdotes of humor among the Denver journalists, helped mask the realization that many of their ranks were bringing a new meaning to "meeting a deadline." Attending many more funerals would become a part of the club's routine as other early founders of the Denver Press Club grew old and succumbed to a variety of ailments.

The call went out to all persons connected with the press of Colorado to meet at the *Republican* newspaper offices to respond to the sudden death of Colonel Charles Brownell Wilkinson, the late editor and proprietor of the newspaper.[60] After his first wife died, Colonel Wilkinson married again in 1868. They moved to Denver in September 1879 when the Colonel became the proprietor and editor of *The Republican* until he sold it November 1880 to the new owners who renamed it *The Democrat*. He had not been in "robust" health for several years but was still able to maintain his commitment to the newspaper. Approximately 8 p.m. while sitting in comfortably at his home at 506 Curtis Street with his wife and several friends, he complained that he could not catch his breath and requested the windows be raised. Within a half hour, Colonel Wilkinson caught his last breath.

While he lay in state at his home; an elaborate cross, wreath, and flowers were provided by his peers from the Denver Press Club. Even his crutches were trimmed with flowers. Colonel Wilkinson was also laid to rest in Cemetery. The services were arranged by a committee of members of the Denver Press Club in "perfect taste, free of sham and ceremony just as the deceased would have directed had time been vouchsafed to him to speak his desires."[61] The Denver Press Club met on January 10, 1881 and passed a report as a tribute to the passing of their esteemed colleague. The final paragraph concluded, "May the Great Proof Reader find, as we believe He will, in his life few doublets of errors repeated, few outs of duties neglected, and receive him into a life whose bright ways are crossed by no lines of sorrow of misfortune."[62]

Much of the benevolence of the early press club was through the generosity of the Denver theater community and the national celebrities that graced the local stages. The public persona of the early Denver Press Club was steeped in theatrical promotions, oratories at civic gatherings, and railroad excursions into the mountains to promote the development of resorts in the fresh air of the Rocky Mountains. Young newspapermen in the East had pangs of envy and risked their meager savings to "Go West, young man" (as popularized by Horace Greeley). The romanticized stories of the West often neglected to describe the economic hardship of being a newspaper pioneer.

Desperate to find relief for scarred lungs or recovery from physical deformities, many newspapermen made the stagecoach (or train excursion in later years) to Colorado. Some young men made incredible efforts to succeed, but others died at a young age without funds for a respectable burial. The benevolence of the Denver Press Club members remedied the misfortune of others by purchasing a plot for eighty dollars in 1882. Located in Lot 51, Block 2 near the main entrance of Riverside Cemetery, press club members fill an unclear number of spaces in the 320-square-foot plot.

The eight-person lot diagram shows the location of seven press-club members, but the corresponding name chart lists four individuals; a fifth includes the notation "no record of grave #." Rod-probing, excavation, or using ground-penetrating radar of 150-year-old cheap wooden-boxed remains are nearly useless in locating any buried remains. The residents known to be interred at Riverside include an odd selection of press club characters. Only the graves of Michael J. Gavisk, O. J. Goldrick, Henry L. Feldwisch and Colonel Champion Vaughan are marked with stones. The memory of their accomplishments is preserved in the soil of the press club.

Michael J. Gavisk arrived in Colorado in 1877 to become the editor of the *Leadville Democrat*, but the two-mile altitude exacerbated his frail health and he moved to the mile-high city of Denver where he became the city editor[63] of the *Rocky Mountain News* when the paper doubled its size to eight pages. His fellow newspapermen were quick to note that Gavisk "carved out for himself the reputation of being one of the best newspapermen in the west, and he is worthy to wear the laurels he has won."[64]

By 1880, Gavisk, now the managing editor of the *Leadville Democrat*,[65] fell into ill health. The *Daily News* noted that his brief control of the *Democrat* was sufficient to earn "a high reputation as a brilliant and successful journalist"[66] and the newspaper rose to become one of the leading newspapers in the state. The *News* expressed their hope that he would continue to edit during his convalescence. The *Daily Republican* was more cynical about the appointment when it noted that "Mr. Gavisk is the forty-third editor that paper has had since its birth."[67] His position was short-lived as Colonel John L. Bartow (former editor of the *Houston* (Texas) *Telegram*)[68] became the new editor of paper as Gavisk's health declined and he could no longer handle the stress of publishing a newspaper.

By early 1881, the governor sought Gavisk's journalistic skills to become the governor's private secretary to replace William G. Smith of Golden.[69] Within a few months, it was reported Gavisk was compelled to "temporarily"[70] leave his desk, despite being confined to his room.[71] His slow recovery enabled him to travel to Manitou[72] where the natural mineral waters were said to have curative powers. The water and rest must have been successful as his next public appearance was with the governor[73] in a Memorial Day parade on the streets of Denver and later on a special train expedition to the Idaho Springs mineral baths with the Colorado State Press Association.[74]

The former city editor of the *Rocky Mountain News* and private secretary to Colorado Governor Frederick W. Pitkin, M. J. Gavisk, was named as industrial editor of the new *Journal of Commerce*[75] but was forced back into two weeks[76] of bed rest in Pueblo by the end of the year.[77] Governor Pitkin left for the Lindell Hotel in Pueblo to spend several days with his friend, expecting the two would return to Denver together[78] six days later. The journey was too difficult for Gavisk and he experienced a relapse of "consumption," a reference to the wasting away of the body attributed to pulmonary tuberculosis.

Gavisk's condition became critical by mid-January[79] and the services of Rev. Father John B. Raverdy were summoned to help him write a will. He originally expressed his desire to be buried in the Catholic cemetery in Denver, "saying that he would then be surrounded by more friends than in any other state or city."[80] On his deathbed, Gavisk did confess that he had little property as an estate, but believed he saved enough for a funeral. Instead of being buried among the Roman Catholics, he privately requested his burial be at Riverside with members of the Denver Press Club as pallbearers. When the club convened, members learned of Gavisk's dire economic situation and offered to bear a portion of the necessary funeral expenses.[81]

His passing on January 14, 1881 once again summoned members of the Denver Press Club to help organize the funeral. His body lay in state in the Capitol where his friends paid their last respects.[82]

"To those who do not understand the relations of journalists," reported the *Denver Republican*, "it is no easy task to explain the unbounded admiration which his brethren of the press felt for Mr. Gavisk."[83] His funeral bier lay in state in the Executive office and was abundantly decorated with flowers from Colorado organizations and individuals. The *Republican* presented a pillow with roses, carnations, and pampas plumes along the border; the center included "30" in immortelles (a long-lasting flower that were common on graves). The numerical reference was to a telegraphy to indicate "good night,"[84] but it was later adopted by newspapers expressing the end of an article at the telegraph editor's desk.

The beautiful floral arrangements that were placed around the bier the previous day were sent East to his relatives and friends.[85] The *Denver Tribune* began raising funds for a graveside monument for the young press-club member; the newspaper started with $50 and Wolfe Londoner doubled the fund with his own contribution. Gavisk's final resting place became the first of eight possible internments at the Denver Press Club's Riverside plot, fulfilling its promise to take care of his funeral expenses.

O. J. Goldrick's extravagant arrival in Denver is described in Margaret McLean Truly's extensively researched biography. Goldrick's appearance as a well-heeled dandy and air of sophistication quickly earned him the moniker of "Professor" by the rough-shod mining and ranching inhabitants of Denver City. He quickly became imbued with the establishment of Denver's first school on the corner of Twelfth and Blake Streets in West Denver. In addition to his teaching duties at the school, Goldrick also freelanced articles for Byers' *Rocky Mountain News* and used the pen-name of "Observer" for a column published in the *Missouri Democrat*.[86] O. J. Goldrick began as a regular correspondent for the St. Louis *Democrat* and the Salt Lake City *Daily Vidette* where his anti-Mormon articles were not well received. He arrived in Denver and edited several local newspapers, including the *Rocky Mountain Herald*.

Goldrick fell ill from pneumonia on November 25, 1882 and was gone by midnight at the age of fifty-three.[87] The *Denver Republican* reported, "Professor Goldrick had hosts of friends—in fact, it is doubtful if he had any enemies. He was a plain spoken, blunt man, but he was neither vindictive or inclined to breed discord among his fellow men. He was a genial man at all times, fond of his joke, or half-serious comments about measures and men, but he meant to do no one an injury, and everybody liked him. He was a man of strong force of character and has been identified with the growth and progress of Colorado for nearly a quarter of a century. He leaves no family; his wife having died a number of years ago. Thousands of people in the West will read the notice of his death with sincere regret."[88]

His flamboyant writing style provided lively news and entertainment to his local and stateside readers, describing weddings as a feast of wild game and locally gathered fruits and berries, reported on dozens of people killed by Kiowa Indians and still wrote with introspection as he watched peaceful Indians peering with curiosity through church doors during services.[89]

The Denver Times further described its colorful peer, "Goldrick is—he has almost reached the point when one must say was—both a pioneer and a curiosity. He has the oddity of kindness and the eccentricity of generosity. Singularly solitary . . . he has lived a queer monosyllabic life, which has had few friends and many acquaintances. With genuine instincts and a reasonable share of intellect, he has outlived his time. He reminds one of a fashion plate which is out of date. The newer time has not known him, and the fault is largely his . . . There is a cordial humanity, a warm kindliness, in his nature which are worth a great deal. His best instincts are voluble, and his worst are dumb. His tongue is quick to praise and stammering in blame. His heart bubbles to his lips at the lightest touch, and he is oddly human in his ways and walks . . . He has been a better man than many who have had better names."[90]

Owen Joseph Goldrick lived his life with dignity but was never portrayed as frugal. Truly's biography described Goldrick as "generous to a fault."[91] His brother, William, sent a dispatch to Denver, requesting Owen's remains be shipped to Delaware, Ohio where he would be reunited with the family.[92] Clara A. Goldrick, a niece of the deceased, also wrote to the press club. "Uncle has no other of near friends than ourselves and we know something of what he would wish done under the circumstances, better perhaps than anyone in Denver. Please take charge, or have some responsible person do so, of all his personal effects. Do not permit any strange hand to touch them. The personal property will you please care for as your own until further instruction."[93]

Goldrick's business affairs were solvent, but "his meager estate did not quite cover his meager bills."[94] When the estate was settled, his tally was $241 short of covering his worldly expenses. Wolfe Londoner, members of the Denver Press Club, and the Colorado Press Association agreed to pay his remaining debts, dissolve the *Rocky Mountain Herald*, and if there were funds left over, erect a monument to Professor O. J. Goldrick's memory at the press-club cemetery plot.[95]

William Goldrick arrived a week after the funeral and expressed his appreciation for the kindness the city and the press club showed to his uncle. For the time being, the nephew decided to stay in Denver and continue publishing the *Rocky Mountain Herald*.[96] Apparently, the newspaper business did not extend through the Goldrick bloodline. By May 1893, the *Rocky Mountain Herald* was being published by Halsey M. Rhoads.[97]

Among the unmarked graves of the Denver Press Club's Riverside plot is the "possible" burial of A. P. "Al" Waite. His name appears on the cemetery card with a question mark attached and no assigned indication of placement within the plot. There is a historical record of Mr. Waite being a composing-room operator, a reporter, and eventually a telegraph editor for the *Tribune* before succumbing to consumption at the age of 29 in 1883. Four years earlier, Waite arrived in Denver to escape pulmonary disease that kept him as a respiratory invalid during his later years. Within a year of arriving in a city where oxygen was crisp, clean, and scarce, Waite began writing equally clear, terse journalism with a keen newspaper instinct. He thought he would only live a couple of months in Denver, but the young man prospered and added a wife during his final year of life. An editorial in *The Denver Times* described him as a young man with "the bitter cynicisms of old age . . . But there was a very warm and tender heart beating beneath this cold exterior. Most of his cynicism was directed against himself and he was full of charity for other's faults, though he did not always acknowledge it."[98]

During the Bill Nye banquet, his awkward conversation with John Leet about the "thirteen superstition" of journalists marching into the event just a few months earlier, was prophetic.

A. P. Waite was an active member of the Denver Typographical Union No. 49, but when he passed away, the *Denver Republican* noted his peers extended their respects only in the form of passing resolutions, arranging the funeral and expressing their sadness to the widow. "The more intimate associates of the deceased," the newspaper reported, "have not been too generous in public expression of fitting respect to the noble memory of one of the cleanest hearts that ever beat in the editorial room, but it is hoped that all members of the Denver press will do homage to his memory by attending his funeral and thus furnish a lasting theme of consolation to the bereaved one in her widowhood."[99]

Internment at the press-club plot must have led to lively discussions in the afterlife. Residents who lived among Colorado's political scribes lay between writers too young to develop permanent ink-stained fingertips, and hardened newspapermen who found their drinking glasses were never left empty. Such posthumous camaraderie must have made the arrival of Colonel Champion Vaughan quite interesting to the perpetual Riverside Press Club underground newsroom when he was buried in the press club lot after his death on January 24, 1884.

In life, Colonel Vaughan brokered his military career into a less-rewarding newspaper life; his obituary noting that he died in poverty as a temperance advocate and political writer. Between 1872-1876, he was an editor of the *Denver Tribune* before becoming the telegraphic editor of the *Rocky Mountain News*. When he wasn't at his newspaper desk, the colonel was in demand as a lecturer for the growing Temperance League movement.

On June 15, 1879 an audience of temperance supporters gathered at the Forrester Opera House to listen to George W. Bain, "a cold-water advocate." The overflow audience filled the seats, spilled over into the aisles, and onto the stage. Vaughan presided over the meeting and introduced the guest speaker. Bain was not described as an "orator" but provided ideas that were "at once unique, original, and striking"[100] about the benefits of sobriety and living in a dry town. In August, the Denver Christian Blue Ribbon Union, the Ladies Blue Ribbon Union, and other area temperance organizers arranged for another temperance rally on August 10, 1879 at the Lawrence Street M. E. Church. Vaughan delivered the temperance address[101] to an overflow crowd seated in the large church sanctuary. By the end of the rally, sixty-seven people signed pledges to abstain.[102]

He received assistance from Sister Eliza and other good people of the local Episcopal churches and became associated with the temperance movement and other moral and religious affairs in the community. Denver temperance advocates were not critical of those who did not abstain from beer, wine or liquor in moderation, but did demand an end to excessive violent drunkenness that disrupted the peace of the evening hours. They asked to protect young boys and children from intemperance and that liquor sales be conducted decently and with unexplained "seductive accessories." This was a popular political platform that appealed mostly to the Republican rather than the Democratic party.[103]

For the hard-drinking denizens of the Denver Press Club, Vaughan was an enigma yet loved by his peers despite his transgression from the ways of the newspaper community. The normally decently dressed and respectable-looking gentleman was a frequent occupant of the Windsor Hotel lobby. Approximately 4 p.m. on January 22, 1884, Champion Vaughan, onetime editor of the *Denver Tribune* passed away, financially destitute.

The Denver Times provided a unique obituary: "A well-known gambler, this morning, paid a negro a dollar to wash the filth from a man who was formed and fitted by nature to adorn almost any exalted station in life. The wreck that sat in the justice's court, unmindful, unconscious of what was going on around him, was Champion Vaughan, who could not have dived deeper in dissipation than he did without reaching hell itself." The obituary continued, "He was a genial, polished and companionable gentleman, a pretty good writer, and a good public speaker. His present degraded condition was brought on by dissipation, though more in opium than spirits. He has long been a confirmed morphine eater. His wife, from whom he has been separated some years, resides in Milwaukee, and she and her relatives are of the highest respectability."[104] He was well educated with an active knowledge of the men and events of the time. "As a writer," the *Rocky Mountain News* reported upon his death, "he was rather harsh and severe, but was one of the most talented editorial scribblers that ever struck the town."[105] The Episcopal churches took charge of the deceased. The final arrangements included Colonel Vaughan's internment within the Denver Press Club plot.

While the other burials were for press-club members who no longer had the funds for a proper burial, Henry Feldwisch's family witnessed an elegant send-off by his colleagues at the *Denver Republican* and *Denver Times* and the highest levels of state-business and political leadership. He died of an unexplained hemorrhage on November 29, 1887, a few days before his 34th birthday. When Feldwisch's heavy rosewood casket was lowered into one of the eight places in the Denver Press Club's Riverside plot, the *Rocky Mountain News* reported that his casket was surrounded by several floral stands including one offering from the Colorado Press Club[106] (once again a possible misprint of the combined names of the Denver Press Club and the Colorado Press Association). The display was a wreath adorned with a "scroll Press badge pendant" with words spelled out in blue immortelles, "The Press." The entire display was surmounted by clusters of tea roses.[107]

Other than a "curiosity" human-interest story published in 1925, no other reference to the Denver Press Club plot at Riverside Cemetery was found in newspaper, club records or any other repository.

The benevolence of the Denver Press Club lasted longer than anyone envisioned as new challenges heralded the 20th Century. The newspapermen would soon be writing about the personal and economic impact of World War I (July 1914-to-November 1918) and the spread of Spanish Influenza as doughboys returned to the States, spreading the European flu throughout the country (January 1918-December 1920).

There would be a decade-long reprieve before Denver would feel the dual-economic impact of the Great Depression (mid 1929-mid 1931) and the "Dirty Thirties" of the three waves of the Dust Bowl storms of the 1930s.

The Great Depression of 1929-1939 prompted the need for additional assistance to press club members as unemployment rose and millions of workers were laid off. In 1937 the Denver Press Club formalized its benevolence program and created the Press Benevolent Association. The new corporation's objectives were "(a) to encourage and develop higher standards of journalism, (b) to assist in the training of promising young men for the newspaper profession, by courses of lectures or otherwise, (c) to stimulate the intellectual life of the community by bringing to Denver notable writers and thinkers from other parts of the country, (d) to visit and assist sick or distressed newspapermen, their wives, widows and orphans, and to cooperate in other worthy charitable and public causes, and (e) all to the end that exchange of ideas may be promoted, a spirit of fellowship and civic responsibility may be fostered, and fine sense of ethics and sportsmanship may be developed, among the newspapermen of Denver."[108]

In order to provide benevolent support to the members and their families and strengthen the role of a Denver Press Club, the new companion corporation to the Denver Press Club created four committees: "(1) a committee on Journalistic Ethics which shall be composed of three members known for their devotion to improvement in standards of journalism, (2) an Education Committee which shall be composed of three members who shall have charge of all lectures and other educational activities of the association in the training of promising young newspapermen, (3) an Entertainment Committee which shall be composed of three members and shall be charged with the duty of arranging for the entertainment in Denver of distinguished writers and thinkers from other parts of the United States, and (4) a Philanthropic Committee which shall be composed of three members and shall be empowered to investigate and act upon all requests for assistance presented to the association in behalf of sick, disabled, or destitute newspapermen or ex-newspapermen and their families and dependents . . ."[109]

When John Leet was reflecting on the frivolity of the Bill Nye Banquet, he was also reflecting on all the friends that he lost during the end of the 19th Century. "But it saddens me to reflect how swiftly the years have flown and that half of those genial spirits have climbed the golden stairs. Half the hands that grasped mine that night are cold, half the hearts that throbbed warmly then have ceased to beat and half the eyes that beamed brightly into mine around that joyous banquet board have long since hid their luster in the grave."[110] The beginning of the 20th Century would also challenge the membership of the Denver Press Club.

1   *Denver Republican*, January 12, 1880, p. 2
2   "Press Club: Second Annual Meeting and Election of Officers," *Denver Daily Republic*, February 9, 1880, p. 4
3   *Denver Daily Republican*, March 1, 1880, p. 1
4   "Coming Events: The Grand Ball of the Press Club on the 31st-Engineers' and Firemen's Balls, Etc." *Denver Daily Republican*, March 23, 1880, p. 4
5   "Memoriam: Action of the Denver Press Club on the Death of W. B. Vickers," (unknown newspaper), March 3, 1880, p. 86
6   "Death of Wm. H. Vickers," *Denver Daily Republican*, March 27, 1880, p. 4
7   "The Press Club Meeting," *Denver Daily Republican*, March 24, 1880, p. 4
8   "Press Club Meeting," *Denver Daily Republican*, March 25, 1880, p. 4
9   "The Last Sad Rites: Funeral Ceremonies of Mr. W. H. Vickers," *Denver Republican*, March 26, 1880, p 4
10 "Denver's Literary Pabulum," *Denver Republican*, May 14, 1880, p. 1
11 "Press Gang Free Lunch," *Denver Republican*, July 7, 1880, p. 4
12 "Press Gang Free Lunch," *Denver Republican*, July 7, 1880, p. 4
13 "The Windsor," *Denver Republican*, July 7, 1880, p. 2
14 "Here They Come: The Journalists Coming From All Parts of the State," *Denver Republican*, July 14, 1880, p. 4
15 "Jaunting Journalists," *Denver Republican*, July 15, 1880, p. 4
16 "Colorado Journalists," *Rocky Mountain News*, July 15, 1880, pp. 4-5; "Jaunting Journalists," *Denver Republican*, July 15, 1880, p. 4
17 *Denver Daily Times*, February 11, 1882, p. 2
18 "A Journalist on a Broncho," *Denver Daily Times*, February 28, 1882, p. 3
19 *Denver Daily Times*, November 17, 1881, p. 4
20 *Rocky Mountain News*, January 15, 1882, p. 4
21 *The Tribune*, January 13, 1882, p. 4
22 *Rocky Mountain News*, December 16, 1882, p. 4
23 *The Castle Rock Journal*, April 12, 1882, p. 2
24 "The Study of Character in a Newspaper Office," *Rocky Mountain Weekly Herald*, May 9, 1893, p. 5
25 "How to Hold a Newspaper," *Denver Republican*, January 15, 1882, p. 2
26 *Daily Denver Times*, August 4, 1884, p. 4
27 "Press Club Meeting: Adoption of a Constitution for the Newspapermen's Club, Yesterday," *Rocky Mountain News*, July 28, 1884, p. 8
28 "Mines, Mining and Stocks in Bare Hills District," *Rocky Mountain News*,

April 22, 1896, p. 9

29 "Stole the Press Desk," *Denver Daily Times*, December 8, 1896, p. 7

30 "Newspapers for Warmth," *Denver Daily Times*, December 17, 1896, p. 7

31 "One of Brodie's Drinks," *Denver Daily Times*, December 21, 1896, p. 7

32 "Woman's Century: Camp Life on the Colorado," *Dallas Morning News*, September 4, 1899, p. 6

33 Ibid

34 Ibid

35 Ibid

36 Ibid

37 Ibid

38 Ibid

39 Ibid

40 "Gopher Editors," *Denver Times*, September 18, 1899, p. 3

41 Ibid

42 Ibid

43 "The Mexican Editors: They Have Concluded to Return by Way of Denver," *Denver Daily Times*, July 11, 1885, p. 2

44 "Editorial Visitors," *Denver Tribune*, May 26, 1883, p. 6

45 *Denver Daily Times*, August 1, 1885, p. 4

46 "The World Do Move," *Denver Evening Times*, February 15, 1888 p. 1

47 "How Typewriters Changed Everything, https://daily.jstor.org/how-typewriters-changed-everything/

48 Ibid

49 "Humor of Bill Nye," *Duluth News-Tribune*, March 8, 1896, p. 9

50 *Nye*, Bill Nye, T. A. Larson, *History of Wyoming*, University of Nebraska Press, 1965 (www.wyominghistory.org)

51 "Death of 'Bill' Nye," *Indiana State Journal*, February 26, 1896, p. 3

52 Ibid

53 "Humor of Bill Nye," *Duluth News-Tribune*, March 8, 1896, p. 9

54 Ibid

55 Ibid

56 "Famous Bill Nye Banquet," John E. Leet, *Denver Times*, February 16, 1902; published in *Newspaper Career of E. D. Cowen*, authors Edwin David Cowen, Charles Arthur Murray, Slason Thompson, Robert Emmett Monaghan Strickland, Charles Elwood Arney, and others; Western Co., publishers; Seattle, Washington, 1930

57 "Famous Bill Nye Banquet," John E. Leet, *Denver Times*, February 16, 1902; published in *Newspaper Career of E. D. Cowen*, authors Edwin David Cowen, Charles Arthur Murray, Slason Thompson, Robert Emmett Monaghan Strickland, Charles Elwood Arney, and others

58 Ibid

59 Ibid

60 "The Press: Meeting at '*The Republican*' Office To-Night," *Denver Republican*, January 8, 1881, p. 1

61 "The Dead Journalist," *Denver Republican*, January 10, 1881, p. 1

62 "The Last Tribute," *Denver Republican*, January 11, 1881, p. 8

63 "Compliments to the *News*," *Rocky Mountain News*, July 20, 1879, p. 4

64 "City of the Plains," *Rocky Mountain News*, September 6, 1879, p. 3

65 "The Close: M. J. Gavisk Assumes Control of the Democrat," *Rocky Mountain News*, June 17, 1880, p. 2

66 *Rocky Mountain Daily News*, April 1, 1880, p. 4

67 *Daily Republican*, June 18, 1880, p. 2

68 *Rocky Mountain News*, July 30, 1880, p. 4

69 *Rocky Mountain News*, January 9, 1881, p. 4

70 *Rocky Mountain News*, April 23, 1881, p. 8

71 *Rocky Mountain News*, April 27, 1881, p. 3

72 *Rocky Mountain News*, May 11, 1881, p. 8

73 *Rocky Mountain News*, May 31, 1881, p. 4

74 "The Journalists' Jaunt," *Rocky Mountain News*, July 14, 1881, p. 8

75 "New Journal of Commerce,: *Rocky Mountain News*, August 14, 1881, p. 4

76 "Personal," *Daily Denver Times*, January 11, 1882, p. 4

77 "At the State House," *Denver Daily Times*, November 19, 1881, p. 4

78 "At the State House," *Daily Denver Times*, January 5, 1882, p. 4

79 *Denver Tribune*, January 14, 1882, p. 4

80 "M. J. Gavisk," *Denver Tribune*, January 14, 1882, p. 8

81 "Meeting of the Press Club," *Denver Republican*, January 15, 1882, p. 4

82 "Death's Dart: It Touches a Well-Known Colorado Journalist," *Rocky Mountain News*, January 15, 1882, p. 2

83 "Death of Michael J. Gavisk," *Denver Republican*, January 15, 1882, p. 4

84 "Tribute to the Dead," *Denver Tribune*, January 16, 1882, pp. 4-5

85 "At Rest: The Funeral and Burial Yesterday of the Lamented M. J. Gavisk," *Denver Tribune*, January 17, 1882, p. 4

86 *In Defense of Professor Goldrick*, Margaret McLean Truly, Summit Trail Booksmith; Vestavia Hills, AL; 2016, p. 23

87 Ibid

88 "An Old-Timer Gone: Professor O. J. Goldrick Dies at Midnight After Several Days Suffering from Pneumonia," *Denver Republican*, November 26, 1882, p. 7

89 *In Defense of Professor Goldrick*, Margaret McLean Truly, Summit Trail Booksmith; Vestavia Hills, AL; 2016, p. 33

90 *Denver Tribune*, November 26, 1882, p. 4

91 *In Defense of Professor Goldrick,* p. 112

92 "Consigned to the Tomb: The Body of Owen J. Goldrick Laid to Rest in Riverside," *Denver Republican,* November 28, 1882, p. 8

93 "Professor Goldrick's Niece," *Denver Republican,* December 2, 1882, p. 4

94 *In Defense of Professor Goldrick,* p. 114

95 "A Pioneer's Funeral," *Daily Denver Times,* November 27, 1882, p. 4

96 *Denver Republican,* December 9, 1882, p. 1

97 "A Paper for the People," *Rocky Mountain Herald,* May 9, 1893

98 "A. P. Waite Dead: The Telegraph Editor of the *Tribune* breathes His Last This Morning," *Denver Times,* May 25, 1883, p. 1

99 "Obsequies of A. P. Waite," *Denver Republican,* May 27, 1883, p. 1

100 "Last Night's Temperance Meeting," *Denver Daily Republican,* June 16, 1879, p. 4

101 "Temperance Topics: A Great Rally to Take Place Tomorrow Evening," *Denver Daily Republican,* August 9, 1879, p. 4

102 "The Blue Ribbon on High: A Grand and Significant Rally of the Temperance Hosts," *Denver Daily Republican,* August 11, 1879, p. 4

103 "The Temperance Demand," *Denver Republican,* August 21, 1879, p. 2

104 "Col. Champion Vaughan," clipping file of the Wisconsin Local History & Biography Articles, unknown Milwaukee WI newspaper, www.wisconsinhistory.org, 1882

105 "Death of Champion Vaughan," *Rocky Mountain News,* January 23, 1884, p. 3

106 "The Journalist's Funeral," *Rocky Mountain News,* December 1, 1887, p. 5

107 "The Journalist's Friend," *Rocky Mountain News,* December 1, 1887, p. 5.

108 Articles of Incorporation Press Benevolent Association, February 11, 1937

109 Ibid

110 "Famous Bill Nye Banquet," John E. Leet, *Denver Times,* February 16, 1902; published in *Newspaper Career of E. D. Cowen,* authors Edwin David Cowen, Charles Arthur Murray, Slason Thompson, Robert Emmett Monaghan Strickland, Charles Elwood Arney, and others; Western Co., publishers; Seattle, Washington, 1930

CHAPTER 4

One of the great trials of the newspaper profession is that its members are compelled to see more of the shams of the world than any other profession . . . Through the editorial and reportorial rooms, all the follies and shams of the world are seen day after day, and the temptation is to believe neither in God, man nor woman. It is no surprise to me that in your profession there are some skeptical men—I only wonder that you believe anything.[1]

The Denver Press Club struggled to find its purpose in the Twentieth Century as Denver likewise struggled to find its place among the more established cities of the United States. Being a social club for the men of the pen was satisfactory for the first thirty-five years, but by the last decade of the 1800s, the national mission of press clubs began to find new roots. The revamped Denver Press Club of 1890 was "already a representative organization, embracing many of the best newspapermen of Denver in its membership," described the *Rocky Mountain News*. "Its object is to cultivate closer and more fraternal feeling[s] among the working newspapermen of the city." When news of the re-invention of the Denver Press Club gradually reached other cities during the next decade, the role of a "press club" and a "press benevolent association" began to meld into a new organizational purpose.

For example, a journalists' club in Baltimore was established to lobby for laws that would "amply protect newspapermen in the preservation of confidences reposed in them."[2] The preamble of the organization stated, "that newspaper writers, upon whom the public depend for important information, should be accorded at least the same protection from being compelled to violate confidences as pastors, counsel, servants, etc."[3]

Colonel Alexander Kelly McClure, one of the founders of the Republican Party and editor-in-chief of the *Philadelphia Times* (1873-1901) added, "With the wonderful advance of everything relating to the growth of population, and the development of industry and wealth, it was only natural that journalism should take the lead, and the result is that to-day our free land has more newspapers than the combined journals published in all other countries of the world, and even when discounted by all the imperfections of our present journalism, and the sensationalism that so often mars the pages of the family newspaper, the American journal of to-day is the greatest and grandest the world has ever known and is daily exerting most beneficent influence in the education of the people, who are the sovereigns of the Republic."[4]

A theoretical change may have been revamping the philosophical image of journalism and the role of press clubs, but an empty spot at the poker table and an empty glass in the hands of a newspaperman were unlikely to succumb to good intentions. During the growing years, the Denver Press Club moved from hotel-to-hotel; thrown out of most of the finest establishments in the city. Even a few private homes, businesses, and other fraternal organizations hosted the club for varying periods. Eventually, club members knew the search for a permanent club house was mandatory, and an obsession to club members for decades.

FUNERAL NOTICE.

A meeting of the Denver Press club will be held to-morrow, Sunday, at noon in the offices of the *Rocky Mountain Herald*, postoffice annex. All members are requested to be present.

LADIES can save money by having hats pressed over: 75 new shapes at Weatherhead's, 1434 Larimer street.

A misplaced funeral announcement for the Denver Press Club
was placed in an 1891 edition of the *Rocky Mountain News*.

Rocky Mountain News, April 25, 1891.

While the building fund grew, new club rooms were rented at 18 Granite Block, the corner of Fifteenth and Larimer Streets, in February 1891.[5] Two months later, they met again, but the announcement was made with a strange notice in the *Rocky Mountain* News. Under the headline of "Died," funeral notices of five former members of the Denver community were listed. Immediately afterward a misplaced headline "Funeral Notice" announced: "A meeting of the Denver Press Club will be held to-morrow, Sunday at the offices of the *Rocky Mountain Herald,* post-office annex. All members are requested to be present."[6]

On October 23rd at the new Broadway Theater, Messrs. M. B. Leavitt (lessee of the theater) H. B. Lonsdale (resident manager) and Mr. J. C. Duff of the Duff Comic Opera Company proposed a benefit performance of Gilbert & Sullivan's *Pirates of Penzance* on behalf of the club's building account.[7] When the tally of tickets was completed, 5,500 patrons filled all the seats of the Auditorium Theater (the free comp list did not apply to this performance).[8] Parquet tickets sold for $1.50, dress circle $1, and balcony seats were 75-cents. Folding chair seats were 35-cents and 25-cents.[9]

The new Granite Block Building, in what is now called Larimer Square, was conducive to Denver's national image, and to the purpose of the Denver Press Club. When a special correspondent for the *Philadelphia Times* came to Denver to research articles, he sought the hospitality of the rooms of the Denver Press Club. He was introduced to Lute Wilcox, the blind editor of *Field and Farm,*[246] a recognized authority on all field-and-farm topics. The Denver Press Club was gaining the reputation as a one-stop opportunity to meet with top decision leaders of the region — many of whom were honorary members of the club and trusted resources for the newspaper community.

*****

Seventy-six men and women of the Mississippi editorial excursion to Denver were a day late in arriving during the summer of 1900. While waiting for their baggage to be brought to their rooms, the president of their association expressed his familiarity with the journalistic sites of Denver and proposed to amend their schedule. "Let's go right up to the cyclone cellar, for we are all powerful dry."[10] A band at the hotel performed only two or three welcoming musical selections before the delegation walked out and marched down Arapahoe Street for a more fluid morning welcome in the cellar of the grocery store where the press club began.

"Down into the cellar under Wolfe Londoner's store they tumbled," *The Denver Times* reported, "and with scriptural suggestiveness, Londoner stood at the foot of the stairway, dividing the throng, sending the men to the right and the women to the left. To the right was a beer fountain embedded in ice, and to the left Flora McCune was presiding over punch bowls filled with Boulder strawberries floating on the non-alcoholic liquid surface. But it only took a moment to learn that a mistake had been made when it was supposed that the ladies were to be satisfied with a frozen punch. A big box loaded with beer mugs and chopped ice looked too tempting to them, and for a while, the bowls were deserted for the Cape Nome beer faucet at the farther end of the cellar."[11]

Londoner entertained his guests with literary sermons while the waters of the Cyclone Cellar fortified his guests. During the editorial gathering, Londoner regaled his guests with an exposition on "The Evil Effects of Mineral Water."[12] For nearly forty years, the Denver Press Club struggled to be more than a social manifestation of the hard-working editors, journalists, and printers of the Rocky Mountains; but the attraction of the Cyclone Cellar kept drawing the club back to Londoner's allure.

*****

Times were changing among the national newspapers. In 1903 Joseph Pulitzer of the *New York World* recognized a need to unify newspaper journalism and donated a million dollars to establish a school of journalism to raise the quality of newspapers.

In 1903, the *Fort Collins Express* editorialized their skepticism of what benefits could be derived from teaching journalism. "The real newspaperman cannot be made. He must grow. Some have a natural aptitude for the profession. Those who do not have this aptitude had better follow some other calling. The idea of grinding out a lot of newspapermen from a common lot of men is an absurdity. If newspapermen were turned out upon the leveling plan of the graded schools, a fine lot of cattle would be the result. The whole newspaper push would deteriorate into a sense of mediocracy. Modern commercialism has had a pernicious effect enough upon journalism without adding the straight jacket process of professional tutelage. There are no great editors anymore. There are some smart alecks and a great many newspaper chumps. . . Journalism isn't in the books. It is not of yesterday, but today. It is the epitome of passing events, and events in journalism must be anticipated, rather than reviewed. The more a man knows, and knows well of things in general, the better journalist he makes. And this necessity for knowledge of a great range of subjects is one of the things that make schools of journalism impracticable. A college education in journalism is a benefit but not an essential. The mind of the journalist is one that must think quickly and think broadly. The discipline of the mind such as is acquired in school or college is a great aid in practical journalism. But the great journalist of the future is the one whose mind is not only stored with a mass of knowledge, but he must be a broad thinker, and be endowed with a moral courage that will break the shackles of precedent, prejudice, selfishness and the pride of ostentation."[13]

Likewise, the *San Francisco Call* chastised the idea of a school of journalism: "After all, young man, your college of journalism [is] in the college of effort, and you must begin at the bottom, no matter what you may acquire in a university. No one knows how a journalist is made, and no one knows how to make one. A machine that will turn out a journalist and give him a degree of that effect may do a good business in degrees and may equip some young men to write after a fashion—without inspiration— folios of sorrow. A great newspaper is a strange, live and unexpected thing that rushes into existence through the night, made by many hands, swayed by many circumstances and born in the rush and delirium of 10,000 thrilling currents racing to their goal from the brain centers of the world. A strange untutored youth standing in the doorway sees something spring out of the confusion, grasps it and is gone. To him it is a thing to sell in a hurry. To you and me, who have watched its birth, it is like the finished model in the sculptor's studio surrounded by the waste and wreck of scaffolding and clay, standing alone in its simple magnificence, the marvelous offspring of science and art—a modern newspaper. To know this thing, to understand how it grows, upon what it feeds, what sustains it and what it means, you must have lived with it; and you shall not know it in any other college of journalism."[14]

The free-for-all among newspapermen was beginning to have legal consequences. At what point did an editor's vitriol provide an opportunity to hide behind the freedom of speech component of the First Amendment to the U.S. Constitution? The New York State Assembly passed an act that changed the law of libel to remove the injustice to which publishers were subjected. The new law, which was expected to spread to the other states, required a complainant file notice of libel with the publishers, providing them with an opportunity to print a retraction. If they refused or neglected to do so, the libel case could proceed to the courts. But if a retraction was made, the presumption of malice was removed, and the burden of proving malice resided with the complainant.

Publishers believed the old libel laws, borrowed from English common law, were no longer applicable to the publishing industry. Early newspaper publishers not only had first-hand knowledge of the accuracy of news-events that they covered; but they also wrote the story, set the type, and distributed the final product. In 1905, when the new libel laws were spreading, it was impractical for a publisher to verify every statement even though the newspapers were considered a public necessity by publishing news of the world that may be worth printing.

"Publishers should be protected against unjust and vexatious litigation concerning publications prompted in no respect whatever by malice," William Stapleton, editor and manager of the *Denver Republican,* editorialized. "At the same time, however, the public is entitled to be protected against those irresponsible publications known as yellow journals, which pay no regard to the truthfulness or falsity of what they may print. But in the effort to hold such pernicious journals to just and adequate responsibility, honest and decently conducted papers should not be made to suffer."[15]

Recognizing the changes in journalism, the newsmen of the Denver Press Club needed to get serious about the welfare of their craft and unite somewhere other than the Cyclone Cellar where they merely swapped stories and engaged in lively games of poker. When twenty newspapermen agreed to provide a united and serious effort, Attorney James W. Kelley scheduled a luncheon at the Albany Hotel in the spring of 1905 and offered to write the new organizational papers to turn the Denver Press Club into an organization similar to the press clubs of the East. Fifty newspapermen gathered around a banquet table at the Albany Hotel to, once again, revamp the purpose of the Denver Press Club.

Denver Press Club members posed at the entrance of the Albany Hotel: (first row, seated: C. C. Williams, Thomas Rooney, Walter J. Davis, John C. Hammond, Edward Keating, John Connelly, T. H. A. McGill, Lee Haney, J. W. Kelley, R. A. Eaton. Second row, seated: Robert C. McElravy, L. J. Kavanaugh, T. H. Howell, J. H. Phillips, E. B. Johnson. Rear group, standing: W. C. Spencer, A. U. Mayfield, Martin Dunn, J. C. Stewart, T. H. Lawrence, S. A. Olympius, W. G. Collins, D. H. Wilson, Jennings Sutor, R. E. Smith, Fred L. Miner, A. W. Sowers, Warren Gilbert, Eugene Taylor, George P. Wallahan (wearing hat), Roy O'Conner, Samuel Wood, Warren Given, Frank Wright, Frank Farrar, Lute Johnson, A. W. Walhser, and H. S. Rogers.

Courtesy of the Denver Press Club

Members of the 1905-1906 Denver Press Club Board of Directors included (standing left-to-right): J. M. Ward (*Denver Post*), R. E. Smith (*Rocky Mountain News*) Treasurer W. C. Spencer (*Republican*), Martin Dunn (*Denver Post*), Eugene Bowles, (*Times*); (Sitting, left-to-right): Vice President Raymond A. Eaton (*Republican*), President Edward Keating (*Rocky Mountain News*), and Secretary W. R. Given (*Rocky Mountain News*).

Courtesy of the Denver Press Club

The reorganization of the Denver Press Club almost didn't happen; the meeting was called to order when a "flash" came over the house telephone that a Northeast Denver man was on a rampage and murdered two people and shot two policemen. Every police reporter and others swarmed from the press club meeting—some on foot, some via trolley car and one in his horse-drawn buggy. Robert Emmett Harvey, the *Denver Post* police reporter, installed a huge Chinese gong on the dash board of his vehicle to help clear traffic on his way to a story. The unusual arrangement was made through his connections at City Hall and drew both envy and derision from other police reporters whom he left in the dust.

After the reporters filed their stories, they returned to the Albany to restore the quorum necessary to reorganize the Denver Press Club.[16] The new officers included President Edward Keating (*Times*), Vice President Raymond A. Eaton (*Post*), Secretary Harry Robinson (*Rocky Mountain News*), and Treasurer W. Clyde Spencer (*Republican*).

The Albany Hotel (1895-1976) hosted many of the events for the
Denver Press Club. It was refurbished and reopened in 1938 after
Denver Press Club's architect, Burnham Hoyt redesigned the
celebrated hotel that once stood on 17th and Stout Streets in Denver.

Courtesy of the author.

When the meeting was over, a plan was made to establish a new
headquarters to provide newspaper writers with sufficient space to host
social functions and entertain prominent visitors to "the Queen City of the
Plains."[17] Despite the hype of the "new" Denver Press Club, the activities
looked the same as the "old" Denver Press Club. The first event was a
"smoker" co-hosted by the Chamber of Commerce and held at the Albany
Hotel. A smoker was an informal gathering of men for the broad purposes
of entertainment, discussion or any other agenda, normally surrounded
by swirls of cigar and pipe tobacco smoke. "It was shown in the talks,"
according to the *Denver Post*, "that the newspaper and its writers are among
the greatest and strongest factors in the country for the upbuilding of the
community and that, although they are often criticized for their modes of
exposures, it is all for the good of their cities."[18]

The following Sunday, a fund-raising performance at the Broadway
Theater brought the Henry W. Savage English Grand Opera Company for
a benefit preview performance the day before the troupe was scheduled to
open at the theater. The event was to begin raising funds to secure suitable

quarters for the press club,[19] and placed the club as a conduit to bring "the most brilliant entertainment of the kind ever given in Denver."[20] Not to be outdone, A. C. Carson, manager of the Orpheum theater, received a wire from Martin Beck, general manager of the theater company—"Say to the Press club that the very best in the entire Orpheum circuit is at their disposal for their big show April 2."[21] The press-club fund-raising performance became the largest local theatre event in the city's history.

Because of the assistance members of the Denver Press Club provided to Catholic institutions of the diocese; James Phelan Cuddy, the editor of the *Denver Catholic,* urged all members of the faith to attend the press club benefit. "No Catholic," wrote Cuddy, "who claims the allegiance of membership to one or any of the organized societies of the church which were established and lived on lines of philanthropy, should forget the members of the press."[22] Judge Benjamin Lindsey, a social reformer and judge of the juvenile court system in Denver, spent $25 of his own money to purchase 100 tickets in the second balcony for the benefit of the newsboys of Denver.[23]

In addition to the grand opera company selections, Walter Juan Davis put aside his role as local newspaperman to launch his debut on stage with entertaining anecdotes and songs that portrayed his role as a "Crossroads Editor."[24] The Mendelssohn Quartet performed, and the duo of Bert Howard and Leona Bland were loaned by A. C. Carson, a former newspaperman and current Orpheum manager to perform an act from "The Stage Manager."[25] More entertainers brought their talents to the press-club benefit. Seven young women, known as "The Pajama Girls,"[26] performed Geisha-inspired Japanese music and dance. By the time the curtain rose; ten acts, drawn from the finest grand opera, vaudeville, and local stages,[27] waited in the wings for their opportunity to perform at the benefit presentation.

Symphonic conductor Rafaello Cavallo took the baton with thirty Denver musicians, while stage hands from various theaters throughout the city provided the stage logistics for the performance. Newly elected Governor Jesse Fuller McDonald and other local dignitaries accepted invitations to attend.

As the final matinee curtain fell, the performers headed down the street to the Albany Hotel where a cast-party dinner was prepared. Amid informal speeches (including one from Justice L. M. Goddard of the Colorado Supreme Court) and impromptu songs from professional entertainers, it was expected that future press-club benefits would become a popular annual feature in the Denver entertainment world.[28]

Just two months into Keating's term as president of the 1905 Denver Press Club, the club's connections with the entertainment industry was tapped for another community program. Governor Joseph Folk, described as Missouri's great reformer, planned to come to Denver to meet with Judge Ben B. Lindsey of the Juvenile Improvement Association. Their objective was to encourage the children of Denver to become active in community service. The Denver Press Club was asked to provide entertainment for the youth conference. The *Denver Post* suggested that Governor Folk be granted an honorary membership.[29]

To announce plans for a new clubhouse,[30] the press club renewed their breakfast gatherings at the new Savoy Hotel in May 1905. A few days later, the Denver Press Club signed a lease for six rooms on the third level of the new Railroad Exchange Building at Seventeenth and Champa Streets. When the construction of the building was completed, the rooms were suitably furnished for the club.[31]

In July, the Denver Press Club's "permanent" club house held a house-warming party; a Dutch luncheon accompanied with music "appropriate to the occasion" (according to the *Denver Republican*). Each member was encouraged to bring a beer stein to leave behind for that member's future use.[32] The "Knights of the Pen," as Wolfe Londoner described the members of the Denver Press Club, turned out in large numbers. The membership rewarded Edward Keating with a silver loving cup for his brilliant leadership in reactivating the club into national prominence as well as for celebrating his birthday the same day as the press-club house warming.[33] One side of the cup bore the words "Presented to President Edward Keating of the Denver Press Club by his Friends," and matched on the other side with the date and the words "For he's a jolly good fellow."[34] The club's patriarch, Wolfe Londoner, was on hand with one of his entertaining speeches for just such an occasion. A. E. Pelton and Louis Hallet, managers of the Curtis Theater company brought several members of the company to entertain the newspapermen.

Unnamed members of the Denver Press Club enjoy a new
tradition of enjoying their beverages in ornate beer steins.

Courtesy of the Denver Press Club

Keeping with the "stein" theme, John Hernan, manager of the Brown
Palace presented a silver stein to the club; Wolfe Londoner provided
two steins. A two-gallon antique German stein was donated by B. Shep
White and J. M. Ward. S. H. Dutton of the Albany Hotel and William
Sexton donated two silver steins and provided salads and sandwiches. The
clubrooms were decorated with donations from the showrooms of Daniels
& Fisher, the Denver Dry Goods company, Joslin Dry Goods, American
Furniture, and the Knight-Campbell Music Company.[35] The club house
included two large reception rooms that could be combined as an assembly
room. There was also a card room and buffet area.

Refreshments were served, and recreation provided under the watchful
eye of the club's new steward who lived alone in Hop Alley near 20th and
Larimer streets. Since the revitalization of the 1905 Denver Press Club,
the rooms were managed by Wong Gum Chung, better known as Jimmy
Wong, "friend of presidents, of governors, of United States senators and
of every man who has worked on the editorial staff of a Denver newspaper
for two decades."[36] At one point, he was the private cook to "Black Jack"
Pershing on the Mexican border[37] and part-owner of a Chinese restaurant
in Cripple Creek. "Big Bill" Haywood, union leader for the Industrial
Workers of the World, informed him that all restaurant employees were

required to join his organization or get out. Wong responded, "We got no employees. We all bosses; all part owners."[38]

Members of the Denver Press Club and the Writers' Club gather in the rooms of the Denver Press Club. The gentleman with a young child was cartoonist Richard F. Outcault, originator of Buster Brown Shoes advertisements and creator of "The Yellow Kid" cartoon that was at the center of the concept of sensationalized "Yellow Journalism." The member seated on the floor, (clasping his hands, seated second from the left) was James Grafton Rogers, professor of law and dean of the University of Colorado School of Law and Assistant Secretary of State. Seated on the floor (with a number 3 written on the picture) in white, was Jimmy Wong, night manager of the Denver Press Club.

Courtesy of the Denver Press Club

Fearing violence, the restauranteurs dissolved their partnership and Wong returned to China with $20,000 in gold coins. He distributed the money into four earthen jars under the floor of his home to guard against bandits, covered the floor with concrete, and instructed his wife to tap only one jar at a time if she needed money; he then returned to the United States. Wong made periodic trips back to China in an attempt to father a son, but only daughters were born. He returned to Denver and became the steward at another Denver club before becoming the night steward for the 1905 Denver Press Club. Renewing his friendship with Denver newspapermen, Wong was often greeted with discouraging news: "Where

Smith? They tell me, He died. I ask Where Jones? They say, He die. I ask Where Doctor Pa'khill? They say, He die." He paused in his conversation and scowled at a young man who had just joined the press club. "Huh! Me, you, big damn fools, we live. Good men die."[39]

To Denver newspapermen, Jimmy Wong was more than just the night manager of the Denver Press Club. Wong was also their source of encouragement during times of misfortune, and to moderate their enthusiasm during times of success. From 1905 to 1927 he was the warm friend and compassionate confidant of every newspaperman in town. He accompanied them through hangovers and broken love affairs, provided wise counsel, and loaned them cash. He was vigilant over his hard-drinking, suicidal, "cyanide kids" and served as a mentor to thrift, industry, moderation, and patience — even though few followed his wise advice. During his tenure with the Denver Press Club, his black hair turned silver and he eventually concluded his service with the knowledge he taught more than one press club member how to be a gentleman. His level-headedness provided him with access to four presidents of the United States, every Colorado governor during his tenure at the press club and was included in articles published in national newspapers by writers who considered themselves friends of the tireless night manager of the Denver Press Club. His salary was reported to be $15 a week.

Newspaper ad-man Lee Casey wrote of Jimmy Wong, "Every good waiter is courteous and considerate by the very nature of his calling because he devotes his life to the service of others. Jim Wong was that, and more. He was the wise and kindly guide of a generation of Denver newspapermen, all of whom learned from him something of the graces of irony and urbanity combined with deep understanding and sympathy. I never knew a better man. I never had a better friend."[40]

Wong's first lesson in fortitude and survival abilities occurred during a conversation with an inebriated club visitor when the club was located in the Railway Exchange Building. When the unnamed guest leaned backward against an open window on the second floor, he landed head-first on the ground below. The fallen newspaperman got up on his own, returned to the second-story press club rooms and continued his conversation with the night steward.

Building owner, James H. Causey was also the owner of the more prestigious University Building, and his building-management sensibilities didn't take kindly to the late-night habits of the Denver newsmen in his other rental space in the Railway Exchange. At all hours of the day or night, renditions of popular melodies and extemporaneous vocal versions emanated from the second floor of the Railway Exchange, often sung in conflicting musical keys.

The press club's whirlwind of activities brought members to the home of Mrs. Mary Elitch Long, the matriarch of her late-husband's amusement park enterprise. One private excursion included a private demonstration of Dr. Carver's sharp-shooting exhibition and his performing diving horses at the original Elitch Gardens site. Dr. Carver provided a short lecture about how the horses were trained, and then the hostess of the Gardens took the newspapermen on a tour of the new features of the Gardens.[41]

New telephone technology also came to Denver in 1905. Installation of the American DeForest Wireless Telegraph Company's "telephone antenna-to-receiver transmission system" was personally supervised by Dr. Lee DeForest who installed the system throughout the 1904 St. Louis World's Fair property. He explained that communications could be established by "tuning in" a receiver in another city before sending the message. One message could also be "broadcast" to an unlimited number of receivers or restricted to one receiver without fear of someone "tapping the wire." With many dispatches being received by newspapers still using the laborious Morse telegraph key of dots-and-dashes, the Denver newspapers watched the "Wireless Telegraph" installation with great interest.[42]

Nearly 300 delegates of the National Editorial Association also arrived in Denver during the summer of 1905 after they concluded their annual convention a few weeks earlier in Guthrie, Oklahoma. The chamber of commerce invited the newspaper editors to visit Denver's community improvements that occurred during the past four decades. Wolfe Londoner previously addressed every meeting of the association during the past fourteen years and was on hand to greet his fellow members. He was joined by Edward Keating, president of the Denver Press Club, who added his own words of welcome.[43]

When the Denver Elks secured their national convention in Denver for 1906, the Boosters' club met at the Albany to start organizing the event. The *Denver Post* reported that "Everybody wanted to get on the committees and everybody was determined to have his own particular club represented in the welcoming body."[44] After a lively discussion during the plenary session, the entertainment committee was composed of six representatives—one each from the Elks, the Chamber of Commerce, the

Denver Press Club, the Real Estate Exchange, the Denver Ad Club, and the Hotel and Restaurant Men's Association.

In 1905, the press club sought to be more assertive when it came to presidential matters during the upcoming national election. Upon the next campaign visit by President Theodore Roosevelt, the press club proposed to honor him with a banquet where he would be elected the first recipient of an official Honorary Membership of the Denver Press Club.[45] The following week, the Denver newspapermen, "almost daily showing themselves to be among the city's strongest 'boosters,'"[46] got together with the chamber of commerce to establish a committee of public-spirited organizations to create a general auditorium committee to stimulate the construction of a city auditorium.

The *Denver Republican* described the value of the new philosophical structure of the press club— "Denver has long needed a press club, not alone to bring about a closer relationship between the newspapermen of the city, but chiefly as a means of affording adequate entertainment for celebrities who visit Colorado," the newspaper editorialized. "It is proposed to have President Roosevelt the guest at a Press club breakfast, and such honors paid to other visiting men of distinction will give the guests of Colorado new cause to remember this state with pleasure. The new club is deserving of all the encouragement that can be given by the public."[47]

President Theodore Roosevelt and associates Dr. Chapman and Mr. Stewart pause in their hunt for bears near Glenwood Springs.

Courtesy of the Library of Congress, *President Roosevelt and his fellow hunters, Dr. Chapman and Mr. Stewart, Rocky Mts., Colo.*, ca. 1905. Photograph. https://www.loc.gov/item/2013651348/.

Colorado's mountainous terrain and ample wildlife for hunting appealed to Teddy Roosevelt. While he hunted his prey, the vehemently partisan press preyed upon the hunter. Newspaper readers feared for the safety of their president. Eastern papers duplicated the ridiculous stories because they had no evidence to the contrary and their readers believed them. One report claimed a bear turned upon Roosevelt, killing the president. Another correspondent, claiming he was from Glenwood Springs, reported the president was in hand-to-claw combat with other bruins; after discarding his rifle, the president ripped into a grizzly bear with a butcher knife, holding on only with the strength of his presidential teeth.

Some publishers in Denver fought back in the name of fair play, for the treatment of their reporting subjects. "And yet," the *Denver Republican* reported, "because of the yellow sheets have never hesitated to sacrifice any and every interest of the state to their own insatiate greed for sensationalism, there is imminent danger that their course, entered into at the very beginning of the hunt, will disgrace the people and bring into question their hospitality and sense of respect due an honored guest."[48]

D. C. Beaman, vice president and general counsel of the Colorado Fuel and Iron Company, Democratic state senator, and cattleman, bristled with the way President Roosevelt's Colorado hunting expedition was being treated by the Denver press. "Such treatment of a high public official on a private recreative trip is shameful and a disgrace to journalism and the state, and the editor who permits its publication is, if possible, more blameful than the correspondent who fabricates it. . ... For the credit of the state the owners and manager of the papers, if the editors will not, should sit down and sit down hard on this infamous way of handling the matter of this hunt which, if properly handled, might be made interesting to the public and acceptable to the subject of it."[49]

The president considered his outings as a means to build his mental and physical strength "in the freedom and the wholesomeness of the out-of-doors as other national leaders have found renewed vigor and power for the work that confronted them."[50]

President Theodore Roosevelt was preparing to leave his hunting camp near Glenwood Springs for more comfortable rooms at The Brown Palace. Housekeepers redecorated the president's hotel room with animal skins, pictures of hunting, and mounted animal heads. Waiting for the president's arrival was a special Honorary Membership card from the Denver Press Club. It was made of gold from a prospect hole on the Moffat Road at the Denver & Northwestern Mining company[51] and bore the engraved press club seal and national coat-of-arms in enamel, the president's name engraved in old English, and the signatures of the officers of the club.[52] The card was designed by Thorwald Sorenson, an employee with the Boyd Park company and former royal-seal engraver to King Oscar II of Sweden.[53]

Federal troops and state militia members escorted the president from Union Station to The Brown Palace Hotel in May 1905. Before the banquet, only one reception was scheduled — a 6:45 p.m. gathering in the Press Club's rooms on the eighth floor of the hotel, close to the president's own suite.[54] At the last minute, the president invited the Denver Press Club members to his own more-spacious private rooms. The members arrived in pairs and President Roosevelt shook hands with each of the 100 members as they entered and were introduced. The two presidents met each other at the door — "Boys, I am so glad to meet you and to greet you," said

President Roosevelt. "The same to you, Mr. President," responded press-club president Keating as they warmly shook hands in welcome.[55]

Before formally addressing the press club members, Orator J. W. Kelley explained the gold and precious stones in the member card were mined shortly after the president's arrival in Colorado, freshly minted in time for this presentation, and it was offered as a sincere tribute of honor and esteem. Kelley continued by promising that newspapermen never hesitate to chastise bad behavior in public office, but also praise good men in the same position. "Please remember," Kelley told the president, "that the newspapermen who know you best, esteem you most."

Keating then addressed President Roosevelt. "Mr. President, I have the honor and it affords me great pleasure to inform you this evening that you have been elected the first Honorary Member of the Denver Press Club. The occasion is doubly pleasant because it is to Roosevelt the individual, not as president, nor to Roosevelt the Democrat, or Roosevelt the Republican . . . It affords me great pleasure to present to you this slight token in the shape of a membership card, because with it is conveyed the high esteem in which you are held, Mr. President, by newspapermen, not alone in Denver, but everywhere. You are truly first in peace, first in war, and first in the hearts of your countrymen."

To the cry of "Hip, Hip, Hurrah!" and three cheers, Keating presented the gold membership card to the president.

"Mr. President [Keating], Mr. Kelley and fellow members of the Denver Press Club," the President began, "I believe I now have the right to so address you. It is with the greatest pleasure that I accept this handsome card. More than anything else the sentiment in which it is tendered appeals to me. I number among my best friends many newspapermen. Always have. I found them loyal and I am deeply touched by this handsome tribute. I shall always remember the Denver Press Club of which I am proud to be a member, and I promise you that I shall come back again and be with you on some future occasion. Next time, I shall be with you for a longer period. I appreciate the responsibilities imposed upon me, and I shall always try and do that which seems fit and best. I shall always do that which is decent as every decent American citizen should do. Gentlemen, I thank you."[56]

Among the Denver Press Club members in the room was Eugène Ysaÿe, a celebrated Belgian violinist and the highest paid artist in the country, was in Denver to continue his national performance tour.[57] He greeted the President in French, a language that Roosevelt spoke fluently.[58]

The Denver Press Club's active relationship with world leaders, prominent organizations and industries, active relationships with communicators in the theater-arts community, and hospitality among newspapermen and their families throughout the country, continued to attract the attention of journalists throughout the world. No longer would the Eastern newspaper establishment consider Denver journalism as folksy commentary set among the cow pies. The Denver Press Club helped show that Colorado could participate in national and world events.

The repeated financial success of the press club theatrical benefits and the support of the community pushed the newspapermen to start searching again for a permanent home. Following a Saturday afternoon executive committee meeting at the Albany Hotel with real-estate agents who had properties that could be modified to serve as a club house,[59] the issue was raised to members the next morning during a brunch at the Savoy Hotel, hosted by hotel managers S. H. Alexander and Charles E. Owen.[60] The ornate meal was scheduled to provide an opportunity for morning and evening newspapermen to be in attendance. The brunch menu included Grape Fruit au Maraschino, Eggs a la Melba, Tenderloin of Beef Bing-Bing, Potatoes Sarah Bernhardt, and coffee.[61]

Pushing themselves away from the table; musty ale, clay pipes, dhuddens (short-stemmed Asiatic pipes) and tobacco were passed around among the seventy newspapermen who had gathered for an hour of unbroken pleasure, camaraderie, and good fellowship "not unmixed with a bit of that Bohemianism which is quite sure to crop out among the always cosmopolitan newspapermen."[62]

City press clubs were not the only newspaper support groups. The International League of Press Clubs was established to represent the working journalists throughout the continent. Charles Emory Smith (1842-1908), Editor-in-Chief of the *Philadelphia Press* and Republican leader, noted the important role that journalism played in American life. "Journalism is allied with every form of intellectual expression," he wrote in the 1904 International League of Press Clubs book, *Bohemia*. "It is the daily exchange of all modern life. Millions find little time for books, but everybody makes time for the newspaper. It is *our* open window *of* the world."[63]

The international organization began in 1892 "to bring together all the newspapermen of the United States for mutual benefit and advancement, but the most immediate work is the establishment of a Journalists' Home for aged and invalid newspapermen who have broken down in the work."[64] Active newspapermen employed by the daily newspapers of large cities comprised membership in the international organization.

The International League of Press Clubs notified Denver Press Club president Keating that the international organization considered the Queen City of the Plains as a contender for the 1906 annual international conference. Its participation in a Denver convention would become a direct benefit for the Denver Press Club and a boost for the overall city.[65] President J. J. Keenan of the international association telegraphed, "Other candidates. But Denver's offer very tempting. Send representatives to Detroit by all means."[66]

Keating responded with his promise that all 125 Denver Press Club members would be in attendance if awarded the convention.[67] The next day, the Denver Press Club took advantage of the al fresco breakfast offered by P. J. Foley, the concessionaire at City Park, to strategize next year's solicitation of the international convention.[68] Charles S. Sprague (*Rocky Mountain News*), Thomas Rooney (*Denver Times*), B. Shepherd White of the American Press syndicate and W. C. Spencer (*Denver Republican*) and one other "ambassador" were dispatched to the Detroit convention armed with a half-ton of "inducements to offer in the way of special attractions"[69] to come to Denver in 1906.

While the five newspapermen were on their way to Detroit, phone calls were placed by the Governor of Colorado, the mayor of Denver, board of aldermen, and the general manager of one of the western railroads also extended an invitation to the international press club. The Denver Press Club brought a large number of badges—a blue oval-shaped gold button with the words "Smile and Push Denver" in "gold" and a white ribbon attached with the inscription "Denver, 1906, a Mile High in the Sky." The competing Wilkes-Barre, Pennsylvania delegation arrived earlier with badges comprised of a white ribbon inscribed with the name "Wilkes-Barre" and a small piece of coal attached to a red button.

"Our badges are solid gold," winked a Denverite.

"Ours are solid coal," replied Pennsylvanian Dan Hart and the battle of the coal against the gold was on.

The delegates were invited to the rooms of the Denver delegates in the Cadillac Hotel and several cases of champagne were opened to influence the delegates.[70]

Contrarian Winifred Black of the editorial staff of the *Denver Post*, bitterly considered the value of press clubs was no longer valid in modern 1905 Denver. "The Denver Press Club," according to Black, "is sending a delegation East to try and swing the Press club convention to Denver this year, if it can be swung. Nice, hopeful, little advertising men, swing high and swing low, more power to the censer [sic]—get the convention—if you can. All press clubs, in-or-out of convention, look exactly alike to me. I never saw one yet, where you couldn't throw a stone right into the most thickly populated part and run no risk at all of hitting a real newspaperman. A press club is one of the funniest things in this funny old joke of a world we live in. Once in a while you'll find a real newspaperman stumbling vaguely and puzzled among the horde of obsequious outsiders, who cling to the magic badge, with the pen on it, as if it meant life to them, but for the most part the press club man belongs to one or the other of three great and celebrated organizations—the sad, sweet Order of the Has-Beens, the tender confiding Order of the Would-Be's, or the Dull and Desperate Band of the Never Was'es. Press clubs, newspapermen, fie, fie brethren, why don't you come out in your real colors and tell us what you really are?"[71] The Denver Press Club's colors were clearly to "boost" Colorado.

In August, the Burlington railroad proposed to boost Colorado as a winter resort for the affluent skiers throughout the country and to increase visitor traffic. Denver set up business-planning conferences with the Denver Hotel Men's Association, the Colorado State Commercial Association and the Denver Press Club.[72] Author Hamlin Garland, a guest of the Denver Press Club, accepted the challenge to promote Colorado's potential for outdoor recreation and proposed a national park in the mountainous White River country of Colorado.[73]

Back at the International League of Press Clubs convention in Detroit when it came to ballot for the 1906 convention; the competing Wilkes-Barre, Pennsylvania's press club recognized that the Denver challenge was too strong. Wilkes-Barre withdrew, and press releases went out that Denver would be host of the 1906 convention for the International League of Press Clubs.[74]

*****

The fall arrival of the golden-yellow aspen leaves throughout the Colorado Rockies was matched by a repeat of one of the oddest excursions of "eight of the most beautiful young women in Texas."[75] The Denver Press Club appointed an eager committee to help entertain Mr. Calkins' winners of the beautiful "Telegram Girls" contest.[76] The ladies were under the chaperonage of A. Calkins, editor of the *Evening Telegram* of Fort Worth and sponsor of the trip. The previous year, Calkins sent ten of the most attractive girls to Denver but chose "beauty rather than popularity" for 1905, insisting that "beautiful women are always popular."[77]

The local newspapermen planned a December 1905 fundraiser at the Broadway Theater to help underwrite the publicity and railroad transportation committees.[78] As word spread of Denver's inaugural press-club-league event, prominent members of the journalistic fraternity throughout the country announced their intention of being in Denver for the conference. By the end of the year, the proposed attendees included Mark Twain (Samuel Clemens), Colonel Joe Wheeler (prominent American military commander and politician), members of the British Institute of Journalism; and delegates from Cuba, the Philippines, and the Hawaiian Islands.[79]

With only eight months before the international press club conference convened, the Denver members paused to welcome Christmas 1905. Guest of honor was Santa Claus who made an appearance at the club rooms that were elaborately decorated with Christmas greenery and a miniature tree trimmed with tinsel and lighted candles. The gifts around the tree were selected for special significance to the recipient's newspaper work, but not revealed in the pages of the newspaper. The *Denver Post* acknowledged that "as each package was unwrapped there were shouts of laughter and good-natured chaffing."[80] Entertainment included Joe Newman, a singer performing at the Orpheum Theater, who belted out several of his own compositions. The revelers reconvened first for a New Year's Day open house in the press club's rooms,[81] followed by a reception at the Railway Exchange Building for the Colorado Editorial Association's meeting the following week,[82] and a speaking engagement before the Colorado Commercial Association banquet at the Albany Hotel.[83]

The Denver Press Club was becoming a strong national organization, causing local and regional politicians to take notice. However, it was the *Denver Post* that warned with a wink that Denver's journalistic watchdogs were ready to pounce with a theatrical satirical performance: "Public men should discontinue their grafting, stop riding hobbles and kill and bury all their idiosyncrasies, unless they wish to be held up for laughter before the multitude by the Denver Press Club which is completing arrangements to give a burlesque of local and national characters at its annual entertainment, during the third week in February" [1906].[84] Club members were poised to parody Denver politics in a show at the Broadway Theater on February 19th[85] in the same way the Gridiron Club and Foundation (founded among journalistic organizations in Washington, D. C.) were skewering political and business leaders since 1885. Of the two burlesques written by local newsmen Frank Lundy Webster, Robert McElravy, Charles Bonfils, Arthur Chapman, Eugene Taylor and James W. Kelley, was a send-up of President Theodore Roosevelt's recent Colorado hunting trip. "What 'Teddy' did, how he did it; what the newspapers men and others did, and how they, perhaps, didn't do it, will be portrayed vividly," reported the *Denver Post*.[86]

The second burlesque on Colorado politics was "when the dignity is taken from under it,"[87] the *Post* vaguely explained. Anyone who had the misfortune to sit through a dreary political convention and see people fight over irrelevant issues, was promised an opportunity to laugh back at those very politicians expected to be in attendance at the theater. "Nobody is spared," the *Denver Post* continued, "no mercy is shown to the public characters who will be caricatured on the stage."[88]

In addition to the two burlesques, Mrs. Otis Spencer played the part of Mrs. Suffering Suffrage in a timely satire of the Suffragette movement. The Mendelssohn Quartet appeared while a quartet of cowboys sang original songs of the West. One of the other features was a staged version of living cartoons with live people playing the roles of characters in the funnies.[89]

The second year of the "new" Denver Press Club began with eighty-five men at the Savoy Hotel for breakfast, followed by the annual election of officers. Edward Keating, managing editor of the *Rocky Mountain News* and *Denver Times* was re-elected president. Josiah M. Ward, city editor of the *Post* was named vice president by acclamation. W. C. Spencer, cartoonist for the *Republican* was re-elected as treasurer. Of the fourteen nominations for the remaining directors, five board positions were elected—Eugene W. Taylor (city editor of the *Republican*), Robert E. Smith (*Rocky Mountain News*), Harry L. Wilbur (*Post*), Charles T. Roehrig (night editor of the Associated Press), and Nelson A. Reinert (*Daily Mining Record*).[90] The treasurer's report for the past year put the Denver Press Club on a sound financial and social standing.

The new advocacy focus of the club fit what one newspaper described as a growing fad. At the April 1906 Chamber of Commerce meeting, the "See America First" campaign kicked off with the usual city boosters. "That a large part of the $300,000,000 annually spent by sight-seeing Americans abroad will be retained at home," said Fisher Harris, executive secretary of the See America First league. "The slogan, 'See Europe if you will, but see America first,' has been taken into every prominent publication in America; also, into the pulpit, the state and national conventions, public and private schools, the colleges and the universities."[91] James W. Kelley of the Denver Press Club was among the members of the small boosting committee for the city. He recognized the upcoming conference of the International League of Press Clubs was going to be a test of Denver's fitness to welcome large groups of tourists. Stepping forward, the Hotel Keepers' Association pledged its "hearty co-operation, financial and otherwise"[92] to help Kelley and the Denver Press Club succeed with the International League of Press Clubs conference.

To spiff up the image of the Denver Press Club, members wanted to wear an official button, but the cost was too prohibitive to accomplish. Harry Lee Wilber and F. J. Kasdorf headed to Colorado Springs to confer with James F. Burns of the Portland Gold Mining Company. Because of the positive relationship he maintained with the press men, Burns promised enough Portland Mine gold to be converted into artistic buttons for each of the attendees.[93]

Three months away from what was described in the newspapers as "the biggest gathering of prominent newspapermen in the history of the country,"[94] the people of Denver raised an additional $10,000 to assure that the visiting writers had a very enjoyable time in the city. A large committee of influential Coloradans proposed a complete tour of the state, with highlights that included high-yielding mining camps, coal fields, agricultural districts, and recreational excursions into the Rocky Mountains.[95] Also, a $1,000 gold brick, donated by former newspaperman and current mine owner, Fred G. Shaffer,[96] was provided as the grand prize for the best story written by an International League of Press Clubs attendee. Shaffer's journalistic background recognized that hundreds of thousands of dollars in advertising for the state would result from the donation of a comparatively "inexpensive" gold bar. The Manhattan Beach (once located on the northern shore of Sloan's Lake) and Elitch Gardens (originally located at 38th and Tennyson) amusement parks also made additional entertainment contributions.[97]

The Denver Press Club also urged President Theodore Roosevelt and William J. Bryan to attend — the president was an author and Mr. Bryan was an editor and publisher.[98] The president kindly turned down the invitation, noting he refused "all proffered engagements during the summer."[99]

The press club took a break from their planning to join the Denver Women's Writers' club[100] for an excursion on the Colorado Midland and the Cripple Creek Short line railroads in late June.[101] Finley Peter Dunne (known by the pseudonym "Mr. Dooley" to newspaper readers) described the Cripple Creek excursions as "the one day trip that bankrupts the English language."[102] After the excursion, the press club announced that the Writers' Club would help provide hospitality for the visiting international press men. The Women's Writers Club, "are well known in social and business circles as active and wide-awake,"[103] reported the *Denver Post*.

Despite working until midnight, the press club met for breakfast with its female counterparts, courtesy of J. T. Foley, the concessionaire at City Park. After breakfast, J. W. Kelley (doubling as publicity chairman for the local Elks Club) presented the press men with what was described as "an immense silver loving cup" in appreciation of the press club "boosting" the upcoming Elks convention in mid-July. The Elks also submitted a check for $250 to be used for the entertainment fund for the international press club convention in late August.

J. T. Foley and members of the Denver Press Club
and the Writers' Club at City Park in Denver.

Courtesy of the Denver Press Club

Foley's press-club breakfast became an annual event. He provided boat rides on the lake and automobile rides around the park when breakfast was over. Bands of professional musicians provided the entertainment while Foley provided detailed information about every attraction on the grounds. As the morning activities drifted into afternoon, the soft Colorado breezes blew in from the lake and across the table that was decorated with fresh-cut roses from the park's flower gardens. Members of the party retreated to the shore of the lake to pose for pictures with the massive loving cup.

The Denver Press Club was a male-only organization of Denver-area newspapermen. The women who wrote for the Denver daily papers organized the Women's Writers Club shortly after the male counterparts revamped the Denver Press Club in 1905. The two press organizations were considered good-natured rivals even to a level of sharing gold. The Denver Press Club received a gold bar from the Portland Mine; the Women's Writers Club likewise received a gold bar from the Silver Age and Franklin mines, two of the largest gold mines in the Clear Creek district, courtesy of W. H. Knowles and J. F. Manning of the Producer Mining company. The gold bar would be melted and reformed into badges for the members of the Writers Club.[104]

The week of August 27 to September 1[105] was set aside for the 1906 International League of Press Clubs and provided the Denver Press Club with additional opportunities to establish partnerships with other clubs to help with the convention. In mid-July, the journalists and editors, some of whom were also members of the Elks Club, found time to admit the local Elks to a week-long open house at the press club rooms.[106] A special press-club badge was created to mark the Elks Club guests when they entered the Denver Press Club rooms — an ornate bar draped with the American flag and a scroll of paper crossed with scissors and a quill was inscribed "Press." From the pendant hung an oblong design with the letters B. P. O. E., the words "Cervus Alces," and the Elk's head and dial with the hands set at 11 between the antlers.[107]

"Without newspapermen," the *Rocky Mountain News* reported, "a big convention such as the reunion now in Denver would not be unlike 'Hamlet' without a Hamlet. Many men of the press are Elks. Most of them are in the service of the daily papers. Others are editors and publishers of Elk journals. All are good fellows; else they would not be among the Best People on Earth."[108] The relationship between the Elks and the Denver Press Club combined into a "Bohemian entertainment" event led by Otto Herres of the press committee of the Elks and James W. Kelley, chairman and official orator of the Denver Press Club. Appropriate to the press club's style of entertaining, the Elks visitors were greeted with recitations, songs, and humor in addition to a feast of food.[109]

The next day, the press club rooms were opened to admit the Montana delegates to the Elks Club conference. The *Rocky Mountain News* described the reception as "playing hilarious music and cheering with voices hoarse from the effort of shouting 'Are you all happy?' who watched their automobile whizz through Denver's streets."[110] One of the spectators was Coal Oil Inspector George Creel of Kansas City; a Missouri politician, friend of Governor Folk, and advocate of the upcoming International League of Press Clubs slightly more than a month away. "Denver, of course, is already probably the best-known city in the country," wrote Creel, "but its attractions have never been set forth in so alluring a way as is being done by the publication committee of the Denver Press Club now sending out matter inviting the press writers of the country to attend the convention of the International League of Press Clubs August 26."[111]

George Creel later became the head of the United States Committee on Public Information, the propaganda arm of President Woodrow Wilson's presidency during World War I before moving on to be a feature writer for *Collier's* magazine.

With the close of the Elks Club convention and the positive relationship established with the Denver Press Club, the *Rocky Mountain News* was quick to assess the benefit of favorable national newspaper relationships: "The trained newspaperman is perhaps the most observing person in the world, and with the exceptional chance of winning $1,000, our visitors will be spurred to the wish to see everything, so that their articles and stories may, by their accuracy and completeness, stand a better show of winning.[112]

Larry Giffen, the publicity agent of the amusement park invited the all-male Denver Press Club and the all-female Writers' Club to breakfast at the Manhattan Beach amusement park. Seventy-five guests found a long line of tables formed as a square frame, not only with good things to eat, but with tools of the trade. Pencils, pots of paste, copy paper, file hooks, pipes, cans of black and red ink, stacks of scissors, scoop-shovels representing "scoops" or exclusive news items; placards inscribed with "cub reporter," and "star reporter," together with mounds of sweet peas, carnations and other flowers.[113] Observers noted this was the third get-together in four weeks for the male and female newspaper organizations. The morning was filled with toasts, songs from the Manhattan Beach entertainers, comedy monologues, recitations, and amateur renditions of songs from the newspapermen and women.[114]

The national attention generated by the International League of Press Clubs convention provided a reputation of excellence upon the Denver journalists. When the press club secretary was visiting Salt Lake City, his peers noted the Denver Press Club is now "one of the most famous organizations of its kind in the country."[115]

As the Denver Press Club huddled for one last meeting before the international conference, word began to filter in from other clubs; six hundred[116] active newspapermen were on their way from around the country.[117] The national press was also buzzing about the creation of a new press organization in Denver — the Amalgamated Order of Mavericks, "a body entirely new and absolutely original with the Denver scribes."[118] For those journalists who were not members of the global organization, a "roundup of the Amalgamated Order of Mavericks"[119] was welcomed into the international festivities. It was expected that the two organizations would merge during the Denver conference.[120] The plan for the new organization came from the fertile brain of Edward Keating, president of the Denver Press Club and his idea of uniting the newspaper workers into one organization for social purposes.

As the *Tampa Tribune* reported,

> The Amalgamated Order of Mavericks will have no red tape requirements for membership beyond the proof that an applicant is a bona fide newspaperman. It must be shown that he makes his livelihood by such pursuits, and although he lives in a golden mansion or is the occupant of a hall room, if his money is made by daily toiling over the business of newspaper making, he will be equally eligible and equally acceptable to those who will seek to have this new organization launched at the Denver meeting.
>
> The promoters believe that a great good can be accomplished through the Maverick order from the clear intimacy and kindlier feeling between newspapermen which must naturally follow acquaintance made and renewed at annual meetings of the association. The newspapermen have never had an opportunity before to meet in a great body, that is the men who work at the business of writing up and editing papers. There are many editorial associations and the like of that, but too often the representation in them consists largely of the business office crowd, and very often the person representing a newspaper belonging to the association is someone having no connection whatever with editing the paper. This fact has become known to the people and oftentimes are heard references in irony of the profession as represented at so-called editorial association gatherings.
>
> The Maverick order will do away with this in a measure. For it will soon become known that only active workers in newspaper making are eligible to membership, and the button of the Maverick worn on the lapel will in the due course of time become the badge of the profession. This, of course, is merely a prediction, for no one has the right to say what shall be the distinguishing mark of service in the profession of newspaper making (the

word journalism is avoided because, according to eminent authority, it has exclusive application to a class).[121]

The Denver Press Club suggested that newspapermen throughout the country come to the International League of Press Clubs convention to discuss this matter. As an incentive, the Denver group offered a literary symposium, a Bohemian night in the Garden of the Gods (with Pikes Peak nearby), a trip up the peak, another to Cripple Creek, and still others over the Moffat road, around the Georgetown Loop (the famous Colorado & Southern road to Silver Plume), and then to the Greeley agricultural district known as the "Garden Spot of Colorado" where everything is raised through irrigation.

White and green[122] became the official colors of the Denver Press Club and were used by local businesses during the International League of Press Clubs convention. The club's meeting rooms were filled with vases of wild flowers harvested from the Colorado high country. The floral bank at City Park was prepared in the design of a broken sword crossed by a pen, representing the expression "The pen is mightier than the sword." The letters DPC for the Denver Press Club were also set in flowers. At Elitch Gardens, a similar display was formed from blooming flowers; the initials ILPC were added to the amusement park garden, providing honor to the International League of Press Clubs.[123]

As the delegates arrived at the train station, the Denver Post Boys' Band led the reception committee and welcomed the delegates with rousing music. The next day, several hundred "mavericks," unaffiliated with a formal press club, were welcomed at the train station with the same degree of fanfare before being escorted by automobile caravan to their hotels.[124] Press club members were taken to the Albany Hotel and newspaper "mavericks" were taken to the second floor of The Brown Palace.[125] The Denver Press Club's rooms served as a 24-hour headquarters to the delegates. The *Rocky Mountain News* published a daily "special edition" of "The Daily Scoop" insert that provided news and humorous tidbits on newspapers to entertain the delegates.

Some confusion developed after the press clubs received word that President Theodore Roosevelt would not be in attendance at the Denver conference. A reporter, staking-out the American House hotel, discovered that a young man registered as "David Gray, New York City, N.Y." was actually Theodore Roosevelt, Jr., the eldest son of the president. The young man was passing through Denver on his way to Glenwood Springs to retrace his father's footsteps on his own hunting and fishing trip. The 20-year old Roosevelt had hoped to leave town unnoticed but failed: "Yes, I dodge reporters because I dislike newspaper notoriety. I am singled out only because I am the president's son. If my father were not the president, no one would notice me. And that would suit me to a dot. I am not better than any other young American. I don't mean to be discourteous. I only want to keep out of the newspapers."[126] Arriving in Denver during one of the largest conventions of national journalists, the young Roosevelt chose an inopportune time if he was attempting to avoid newspaper attention.

In a gushing tribute to the newspapermen arriving in Denver, the *Rocky Mountain News* editorialized its role in society.

> There are not many people who give much time to thinking just what place in the world's calendar should be assigned to the knights of the daily press. Personally, they write their names in water—for the average worker finds his most strenuous effort endures perhaps for three hours; occasionally some torch is struck that throws its light for a longer period, but on the whole the game is one of ditch digging.
>
> There is not much acting in the day of the man who gathers and prints the news, though plenty of action punctuates the hours. But the same chap is the supreme dramatist of life. He sets up his show often without the accessories of scenery, devoid of enhancing trappings, unheralded by music, stripped of the illusions that do hedge the mimic stage. Theirs is to chronicle the doings of the stage on which the world's everyday drama is being enacted. The men and women of the press are the exponents of all that is transpiring today, tomorrow and the day after.
>
> It is theirs to press their fingers tightly on the feverish pulse of life's activities and not the heart throbs of the race; to mark the comedies and tragedies that are taking place all during the twenty-four hours of the day; to listen to the howls and yells of the stock exchange, to tell in unimpassioned, impersonal form the story of great losses

endured, and fortunes won on a tick of the wire; how frenzied finance lifts men to the summit of power and hurls them to ruin and despair. . . The joy, the gladness, the wholesome mirth of this world are run in upon the scenes following close on the trail of tragedies and tears. Trained to seeing broadly and swiftly, to gathering into the embrace of a glance the surface and hidden features which shape events, they have a language of keenness and economic strength in which to tell the story of their find. No breath-taking sentences, no waste of time on elaborate diction, they write that they who run may read the story of emotions, impulses and all the situations in which humanity is involved.[127]

The dinner was an informal affair, described as "one of the most pleasing of its kind that has ever been given in Denver," according to the *Daily News*. People known in the literary world were in attendance and fraternized cordially with any guest who chose to attend the affair. "There have been many elaborate dinners in Denver in the past," continued the *Daily News*, "but for genuine pleasure and the best of everything, nothing ever excelled this."[128]

The 400 official delegates overwhelmed the small rooms at The Brown Palace and spilled over to the Denver Press Club rooms in the Railroad Building. As promised, the late-night doors of the Denver Press Club were thrown open to a throng of guests, and it was likely that many of the guests who saw the sunset over the Rocky Mountains also saw the sunrise over the plains east of Denver. "The crowd which packed the three rooms, almost to the point of suffocation," reported *The Daily News*, "was entertained with theatrical 'stunts' rendered by some of the best professional talent in the city."[129] The evening empties were cleared away to make room for lunch and other refreshments. The press-club quarters were too small to accommodate the crowd, so a "pass in and pass out" system of staggered admission was courteously maintained throughout the day. "For five hours," *The Denver Times* reported, "the fun and the mental frolics continued . . ."[130]

A literary symposium at the Broadway Theater brought nationally known literary figures to participate in the International League of Press Clubs convention. Elbert Hubbard (1856-1915) was an American publisher, artist and philosopher. Originally a traveling salesman for the Larkin Soap Company, Mr. Hubbard more famously was known for founding the Roycroft artisan community in New York and for his eccentrically published literary books and magazines. One of his magazine covers was published on brown butcher paper because he said there was literary "meat inside."

Opie Pope Read (1852-1939) was a newspaperman, author, lecturer, and co-founder of the folksy comic newspaper, *The Arkansas Traveler,* but he earned a more-serious national reputation for his coverage of the 1878 outbreak of yellow fever in Tennessee as published in the *New York Herald.* He was an active lecturer and Chautauqua performer and appeared in the 1920 silent film *Birthright.* In a Mark Twain style, Mr. Read provided unflattering views of orthodox religion, and his personal views of golf, fishing and poker. S. E. [Samuel Ellsworth] Kiser, a Chicago poet, humorist, and newspaperman; and W. D. [Wilbur D.] Nesbit, a humorist and *Chicago Tribune* columnist, and others also participated in the literary symposium.

At the conclusion of the Broadway Theater high-brow literary event, a specially selected late-night gathering met at the Denver Press Club for a less sophisticated stag party.[131]

The growing tension in Europe in 1906 did not escape the international journalists. One of the delegates was Mrs. Belva Lockwood of Washington, D. C. She aspired to be president of the United States (receiving 5,000 votes when pitted against Grover Cleveland and James Blaine), was a prominent lawyer, suffragist, politician, educator, and author, but was homeless by the age of 80. The international journalism league appointed Mrs. Lockwood to be an envoy-of-one to attend the peace conference later that year in Milan, Italy to present her resolution from the Denver conference:

> Whereas, the increase of militarism in the countries of the old world, always a menace in times of peace, is becoming a burden to the common people there, more than in our own country, who must always bear the expense of a war, both as to money and to life;
>
> Therefore, be it resolved by this International League of Press Clubs, that we send our congratulations to the Fifteenth Universal Congress of Peace at Milan and will aid them by our influence and our pens to secure a

reduction of armaments and the adoption of an approved arbitration treaty that will accommodate itself to the needs of all nations.[132]

James R. Noland of the Denver Press Club also presented his own resolution to the international group and it was referred to the Committee on Resolutions:

> Whereas, there are stage productions in which the newspaper reporter is portrayed as a silly, asinine personage, without brains, and as this presentation has a decided tendency to cheapen the craft in the eyes of the general public, be it,
>
> Resolved, that the International League of Press Clubs, in convention assembled, agrees as an association and as individual members to discourage all stage productions in which the newspaper writer is caricatured, and be it further
>
> Resolved, that the International League of Press Clubs in convention assembled, requests writers of magazine stories and others in general to portray newspaper reporters as intellectual, prosperous women and men of real life, rather than the pernicious class of past fiction, whose only aim in life has been made to appear to be the dodging of creditors or the procurement of one meal a day.[133]

On Thursday, the International League of Press Clubs was escorted to the irrigation region in the north-eastern section of the state. As 1,200 delegates boarded a train to the agricultural lands, men with megaphones described the sugar factories and thousands of acres of sugar-beet fields as the train passed.[134] The importance of the namesake of the town of Greeley in this part of northeastern Colorado was proudly elucidated to the visiting newspapermen.

Horace Greeley (1811-1872), owner of the *New York Tribune* and the *New Yorker,* was one of the founding fathers of the Republican Party in 1856. Three years later he headed to Denver to write about the Colorado gold rush from the perspective of the people and its effect on the land and water. In 1870 he financed a utopia colony led by Nathan Meeker, the agriculture editor of the *Tribune*, which later developed into the current community of Greeley, Colorado. Horace Greeley's utopian experiment was composed of large canals constructed to carry water to irrigate a vast area of land that was once considered desert. A classic example of enterprise and patience, the delegates were shown that Colorado had more to offer than just mining and that agriculture had outgrown that of mining in the Centennial State.[135]

The trainloads of delegates joined locals for Longmont's parade that concluded in the central park where tables holding 6,000 slices of pumpkin pie and other light refreshments were prepared. Entertainment was provided by local bands and a side trip was made to the track for a series of horse races. Late that afternoon, the delegates to the International League of Press Clubs boarded their special train back to Denver amid a royal send-off by the people of Longmont.[136]

While the agricultural excursionists were on their train ride, others remained in Denver under the questionable guidance of Wolfe Londoner. Approximately forty people packed themselves into the infamous Cyclone Cellar under the Londoner store, listened to Mr. Londoner's tales of Eugene Fields' days as a reporter in Denver, and enjoyed a feast provided by Denver's esteemed full-time grocer, part-time reporter,[137] and perpetual story-telling host.

The International League of Press Clubs took a "round the horn" train excursion up to Cripple Creek, over to Cañon City (where Colorado peaches and apples were distributed to the delegates), and on to Salida where the Monte Cristo Hotel prepared a dinner of mountain trout. The group split between those who wanted to visit the top of Marshall Pass and those who just wanted to search for mountain oxygen. At 6:30 p.m. the train continued along the Denver & Rio Grande railroad to Glenwood Springs. As they traveled the road from Salida, "the travelers saw the cañons by moonlight, and the silver sheen of the lunar light seemed as a message from another world."[138]

The delegates arrived in Glenwood in fairly good condition. Professor John Phin of Paterson, New Jersey was taken "suddenly and seriously" ill as the constant traveling and high altitude challenged the lungs of the 75-year-old editor of the *Shakespeare Monthly* and chemist of considerable fame. He was taken to the Hotel Colorado upon their arrival in Glenwood Springs, attended through the night by Dr. and Mrs. Davis, and was able to leave with the rest of the group the next day. Others welcomed the opportunity to take a late-night or early-morning dip in the hot springs pool that was opened for the travelers.

Novelist Opie Read almost missed the train's departure. At the Hotel Colorado, an ornamental pool was stocked with local trout. Read chose to skip the regular breakfast menu to try and catch a trout for breakfast. He was able to catch a one-pounder, but as he lifted it out of the hotel pool, it wriggled off the hook and fell back into the water. Read made a lunge for the elusive fish, "but found the water would not hold him up," according to the *Denver Post* correspondent who accompanied the press-club group. "The result was a great splash, consternation among the other guests, and an angry author floundering around in four feet of water."[139] After a quick change into dry clothes, Read returned to the dining room where the hotel kitchen had a dish of cured fish waiting for him for breakfast. He announced that he didn't care if there was another train if he missed the special train — he was going to savor the breakfast trout prepared for him.

The final banquet was described by the local press as surpassing the scope of the Roosevelt banquet. After two hours of feasting on food and drink; another hour of toasts, songs, and "jollity" entertained the celebrants. It was nearly ten o'clock when the 400 guests walked upstairs to the eighth floor to The Brown Palace's banquet room that was ablaze in color. Matrices (sheets made from inked metal hot-type forms in the newspaper composing rooms) from all the large daily newspapers around the country were sent to the Denver Press Club and displayed on the walls of the banquet room. An orchestra, hidden behind a wall of palms, provided accompaniment to the delegates who often broke into spontaneous song during the get-together.[140]

Upton S. Jeffreys, editor of the *Post-Telegram* (Camden, New Jersey) and delegate from the Pen and Pencil Club of Philadelphia, was entertained by the Denver Press Club until urgent business forced him to cut short his trip in Denver. Before leaving, Jeffreys rhetorically asked, "Why drink champagne in Denver when you breathe it? I call this a champagne atmosphere. It permeates you, thrills you, makes dull care go away . . . The delegates to the International League of Press Clubs' convention were simply carried off their feet and taken up to the seventh heaven of happiness by Colorado hospitality. When it comes to expressing appreciation of the open-hearted welcome and lavish entertainment bestowed, they are at a loss to find words with which to adequately portray their feelings. The golden hours spent in Colorado can never be forgotten."[141]

During the excursion into the mountains, delegates passed the hat to purchase a going-away gift for the Denver Press Club's hospitality during the past ten days. Over $175 was initially raised to purchase a $225 punch bowl. The donors promised that it would be engraved with the name of every subscriber to the purchase price of the gift.[142]

The objective of bringing the national press together in the Queen City for a symposium steeped in positive good will and camaraderie was clear in the William Stapleton's editorial column of the *Denver Republican*. Denver considered itself as a "convention city" and wanted to be the best. For years, the state had the reputation, perpetrated by the local newspapers that chose to cast a false-light upon the state to politically benefit the publishers, of being in terrible economic position.

"The picture painted for home use," reported Stapleton in the *Denver Republican*, "has naturally been transferred to the outside until we can scarcely find fault with Eastern papers which accept the portrayal as representing true conditions in the state. The visit of the newspapermen will go far toward overcoming this evil. They will be able to see for themselves that no more prosperous a state exists nor one whose people have more cause to be satisfied with their place of abode, their opportunities and the conditions for prosperity which confront them. They will know more of Colorado when they get home and understand that these periodical attacks upon the integrity of the state government and the sanity and character of the people who live here mean nothing more than that a clique of politicians who never build up can only hope to gain their own selfish ends by tearing down, killing off enterprise and misrepresenting conditions."[143]

Nearly a score of articles was published as part of the Denver Press Club's competition for the best-published article written by a visiting member of the International League of Press Clubs. The gold bar that was offered as the prize was cashed at the United States mint and divided among the winners—Guy L. Ingalls (*Free Press,* Detroit, Michigan, $250), Opie Read (*Inter-Ocean,* Chicago, $250), Merton Q. J. Keyes (*Star-Chronicle,* St. Louis, $200), R. M. Brinkerhoff (*Blade,* Toledo, $175), and Lewis G. Early (*Times,* Reading Pennsylvania, $125).[144]

The *Wilkes-Barre Times* (Pennsylvania) reported that the Denver Press Club spent $40,000 in entertainment for the event. (The *Times Picayune* of New Orleans reported the expenditure as only $10,000.[145]) Entertainers and transportation services doing business in Colorado donated nearly all of the entertainment budget. Even though the convention only lasted four days, many of the newspapermen and women extended their stay for an additional six days of sightseeing.[146]

1   "The Study of Character in a Newspaper Office: From a sermon by the Rev. DeWitt Talmage, to Journalists," *Rocky Mountain Weekly Herald,* May 9, 1883, p. 5

2   "The Rights of Newspaper Writers: Appeal for Their Protection Against the Violation of Confidence," *New York Times,* February 3, 1895

3   Ibid

4   "Bohemia," Charles Emory Smith, *Bohemia: Official Publication of the International League of Press Clubs for the Building and Endowment of the Journalists' Home,* Alexander K. McClure, editor-in-chief; The International League of Press Clubs, Philadelphia, 1904, p. 26

5   "Coming Events, *Rocky Mountain News,* February 10, 1891, p. 3

6   "Funeral Notice," *Rocky Mountain News,* April 25, 1891

7   *Rocky Mountain News,* October 16, 1890, p. 4

8   "Broadway," *Rocky Mountain News,* October 20, 1890, p. 7

9   Advertisement, *Rocky Mountain News,* October 23, 1890, p. 3

10 "Editors in Town," *Denver Times,* June 28, 1900, p. 2

11 "Editors in Town," *Denver Times,* June 28, 1900, p. 2

12 *Daily Journal* (Telluride, Colorado), June 12, 1903, p. 1

13 "As to Journalism," *Fort Collins Express,* September 9, 1903, p. 2

14 "Makers of Newspapers," signed "The Schoolmaster," *San Francisco Call,* December 27, 1903, p. unknown

15 "A Reform in Libel Laws," *Denver Republican,* April 14, 1905, p. 4

16 *Denver Times,* March 25, 1882, p. 4

17 "Newspapermen of Denver Organize a Press Club and Elect Board of Officers," *Denver Republican,* March 6, 1905, p. 3

18 "Genuine Boosters," *Denver Post,* March 16, 1905, p. 3

19 "New Press Club Will Smoke Up with the Chamber of Commerce," *Denver Post,* March 14, 1905, p. 9

20 "Grand Opera Stars at Press Club Benefit," *Denver Post,* March 19, 1905, p. 11

21 "Orpheum's Best for the Press," *Denver Post,* March 23, 1905, p. 2

22 "Denver Catholic Urges Readers to Attend Press Club Show," *Denver Republican,* April 2, 1905, p. 2

23 "Newsboys are to Attend the Show," *Denver Republican,* March 28, 1905, p. 5

24 "Star Acts are Promised for the Press Club Show," *Denver Republican,* March 26, 1905, p. 8

25 "Big Programme is Arranged for Denver Press Club Show," *The Denver Republican,* March 29, 1905, p. 4

26 "Denver's Famous Pajama Girls are to Appear at the Big Press Club Show,"

Denver Republican, March 27, 1905, p. 8

27 "Big Press Club Show Will be Given at the Broadway Theatre This Afternoon," *Denver Republican,* April 2, 1905, Sec. 2, p. 1, Sunday edition

28 "Press Club Show a Big Success," *Denver Republican,* April 3, 1905, p. 10

29 "Folk Is to Visit This City," *Denver Post,* June 1, 1905, p. 11

30 "Press Club Banquet at the Savoy Hotel," *Denver Post,* May 20, 1905, p. 16

31 "Press Club's Rooms in New Building," *Denver Post,* May 25, 1905, p. 14

32 "Press Club Will Have House Warming To-Night," *Denver Republican,* July 1, 1905, p. 3

33 "Press Club rooms Opened," *Denver Post,* July 2, 1905, p. 3

34 "House Warming of Denver Press Club," *Denver Republican,* July 2, 1905, p. 12

35 "Newspapermen Give Housewarming to Celebrate Opening of Clubroom," *Rocky Mountain News,* July 2, 1905, p. 9, Sec. 2

36 "Jim Wong, Father Confessor of Newspapermen, Gets Vacation," *Rocky Mountain News,* December 19, 1922, p. 9

37 *Thunder in the Rockies,* Bill Hosokawa, William Morrow & Co., Inc.; New York, 1976, p. 511

38 *The Wildest of the West,* Forbes Parkhill, Sage Books, Denver, 1957

39 Ibid., pp. 115-116

40 *The First Hundred Years: An Informal History of Denver and the Rocky Mountain News,"* Robert L. Perkin; Doubleday & Company, Inc., Garden City, New York, 1959, p 511

41 "Mrs. Elitch Long Will Entertain Press Club," *Denver Republican,* May 26, 1905, p. 5

42 "Wireless Message Received by the Republican from Boulder," *Denver Republican,* April 7,1905, p. 3

43 "Editors From Every Section of the Country are Given a Real Taste of Denver's Best Hospitality," *Denver Post,* July 4, 1905, p. 14

44 "Bugles to Ring Loud When the Elks Return," *Denver Post,* July 14, 1905, p. 3

45 "May be a Guest of the Press Club-President Roosevelt Will Receive an Invitation to Breakfast and be Elected Honorary Member," *Denver Republican,* March 20, 1905, p. 1

46 "Pull of the Press—Newspaper Tow Line to drag Auditorium Out of Quicksands and Push it to Completion," *Denver Post,* March 21, 1905, p. 10

47 "The Denver Press Club," *Denver Republican,* March 26, 1905, p. 6

48 "Yellow Journals Have Already Begun to Fake," *Denver Republican,* April 17, 1905, p. 1

49 "Beaman Displeased with Local Papers—Stores From South About President's Trip All Right, He States, but Colorado Editors Should be Disciplined," *Denver Republican,* April 14, 1905, p. 10

50 "Plans for Stay of President in Denver," *Denver Republican,* May 7, 1905, p. 1

51 "Gold Membership Card to be Given Him," *Denver Post,* May 6, 1905, p. 3

52 "President Joins the Press Club," *Daily News,* May 5, 1905, p. 2

53 "Gold Membership Card to be Given Him," *Denver Post,* May 6, 1905, p. 3

54 "Troops to Escort the President," *Denver Republican,* May 6, 1905, p. 1

55 "Denver Press Club's New 'Fellow Member,'" *Denver Times,* May 9, 1905, p. 9

56 "President Initiated in the Denver Press Club," *Daily News,* May 9, 1905, p. 3

57 "Ysaye, the Highest-Priced Artist to Visit Denver this Season," *Rocky Mountain News,* May 6, 1905, p. 10

58 "President Delighted to be Member of Press Club," *Denver Post,* May 9, 1905, p. 5

59 "Press Club Members to be Guests of the Savoy," *Denver Post,* April 27, 1905, p. 8

60 "Press Club Breakfast," *Denver Republican,* 30 April 1905, p. 5

61 "Denver Press Club Entertained in Royal Style by Gracious Hosts of Magnificent Hotel Savoy," *Rocky Mountain News,* 1 May 1905, p. 5

62 "Denver Newspapermen the Guests of Savoy Management," *Denver Republican,* 1 May 1905, p. 8

63 "Bohemia," Charles Emory Smith, *Bohemia: Official Publication of the International League of Press Clubs for the Building and Endowment of the Journalists' Home,* Alexander K. McClure, editor-in-chief; The International League of Press Clubs, Philadelphia, 1904, p. 9

64 "Delegates Home from Press Club Convention," *Wilkes-Barre Times,* July 24, 1905

65 "Press Club Wants Meeting of International League in Denver," *Denver Republican,* July 15, 1905, p. 4

66 "Pencil Pushers May Come to Denver," *Denver Post,* July 17, 1905, p. 3

67 "Press Club Will Get Convention," *Denver Times,* July 15, 1905, p. 10

68 "Denver Is After It," *Denver Post,* July 15, 1905, p. 2

69 "Denver Likely to Get Press Clubs," *Denver Republican,* July 17, 1905, p. 3

70 "Delegates Home from Press Club Convention," *Wilkes Barre Times,* July 24, 1905

71 "When the Press is not the Press," Winifred Black, *Denver Post,* July 17, 1905, p. 4

72 "To Know Colorado as winter Resort," *Denver Post,* August 1, 1905, p. 8

73 "Personal Mention," *Gazette-Telegraph,* August 8, 1905

74 "Press Clubs to Meet in Denver," *Denver Republican,* July 21, 1905, p. 4

75 "Beautiful Texas Girls Will be Here Tuesday," *Denver Post,* September 3, 1905, p. 17

76 "Denver Likes Telegram Girls," *Fort Worth Star-Telegram,* September 15, 1905, p. 5

77 "Beautiful Texas Girls Will be Here Tuesday," *Denver Post*, September 3, 1905, p. 17

78 "Press Club Convention Coming to This City," *Denver Post*, September 12, 1905, p. 6

79 "Press Club Promises a Record Meet in Denver," *Denver Post*, October 30, 1905, p. 5

80 "Boys Once Again," *Denver Post*, December 25, 1905, p. 2

81 "Joyous Bells Herald Dawn of New Year of Great Prosperity," *Denver Post*, January 1, 1906, p. 1

82 "Denver Press Club to Entertain the Editors," *Denver Post*, January 6, 1906, p. 3

83 "Pledged to Upbuild the Whole State," *Denver Post*, January 7, 1906, p. 2

84 "Exposure to Music," *Denver Post*, January 15, 1906, p. 14

85 "Denver Press Club Members on Boards," *Denver Post*, January 19, 1906, p. 18

86 "Some of the Funny Features at Press Club Show on Monday," *Denver Post*, February 17, 1906, p. 8

87 Ibid

88 "Newspapermen Will Tread the Boards Night of Feb. 19," *Denver Post*, February 5, 1906, p. 3

89 "Stampede for Tickets to Press Club's Show," *Denver Post*, February 15, 1906, p. 2

90 "Press Club Elects Officers and Opens its Second Year," *Denver Post*, March 12, 1906, p. 12

91 "See America First is Becoming a Fad," *Denver Post*, April 3, 1906, p. 6

92 "Hotel Men Will Help Press Club Entertain," *Denver Post*, April 12, 1906, p. 10

93 "Donates Solid Gold Buttons to Denver Press Club Members," *Denver Post*, May 27, 1906, p. 16

94 "Inestimable Value of Press Club's Meeting," *Denver Post*, May 29, 1906, p. 5

95 "Press Club Convention at Denver," *Wilkes-Barre Times*, July 3, 1906, p. 12

96 "Business Men to Aid the Press Clubs' Convention," *Rocky Mountain News*, July 6, 1906, p. 3

97 "Newspapermen Will Be Given a Royal Time Here," *Denver Post*, June 18, 1906, p. 6

98 "Want President to Attend," *The Ogden Standard*, July 6, 1906, p. 7

99 "Declines the Invitation of Anti-Trust League," *San Francisco Call*, July 6, 1906

100 "To Be Guests of Railroads," *Gazette-Telegraph*, June 24, 1906

101 "Newspaper Folks Take Trip Around the Peak," *Denver Post*, June 23, 1906, p. 14

102 *The 1967 Denver Westerners Brand Book*, "The Denver Press Club," Cecil R.

Conner, The Westerners, Denver, 1968

103 "Writers' Club to Help Press Club in Entertaining," *Denver Post*, June 27, 1906, p. 10

104 "Women Writers Given Gold Bar," *Rocky Mountain News*, July 2, 1906, p. 7

105 "The Press Gang: Will Round Up at Denver in Fine Style August 27," *Tampa Tribune*, July 8, 1906, p. 8

106 "Press Club Will Keep Open House for Elks," *Rocky Mountain News*, July 10, 1906, p. 6

107 "Many Journalists Among Delegates," *Rocky Mountain News*, July 17, 1906, p. 3

108 Ibid

109 "Press Club Gives Visitors a Treat," *Rocky Mountain News*, July 18, 1906, p. 5

110 "Throw Open Club to Montana Elks," *Rocky Mountain News*, July 19, 1906, p. 8

111 "Denver Sets the Pace for Kansas City," *Denver Post*, July 21, 1906, p. 2

112 "Newspaperman is Good Advertiser," *Rocky Mountain News*, July 29, 1906, p. 11

113 "Newspaper Writers Larry Giffen's Guests at Manhattan Beach," *Denver Post*, July 16, 1906, p. 5

114 "Press Clubs are Guests of Giffen," *Rocky Mountain News*, July 16, 1906, p. 2

115 "Today's Bunch of Town Gossip," *Salt Lake Telegram*, January 5, 1907

116 "Newspapermen to Tell World About Colorado," *Denver Post*, August 12, 1906, p. 9

117 "Noted Writers to Attend the Press League's Meeting," *Denver Post*, August 12, 1906, p. 33

118 "The Amalgamated Order of Mavericks," *Tampa Tribune*, August 12, 1906, p. 3

119 "Press Club Convention at Denver," *Wilkes-Barre Times*, July 3, 1906, p. 12

120 "Newspapermen to Meet," *The Saginaw Evening News*, July 3, 1906, p. 1

121 "The Amalgamated Order of Mavericks," *Tampa Tribune*, August 12, 1906, p. 1

122 "White and Green Official Colors of Press Club," *Denver Post*, August 18, 1906, p. 8

123 "Set Floral Pieces in Place at Resorts, *Denver Post*, August 22, 1906, p. 5

124 "Great Week for Writers," *Rocky Mountain News*, August 26, 1906, p. 1

125 "Newspapermen Will See It All," *Denver Post*, August 26, 1906, p. 2

126 "Theodore Roosevelt, Jr., Traveling Under the Incognito 'David Gray,' Spends Night in Denver," *Daily News*, August 24, 1906, p. 5

127 "Newspaper Writers Life Supreme Dramatists," *Rocky Mountain News*, August 26, 1906, p. 4

128 "Officers Given Dinner at Savoy," *Daily News*, August 28, 1906, p. 6

129 "Local Press Club Gives Reception," *The Daily News*, August 28, 1906, p. 6

130 "Press Banquet Most Brilliant Affair in the History of Western Newspaperdom," *The Denver Times,* August 31, 1906, p. 2

131 "Press Clubs Work to Aid Peace Movement," *Salt Lake Tribune,* August 29, 1906, p. 1

132 Ibid

133 Ibid

134 "Banquet and Trip for the Visitors," *Denver Republican,* August 31, 1906, p. 5

135 *Weekly Courier* (Fort Collins, Colorado); August 22, 1906, p. 5

136 "Thousands, Including Press Club Delegates Eat Pumpkin Pie as Longmont's Guests," *Denver Republican,* August 31, 1906, p. 4

137 "Banquet and Trip for the Visitors," *Denver Republican,* August 31, 1906, p. 5

138 "Writers Visit at Glenwood and Leadville," *Denver Post,* September 3, 1906, p. 11

139 Ibid

140 "Newspapermen on a Jaunt," *Denver Post,* August 31, 1906, p. 2

141 "Denver Ozone Like Champagne, Says Mr. Jeffreys," *Denver Post,* September 4, 1906, p. 11

142 "Punch Bowl is Presented Press Club By Guests," *Denver Post,* September 4, 1906, p. 10

143 "The Coming of the Newspapermen," William Stapleton editor and manager, *The Denver Republican,* August 27, 1906, p. 4

144 "Prize Stories On Colorado," *Daily Illinois State Register* (Springfield, Illinois), February 11, 1907, p. 1

145 "News and Notables at the New Orleans Hotels," *Times Picayune,* February 23, 1907

146 "Were Royally Entertained," *Wilkes-Barre Times,* September 10, 1906, p. 8

CHAPTER 5

Printing paper has advanced over one hundred percent in the last two years. The other day printers' wages in Colorado, took a jump up of ten to fifteen per cent, and now we have a circular from all the prominent type founders in the United States, announcing an advance upon everything in their line from twenty-five to thirty per cent. Under this state of things there is a poor prospect for printers getting rich right away. Patrons are requested to consider these facts when they think our prices are steep, although in most things they have not advanced a particle.[1]

By the end of 1906, the news coverage of the Denver Press Club returned to the local journalists and to less-grandiose events. For some members, it provided them with an opportunity to expand their talents outside the newsroom. During the year, one twenty-five-year-old Denver Press Club reporter channeled his talents to write poetry. After his mother died when he was quite young, Alfred Damon Runyon received his youthful education in the printing office where his father worked. When he was in his teens, young Runyon ran away to the Philippines with a Minnesota regiment among the first American troops. There, he gathered experiences that gave him material for verse and stories as "the Kipling of American army life."[2] National magazines were quick to pick up Mr. Runyon's poetry that supplemented the news coverage and columns that he wrote for the Denver newspapers and his hometown *Pueblo Chieftain*.

A scrappy young man, five-foot-six and weighing approximately 125 pounds, he had mixed success as a soldier from Pueblo, Colorado but was confined to his tent for most of the war to protect him from the ravages of war in the Philippines.

The war left him a hard-drinking young man; on several occasions the *Chieftain* editor threatened to fire him for his inconsistent job performance and dependability. Oddly, he moved on to the *Colorado Springs Gazette* in a town that was known for its temperance. Runyon quickly discovered that a drugstore with a bar secreted in the back room was located just down the street from the newspaper office. The Elks Club of Colorado Springs also had a large bar and a running poker game for the members. Another block away was MacRae's restaurant where whiskey was served in coffee cups. With only a newspaperman's salary to work with, Runyon could develop moderate tabs at all three places without angering the bartenders about the unpaid bills.

Jimmy Breslin's biography of Damon Runyon explained, "When Runyon was missing from work, he was in bed in his room, unable to move. He had a body that begged for whisky but could metabolize almost none of it. The alcohol turned into formaldehyde, which is the reason, based on medical knowledge, that people say they got 'pickled' or 'embalmed' last night. Runyon's hangovers lasted for days and often a week. The illness from whisky, and the simultaneous burning need for it, often lined up on either side of his skull and raced at each other, illness against uncontrollable thirst. The resultant explosion being awful."[3]

Runyon and fellow journalist Cecil Conner would get into drink-infused fights in the newsroom; Runyon once stabbed Conner with long bladed scissors used for cutting copy. After drying out, the two would go off on a news assignment but end up over a liquor barrel. After being confronted by the city editor upon their return, the Pueblo City Directory for 1904-1905 merely stated Runyon "Moved to Denver."

The *Denver Post* accepted Runyon's news-reporting skills, and on the second day of work, he noticed Charles Van Loan was taking a drink of water out of a pitcher. As Breslin continued, "Now, there are many ways that people take in water, but the drinker's gulp, with the hand shaking the cup of folded copy paper as if it contained ice, tells you more about the person than a complete biography." Runyon learned that Van Loan's drink of choice was something called "North Platte," a beverage of no known recipe to modern bartenders. He soon developed a running tab for North Platte at the Denver Press Club bar where he would self-medicate himself into a melancholy stupor. "Runyon sat motionless on the stool and dreamed," continued Breslin's biography. "He also was exceptionally gloomy. He never had known that an inspiring thought weighs as much as a sack of cement, and if you have enough inspiring thoughts, you can't square your shoulders at the bar."[4]

Runyon was not the only heavy drinker among the ranks of the newspapermen in Denver. "Western newspapering reflected the still restless heritage of pioneer times," wrote Gene Fowler in *Skyline*. "Some journalists drank too much, others did not. An editor's main concern was whether or not a man brought back the story to which he had been assigned. What you did in your off hours was a matter to be resolved by yourself, your bartender, your sweetheart, your pastor, or the undertaker."[5]

Another of the Denver Press Club's most prestigious guests at the end of the year was "The Honorable S. Claus, Great Northern Land, N. P."[6] who was scheduled to make his popular visitation to the press club's rooms. The adults in attendance remarked how much the jolly bearded gentleman bore a striking resemblance to C. W. Varnum. His assistant, Kris Kringle, looked like John Stuart Jackson, son of J. S. Jackson, MD. Writers, from the cub reporter to the managing editor, were provided with cigars and humorous gifts of the season. In return, Henry Doherty of the Denver Gas & Electric Company provided the press club with a handsome bearskin rug.[7] The following day, the club rooms hosted a public open house to imbibe in refreshments of the season.

It's not clear what year it was when the *Denver Post* hired Damon Runyon from the *Rocky Mountain News* but it was the same year the newspaper purchased the first motor-driven delivery truck seen west of Chicago. To celebrate the two new acquisitions, the *Post* chose to celebrate the Christmas delivery to benefit the children of the city. The plan was that the red truck, containing gifts, would pull up to the newspaper office and Santa Claus (played by Damon Runyon) and cartoonist "Doc Bird" Finch would assist in the distribution of presents. Runyon was too skinny to be believable as Santa Claus. The Albany Hotel donated pillows to fatten the already inebriated Runyon. To an unknown audience, he was found belting out one of his own poems that was inappropriate for the holiday, "What Happened to My Seester, Meester?" about the seduction of a Mexican lass by a New York gambler, to the chagrin of the lass's brother.

Gene Fowler continued the story. "Doc Bird had been fitted out with a feathered costume. Over his head and face was a papier-mâché bird's noggin with a huge beak. The solid headpiece would keep Mr. Finch from drinking while on duty. But Doc Bird had placed an uncorked quarter of rye whiskey inside the mask. Whenever he desired refreshment—which was often—he would point his beak to the sky, and swallow as the other birds did."[8]

By the time the drunken Santa and tipsy feathered assistant arrived at the *Denver Post,* the owners of the *Post* beamed down at the crowd of happy children that greeted the truck and the cantankerous red-cheeked Santa. Smiles turned to fear as Santa stumbled out of the truck, kicking several children out of his way. Instead of a chorus of "ho-ho-ho's" Santa slurred, "Get outta here, you noisy brats!" Before the shocked parents could close in on Damon Runyon to lynch him, Police Chief Hamilton Armstrong and several men-in-blue came to the rescue of the slumped-over Santa who had fallen into a stupor once again. "Doc Bird waddled out of view, his beak pointed toward the sky," continued Fowler. "There were threats to cancel subscriptions. The police eventually distributed the presents, but it is said that several of the children became atheists that day."[9]

When Runyon was transferred from the city beat to the sports department, he spent his time late into the evenings at the press club. Van Loan was summoned to help night steward Jimmy Wong corner Runyon in the poker room, trying to calm down "Demon" Runyon as he was now known. After being fired from the *Post,* he begged for re-employment at the *Rocky Mountain News.* After a series of additional alcoholic incidents, Runyon was sent to a hospital where he dried out for the last time and stayed on the wagon without sharing news of his sobriety with his readers. He rode the wagon off to New York where he continued his professional reputation as a journalist and the author of *Guys and Dolls.*

Damon Runyon and Night-Steward Jimmy
Wong at the Denver Press Club.

Press-club lore claims that many of the characters that found their way into the quintessential play of the underbelly culture of big cities were taken directly from Damon Runyon's days as a beat reporter (and off-duty alcoholic) in Denver.

Runyon had a love of dogs and was offered a Brussels Griffon dog by boxer Jack Dempsey while they were both in Denver. But when Runyon relocated to New York, he was given a pair of whippets that stayed with him in the Big Apple and traveled with him to Runyon's retirement home on Hibiscus Island, Dade County, Florida. Gene Fowler explained, "The whippets . . . had been a going-away present from one of his neighbors, a Mr. Alphonse Brown. Mr. Brown was a retired Chicago businessman of sorts. Just recently, under the more familiar name of Al Capone, he had been invited by his Uncle Whiskers to take a long holiday on another island, Alcatraz. The sport of dog racing was impractical there, because of the rocks."[10]

For others, the Denver Press Club provided an opportunity to bring diverse points of view to a forum of civil political and social discourse. Eugene V. Debs, twice a candidate for president of the United States on the Socialist ticket, was touring the Rocky Mountains on behalf of William D. Haywood who was sitting in a Boise, Idaho jail in 1906. Mr. Haywood was charged with complicity in the assassination of ex-Governor Frank Steunenberg of Idaho. Mr. Debs drew large crowds and was invited to present a non-political address at the Denver Press Club.[11] Many of the press club members were personally acquainted with Mr. Debs as well as personal friends with Mr. Haywood.[12]

The annual Denver Press Club's "Foley's Breakfast" invitation greeted the members in the early weeks of 1907. J. P. Foley, the concessionaire at City Park, expanded the active membership to include former members of the Denver Press Club who were seeking their fortune in the Goldfield mining camps in Nevada.[13] Foley, likewise, had financial interests in the Clear Luna Mining Company in Goldfield and befriended the journalistic ex-patriots in Nevada.

Back in the club rooms of the Railway Exchange Building, the press club was planning their third annual stage show. "Forty neatly-costumed, highly-polished well-trained minstrels"[14] stepped in front of the stage lights of the Broadway Theater of the afternoon of Friday, January 23, to perform "The Minstrels in Venice."[15] The minstrel show became a matter of lampooning local officials and events, with dancing, new songs, parodies, and jokes geared to the local establishment. On each end of the show were four black-faced comedians dispensing the fun. Once the curtain was raised, one skit began on the heels of the previous one.

Former Denver newspaperman Harry Lee Wilber was one of the new miners at the Goldfield camps in Nevada. He gathered a delegation of a dozen newspapermen attending the Trans-Missouri Dry Farming Congress in Denver, and timed the visitation to enable the former newspapermen to attend the minstrel show at the Broadway Theater.[16] The popularity of the show prompted the press club to announce a matinee as a second show, and offered the tongue-in-cheek grave announcement: "The press club boys . . . do not expect their show to take the place of the symphony concerts."[17] Invitations were sent to the Western Stock Show and the Colorado State Senate—the latter willing to adjourn early to attend the press-club event.

The *Denver Republican* reported, "The tastes of a people and the degree of civilization and refinement of a nation are frequently told more emphatically by the national songs than through any other of the many standards by which relative merit has been judged through the ages. As with the nation, so with states in our own country."[18] Among the important debates confronting government officials, two state songs split the allegiances of the legislators. One was composed by Colorado Springs musician Maude McFerran Price, social leader and renown for her open-hearted hospitality. Her catchy musical offering was known simply as "Colorado." The second selection, written by local federal employees C. H. Scoggins and Charles Avril, was entitled "Where the Silvery Colorado Wends Its Way." The producers of the Denver Press Club minstrel show decided to perform both state-song nominees and let the audience determine which would become the official state song; the legislators in attendance would be entitled to one vote in this representative form of the state-song popularity contest.[19]

When the two Colorado state-song nominations were sung, the audience applause was so evenly matched that the decision had to be remanded to the second-show audience.[20] There was no reference published how the second audience voted, however another song, "Pretty Mary Carey," was written by Lucius H. "Lute" Johnson and was performed by the press-club minstrels. When Johnson and the press-club minstrels were practicing in the club's rooms, the press agent for Al G. Field Minstrels[21] heard the rehearsal and acknowledged its suitability for stage singing. He procured an orchestration and rushed it special delivery to Mr. Field with the recommendation that the song be considered for the Orpheum national circuit.[22]

Johnson was a prolific writer, born in Mt. Vernon, Illinois in 1863 and arrived in Denver on his twenty-first birthday. He was self-educated and single, and became a mining-beat editor, Sunday editor and editorial writer for the *Denver Republican*. He later moved to the *Denver Post* as a special writer, but found time to write a book, *A Spare Million* in 1911; several dramatic stage productions that included "Magnolia Planation," "Nada," and "Miss Forty Four." In addition to writing "Mary Cary," he penned two other songs—"Little Coon," and "Lullaby." In his spare time, he wrote short stories for magazines.[23]

The press club event was the first black-face performance by amateurs on the local theater stage. As the *Denver Republican* reported, "Certainly no one but the most captious critic could find room for complaint. The program was full of ginger and was well diversified throughout. It ran the gamut of up-to-date minstrelsy, including bright repartee, splendid vocal efforts and numerous features of the plain, every day, but always reliable minstrel show character."[24]

In 1907, the Denver Press Club collected a "fine collection of [original artwork] that decorate the walls of the Denver Press Club." The only known example of that collection was an Orientalist oil painting on wood by Belgian artist Jan-Baptist Huysmans, purchased for the club by associate member Verner Z. Reed of Colorado Springs. The painting depicted the interior of a Turkish seraglio with three "languorous inmates and luxurious furnishings,"[25] according to the *Denver Republican*. None of the paintings that once hung in the press club rooms is still on the walls of the present press club. Huysmans paintings currently fetch $300,000 to $500,000 at art auctions.

Club president James R. Noland promoted greater use of the club to the members in 1907. In a printed form letter, he reminded members that the club maintained copies of all the daily newspapers and magazines. The club library had more than a thousand works of fiction, history, travel, as well as "the works of all the standard writers." The library was isolated from the din of other club activities, well illuminated, and comfortably furnished. The hours of operation of the press club were changed from noon until 6 a.m. the following morning on weekdays and opened two hours earlier on Sundays.

"Only the purest and best liquors and wines are handled in the buffet," the form-letter to the press-club members continued. "These are not sold for profit, and if you want liquors of any kind for medicinal or family use, it will pay you to purchase your supplies at the club, because you not only secure pure goods but they are sold at about 25 per cent under the retail price."[26]

The club's notoriety as an internationally prominent press club was putting stress on the three rooms in the Railway Exchange Building. At the March 1907 annual meeting in the Bohemian room of the Albany Hotel, the club proposed leaving the present location "to a more desirable location, the establishment of a permanent building fund, and the securing of an extensive library."[27] The 100 members[28] in good standing was the largest membership since the club began in 1867.

The New York Hippodrome was an entertainment center with
a capacity nearly double of the Metropolitan Opera. Circus
acts drew audiences from around the country. To promote
the 1905 opening, promoters sent "Little Hip" to Denver.

Courtesy of the Denver Public Library, Western
History Collection, Call #X-28840

When the members arrived for the meeting, they were treated by
"Little Hip." the smallest elephant in the world and headliner at the
Orpheum theater that week. As the *Denver Republican* reported, "Hip
will be on deck at 11:30 to give the newspaper boys the glad hand as they
enter the breakfast hall but will not be able to remain throughout the meal,
as he has a date to go automobile riding with a party of women at noon."[29]
He was accompanied by the guest-of-honor Al G. Field of the Orpheum
minstrels and several entertainers from his company.[30]

James W. Kelley, newspaper reporter and city passenger agent for the
Moffat Road[31] project into the mountains, was chosen as the new president
of the club with the acknowledgment that the treasury was in good shape
and all indications were for a year of prosperity for the club. The *Denver
Republican* reported about the financial picture at the annual-meeting
breakfast. "The spirit of good fellowship and jollity which no tribe on earth
is more capable of producing and enjoying than the men who get out the
daily papers, was let loose with the appearance of the Belle-flowers and

whipped cream, and prevailed clear down through buckwheat cakes and syrup, to coffee and cigars, at which point the tables were clear for action and the transaction of business was taken up."[32] Mr. Kelley promised that "frequently recurring entertainment in the club rooms" and other activities would be inaugurated in 1907 and "everything possible will be done to make the club one of the popular and important organizations of the city."[33] The vice president was Lucius M. "Lute" Wilcox.[34]

The reputation of journalism was beginning to change. A style of newspaper reporting that emphasized sensationalism over facts was one of many factors that prompted the United States and Spain to engage in war in Cuba and the Philippines. Its origins had nothing to do with reporting, but everything to do with the attempt of William Randolph Hearst of the *New York Journal* to steal cartoonist Richard F. Outcault from Joseph Pulitzer's *New York World*. The popularity of Outcault's cartoon strip about New York's slums was printed in color and featured the strip's well-known character known as "The Yellow Kid." The fierce bidding war between Pulitzer and Hearst and the sensationalized style employed by the two publishers with exaggerated or even fictionalized stories that peaked in 1898 during the sinking of the U.S. battleship Maine, in Havana Harbor, was an incentive to launch the Spanish-American War. The publishers printed rumors of plots to sink the ship, even though the U.S. naval investigation later indicated the ship had inadvertently hit a mine in the harbor. The commercial exploits of the two publishers to sell papers blended the two situations to describe sensationalized newspaper reporting as "Yellow Journalism."

In 1905 when President Roosevelt was hunting in Colorado, his staff expressed dismay at the sensationalized accounts of the president's exploits in hunting bear and chastised the Colorado media for exploiting the trip with gross exaggerations. Two years later, the practice of Yellow Journalism reached an international level when William T. Stead, editor of the London-based *Review of Reviews*, spoke at the rededication ceremonies of the Carnegie Institute of Pittsburg. Mr. Stead recommended that writers, making false or misleading statements in headlines or the body of text "which were calculated to inflame national animosity against the neighboring nation and so to endanger the maintenance of peace,"[35] should be sent to prison as found by a jury of twelve.

The Colorado Editorial Association met in the clubrooms of the Denver Press Club in 1907 to adapt changing directions in journalism and to prepare for a conference later that year.[36]

"Good fellowship, plenty of everything that makes a pleasing meal, and a recurring element of surprise, all contributed materially to the success of the breakfast given by the Denver Press Club,"[37] reported the *Denver Republican* when the club met in the banquet hall of The Albany Hotel. The entire Denver membership was in attendance in addition to fourteen members[38] from the Pikes Peak Press Club and women newspaper writers from the Writers' Club.[39]

Men and women reporters possibly at the *Rocky Mountain News/Denver Times* newsroom.

Photo by Harry Mellon Rhoads. Denver Public Library, Western History Collection, Image File # ZZR700185711

Despite the strong relationship between the men of the Denver press work and their silent partners among the women who also were newspaper writers, there was a public and social separation between the genders. In the invitation to the various writing groups, nothing was mentioned of any inclusion of the women writers. With a flair for suspense, the gentlemen of the press entered the breakfast room and noted that one chair at each table was "reserved" for a yet-to-arrive guest. When the gentlemen were seated, the lights were turned out and "the fair associates of the news-gatherers,"[40] were escorted into the room. The lights were switched-on and an assembled orchestra "did its prettiest" while the men cheered the arrival of the members of the Writers' Club.

After the breakfast plates were cleared away, Denver Press Club President J. W. Kelley welcomed the former and current presidents of the League of International Press Clubs in front of the 200 diners,[41] and provided some ideas for the relationship between the local press club and their international counterparts. Likewise, Winifred Black, a prominent newspaper woman, spoke on developing a closer relationship among the wives and families of newspapermen and to seek a means of enhancing the relationships among the press-club fraternity. After the impromptu discussions were finished, the Twenty-First Infantry band from Fort Logan, under the direction of Bandmaster Graves, marched into the room to provide a rousing morning concert.

The relationship between the Denver Press Club and the Writers' Club developed a personal level when it was announced that Denver Press Club President Kelley and Miss Evelyn Brown (Society Editor of the *Denver Post,* former child actress, and member of the Writers' Club), were married. Kelley once served as drama critic of the *Republican* before becoming the railroad editor of the paper. He then moved on to the passenger office of the Moffat Road.[42] Kelley was a Catholic and Brown was a Christian Scientist; after a hurried compromise, Rev. R. F. Coyle, pastor of Central Presbyterian church officiated over a ceremony "bitterly opposed by Miss Brown's parents." Brown had been given an assignment to attend an automobile race, but the editor received a call mid-afternoon and learned that "Mrs. Kelley" could not cover the races due to "another assignment"[43] at the starting line with Rev. Coyle and Mr. Kelley.

The Denver Press Club was familiar with the train excursions into the mountains. F. D. Fowler, president of the Eldorado Springs resort, initiated a "splash" for the club which he expected would become an annual event. "Those aquatically inclined who have entered in the water sports have been practicing in their home bath tubs for the past month and promise to make the fish look like 30 cents,"[44] reported the *Denver Republican.* "The acrobatic members of the club are telling their friends to bet on them to beat Professor Baldwin, who is scheduled to walk a cable across the gorge. There will be a band in attendance to help the frivolous trip the light fantastic." At noon, a complimentary buffet was provided by the management of the hot springs resort.

Many years later, the son of one of those attending the event reflected on his youthful experience. Colorado's Poet Laureate Thomas Hornsby Ferril accompanied his father that day, "For entertainment, the famous tightrope walker, Ivy Baldwin, walked across Boulder Canyon; prompting myself and my friends to emulate him for weeks, stretching ropes between trees and attempting to balance on them."[45] Years later, a much older Poet Ferril had a chance to meet Ivy Baldwin at the Denver Press Club when the daredevil was promoting his new stunt talents as an accomplished aerial balloonist.

In another rail excursion, twenty-five to thirty members of the Denver Press Club climbed aboard a special Midland train to Leadville with the sixty-five-piece *Post* band[46] complementing the rhythm of the rails. An exotic side-trip to the Yak Tunnel included a fifty-mile-an-hour train ride that led to an underground cavern[47] where lunch was served two miles underground. Above ground, the two-mile high community was hosting a reception for Colorado Elks Club members. Thirty donkeys from Mr. Fowler's stable were brought out and coupled with press-club members for a donkey race; the winners received leather medals.[48] After the newspapermen held a business meeting, the men and their spouses, and members of the Writers' Club attended a field day and athletic carnival where a rock-drilling contest, a tug-of-war, and a baseball game between the Elks teams of Leadville and Victor were featured.[49] That evening, a smoker was held with a ten-round boxing match between Kid Texas and Young Erlenborn of Denver, a minstrel show, and other features.[50]

The special train and the press club almost got into more hot water on the Argentine Central Railway than in the mineral baths in Idaho Springs. According to the "rules of the road," no trains on the Argentine were supposed to travel on Sunday. Saturday afternoon, the press club group traveled to the 14,000-foot peaks as guests of the Colorado & Southern and Argentine Central railways; they arrived in Silver Plume (the terminus of the Colorado & Southern and the beginning of the Argentine Central) just a few minutes before the evening clock struck midnight. The press club entourage was able to switch to the more liberal railroad lines that accepted the celebrants, and they arrived in Denver at 4 o'clock Sunday morning.[51]

Another group from the Denver Press Club was selected to travel to Birmingham to watch their former press club president lead the International League of Press Clubs.

The Denver club was collecting photographs to adorn the club walls—portraits of Mark Twain, Henry Watterson (editor of the *Louisville Courier*), William Randolph Hearst (*New York Journal* and *American*), William Jennings Bryan (*Commoner*), Arthur Brisbane (*American)* and other journalistic notables.

Club President J. W. Kelley, on behalf of the 200 Denver members, wrote to Samuel "Mark Twain" Clemens reminding him of his golden days as a newspaper worker in Nevada. "Time has mellowed the memory of that time and you are now looked upon as a person who would be above such a thing. We trust; however, you will not let the dead past get to [sic] busy burying its dead that it will spade under the love you had—or we suppose you had—for the West. Can't you take a photograph and write your name across it and mail it to us? We will esteem it highly and it will inspire many of the boys to do greater things. You are a mighty cheerful personality and to look at your pictured face and ponder on your deeds will do us all good."[52]

Twain's photograph bore the inscription "Dean of the planet's journalism; joined the guild in 1849, aged 14, and has not broken the connection in 58 years."[53] Additionally, a collection of original drawings from many national cartoonists were added to the club walls. None of these wall hangings have survived today's press club.[54]

Once again, the press club members were fed and entertained by the proprietors of the Albany Hotel with "corn" as the culinary focus—corn whisky cocktails, a menu in the shape of an ear of corn, corn-meal mush, corned beef hash, corn fritters (with corn syrup), corn bread, parched-corn coffee, and finally the distribution of corn-cob pipes.

Throughout the morning festivities, various members rose to speak on different subjects. Meyer Friedman, president of the Chamber of Commerce was featured with a talk on "The Press Club and its Relation to Booster Organizations."[55] The Denver Press Club membership chose to assist in "boosting" the resources of Colorado by canvassing the hotel, railway, and commercial interests within the state. As reported by the *Denver Post,* "The Denver Press Club is an organization of active newspapermen of this city and state and they propose to closely identify themselves in every way possible with the other movements for the betterment of conditions and the development of the state.[56] "Hotels, resorts and places of amusement will be asked to make specially [sic] low rates, railways will be asked for transportation facilities and the cooperation of the local chamber of commerce will be sought, so that the visitors may be given a maximum of enjoyment at a minimum cost," reported the *Editor and Publisher*. "A bureau will be opened at the club headquarters to which the visitors will come on arrival in Denver. They will be expected to bring credentials showing them to be actual bonafide [sic] writers in the editorial departments of newspapers or other publications, regularly employed and on vacation. To them, the club will issue cards of introduction which will entitle them to special rates and consideration wherever they may desire to go. Vacations will be planned for them if desired, fishing, hunting or exploring trips. If a man wants to see Colorado farming at its best, a card to the chamber of commerce at Rocky Ford or Greeley or Fort Collins or Monte Vista or Grand Junction will assure that the visitor will be received with open arms and shown the best there is to be shown. The same policy will be followed as regards the mining camps. An effort will be made to secure a constant supply of fresh photographs to illustrate articles on Colorado."[57]

Theatrical comedian James T. Powers and the Denver Press Club joined efforts to devote one performance during the week-long performance of "The Blue Moon" as a building fundraiser for the club on December 3, 1907, at the Broadway Theater.[58] "Blue Moon" was the story of a British regiment in Central India and their effort to find a young English girl who had been kidnapped many years previously.[59] Instead of relying on the talents of the local newspapermen, the press club decided to call upon professional actors from the Shubert theatrical producers.[60] Wealthy friends of the newspaper boys who sold editions on street corners as their sole source of income, were buying tickets and turning them over to the often homeless children.[61]

The Republican Club scheduled a smoker the night of the press club's "Blue Moon" fundraiser but postponed their smoker so it would not conflict. A meeting of the board of aldermen was also scheduled, but the municipal lawmakers also decided to postpone their meeting to attend the press club show.[62]

*****

The success of the Denver Press Club's ability to host the largest conference held in the city's young history attracted the attention of the Democratic National Committee. A year after the International League of Press Clubs convention, the Democrats began looking at Denver to host their party's national convention in 1908. Denver Press Club president James W. Kelley pledged the support of their membership to entertain the visiting newspaper correspondents and promised to provide free transportation for every accredited Colorado newspaperman if the convention was held in Colorado.[63] More than 400 newspapermen[64] from national and local newspapers (and their wives) were expected to be in attendance. A consolidated national "newsroom" of fifty rooms was located a city block from the convention on two floors of the Denver Chamber of Commerce Building[65] and was fitted with telegraph terminals, typewriters, and paper. Within a few months of planning, the entire three-story-plus-basement building was turned over to the Denver Press Club and equipped with five hundred news desks, a complete photographic studio and photo lab, and both Western Union and Postal Telegraph wires and operators.[66]

At the January meeting of the Denver Press Club, members passed a resolution endorsing the national journalistic support for the region: "The party having this work in charge must be big enough to understand the value of the story and must have state pride enough to handle them in such a manner as to produce the best results throughout the east. Naturally the best results in the east will be the bringing of a tremendous crowd to Denver. The size of the crowd depends almost wholly upon the character of the stories sent out. The Denver Press Club believes that [A. W. Sowers, general press agent for the convention] is the man to handle this work and has unanimously endorsed him and will go down the line for him."[67]

Newspaper photographers from 1907: Charles Mace (*Rocky
Mountain News*), Joe Langer (*Denver Post*) Stuart Mace (*Denver
Times*), and an unnamed Associate Press photographer

Courtesy of the author

The year 1908 was expected to be a substantial boost for Denver. The
Democratic National Convention in July was expected to draw 30,000-
to-75,000 people; the Odd Fellows convention in September anticipated
30,000 people; the National Western Stock Show always drew a large
crowd, and the 10,000 predicted for the American Federation of Labor
convention would be the five-digit attendee leaders.[68] Several national
newspapers attempted to portray Denver as inadequate to accommodate a
national political convention. In response, the Denver Press Club passed
another resolution that Denver hotels were modern and there were enough
of them to comfortably house any size crowd that expected to come to the
city during the convention.[69] Instead of formal entertainment, banquets,
and listening to speeches that may or may not be of interest to their
guests; the Denver Press Club chose to allow the entire state to provide
entertainment for the visiting dignitaries and guests. This was the first

occasion for most visitors to have first-hand access to the business and tourist opportunities provided throughout Denver and Colorado.[70]

To make transportation easier, the Santa Fe and Burlington railroads each contributed $2,000 to the Denver Convention League, and the Rock Island contributed an additional $1,000.[71] National magazines solicited scenic views of Denver and Colorado to illustrate promotional articles about the resources of the city and state. Samuel F. Dutton of the Albany Hotel proposed the Convention League promote the "unlimited entertainment" available around the convention site. The Denver Press Club was in charge of picnics, receptions, dinners, and banquets for the benefit of the national and international members of the press.[72]

Motorized omnibus vehicles began to appear on the streets of Denver, taking tourists to scenic spots throughout Colorado.

Courtesy of the author

The proposed sightseeing and entertainment programs included "Seeing Denver" and "Seeing the Foothills" trolley cars and automobiles that brought guests to Golden, Colorado. City Park was alive with band concerts in the afternoon and evening, boating on the lake, visits to Elitch Gardens with their rustic theatre and famous stock company, an alternative visit to Manhattan Beach with their theater at Sloan's Lake, the Tuileries, and new Lakeside resort for outdoor amusement entertainment. The Colorado & Southern Railroad brought people over the famous Georgetown

Loop to Silver Plume where the Argentine Central Railroad connected to bring guests up McClellan Mountain's "Switzerland Trail" to Ward and Eldorado Springs surrounded by perpetual snow on the Continental Divide. The Denver & Rio Grande, Colorado Midland and Cripple Creek Short Line transported guests to Pikes Peak from the Manitou mineral springs. Other train excursions traveled to the mining camp of Cripple Creek or Royal Gorge from Colorado Springs. The Colorado Midland's "Wild Flower" excursion provided guests with the opportunity to sight the best views of the wild mountain flowers while other excursions headed to Glenwood Springs' hot-cave baths and swimming pool and on to Grand Junction's fruit orchards and the "High Line" irrigation canal on the western slope of Colorado.[73]

The annual convention of the Colorado State Editorial Association, marketed as "the [sixty] men who mold the public opinion of their communities—the men who exploit every new and worthy enterprise— the men who make known to the world the wonderful possibilities of Colorado—the men who keep their ears to the ground and their hands on the pulse of the town in which they live" started the year off with their annual convention (and smoker) in Denver. Each activity was presided over by toastmaster and Denver Press Club president J. W. Kelley[74] and hosted in the rooms of the Denver Press Club.[75]

"Denver seldom has occasion to welcome and entertain a more representative body of men—all shades of political belief and from all sections of the state, representing the mining industry and that of the fruitful fields of Colorado,"[76] editorialized *The Denver Times*. "They are also the best exponents of personal journalism in this country, not in the offensive sense of personalities, but men who conduct papers that are looked upon as expressing the personal views of their editors. Just as people used to take the *New York Tribune* to find out what Horace Greeley thought, or the *New York Herald* to get the view of the elder James Gordon Bennett, or the *Courier-Journal* to see what Henry Watterson had to say, so they take and read these out-of-town Colorado papers, sure they will find some words of guidance from the editor whom they know and whose opinion they respect. The busy city man hasn't the time or the evening fireside, many of them, where the paper can be read from beginning to end, but these editors who are in Denver now, they have a constituency much to be desired and an opportunity possessed by few men to form convictions and thus to sway communities."[77]

The March 1908 annual meeting of the Denver Press Club treasurer's report stated there was over $3,500 in the club's coffers and the clubhouse was free of debt. With a financial edge on the books, the Denver Press Club's annual meeting began serious contemplation for building their own exclusive club house.[78] The club was considered "by far the most representative strictly newspapermen's organization in America"[79] with a membership of 178 members[80] either currently engaged in newspapers or former members of the craft. It was clear that a new press-club building would have a library; Samuel H. Wood donated a hundred rare books to form the nucleus of the new reading room. Additionally, a smoker was scheduled later that month with every participant donating a book or set of books to fill the shelves.[81] Guests at the smoker included Al G. Field, the minstrel playing at the Tabor that week,[82] and C. C. Hamlin of the Colorado Bar Association;[83] and presided over by Senator J. C. Burger[84] at the Railway Exchange Building.[85]

For a more sophisticated event, the Young Men's Christian Association invited thirty members of the Denver Press Club, their wives, and lady friends to an impromptu musical program in their new building. Frederick Starrett[86] of the YMCA arranged the presentation in appreciation for the support of the newspapermen while the organization was soliciting funds for the building.

The death of Denver Press Club favorite, Bill Nye, prompted interest in erecting a memorial to its favorite political satirist. Frank T. Searight of the *Los Angeles Herald* and president of the American Press Humorists' Association proposed their sixth annual convention to be held in Denver where Searight accepted a permanent post with the *Denver Express*. "Denver not only is pleased over the prospect of another Bill Nye monument-fund entertainment by the American Press Humorists such as was given at the Auditorium in Los Angeles last fall," explained Mr. Searight, "but they are enthusiastic over it. The reason is that this was Nye's stamping ground. This was the place where he used to congregate with that other noted Denverite, 'Gene Field, and those fellow-geniuses Rothacker, Will Visscher, Bill Barlow and James Barton Adams. In fact, Denver looks upon Bill Nye as a Denver man and wants to pay tribute by boosting the monument project."[87]

At the August 24-29 convention of the American Press Humorists' Club in Denver, a public-entertainment fundraiser was arranged at the Baker Theater. Manager McCourt of the Tabor, Broadway and Baker Theaters donated their box-office receipts of all three theaters for the conference. Several humorists of that era were loaned by other theaters for the fundraiser for the Bill Nye monument fund. The Denver Press Club provided an open house with hospitality assistance from the Denver Woman's Press Club.[88]

While plans for a convention of humorists was being organized, the national political convention was just months away, and the guest list was developing. Williams Jennings Bryan returned to Colorado after an absence of nearly three years.[89] The day before the April 7 reception at the Denver Press Club was awkward for Mr. Bryan. His arrival at Union Station and automobile transportation to the University of Denver was greeted by a smattering of pedestrians who looked upon the motorcade with indifference and non-recognition of the Democratic presidential front-runner.[90]

The banquet for Mr. Bryan at the El Jebel Temple banquet hall, was disrupted that evening when more than fifty waiters went on strike against the caterer and the affair was canceled before dinner was served.[91] Members of the Denver Press Club recognized their banquet was in jeopardy and left their dining tables to begin waiting tables. Prominent members of the Democratic party also rose to carry dishes and trays to the amusement of the other dignitaries. Once dinner was served and devoured, the only speech began at ten-o'clock in the evening as Denver Press Club member and former Congressman John F. Shafroth introduced the guest of honor, William J. Bryan, candidate for U.S. President.[92] The following morning, Mr. Bryan met with party leaders and stopped off at the rooms of the Denver Press Club to express his gratitude before leaving on the Burlington Railroad to return to Lincoln, Nebraska for a week of rest.

Normally, the men of the Denver Press Club provided the frequent bouts of entertainment for members of the club. With the upcoming National Democratic Convention in the planning stages, the wives of the press club rose to the occasion to help maintain the press club entertainment traditions. Ida Matthews, the wife of club president James R. Noland, was a pupil of Prof. S. C. Bennett of New York and Vernon Stiles of the Savage Opera company. She performed her first public operatic appearance in

Denver on behalf of the Denver Press Club at a breakfast performance for the members.[93]

*****

Excitement was felt throughout the City of Denver as the Denver Auditorium was due to open in June. W. H. Merman, the Chicago contractor, was away from the project during April, but still found time to optimistically meet with the Denver press: "It is very hard to estimate the exact amount of work done on such a building when foundations and plans are taken into consideration, but I should say that we have 90 percent of the work done in value and 95 per cent in time. The Democratic National Convention could open its session on June 1st if that was the date set."[94] Mr. Merman's projection was only a few days off as construction workers wrapped up on 6 June, a month ahead of the actual opening of the Democratic National Convention on 7 July.[95] A more-pressing problem could not be resolved. An anonymous donor offered the services of a fully stocked bar in the Auditorium near the committee rooms, but far enough from the assembly hall; the auditorium committee wisely turned down the generous offer. The nearest licensed saloon was a block away and no temporary alcoholic bars were allowed any closer, but non-intoxicating beverages were allowed close to the Auditorium Theater.[96]

With only a few weeks before the convention delegates began arriving, it was time for the Denver Press Club to relax. Together with the Writers' Club, the men and women of the press traveled to Lakeside Amusement Park, known as "the White City" because of its illumination of thousands of white electrical lights at night. The entertainment began with breakfast at the lake followed by a full day "devoted to seeing the wonders of the magnificent resort"[97] west of Denver.

The streets of Denver were lavishly decorated for the 1908 convention. Each state in the Union, Alaska, the Philippine islands and other distant possessions of the United States was given one downtown block to be adorned with decorations portraying their state or region. Fifteenth through Seventeenth Streets were divided into block lengths with the state coats of arms for each state suspended above the street and outlined in tiny electric lights. Seventeenth Street was strung with electric light strings and large American flags; Sixteenth Street was festooned with more large American flags hung across the street and the ornamental poles were draped in the national colors.[98]

Seventeen of the 100 members of the Gridiron Club from the Washington club of newspapermen were in attendance in Denver. The group began approximately twenty years earlier and dedicated themselves to meet occasionally, have fine dining, and entertain themselves "in their own particular way."[99] Admission to the club was by invitation only and whatever happened or was said at the Gridiron Club had to remain at the club.

The *Rocky Mountain Daily News* reported "'Big' men, big in the sense of accomplishment in the world at large, are no particular novelty in the rooms of the Denver Press Club, because all the 'big' men of the nation who have ever been in this city have been guests of the club, but last night there was a collection of men of note at the club headquarters in the Railway Exchange, which almost eclipsed all other occasions."[100] William Jennings Bryan often boasted about his last visit to the press club where his autographed photograph now hung on the walls.

American playwright Augustus Thomas was likewise welcomed to the Denver Press Club during the convention. The Denver Press Club and the Writers' Club invited a select group of noted guests to attend a breakfast in honor of Mr. Thomas as one of the greatest playwrights and orators. While the intention of the gathering was to hear Thomas speak on theatrical plays and the political convention, his talk drifted to the topic of telepathy. He described the phenomena of "mental pictures" of one mind communicating with another as demonstrated by a spate of "mind readers" who were popular stage entertainers at the time.[101]

To keep the visiting journalists busy, the Denver Press Club was joined by the Pikes Peak Press Club of Colorado Springs and the Cripple Creek Press Club to visit several gold mining districts.[102]

William Randolph Hearst's train from Chicago left for Denver at 1 p.m. on Tuesday but was delayed by ten hours due to a freight-train wreck on the line. The new estimated time of arrival would have been midnight and too late for his appearance before the delegates at the Democratic Convention. The *Denver Post*, with the cooperation of the Burlington Railroad, arranged for a special train with double-header engines to meet Mr. Hearst in McCook, Nebraska and transported him over tracks cleared of all train traffic and into Denver at the incredible speed of seventy-five to eighty miles per hour. Between the power of the twin engines and the power of the press, the special arrangements enabled Hearst to speak in Denver in a timely manner. He was able to reach Denver's Auditorium Theater with only few minutes to spare.[103]

The press club's participation in the National Democratic Convention once again earned accolades from journalists throughout the country. Denver had reason to be proud of its success in competing with the East Coast press clubs and substantially larger news organizations.

With the summer festivities successfully completed, the Denver Press Club resumed its responsibilities out of the late-Fall Colorado elements. Excavation on the foundation of the Temple of Commerce building was scheduled to commence January 1, 1909 and open a year later. Bonds to fund the project were sold through the Colorado Income Realty Association, a company formed by several commercial organizations. Housed in the building that was later renamed the Chamber of Commerce building, office space for the chamber, the Traffic Club, the Real Estate Exchange, the Manufacturers' Association, the Colorado State Commercial Association, and the Denver Press Club was provided. The journalists expected to have rooms on the eighth floor as a result of the Denver Press Club's $10,000 investment in the building.[104]

Meanwhile, at the existing press club rooms in the Railway Exchange Building, Attendant Joe Diner was over-seeing a pool tournament with twenty-nine men participating in what the *Denver Republican* described as "some weird and wonderful pool playing, interspersed with several exhibitions of a really meritorious character, featured the opening of the handicap tournament at the Denver Press Club."[105] For two days, Diner was struggling to determine how many games would actually be played — his estimation was the pool tables would have 190 games played upon the green felt.[106] Joe Diner was the first notable day-manager or attendant of the Denver Press Club because of his straight-forward way of handling nearly any situation brought to the club. One story about Diner involved a phone call he received in 1908:

> "'Say,' said a feminine voice, 'where are Mr. Brown's pants?'
> 'I don't know,' replied Joe. 'Hasn't he got 'em on?'
> 'Please don't get fresh,' said the woman. 'Send Mr. Brown's pants up at once.'
> 'All the pants here are in use,' said the attendant.
> 'Well, what have you done with Mr. Brown's pants?'

'I never done nothing with them.'

'Haven't you pressed them?'

'No ma'am. We don't press pants here.'

'What place is this?'

'This is the Denver Press Club. It is where the newspapermen hang out.'

'Oh, I guess I made a mistake,' said the woman.

She thought the Denver Press Club was a clothes pressing place."[107]

New products frequently got a try-out at the Denver Press Club as an obvious attempt to gain free marketing on the pages of local publications. P. J. Hall, Denver agent for the Chicago Film Exchange brought the newly invented Ikonograph,[108] a portable five-pound hand-crank moving-pictures projector that advertisements claimed could easily fit into a suitcase and used an acetylene generator, electric light or ordinary gas to illuminate the 17.5mm film. Advertisers claimed it was unequaled for fairs, entreatments [sic] or lodge rooms.

Denver's version of the Washington, D.C. 'Gridiron Club' was initiated in 1908 when Denver Press Club President Thomas M. Hunter was appointed "roast master" for the December event at the Albany Hotel. "It is to be a 'gridiron sizzle,'" the *Denver Post* reported, "and the flesh pots will be made to boil with the hide and hair of the men selected for the slaughter."[109] Before the "sizzling of souls," a pre-Gridiron breakfast group was entertained by the Albany orchestra with light music and the vocal renditions of Mrs. Otis B. Spencer.

Denver Press Club photo

The menu card for the first Gridiron dinner at the Albany Hotel was printed in the likeness of a lobster. Before the first plate was placed before the newspapermen, the hotel apologized. When hotel managers Dutton and Epstein sent the menu to the printer with the instruction the card should be printed in a shape of a ham hock to reflect the key ingredient of the breakfast fare. The printer, the Carson-Harper Company, was out of ham pictures and arbitrarily substituted a lobster in its place.[110]

Each year, the press club conducted a theatrical fundraiser where prominent men and women from the literary, social and political world came together to show appreciation for the role the Denver Press Club played in boosting the community. In reality, when the club's coffers were low, the press boys chose to put on a show to raise money for the club. The 1908 event was a play written by Eugene Walter, a former Denver newspaper reporter. "The Wolf" portrayed the story of a girl "Who loved unwisely and was sent to death by her lover in the Canadian Hudson Bay country. Her half-brother seeks her betrayer and finds him attempting to take advantage of the girl loved by the half-brother. He rescues her, the villain follows the pair and a duel follows in the dark. The audience hears but does not see the life and death struggle. Finally, there is a dying moan and the listeners know that one is dead—but which one?"[111] the *Denver Post* revealed before the show opened in Denver.

To create the most modern special effects for the performance, recording experts brought their equipment to the Bronx Park Zoological garden in New York and positioned a horn to record the yelps and howls of the wolves in the zoo. The record was made permanent and played with startling effect at various times during the performance of "The Wolf." "This is undoubtedly the first time such an idea has been used," reported *The Denver Times*, "and marks the dawn of a new era in the production and working of mechanical stage effects."[112]

The net receipts from ticket sales were supplemented by advertising in an elaborately bound program. Cecil R. Conner (a press-club member whose fame included attendance at more than fifty years of press-club annual meetings), explained that the advertising came from voluntary sources and a few sources that had pressure put upon them from more assertive press-club members. The program was profusely illustrated with contribution from press photographers and cartoonists, and poetry supplied by artistically challenged newspaper scribes.[113]

Before the end of the year, the Denver Press Club was the guest of the Denver Athletic Club where the members from both clubs were the subject of two hours of roasts "of the laugh-provoking sort that drive away worry wrinkles and beget humor lines."[114] Governor-elect John Shafroth was in attendance and fielded many of the political blows, but still found a few kind words for his roasters. He told the journalists that their profession had grown to be the most powerful calling because the men and women of the press believe they are swayed by good impulses.

On Christmas Eve, members of the Denver Press Club and their families gathered around the club's unusual Christmas tree. A handsome present for each child was attached to the branches, distributed with the assistance of four Santa Clauses. Some of the children may have been old enough to question why there were four men who bore an uncanny resemblance to club members E. O. Russell, Alfred Damon Runyon, Gray Richardson and Edward Wilson. For the adults, guests were treated to musical entertainment, Bide Dudley's humorous stories, the oratory talents of James Kelley, and silent moving pictures. According to the club's house committee, "it was the most successful family Christmas entertainment the club has ever given."[115]

The Denver Press Club was still eager to maintain their own club house; the annual theatrical fundraiser added to the $3,000 already in the 1909 building fund. On May 28, Denver's "Rector Cafe" in the Ernest

Cranmer Building (17th and Curtis Streets) opened under the short-lived ownership of the Denver Press Club as a means of increasing revenue for the building fund. E. J. Flynn, manager of the Rector Cafe company, owned a chain of cafes in all the leading cities.[116]

The mid-July 1909 temperature and excessive humidity in Denver prompted thousands of people to get out of the city and into the mountains or down to the Clear Creek and Platte cañons. The *Denver Post* described it as "one of those regular way down East' summer days, where you boil and swelter, wilt your collars and lose your temper."[117] The Denver Press Club arranged an excursion to Riverview in Platte Cañon for approximately one hundred local newspaper people, their wives, mothers, sweethearts, and children to coincide with the club's annual picnic. The Colorado & Southern railroad provided three large observation coaches to accommodate the group.

Leaving Denver at 8:15 a.m., the picnickers had six hours in the mountains where basket lunches were spread under the shade of the trees on the mountain side. A few of the more-energetic club members kept busy with an impromptu game of baseball. Club steward Joe Diner served ice cream and lemonade to help cool the guests from the heat.[118] Baseball was becoming a popular sport in Denver. If you believed the Denver Press Club members, they would have claimed to be candidates for professional ballplayers in their younger days. The Colorado Hotel Clerks Association finally called the bluff of the newspapermen and challenged the Denver Press Club to a ball game at the Broadway park.[119] Other groups also stepped up to challenge the press club. As always, the Denver newspapers did not publish the outcomes of those challenges, possibly to avoid any humiliation in their own publications.

In late-August, the Denver & Rio Grande Railroad brought press club members and friends to Pinecrest, a new resort on Palmer Lake. Each guest was given a gold stickpin by the railroad hosts; the Carson-Harper Company offered another stickpin to the winning baseball team captain who won the *Post-Republican* v. *News-Times* game.[120] By 1910, the newspapers recognized that club life was an attractive feature of life in Denver. Among the leading social organizations were the Denver Club, the Athletic Club, the Denver Press Club, the University Club and of course, the Woman's Club.[121]

1   *Daily News,* March 12, 1864, p. 4

2   "Denver Writer Rapidly Forges to the Front as a Poet," *Denver Republican,* December 30, 1906, p. 1

3   *Damon Runyon,* Jimmy Breslin, Ticknor & Fields, New York, 1991

4   Ibid

5   *Skyline,* Gene Fowler, Viking Press, New York, 1961, p. 21

6   "Santa Claus at the Press Club," *Denver Times,* December 24, 1906, p. 4

7   "There Never Was Such a Christmas Day in Denver," *Denver Post,* December 25, 1906, p. 4

8   *Skyline,* Gene Fowler, Viking Press, New York, 1961; p. 22

9   Ibid., p. 23

10 *Skyline,* Gene Fowler, Viking Press, New York, 1961; p. 277

11 "Debs is Giving Patterson Bad Case of Heart Failure," *Denver Post,* November 4, 1906, p. 2

12 "Debs Well Entertained," *Gazette-Telegraph,* November 6, 1906

13 "Wage Question Not Worrying Nevada Miners," *Denver Post,* January 2, 1907, p. 10

14 "Press Club Will Give Clever Minstrel Show," *Denver Republican,* January 8, 1907, p. 3

15 "Newspapermen Will Give Minstrel Show," *Denver Post,* January 9, 1907, p. 6

16 "Goldfield Will Send Delegation to Big Minstrels," *Denver Post,* January 19, 1907, p. 10

17 "The Press Club Minstrel Show," *Denver Republican,* January 20, 1907, p. 27

18 "Press Club Show to Settle Contest," *Denver Republican,* January 24, 1907, p. 8

19 Ibid

20 Ibid

21 "Song Hit of the Press Club Show Gets Into Bill of Real Minstrels," *Denver Republican,* March 31, 1907, p. 13

22 "Newspaperman's Song Making Hit," *Denver Republican,* February 10, 1907, Part 4, p. 33

23 *Who's Who in America,* Volume 11, edited by John William Leonard, Albert Nelson, Marquis Publishing, p. 1519

24 "Newspapermen Prove Past Masters of Minstrel Art at Press Club Show," *Denver Republican,* January 26, 1907, p. 8

25 "Beautiful Picture, Portraying the Interior of Turkish Harem, is Presented to Press Club," *Denver Republican,* February 5, 1907

26 Form letter from James R. Noland, president of the Denver Press Club Board of Directors, circa 1907

27 *Saguache Crescent,* February 28, 1907, p. 5

28 "Press Club Will Give Annual Breakfast and Hold Yearly Election," *Denver*

Post, March 9, 1907, p. 8

29 "Newspapermen Entertain Baby Elephant at Press Club Feast," *Denver Republican*, March 10, 1907, p. 23

30 "Install Officers of the Press Club," *Denver Republican*, April 1, 1907, p. 8

31 "James Kelley New Head of Press Club," *Denver Times*, March 1907

32 "New Heads for the Press Club," *Denver Republican*, March 11, 1907, p. 10

33 "Press Club Plans Year of Activity," *Denver Republican*, April 2, 1907, p. 12

34 "Lucius M. Wilcox, Denver's Blind Author, Writes Book on Irrigation," *Denver Post*, April 21, 1907, p. 51

35 "Denounces the Yellow Journalist," *Denver Republican*, April 13, 1907, p. 1; "Yellow Journalism the Fear of Peace," *Denver Times*, April 13, 1907, p. 10

36 "Editors Meet in rooms of Denver Press Club," *Denver Republican*, May 18, 1907, p. 11

37 "Press Club Entertains Friends From the City and the State," *Denver Republican*, May 20, 1907, p. 4

38 "Press Club is Entertained," *Colorado Springs Gazette*, May 20, 1907, p. 5

39 "Press Club Entertains Friends From the City and the State," *Denver Republican*, May 20, 1907, p. 4

40 Ibid

41 "Denver Press Club Entertains Friends," *Denver Times*, May 20, 1907, p. 7

42 "Newspaper Workers in Romance of Real Life," *Denver Post*, June 2, 1907, p. 13

43 "Society Editor Couldn't Cover Races Because She Had Eloped and Was Married," *Omaha (NE) World Herald*, June 2, 1907, p. 1

44 "Press Men Guests at Bathing Resort," *Denver Republican*, June 3, 1907, p. 10

45 "Press Club All Set for Diamond Jubilee Bash," Dolores Eyler, *Rocky Mountain News*, October 31, 1980, p. 35c

46 "Denver Boosters Ready to Yell for Leadville," *Denver Post*, June 12, 1907, p. 2

47 "Leadville is Ready for the Great Spread," *Denver Post*, June 11, 1907, p. 5

48 "Newspaper Folk Take First Annual Splash," *Denver Post*, June 9, 1907, p. 24

49 "Denver Boosters and Members of Press Will Make Leadville Howl," *Denver Post*, June 7, 1907, p. 8

50 "Leadville Prepares for Elks," *Gazette-Telegraph*, June 10, 1907

51 "Press Club Nearly Causes Road Violation," *Denver Times*, August 1907

52 Letter from J. W. Kelly, Denver Press Club, Railway Building, Denver, Colorado to Samuel Clemens, May 28rd [sic], 1907

53 "Press Club Chooses National Delegates," *Denver Post*, June 24, 1907, p. 4

54 "Press Club Receives Photo of America's Great Humorist," *Denver Republican*, June 24, 1907, p. 24

55 "Members of Press Club Feed on Corn in Various Desguises [sic]," *Denver Republican*, July 1, 1907, p. 3

56

57 "What is the South Doing," *Evening Times,* November 19, 1907

58 "Powers to Give Press Club Show," *Denver Post,* November 13, 1907, p. 6

59 "James Powers in Blue Moon at the Broadway," *Denver Times,* November 30, 1907, p. 8

60 "Press Club Show Dec. 3 is Headed by Famous Comedian: Jimmy Powers in Brilliant Opera, 'The Blue Moon,'" *Denver Times,* November 13, 1907, p. 3

61 "Fashionable Denver at Press Club Show," *Denver Times,* November 27, 1907, p. 2, Extra Edition

62 "Big Events Postponed for Press Club Show," *Denver Times,* November 30, 1907, p. 11

63 "Denver Will Entertain Her Visitors As They Have Never Imagined," *Denver Post,* December 15, 1907, p. 16

64 "Press Club to Help Entertain," *Denver Post,* December 23, 1907, p. 12

65 "Arrangements On Tap By Denver Press Club," *Anaconda Standard* (Anaconda, Montana), February 10, 1908, p. 7

66 "Denver Prepares to Play Host," *New York Times,* April 12, 1908

67 "Denver Press Club Preparing to Boost State of Colorado," *The Chieftain,* circa February 1908

68 "Conventions Coming to Denver," *Castle Rock Journal,* January 3, 1908, p. 3

69 "Hotels of Denver: Press Club Declares that They are Ample for any Convention Needs," *Grand Rapids Press,* February 11, 1908

70 "The Denver Press Club's Hospitality," editorial by the *San Franciscan Examiner,* July 9, 1908

71 "Railroads Aid Convention," *Littleton Independent,* March 13, 1908, p. 7

72 "Magazines Want to Help Boost Denver," *Denver Post,* March 3, 1908, p. 7

73 "Denver a Great Place: Information Concerning the Place Where Convention is to be Held," *The Daily Record [Greensboro, NC),* March 4, 1908, p. 2

74 "Editors of the State Share With Cattlemen Royal Dinner Welcome," *Denver Times,* January 20, 1908, p. 3 Extra

75 "Editors Gloat Over the Death of Laton Bill," *Denver Post,* January 21, 1908, p. 6

76 "Editors of the State Share With Cattlemen Royal Dinner Welcome," *Denver Times,* January 20, 1908, p. 3 Extra

77 "Editors of the State Share With Cattlemen Royal Denver Welcome," *Denver Times,* January 20, 1908, p. 3 Extra

78 "May Build Club House," *Gazette-Telegraph,* March 9, 1908

79 "Leaders Chosen by Press Club for New Year," *Denver Post,* March 9, 1908, p. 5

80 Ibid

81 "Press Club Honors Officers," *Denver Post,* March 14, 1908, p. 8

82 "Press Club Tenders Smoker to Al Field," *Denver Post,* March 18, 1908, p. 6

83 "City Briefs," *Colorado Springs Gazette,* March 24, 1908, p. 3

84 *Denver Post,* March 24, 1908, p. 7

85 "Coming Events," *Denver Post,* March 24, 1908, p. 10

86 "Smart Set is Busy in Whirl of Society: Plan Many Musicals and Entertainment," *Denver Post,* Society Section, p. 6

87 "Humorists Want Denver," *Los Angeles Herald,* March 30, 1908

88 "Funny Writers Will Help the Nye Monument," *Denver Post,* August 11, 1908, p. 6

89 "Bryan Given Ovation: Throngs at the Depot and Along the Streets His Car Must Pass," *Denver Post,* April 6, 1908, p. 1, 2

90 229 "Bryan Given Ovation: Throngs at the Depot and Along the Streets His Car Must Pass," *Denver Post,* April 6, 1908, p. 1, 2

91 "Bryan Banquet a Fluke," *Charlotte Observer,* April 7, 1908, p. 4

92 "Bryan Talks to Democrats at Dinner," *Idaho Statesman,* April 7, 1908

93 "Press Club Officers to Entertain the Members," *Denver Post,* April 19, 1908, p. 31

94 "Rushing the Auditorium," *Colorado Transcript,* May 7, 1908, p. 7

95 "Denver's Big Auditorium Completed," *Daily Journal* [Telluride, Colorado] May 23, 1908, p. 1

96 "Bars Barred From Denver Auditorium," *Daily Journal* [Telluride, Colorado] May 27, 1908, p. 1

97 "Newspaper Workers Entertained at the White City," *Denver Times,* June 22, 1908, p. 4

98 "Denver Will be Decorated," *Breckenridge Bulletin* [Breckenridge, Colorado]. July 4, 1908, p. 6

99 "Seventeen of Gridiron Club at Convention, *Sunday News-Times,* July 5, 1908, Sec. 1, p. 11

100 "Visiting Writers Entertained by Press Club," *Rocky Mountain Daily News,* July 8, 1908, p. 4

101 "Newspaper People Meet Thomas at Breakfast," *The Daily News,* July 13, 1908, p. 5

102 "Visting Writers Given Real Treat," *Denver Post,* July 13, 1908, p. 4

103 "Hearst Speeds Denverward on Special Flyer," *Denver Post,* September 30, 1908, p. 4

104 "Work on Temple of Commerce to Begin January 1," *Denver Post,* November 24, 1908, p. 4

105 "Wonderful Work of Press Club Experts," *Denver Republican,* December 1908

106 "A Hard Problem: Smoke Wreaths," Bide Dudley, *Denver Post,* November 26, 1908, p. 14

107 "A Slight Mistake," *Denver Post,* June 6, 1908, p. 12

108 "Moving Pictures at Press Club Smoker," *Denver Post,* December 2, 1908, p. 8

109 "Press Club Plans 'Gridiron Sizzle,'" *Denver Post,* December 10, 1908, p. 3

110 "Lobster on Menu Card is Only One at Press Club Banquet," *Rocky Mountain Daily News,* December 14, 1908

111 "Press Club Benefit Will Be Denver Newspaperman's Play," *Denver Post,* December 16, 1908, p. 9

112 "Realistic Wolf Howls, Obtained by Phonograph for Stager Effect," *Denver Times,* December 1908

113 *The 1967 Denver Westerners Brand Book,* "The Denver Press Club," Cecil R. Conner, The Westerners, Denver, 1968, p. 136

114 "Press Writers Breakfasted by Athletic Club," *Denver Post,* December 21, 1908, p. 3

115 "Denver Newspaper Folk Gather Round Their Yule Tree, *Rocky Mountain News,* December 25, 1908

116 "Denver Press Club to Open Rector Cafe," *Denver Post,* May 28, 1909, p. 18

117 "Crowds Throng Parks and Hills to Escape Heat," *Denver Post,* July 12, 1909, p. 4

118 "Denver Press Club Held Its Annual Picnic at Riverside," *Denver Post,* July 12, 1909, p. 5

119 "Press Club Field Day Will Be Hummer," *Denver Post,* August 21, 1909, p. 7

120 "Newspapermen To Have Outing at Pine Crest," *Denver Post,* August 28, 1909, p. 8

121 "Phenomenal Growth of Denver Shown By Building Records," *Denver Post,* December 26, 1909, p. 45

CHAPTER 6

The Press is at once the eye and the ear and the tongue of the people. It is the visible speech, if not the voice, of the democracy. It is the phonograph of the world.[1]

The 1910 Denver Press Club began the new decade with a reception held during the club's open house on New Year's Eve[2] in the convention hall of the Albany Hotel. At the March annual membership meeting a few months later, the club elected Colonel John S. Irby, secretary to Mayor Speer and former newspaper editor, as the new president of the Denver Press Club. The first item on the agenda of the new president was to prepare to move into the club's new quarters in the Kittredge Building.[3] On March 31, the wives of the press club members and members of the Writers' Club spent the afternoon in an informal open house in the new club rooms at 16th and Glenarm Place. In the evening Al G. Field and his theatrical company of minstrels climbed to the second-story rooms of the latest home of the Denver Press Club.[4] Before the moving boxes were even unpacked, the club was preparing to build their permanent home. The fund to purchase lots and construct a club house was growing, and the new club administration proposed to break ground for a permanent club house later in 1910.

As a community-awareness project, the newly elected officers donned their kitchen aprons and tendered a complimentary breakfast to the rest of the press-club membership when they gathered at 10 a.m. on April 10, 1910, at the Auditorium Hotel. "One of the unwritten laws of the organization," reported the *Denver Post*, "is that the genial hosts shall take the best they can get from the membership on that occasion, and, besides that, they have to pay for the eatables and drinkables that the grillers consume."[5] Twenty-three new active members, one non-resident member, and one associate member were welcomed at the brunch.

*****

Despite the onerous date of Friday the Thirteenth, auto-daredevil Barney Oldfield accepted the invitation of the Denver Press Club to appear in May.[6] On May 13-14, 1910, the press club arranged for a street parade and an exhibition electric-car race from Overland Park in Denver to the town of Sedalia and back.[7] The actual race took place on the scientifically banked turns of Overland Park's oval wooden track. Mr. Oldfield's manager examined the oval track and acknowledged it was the best oval track in the country, more than capable of taking on a caravan of Mr. Oldfield's "supe'd up" cars, entrants by Denver auto dealerships, a few motorcycles, and any of Denver's "society folk" who wanted to participate.

Berna Eli "Barney" Oldfield was a bicycle racer who was influenced by Henry Ford to race Ford's 999-racecar. In 1903, Oldfield broke the mile-a-minute barrier at 59.75 seconds in Indianapolis.

Courtesy of the author

"Cars these days," Mr. Sloan (Oldfield's manager) explained, "are designed for both gravity and centrifugal force, and this track will enable a careful driver to attain any speed without danger. After you have used up the force of gravity in rounding the curves the centrifugal force is to be reckoned with and the extreme high-power cars, also designed to resist the atmospheric pressure, which is a part of the gravity, is gone. Then it is a matter of swing or, in other words, taking the curves. We are confident to state that we will have cars for which your Overland track will be child's play to make miles in many seconds less than a minute and show the value of expert driving."[8]

On April 20, the Denver Press Club's entry into the sporting world went up in flames as the Overland club house, grandstands, and adjoining buildings burned to the ground. Boys working on the park grounds discovered the fire and notified Captain Grimes of the Englewood volunteer fire department who enlisted support from the Denver Fire Department. There were no fire plugs near the park and the only fire engine equipped to draw water from an irrigation ditch, was one the city ordered to the scrap pile because the department believed it was no longer useful. The all-wooden grandstand was engulfed in flames before the old fire truck reached the park. Officers of the fair association promised a modern grandstand would be built in time for the Barney Oldfield races.[9]

"There isn't any organization with more stamina than the Denver Press Club," reported the *Denver Post*, "which has started out to put up a new building, and has arranged a series of auto races and a display of airplanes at Overland park . . . When the grandstand burned, the Press club managers started in to provide for the contingency before the ruins had quit sending up their fits of flame every time a fresh breeze would fan some part that was not entirely destroyed."[10] The new grandstand was made of concrete reinforced with steel.

As the auto-and-air show drew nigh, Barney Oldfield and "his monster 100-horse-power Benz racer" joined $60,000 worth of other big cars that were racing with other professionals in California. Motorcycle factories also shipped "a large number" of cycles especially built for racing; and a local auto race and novelty stunts for electric cars were added to the entertainment bill.[11] So that spectators could witness the full impact of the speed, the Denver Press Club moved their auxiliary grandstand several hundred feet back up the course where Mr. Oldfield was expected to reach his maximum speed.[12] In a subsequent article, the *Denver Post* reported that Mr. Oldfield and "his monster 100-horse power Benz racer" will attempt to break the world's records for the mile and two-mile races and cross the finish line at one-hundred miles-an-hour as an estimated crowd of 25,000 people cheer the racer.

The city turned out to support the press club's building fund. Even the Daniels & Fisher store advertising included an open-letter within their advertisement in the *Denver Post:* "Dear Everybody: There's a lot of truth in the modern saying—that all things come to him who hustles while he waits! For instance, those top-notch hustlers—the Denver Press Club— instead of simply waiting for a Club House are helping matters along by holding races out at Overland Park. Just as we, while waiting for our new building, expect to do an unusual amount of mercantile hustling. . ."[13]

The success of the Barney Oldfield races brought a change from railroad travel to an increased enthusiasm for the automobile. A night-time trip between Denver and Colorado Springs became a popular challenge and the Denver Press Club was quick to accept an invitation of the Pikes Peak Press club to attend a dance on May 17 in the pavilion at Stratton Park in Colorado Springs.[14]

The go-to getaway place for motoring tourists, visiting pleasure seekers, locals, and the Denver Press Club was "Mt. Morrison and the Region of Peaks, Parks, and Rocks."[15] John Brisbane Walker, promoter and president of the company operating the pleasure resort invited members of the Denver Press Club and the Writers' Club to hold their annual outing and picnic on Mt. Morrison on June 26. Mr. Walker purchased *Cosmopolitan Magazine* in 1888 and sold it to William Randolph Hearst in 1905 for a reported $1.0 to $1.5 million which was reinvested in land investments in the Morrison area.

Denver Press Club members and their families were
often guests of the narrow-gauge railroads that connected
Denver with mountain tourism amenities.

Courtesy of Denver Public Library Western
History Collection, Call No. Z-3472

Instead of describing the day as a "picnic" or "outing," the event was
billed as a "scramble." The reference was to adventurous rambles into caves,
and over boulders that would be required to enjoy the entire park and the
natural beauties of the area. Mt. Morrison is the "tall hump of slag" west
of today's Red Rocks amphitheater. In the 1890s a funicular railway was
built and brought visitors to the top of the 7,881-ft. "mountain," and the
"summit" served as a popular picnic area with beautiful views of the city
and plains to the East.[16]

The newspapermen brought their wives and sweethearts to join
members of the Writers' Club as they were all escorted to the Denver
train station. T. E. Fisher, passenger agent of the Colorado & Southern
railroad, arranged to provide two special train-cars to bring many of the
guests to the Red Rocks park; others provided their own transportation
with private horseless carriages. Once they assembled at the park, the larger
group separated into small groups, climbing over the rocks and searching
for shady nooks. After a basket luncheon, the inclined railroad was started,
and Mr. Walker escorted the party to the summit where the party was
welcomed at the Mt. Morrison Casino and grand hotel originally built

by former Governor John Evans in 1874. It was demolished in 1982.[17] At sunset, a dinner was served on the broad veranda of the hotel.[18]

The following month, another train excursion brought the Denver Press Club and their families to Pinecrest, "a cozy retreat just south of Palmer Lake."[19] Once the Rio Grande train left the party at the resort depot, the guests were treated to a natatorium [building with a swimming pool], billiards, pool and bowling. Basket lunches and fried "springers" [fried chicken] were served under the pine trees overlooking the lake.[20]

The Denver Press Club's support of the Rocky Mountain network of rails earned them an opportunity to initiate a new motor-car that arrived for use on the Denver, Laramie & Northwestern railroad. The oddly shaped rail car had the appearance of an Airstream mobile-home trailer, insulated with a new substance made from a combination of spun glass and fiber held between the steel outer-shell and 1.5-inch boards on the interior. Described as "a boat" or "steel projectile,"[21] the steel railroad car was built to provide uniform interior temperatures in winter or summer and provide the traveling public with railway travel impervious to a shock of any kind in time of a railroad emergency.[22]

The Denver Press Club wanted to rekindle their friendship with a past president. A telegram was sent to Colonel Roosevelt, who recently returned from a business trip to Europe. "Honorable Theodore Roosevelt . . . The Denver Press club sends 'greetings on your return to America after your remarkable tour of the effete East. We urge you to come to Denver, a live one, be [the] guest of Press Club and tell us to our face what you think of us. The earlier the better we like it. John S. Irby, president."[23]

Colonel Irby, president of the Denver Press Club sent a second telegram to Colonel Theodore Roosevelt expressing the club's desire to entertain "its only honorary member" with a cowboy breakfast[24] at the Interstate Fair and Exposition grounds in August 1910. Colonel Roosevelt appreciated one-on-one camaraderie instead of "the pomp and glory of pageants and hero worship"[25] "In a way," the *Denver Post* reported, "it is of a private nature between him and the Press Club, yet it conveys by its very appropriateness the sentiment of the Western people."[26] On July 15, Colonel Roosevelt telegraphed Colonel Irby, accepting the press club's invitation to attend the old-fashioned cowboy breakfast on August 29.[27]

Silver Dollar Tabor, daughter of Senator H. A. W. Tabor being
presented to President Theodore Roosevelt by Sheriff Alexander
Nisbet and Senator Irby, president of the Denver Press Club at the
Chuck-wagon breakfast given by the press club on August 29, 1910.

History Colorado, BPF-Tabor Family Collection, Scan # 10048654

Gifford Pinchot, former federal forester under the Taft administration, arrived early in Denver to smooth out the logistics for Colonel Roosevelt's arrival. Several organizations attempted to out-plan the others for the benefit of Roosevelt's entertainment. Mr. Pinchot met with representatives from the Colorado Live Stock Association, the Denver Convention League, the Spanish-American war veterans, and the Denver Press Club; and negotiated the planned entertainment to the satisfaction of the groups vying for Roosevelt's attention.[28] He was scheduled to arrive in Denver at 10:30 and would be taken to a stand on Sixteenth Street to review a parade of Spanish-American war veterans. To fortify the former president's energy the Denver Press Club scheduled a chuck-wagon breakfast at Overland. After a short rest, the former president traveled to the Auditorium for a public address at 2:30 p.m. followed by a meeting with the veterans. The Colorado Livestock Association provided Roosevelt with a banquet at El Jebel temple in the evening. After an evening's rest, his train left Denver at 8 a.m. the next morning.[29]

The press club sought to present the cowboy luncheon (a slight scheduling problem moved the feast to the noon hour) with as much authentic detail as possible. A delegation of 500 cattlemen was dispatched onto the plains to gather organic bovine cooking material for the feast to bring memories back to Colonel Roosevelt when he rode the ranges;[30] wood and coal for cooking purposes were often hundreds of miles away[31] and the sun-dried cow-patties burned nicely as aromatic fuel. Jim Scott of Deer Trail and Harry Grant of Fort Collins, two old-style cow-camp cooks, prepared the food just as it was prepared for the spring and fall roundups from their two chuck wagons.[32] Mr. Scott's driver of the four-mule team was "Whistling Jack" Thompson, "… 60 and 'ode years of age, is still 'husky' and he carries with him the same old sheaves of impenetrable whiskers that the north winds have tackled in vain."[33]

"On the night before last," Scott related to the *Denver Post*, "the mule team attached to the chuck wagon ran away and went seven miles full chizzle before we could get them stopped. Of course, about half the stuff in the wagon hopped out and was lost, but we took it out of the hides of them dumb fool mules when we got 'em stopped."[34]

"Pot Luck with the 'boys.'" President Theodore Roosevelt supervises how the steaks are being cooked over a fire made from prairie cow pies. Roosevelt was the guest of the Denver Press Club in an authentic Chuck-wagon feast prepared in his honor.

Courtesy of the Library of Congress, Underwood & Underwood, publisher. "Pot luck with the 'boys'– President Roosevelt's cowboy breakfast, ca. 1903. Photograph https://www.loc.gov/item/2010647452/.

The official camp cook for the Denver Press Club chuck-wagon luncheon was Louis Callahan, described as "the wealthiest Negro in Colorado—half darkey, half Indian,"[35] reported the *Beaumont Enterprise and Journal.* He had his own ranch, bank stock and a net worth of $40,000, "but lazy mussy, he's just a camp cook and a good one," continued the *Denver Post.*[36]

"Well, such, it was along reboot 1874 when I struck Colorado," Mr. Callahan told the *Post,* "and yit, while I done worked hard in it, I don't begrudge nuthin that I did. And when it comes term cookin'—well, I don't know as anybody wants to give me no handicap."

When Colonel Roosevelt's press-club escort picked him up at his hotel (where he changed his city clothes for attire more appropriate for a chuck-wagon luncheon), he implored his hosts to "just let me be a reporter" at the luncheon. The chit-chat between the reporters at Overland Park and the former U.S. president mentioned the Spanish-American War veterans and livestock people who were in attendance, but Roosevelt reserved a few special comments for the members of the Denver Press Club. "But this bunch of newspapermen, did you ask me? Well, you know they are dandy. I know of no feature of my Western trip that I will enjoy more. When I left the White House I called in all my newspaper friends and told them good-bye. There are a number of them here today, and you know I am glad to see them. Everybody always calls me a press agent, but it is the square deal you fellows have given me that made that reputation. Love you. Well, you can just tell the whole world that I am one of you, even if, as I heard the term used the other day, 'graphite propelling' has never been my profession."[37]

Sitting under the cool shade of the trees at Overland Park, Colonel Roosevelt was surrounded by sheriffs, newspapermen, and their guests. As the former U.S. president worked his way up to the chuck wagon, he was greeted with "Now, you all, jets stan' back a little ways, will her, please, gemmun, an' lemme he'p de Cunnle to some o' de fines' beef what he evan flung his lip ovah," challenged head-cook Louis Callahan, "who is about the color of a 20-year-old meerschaum."[38]

With a cup of steaming coffee, a huge piece of steak, a tremendous potato and two tall biscuits, the former U.S. president sighed in satisfaction, grinned and merely commented, "That's bully." Denver Press Club president Colonel John S. Irby rose and addressed their distinguished fellow journalist. "Colonel Roosevelt, we are glad you are here. The newspapermen of Denver understand and love you. We are glad—yes, delighted—that you are the only honorary member of the Denver Press Club. When we elected you to that position we placed the standard so high that we have never been able as yet to duplicate it. Our only regret is that you are not an active member of the press club, and hope some day you will qualify by becoming a resident of Denver. We extend you a genuine Colorado welcome and assure you that wherever your duty calls you we are looking to you yet for much additional good to come out of your great influence."[39]

The Denver Moving Picture Theater on Seventeenth Street (between Curtis and Arapahoe) was able to exhibit a two-reeler of Colonel Theodore Roosevelt's visit to Denver. The second reel showed the former president dining at the chuck-wagon dinner with Mr. Pinchot and Mr. Garfield, followed by a broncho-busting contest with Dode Wykert riding "Sam," the winner of the *Denver Post* trophy. "The Great Horse Race of 1908" was sponsored by the newspaper as a 500-mile route from Evanston, Wyoming to Denver. Mr. Wykert was a Greeley, Colorado native and one of the twenty-five pairs of racers. After covering 565 miles in 152 hours and 18 minutes, the $300 prize and two pairs of cowboy boots were awarded to Wykert, a silver-trimmed saddle to the pair, and "Sam" was granted the privilege of grazing on the State Capitol lawn.[40]

*****

In August 1910, negotiations began for the purchase of the lot on Glenarm Place between Thirteenth and Fourteenth streets, opposite the Denver Athletic Club. The lot, valued at $7,500, had a two-story brick residence that could be remodeled into a temporary club house until a permanent home was erected for the Denver Press Club.[41]

There was a dispute whether the Barry family had any title to the building. The club had to sue to clear the title of the property through Attorney Hamlet J. Barry (manager of Denver Water Board and member of the law firm of Calkins, Kramer, Grimshaw and Harring)[42] against James Barry and his unknown heirs. "The complaint sets forth Barry or his heirs allege to have an interest in the property and the Denver Press Club having purchased the property in fee simple, desires the cloud removed from the title. The court is asked to have Barry, or his unknown heirs appear and present the nature of their claims; that it decrees they have no interest in the estate; that the Denver Press club be adjudged the sole owner in fee simple and that Barry and his heirs be forever enjoined from asserting any claim to the property."[43]

A little over a month later, the legal column of the *Denver Post* noted that Lot 9, Blk 198 real estate had transferred from Victor R. Olmsted (Denver Real Estate Exchange member and president of Thompson-Olmsted Investment Company) to the Denver Press Club for the valued amount.[44] *The Denver Times* clarified that the purchase was for investment purposes and <u>not</u> as the site for the proposed home of the Denver Press Club.[45] The *Denver Post* then reiterated that the club would neither occupy nor remodel the residence; instead, it was intended to be leased until the club deemed it timely to build a large clubhouse at that location.[46]

The benevolent side of the Denver Press Club was shown once again when a massive explosion destroyed the *Los Angeles Times* building in 1910, killing twenty-one people and injuring many others. The explosion was the result of a fight between the Bridge-and-Structural Iron Workers Union and publisher Harrison Otis who was the leader of the Merchants-and-Manufacturing Association, a powerful group of business owners with strong anti-union political connections.[47] Denver Press Club President John S. Irby forwarded a telegram, "The Denver Press Club extends to you and the families of the men killed in the destruction of the Times Building its sympathy. Please advise us if the club can be of any assistance to you or the members of the families." General Harrison Gray Otis (president and general manager of the Times-Mirror Company) responded, "Thank you greatly for your telegram of sympathy. The Times needs no assistance itself but will accept same for families of the slain."[48]

The Denver Press Club was able to relax by the end of 1910 with a pair of Christmas trees provided and decorated by their friends in Bear Creek Cañon for the members and their families during holiday celebrations at the Albany Hotel.[49] The *Denver Post* oddly described the purpose of having Mr. and Mrs. Kris Kringle at the press club holiday party: "Not often is it that Mrs. Kris Kringle gets away from home, for she has so much to do in helping her husband get the good things together for the little ones, but on this occasion she said she just would come anyway and see the children of the newspaper boys and look after those of writers who have been called from this life."[50]

Mrs. James R. Noland provided several songs while Melville Gideon and Mabel Bunyea, vaudeville stars with the Orpheum circuit, were also on hand to provide "some rare entertainment."[51]

One of the newer members of the Denver Press Club was a young sports-writer on the boxing beat that was gaining popularity in Colorado. Abe Pollock was a part-time referee and full-time writer who was able to work the press club away from the theater crowd and draw them into the ring. "Plans are being laid to throw Denver wide open to pugilism," reported the Sidelights on Sporting Stage article in a North Dakota newspaper. "Whether or not the bout scheduled for today between Jack (Twin) Sullivan and Johnny O'Keefe is pulled off in Edgewater, where it was originally proposed, or in Denver, it is proposed at an early date to stage fights between fighters of national reputation in the auditorium. The promoters are said to be planning to use the Denver Press Club as an entering wedge."[52] A couple of weeks later, the club's first sponsorship of a boxing exhibition between Johnny O'Keefe of Denver versus Jimmy Gardner of Lowell, Massachusetts was booked for the Auditorium Theater. As the *Denver Post* reported, the press club secured "a number of athletic acts of much merit [that] will make the program one of the best of its kind that has been staged in Denver in many months." [53]

The bout was almost stopped before the boxers were able to enter the ring; District Judge Carlton M. Bliss refused the injunction by the Christian Citizenship Union which sought to prevent the "glove contest" between the two boxers. The Christian Citizenship Union sent letters to the pastors of local churches, asking them to contact Mayor Speer and urge him to withhold his consent for the use of the Denver Auditorium as a boxing arena on the grounds that it was a public building. Judge Bliss stated that the district attorney's office would send representatives to be at ringside to assure that if the boxing laws were violated in any way, "everyone connected with the affair would be arrested."[54]

Proceeds from the "athletic contest" (as the boxing match was now known) were to go toward the building fund for a press club-house on the lot they purchased several months ago. To meet the critics of the boxing exhibition, the Denver Press Club assured the Christian Citizenship Union that the event would be combined with a juggling act that will open the program, followed by a wrestling match between Gehring and Sloan or Harrison. Mike Malone and Bedt Erlenborn will box, followed by Kid Goodman against Charley Pierson, the "Fighting Newsboy." The team of Hanlon, Dean & Hanlon will also appear in an acrobatic stunt. The ten-round boxing demonstration would conclude without a decision— "The science of defense will be given a practical demonstration by them. There will be nothing brutal in the show. It will be a clean exhibition of scientific boxing."[55]

The *Denver Post* reported the Denver Press Club exhibition, "The managers of the entertainment have made every effort to keep anything in the least objectionable from the program and promise that the show will be clean and well-handled from start to finish. The club caters to the best class of people and the performance tonight is expected to appeal strongly to all those who favor clean and well-governed sport."[56]

After completing six of the scheduled ten rounds, the "demonstration" was ruled as "no decision" per prior agreement.[57] The headlining boxers Jimmy Gardner and [Johnny] Jack O'Keefe were arrested on a warrant issued by the district attorney's office on the charge of violating Denver's law against prize fighting. The warrants were requested by Attorney Edwards for the Christian Citizenship Union. The two boxers appeared before Justice of the Peace C. J. Gavin and each paid $200 bond to appear the next morning before the judge.[58] "We will take the case through the courts, if necessary, and get a final decision," said Burt Davis, representing the boxers. "It is our claim that the affair was a sparring contest and therefore within the law." Officers of the Christian Citizenship Union said their representatives claimed the bout was "nothing more or less than a prizefight," citing the referee's decision in the sixth round when O'Keefe was "all but out" as assurance that the exhibition was essentially a prizefight.[59] The outcome of the case was not found in the Denver press. Judge Bliss passed away the following year.[60]

The newly elected president of the 1911 Denver Press Club, James R. Noland; and Harry Lee Wilbur, chairman of the entertainment committee; sent invitations for a "rabbit egg" hunt on Easter Sunday in Cheeseman Park for the children of press-club members. The invitations included pictures of bunnies and verses about the rabbits and egg hunt.[61]

While the Denver Press Club children were searching for Easter eggs, the men of the press club continued to explore the future. In 1911, people were aware that Orville and Wilbur Wright's machine flew along the Rio Grande carrying war dispatches for the first time in North America. The Denver Press Club and E. J. Carlin of the Wright Bros' corporation were in the midst of negotiations to establish an airplane factory to build biplanes, monoplanes, engines and supplies, and eventually, establish an aviation training school in Denver. Mr. Carlin's company represented seven types of airplanes and a racing automobile that competed with a Blériot monoplane.

Carlin and the Denver Press Club proposed a plan for a three-day meet that would include cross-country flights and attempt to set new altitude records. In addition to a cast of international aeronautical celebrities, Carlin promised a contest between the flying machine and the automobile with the airplane's propellers "so close to the auto that it takes a man of wonderful courage to keep his hands steady at the wheel."[62] The cost was $6,000 per day for the three-day meet. Within three days of the negotiating session, the contract was signed, and the flight troop was in Denver preparing for the show.

As the *Denver Post* reported: "By far the greatest and most spectacular aviation meet that Denver has ever had a chance to see is to be held at Overland Park Friday, Saturday, and Sunday of this week, under the management of the Denver Press Club. By putting up a large bonus, the press club, through the active efforts of its president, James R. Noland, today concluded arrangements with the world renowned Moisant International Aviators, incorporated, and the famous flyers who have excelled all others in the world in the accomplishment of unparalleled feats in aviation are all here on the ground, and with their corps of thirty employees are perfecting every detail for the opening of the splendid exhibitions on Friday."[63]

Instead of the normal admission price of $1.00 to $1.50, the Denver Press Club insisted the price of general admission be 25-cents so that even low-wage, working families could attend. If the exhibition was canceled on one of the three days, the ticket-holder could attend any of the other days or get a refund at a designated bank.[64] After two days of scheduled events, only one ten-minute flight was airborne, and the thousands of people in attendance failed to accept grounding the airplanes due to weather. "It's cold feet that's the matter with 'em—not the wind!" cried one man in the grandstand. Others shouted "Rotten!" with a voice of disgust as they walked out of the park. On the night before the last performance date, the Moisant aviators and their manager quickly left the city to set up for another "meet" in Newton, Kansas.[65]

The Denver newspapermen prepared for another race of a political kind.

New Jersey Governor Woodrow Wilson was circulating through the country to advance an exploratory national campaign of issues. His Colorado itinerary included a program on "Labor" during his stopover in Pueblo, Colorado; "The Initiative Referendum and Recall" in Colorado Springs; and "Trusts and the Tariff" for his final stop in Denver. President Roosevelt's previous bully-good endorsement of the young state and the hospitality of the Denver Press Club whetted the attention of the governor. The press club quickly rose to the prospects of entertaining another prominent political figure and proposed a welcoming banquet but debated the most hospitable way of welcoming the governor.

Recognizing Governor Wilson as an educated man of letters and a learned Princeton professor of ancient Greek, someone within the Denver Press Club suggested that their invitation to the governor be written in Greek. A Colorado Springs newspaper recognized the danger of undertaking such a daunting task: "The Denver Press Club, with a reputation for originality to sustain, conceived the idea of putting a request for the honor of Governor Wilson's presence at a reception, tendered him tonight, in that language, which made the 'Anabasis' a hard and rocky road for its members in the days of their boyhood. None of the members would attempt the translation, and the occupant of the chair of ancient languages at a local institution was appealed to. 'Translate this into Greek? Why certainly. Delights,' he told the committee that waited on him. 'To whom is this to go? Oh, Governor Wilson? That changes the aspect of the situation. Governor Wilson, you know, is one of the greatest authorities on Greek in the country. Bless my soul, if he should detect some slight error, I should never get over the humiliation. You will understand my refusal, won't you gentlemen. Good-day.'"

Several professors of the Greek language arts were solicited to assist in the ancient script: "To requests from the Denver Press Club to indite [sic] a short epistle to the New Jersey executive and former Princtown [sic] professor couched in phrases with which Demosthenes was wont to toy," wrote the *Colorado Springs Gazette*, "these erudite gentlemen have returned the polished and rhetorically correct equivalent of 'Nay, nay, Pauline.'" [A popular song title at the turn of the previous century.]

An anonymous press-club scribe drafted the invitation to Governor Wilson "in 'newspaper' English."[66]

Editors from newspapers throughout Colorado were invited to make the Kittredge Building rooms of the Denver Press Club their home, especially when the club became a magnet for national politicians and entertainment celebrities. "The club is noted throughout the country for its hospitality," reported the *Denver Post*, "and it is one of the strongest organizations of its kind in the United States." Wilson's first visit to the Denver Press Club was May 8, 1911; his second on October 13, 1912; and a third in 1915. The *World* newspaper claimed Wilson also visited in 1919.[67]

Wilson's first welcoming party was more raucous than dignified. After a welcoming dinner, the libations must have certainly flooded the attendees. "A revel of frenzied enthusiasm swept over 800 men at El Jebel temple last evening,[68] reported *The Denver Times* on May 9, 1911. "Eight hundred men, half of whom were college grads, mounted their chairs, yelled, shrieked and pummeled the tables with their fists when an eminent political reformer, a noted educator and a probable presidential nominee arose to address the assembly. . .. Twelve college alumni delegations kept the great hall in a din of college songs and cheers that reverberated and echoed for blocks around. It was a veritable stampede of sentiment toward the achievement of a courageous figure, who, as if unconscious of the wave of hilarity he had created, sat facing them, reposed and implacable."

President Woodrow Wilson sits among the members
of the Denver Press Club on September 25, 1919.

Courtesy of the Denver Public Library, the Harry M.
Rhoads Photograph Collection, Call #RMN-043-7100

Included in the governor's more dignified 1912 Denver schedule was a ten-minute visit with the Denver Press Club in the Kittredge Building.[69] They overflowed the confines of the club rooms, forcing some of the party to sit in a circle on the floor around the governor. "The newspaper boys were alternating their stories with various liquids, carefully handing the governor each time a lemonade, a white soda or something else 'soft.'" The indoor campfire stories became better, and Governor Wilson and his hosts became friendlier and more relaxed. By the third or fourth round, the guest of honor noticed he was the only one who was being serviced non-alcoholic beverages while his hosts were served adult beverages. Finally, with a mischievous grin, Governor Wilson chastised his hosts; "By birth, I am an American, by paternal parentage I am Irish, but by thirst I am Scotch."[70] The assembled newspapermen let out a collective whoop and a fresh round of full-strength drinks, including the club's best scotch whiskey, accommodated the governor's thirst.

Governor Wilson claimed his appearance was not particularly tied to the upcoming presidential elections, but it was becoming clear that Governor Wilson was interested in becoming President Wilson. "I want to say that I have a feeling that might be described as a yearning," the candidate explained while addressing a dozen Denver Press Club members, "yearning because I realize the responsibility that rests one to make good if elected president."

When the governor finally got to the Albany Hotel for a dinner in his honor, the main course included trout that was caught during a recent Denver Press Club fishing trip on the Gunnison River. *The World* published a comment that when the press club gave a dinner in Woodrow Wilson's honor, the members and the governor would retire to the club for an exhibition of gubernatorial billiard playing that included fancy trick shots that would have been the envy of professional pool sharks.[71]

On December 14, 1913, President Woodrow Wilson was elected to become the third honorary member of the Denver Press Club, but it took an additional five years before the card could be presented to him. The roots of the press club were distinctively a newspaper writers' organization and even an honorary membership required the recipient be prominent with a newspaper or literary background. The Denver Press Club cheekily suggested the upcoming Brand-Iron Club dinner on January 19 would be a nice way to recognize the western stock-show festivities that were being developed.[72] The press club began refining a solid gold membership card from the Colorado mines to be engraved by Jos. I. Schwartz, a local jeweler.[73]

In 1915, the Denver Press Club encouraged the now-President Woodrow Wilson to be a guest of the newspapermen. Congressman Keating, the former president of the press club who began the club's golden age in 1905, conveyed the invitation personally to the president.[74] The president did accept the invitation on his way to the Pan Pacific International Exposition in San Francisco.[75] The club members noticed that Woodrow Wilson always called at the Denver Press Club before filling any other engagements.[76]

Sports returned to the Denver Press Club's social calendar. The May 27, 1911, opening of the Tuileries Track; a one-third-mile, wooden, circular motorcycle track at Lakeside's White City, built at a forty-seven-degree angle. Press-Club President James R. Noland opened the outdoor sporting venue by firing the opening gun to start the first race.[77] Special arrangements were made for the members of the press club to be in attendance. The Lakeside Motordrome was described by the press as a more-civilized track. Like the rest of the amusement park, it was illuminated with electric-arc lamps "making for whimsical nights of entertainment and competition."[78]

General Manager Frank Burt, and the officers and directors of the Lakeside Realty and Amusement Company, invited over 200 members of the Fourth Estate and their families to a special performance of "In the Bishop's Carriage" starring Miss Beulah Pointer in the Casino Theater at the White City.[79] During the first intermission, James R. Noland of the press club presented Miss Pointer with beautiful floral gifts, from both the Denver Press Club and park management. "At the conclusion of the play," the *Denver Post* reported, "the guests were entertained by the management with a luncheon spread on the balcony of the theater and the various concessions were given over to the amusement-seeking crowd, who almost forgot to go home."[80]

The enlarged rooms on the second floor of the Kittredge Building [16th and Glenarm Place] provided adequate space for the Denver Press Club to discuss the upcoming trip to a fishing camp. Once again, the Women's Writers' Club was invited to join the boys along the Gunnison River, five miles north of the town of Gunnison on Colorado's Western Slope. The Henry and Angie Crooks Ranch operated along the Gunnison River where the pressmen found excellent trout fishing. The only way of accessing the camp was by traveling the Denver & Rio Grande standard gauge line to Salida and then the narrow gauge west to Gunnison.

There was sufficient room for twenty people to be at the camp with tents pitched in "a quiet grove, shady and inviting; and wings, hammocks, and other similar devices will make the place as comfortable as is possible."[81] A central dining hall was erected for evenings filled with dancing and parties. A piano was added to the list of camp equipment along with quoits, croquet, archery and target-shooting paraphernalia. "Then, too, there is a small stream right at hand that is filled with small trout easily caught by even a child," President Noland's form-letter message to the members noted. "And there is a dairy a quarter of a mile from the camp site where fresh milk, cream and butter may be had at any time."[82] Members could receive lodge and boarding for $1 per day for adults, and half-price for children between five and twelve, and twenty-five cents for children between one-and-five. No reference was made about accommodating teenagers, even back in 1911.

Credit and identifications cards were issued by club-member Charles Roehrig and only covered camp expenses. Each camper was required to provide their own blankets, sheets, and pillows that could be carried on the train or checked-through as additional baggage. As a special precaution, a "secret invitation committee" was created to pass on names of non-members of the club who may try to make reservations for the press club's permanent fishing camp. Members were welcomed to bring guests, but they would have to request their credit and identification card.

"Muffled music of many phantom violinists lulls the campers to sleep nightly," explained James R. Noland, club president. "Our camp is on a beautiful island that is studded with great shade trees set in an undergrowth of wild roses. The Gunnison tears along not more than ten feet from our assembly hall. Two smaller streams are on the other two sides of our V-shaped islet. According to an Indian legend . . . a party of prospectors in the days of very long ago were drowned while fording the river at a point where the bridge now stands, a mile above the camp. Three of the gold seekers were violinists and carried their instruments with them. The subdued, dreamy, soul music was noted every night thereafter by the Indians who were encamped on what is now known as the Press Club Island. 'Talk about taking dope of one kind and another for sleeplessness,' says Marshal Jennings, 'why that music will lull the most nervous person in the world to sleep in five minutes. It's the most wonderful thing I have ever heard.'"[83]

Gunnison Marshal Jack Jennings, guest of the Denver Press Club fishing camp, explained that Gunnison was freed of "gun-toters." He explained that border law prevailed, and shootings were common occurrences; since prohibiting gun fights in his western town, peace has returned to the Western Slope. [Arizona and New Mexico had yet to be admitted to the United States in 1911. They became the 47th and 48th states the following year. Gunnison was just 150 miles north of the border.] When asked for an explanation, the marshal replied, "I don't allow anybody in the city of Gunnison to pack a revolver. I have played no favorites in this respect, and if application is made to the city authorities by anyone for permission to carry firearms, it is referred to me. . . .. If no guns are carried about the streets of Gunnison, there will be no shooting scrapes in Gunnison."[84]

The fishing camp was supposed to be a permanent addition to the Denver Press Club's real-estate holdings. Along with the initial outing, a substantial unnamed prize was to be awarded to the person who left the camp with the best "fish story." If anyone could tell a whopper of a fish tale, Wolfe Londoner was the most capable.[85]

"It was like this," Mr. Londoner's tale began on a day that just happened to fall on his birthday. "The boys had arranged to entertain a number of friends from Gunnison and the adjoining ranches with a sort of Fourth of July celebration, to end with a display of fireworks that night. Well, believe me, we had the celebration all right enough—also the fireworks. And it was the latter that frightened the trout to death and gave us an abundance for a big fish fry. You see, the camp is in a beautiful spot along the Gunnison River on Cottonhurst, the ranch of Mr. and Mrs. Henry S. Crooks, five miles north of Gunnison. The Press Club boys of Denver, with their usual system of doing things right, erected a big inclosed [sic] pavilion as the central loafing or lounging place. This building is right on the banks of the river, and it was there we congregated for the fire-works. Well! The bombardment lasted thirty minutes and included skyrockets, roman candles, bombs, and all that sort of plowed over the river, the moon came out things. And just as the last rocket exploded we saw that the water was sort of iridescent with floating objects. Observing closely, we saw that the unusual rainbow color effects were caused by countless numbers of mountain trout. The rest was easy."[86]

Investigative journalists discovered a "scandal" among the fishing newspapermen in Gunnison. The Denver & Rio Grande Railroad claimed it billed a box of cornfed trout. "The [Denver Press] club went for an outing along the Gunnison River," according to the D&RG. "It happened that a farmer on the bank was in the habit of scattering corn near the river for his chickens. But the chickens lost out on their rations because the trout climbed on the bank and carried off the greater part of the grain. The members of the club gathered in the well-fed fish and shipped them to their friends in Denver."[87]

The *Oregonian* continued the story, "The farmer put in a coarse-screen wire netting along the river bank. This kept out the larger trout, but the latter, growing wise, sent in the smaller fish through the netting and they brought out the corn, with the result that the farmer was obliged to change his screen to a very fine mesh." As a result, the supply of cornfed-trout was exhausted before the season was half over. The Honorable James W. Kelley of the Denver Press Club and other legal representatives of the Press Club were exploring the constitutional right of the farmer to erect a close-mesh screen along the waterfront and it is to be hoped that this question will be adjudicated in favor of the club."[88]

The fishing camp was only half of the new relationship with the Gunnison Valley; a challenge was issued, and a semi-pro baseball game was held at Broadway Park between the towns of Gunnison and Salida. The Denver Press Club sponsored the event and sold over 3,000 tickets in Denver alone, and helped arrange special trains to bring additional baseball fans from nearby towns. "Gunnison and Salida backers are still placing many wagers on the result of the game," reported the *Denver Post*, "and a victory for either team will be the means of several thousands of dollars changing hands." On the record, the Denver Press Club put up a $500 purse sweetened with a side bet of $1,000 between the fans of Salida and Gunnison.[89]

Ingenuity wasn't restricted to the creative pens of press-club members that year. Two engineering students at the University of Colorado indirectly got into the newspaper business in 1911. John Cummings McBride of Winnipeg, Canada and Thomas A. Blair of Montrose perfected a newspaper vending box that dispensed a newspaper as fast as a nickel was dropped into the slot. Their 10x12x18-inch dispensers held twenty-five newspapers. McBride was a newspaper agent in Boulder and envisioned placing the machines in train depots, street corners, public spaces, and waiting rooms. "The paper will be dry in wet weather and as crisp as if it had just come from the press,"[90] explained *The Denver Times*.

The 1911 Annual Denver Press Club picnic-basket event at a grove near Fort Collins included the club members and their families,[91] and the ladies of the Writers' Club of Denver. The early September event provided an opportunity for the newspapermen and women to be guests of R. S. Ruble,[92] assistant general passenger agent for the Union Pacific railroad and participate in the formal opening of a new rail line to Fort Collins while aboard a special train provided by the railroad.[93]

Lindenmeier Lake's manager, William Lindenmeier, provided the location for games, bathing, boating, racing and other amusements for most of the day. The two-hundred Denver guests were met by Mayor Jesse Harris of Fort Collins and many county officials. Unfortunately, a brief drizzle prevented the scheduled open-top automobile ride throughout the city in the afternoon.[94] The party was quick to adapt to the weather and was directed to the dance hall where dancing ruled the afternoon. Jesse Harris O'Brian, with his bagpipe and Scotch uniform furnished by Mayor Harris, played for several hours to entertain the visitors.[95]

*****

Several U. S. presidents came from journalistic backgrounds, the once-preferred source of a broad knowledge of many things that a president may need to understand. After the successful relationship with President Teddy Roosevelt, the Denver Press Club was excited to learn another president with printers' ink in his veins was coming to Denver.

When William H. Taft accepted the Denver Chamber of Commerce's invitation to Denver, Lucian Wheeler of the government secret service met with a special committee of the Chamber of Commerce, and President James Noland and Secretary John O'Brian of the Denver Press Club. A minute-by-minute schedule of engagements for the nation's chief executive's seventeen-hour stay in Denver was negotiated. The detailed itinerary was scrapped when eight-inches of rain fell over northeastern Kansas and eastern Nebraska[96] creating floods and washouts along the president's route. The deluge delayed President Taft's arrival from Sedalia, Missouri for two hours; last minute revisions throughout the president's schedule became a necessity.[97]

The Chamber of Commerce was responsible for taking care of the president and his staff; the press club was responsible for entertaining the correspondents traveling with the president on the special train. For most of the day, the Denver press succeeded in "kidnapping" the newspapermen who were following the president, providing them only with enough time to satisfy their bosses back east with an occasional dispatch from Denver. Among the best-known newspapermen of a day were Robert T. Small and Robert Dougan, Washington correspondents for the Associated Press. "Bobby Small also carries a camera of the lightning-action sort," reported *The Denver Times*, "and furnishes pictures of the President's tour to illustrated magazines."[98] Other reporters were E. R. Sartwell of United Press, Sevellon Brown of the Washington bureau of the *New York Sun* Press Association, Royal Kent Fuller of the *New York Herald*, George G. Hill of the *New York Tribune*, Gus J. Karger of the *Cincinnati Times Star*, H. F. Taff who was manager of the Washington office of the Western Union Telegraph Company, and C. E. Colony of the Boston & Albany railroad.

The sixteen members of the Washington press corps were the guests of Charles McAllister Wilcox, treasurer of the Denver Press Club and manager of the Daniels & Fisher department stores, at a luncheon in the Blue Room on the fourteenth floor of the Fisher Tower in Denver. The room was decorated in blue and white, with white chrysanthemums and American Beauty roses on the tables that were arranged so that diners could gaze upon the city and mountains.[99]

While the president was being dined at the Denver Country Club and in the home of Crawford Hill at Tenth and Sherman Streets,[100] the press corps was entertained at the Albany Hotel and The Brown Palace.[101] Crawford Hill was the son of the founder of Colorado's smelting industry; his mother was one of the founders of the Young Women's Christian Association of America.

Editorial cartoonist acknowledged President William Taft's girth and his hectic Denver schedule that included Honorary Membership in the Denver Press Club.

Courtesy of the author

After a reception at the Denver Country Club and a presentation to the Public Lands convention at the Auditorium, President Taft met with members of the Denver Press Club at their rooms in the Kittredge Building for twenty minutes before heading to The Brown Palace Hotel to meet with a delegation of prominent Republicans and businessmen.[102] The brief meeting with the press club at 2:30 p.m. was informal, but confined exclusively to the members of the club, as specifically requested by the U.S. president and the secret-service men. Denver Press Club President James R. Noland was scheduled to present President Taft with a solid gold card, acknowledging he was inducted into the Denver Press Club as the second Honorary Member on October 3, 1911. (Another newspaper stated that former club president and Senator John Irby made the presentation). The value of the card, at that time, was $100 in nearly virgin gold. "It is expected that Mr. Taft will speak about ten minutes at the Press Club," reported the *Rocky Mountain News*, "but what he may have to say will not be published to the outside world."[103] The next day, the newspaper rescinded its expectation of secrecy and published the president's acceptance speech made at the press club. The president chose to introduce himself to the newspapermen with a little ditty — "Father calls me William, Sister calls me Will, Mother calls me Willie, But you fellers call me Bill."[104]

Mr. Chairman, Mr. Speaker and Gentlemen of the Press Club.

I am very much honored by being made an honorary member of your club, and I am more honored even by the very kindly words with which you accompany the communication. I cannot mistake the soft tones of a man who comes from south of the Mason and Dixon line, nor the expression of good fellowship that finds equal source in that part of our country.

I am glad to be a member of the Press Club because I was once a newspaperman myself. I have kept that as confidential as circumstances required. But I was a reporter on the *Cincinnati Times* and again on the *Cincinnati Commercial*, and did what they called the law work of those papers, and stood about the courthouse, and, as a budding lawyer, gathered inspiration, such as I could get, from the decisions of the local courts and the methods of trial pursued by successful jury lawyers. . .

I am glad to be in Denver, and I want to congratulate the Denver Press Club on having such a pure air to breathe, which I doubt not elevates the tone of the press. I infer from your pictorial pages that you have got the artistic here, high up in the mountains from the presence of the mountains. I am not able to congratulate you always on your subjects, but I have observed that in the delineation of your president, you prefer the curve of beauty to any rigid straight lines.

I am on a long trip, and I am happy to bring into the Press club a collection of newspapermen who are my associates in the trip, and who accompany me for differing reasons, but between them all I have no doubt that the public will ascertain just what does occur to me, and from their united judgment thrown together, as Jonathan Bourne [Jr.] [U.S. Senator, Oregon, 1903-1913] throws together the citizens in order to get a composite citizen you may get a composite result that will give the exact fact.

It is, of course, pleasant to have associated with you members of the press in whom you have confidence. The experience that I have had in Washington with the Washington correspondents has been such as to give me a very warm circle of acquaintances among the correspondents — men in whom I have great confidence— men whose duty it is to criticize the administration, some of them, whenever occasion arises, but men who do it with that reluctance that ensures a judicial poise in what they do.

Of course, when one goes into public life one expects to be criticized, and he cannot complain, either of unfairness or misstatement, because there is so much to be stated that error must creep in, but, on the whole, the net result, after all—if you give the people and the press time, six months or a year—finally oozes out, and I think the result is one that historians and those who are in favor of substantial justice cannot complain of. I am sure that is the result in Denver among the press and elsewhere. Every once in a while, your fist doubles, and you would like to hit somebody, but as you are in a position where you can not gratify that sentiment, and therefore, are entirely safe; you do not do it—you wait six months or a year, as we propose to in our peace treaties, and then the thing is forgotten, and has made no mark, and I hope has left no scar.

My friends of the Denver Press Club, I thank you for giving me an opportunity to meet you, for including me in your membership, second to Colonel Roosevelt whom I have followed for years, and hope to continue to follow, and an association with whom I shall always deem a very high honor.[105]

President Taft's appearance in Denver marked the innovation of a motorcycle squad comprised of six patrolmen, two of whom would ride ahead of the presidential carriage, two on either side of the vehicle, and two trailing the car. This formation of protection remained with the president until he departed the city.[106]

The end of the year 1911 brought a royal celebration of a different type. Miss Alberta Smith of Montrose was in Denver leading the popularity contest for queen of the apple domain. The winner was crowned the Apple Queen in a ceremony at the Auditorium Theater followed by a dance provided by the Denver Press Club.[107] The competition became acrimonious as it became apparent that votes were being bought by handing out free apples to prospective voters. "The rivalry between the young women has affected their followers," reported the *Rocky Mountain News*, "and the accusation was made that apples were being given away for a coupon; that one queen's follower was passing cards at the show and personally soliciting votes for his girl; still, another declaration was that there were 'knockers' [a person who continually finds fault] out on two or three of the girls."[108]

To close out the year, Mrs. J. P. Wright of the Detention House on 28th Avenue provided fifteen children from the institution, with a festive Christmas holiday. They were joined by children from the Denver Press Club to fill the club rooms in the Kittredge Building with 50-to-75 children. Santa was on hand as the name of each child was read and a trail of wide-eyes and cherubic rosy cheeks stepped forward to receive his or her present from the large bearded man in the red suit.[109]

The new year began on a benevolent note. In January 1912, Thomas K. Mackall, a 36-year-old sporting editor of the *Denver Republican* succumbed to a thirteen-month illness. The former board member of the Denver Press Club was a newspaperman for thirteen years, beginning with four years on the *Democrat* in Lorain, Ohio. He then advanced to the *Cleveland Leader* in Ohio until 1907 when he moved to the Cleveland office of the Associated Press. For the benefit of his health, he moved to Denver to work for a short time with the Associated Press and as the sporting editor of the *Republican*. He left a wife and three small children.[110]

To help the widow's family, the Denver Press Club brought James Mature who defended his title as the champion three-cushion billiard player of Colorado against Arthur Endicott in an exciting tournament at the Kenmore Hotel. Managers Pop Kline and Harry Wolf of the Kenmore turned the considerable proceeds over to the family of Thomas K. Mackall.[111]

The Denver Press Club recognized the potential partnership that could be established between the public schools and the working press. Mrs. Mary C. C. Bradford, county superintendent of schools; W. K. McAllister, general agent of the Southern Pacific Railroad Company; and C. E. Hager, secretary of the Denver Press Club served as the jurors to select the winner of the Lincoln Essay Contest. The Syman Brothers Jewelry Co. furnished a gold watch for the boy and a diamond ring for the girl who wrote the best 500-word essay about the life work and character of Abraham Lincoln.[112] Within two weeks, hundreds of essays flowed into the offices of the *Denver Post*.[113] Winners were Helen Coontz, a high-school student in Fort Morgan; and Elmer Rudolph Wall, a high-school pupil from Ouray.[114]

The club's annual Easter-egg hunt continued in 1912 on the grounds of Elitch's Gardens. Judge Gavin served as master of ceremonies, herding the children through the grounds of the amusement park.[115]

For the adults, pugilists Howard Baker and Jimmy Gardner arrived to box at the stock yards in Denver on 26 April under the auspices of the Denver Press Club,[116] apparently without fear of arrest as occurred the previous year.

Never a group to pass up a publicity gimmick, the Denver Press Club welcomed Willie Ritchie, lightweight champion of the world to meet Alphonse P. Ardourel, champion of the Colorado legislature, for a boxing exhibition in the club rooms in the Kittredge Building. Promoting

Representative Ardourel as a fight promoter would do, the *Rocky Mountain News* explained "Ardourel brings to the contest brawn, brains and a little experience in the ring. He is a member of the house of representatives from Boulder County, and a champion of progressivism in the Nineteenth General Assembly. He is short, solid, quick as a cat, clean of habit. He never smokes nor takes a drink."[117] When asked if his wife approved of his exhibition fight against the lightweight champion of the world, Ardourel said he could not train because if his wife found out about his upcoming fight, "she would have planted a knockout upon his pugilistic ambitions,"[118] the *Rocky Mountain News* reported.

The Colorado & Southern Railway serviced the foothills town of Morrison, Colorado. A special train was put on the route to accommodate one of the Denver Press Club excursions into the Red Rocks area.

Library of Commerce: Chamberlain, W. G., photographer. Morrison, Colorado, ca. 1878; https://www.loc.gov/item/94595139/

In late July (1912) approximately 200 press club picnickers boarded a special train to the town of Morrison aboard the Colorado & Southern Railway. General Manager James Randolph Walker took charge of transporting the group up the incline railway to the top of Mt. Morrison. After lunch, the party was entertained by the 24th Recruiting Company.

The military band from Fort Logan was provided by Lieutenants W. F. Wheatley and Robert Sterrett and performed in the natural auditorium of Red Rocks Park.[119]

The world of newsmen in the early 1900s wasn't all happiness, social excursions, and exciting sports and entertainment. When the camaraderie and free-flowing libations from the bar ceased to mask the pain, newspapermen sometimes tapped into the drug markets used by the ladies of Denver's brothels for laudanum and other pain-numbing drugs. But even such consequential addictions sometimes carried an element of gallows humor for the hardened press-club members.

Paris B. "Monty" Montgomery was a meticulous police reporter but prone to bottomless melancholia during his off hours when he would join Bill Collier at the Denver Press Club for libations during which time they would try to induce the other to "climb the wagon" [of sobriety]. Bill Perkin, author of *The First Hundred Years: An Informal History of Denver and the Rocky Mountain News* explained that "Monty" normally wasn't a jovial type of drinker. "Alcohol plunged him deeper into his despair, and he had frequently threatened and several times attempted suicide."[120] When Collier received a phone call from an undertaking parlor a block from City Hall, it wasn't a big surprise. "Prepare yourself for a shock, Bill. Poor Monty has been run down and killed by a runaway. Better come over right away."

Collier was at Johnny Gahan's saloon on Fourteenth Street and ran to the mortuary. The attendant led him past several sheet-draped corpses to the slab at the end of the room. The sheet was drawn back to reveal his naked friend, body amply dusted with talcum powder. Collier bent over the body and wept for their friendship. "It's all my fault," he blathered, "It couldn't have happened if he'd been sober, and I could have made him quit drinking, but I didn't. I feel like a murderer." As the salty tears fell on the body, the corpse couldn't restrain a giggle.

Realizing the ruse, Collier snatched a wooden mallet that was used as a door stop and pursued the resurrected Monty around the room, out into the alley, up 16th Street to Curtis where the crowds of theater-goers were leaving the Tabor Opera House. The chalk-white, stark-naked, tubby little Montgomery ran screaming down 16th street just a few steps ahead of his irate friend.[121] A police officer disarmed Collier and draped his overcoat over the exposed, shivering, cadaverous prankster.

Collier was quick to provide revenge. Under the guise of their friendship, he retrieved Monty's clothing from the coroner while the instigator was cooling his heels in jail and threw them into the nearby Cherry Creek. Other newspapermen procured Monty's other clothing from his room and left him with nothing. Once the whole incident was finished, Monty's only comment was "A mallet in an undertaking shop! What do they use it for? I don't get it. I just don't get it."[122]

A few months later, the twenty-eight-year-old Montgomery gloomily watched a poker game where Colonel Gideon B. McFall was dealing and several paychecks of fellow journalists (including Gene Fowler) were on the table. Monty finally rose and announced that he was "tired on the inside" and sat down on a chair under the polar-bear trophy on the wall. Cecil R. Conner's version of the story described Paris "Monty" Montgomery sitting next to the night manager who was pumping out some tearful tunes on a player-piano. Here the two versions of the story come together. Without anyone noticing, Monty opened a small packet and swallowed the contents and immediately dropped dead. In the original version of the story, Denver Press Club night manager Jimmy Wong came around to refresh drinks and cried out, "Monty got blue face!" With nary a moment to mourn the passing of their friend, Colonel McFall suggested the chips on the table be swept up for a funeral fund.[123]

"The usually impassive Oriental was greatly impressed by the potency of potassium cyanide," continued Cecil Conner. Later in the club history, another club member used concentrated lye as a means to end life's vicissitudes, according to Conner. The only comment from one of his fellow writers was "Why did he use *that* stuff?"[124]

Other press-club deaths came more naturally, but not any easier to accept. To generations of newspapermen, the father of the Denver Press Club was Wolfe Londoner. For decades, the little, rotund figure of the affable town grocer was seen at nearly all press club excursions and other events. For forty years, he excelled at writing advertisements for his grocery-store business to help subsidize Denver newspapers. As John E. Leet of *The Denver Times* reported, "Strictly speaking, he is not a newspaperman, but is a wealthy grocer. But he has contributed miles of ideas anonymously to the papers, is commissary of all junketing trips, is liked by all journalists and is, altogether, an indispensable institution. He is a landmark. Before he was old enough to vote he was clerk of Lake County, in California Gulch days. He has been county commissioner and mayor. This last experience soured him on politics. The rascally politicians who counted him in without his knowledge counted him out in the courts when they found that they could not use him to further their corrupt schemes."[125]

Near the end of 1912, the Denver Press Club joined hundreds of other Denver admirers of Wolfe Londoner whose body lay in state during the noon hour at the state capitol. An honor guard of National Guardsmen escorted the casket from the Londoner home to the state capitol and back again where funeral services commenced at 2 o'clock.[126]

*****

Five hundred Coloradoans held a picnic at the Mission Cliff pavilion in San Diego in January 1913. The secretary of the Denver Press Club sent a telegram that was read to the group, offering good wishes for the San Francisco 1915 Pan Pacific International Exposition.[127] Colonel D. C. Collier served as president, director-general, and overall moving spirit of the upcoming international fair. He was originally a Colorado native who kept in touch through the *Denver Post* editions that were forwarded to him in San Diego. The Panama-Pacific International Exposition celebrated the completion of the Panama Canal, celebrated San Francisco's recovery from the devastation caused by the 1906 earthquake and fire; and provided an opportunity to bring international ideas and thinkers together.

After the near-destruction of the city, San Francisco needed the power of the newspapermen to "increase tourism, settlement, and investment, and spur development and cement the Golden State as a trade gateway between Europe and Asia through the newly opened waterway."[128] Likewise, Denver's use of the newspapers helped transform Colorado as a gateway to the West.

Colonel Collier and the Denver Press Club found a common element of community "boosterism" as a means of helping each other—the Denver Press Club could help promote the Pan-Pacific International Exposition and the PPIE could help promote "the last and greatest council of the red men of North America," that occurred at the same time, according to the *Denver Post*.

"I figured from the outset that what would be good for Denver would be good for San Diego in 1915," explained Colonel Collier. "I figured further that the proper thing to do would be for us to boost your Indian pageant in all our advertising matter. And so we have arranged to give the 1915 Indian pageant a liberal mention in all the millions of circulars and other advertising matter, including our letterheads and envelopes, not to mention 5,000 newspapers, from now until our exposition opens."[129] In response, president William R. Collier of the Denver Press Club and other associations joined Buffalo Bill Cody's promise to Colonel Collier: "Our Denver people should reciprocate by giving mention of the San Diego [Francisco] exposition . . . It should be tit-for-tat and even then we could not return even so much as one-half of what you propose to do for us."[130]

The western boosterism was interrupted while Colonel Collier was in Denver to meet with the Chamber of Commerce, real estate exchange, and state legislature. Eight companies of firemen fought for four hours to subdue a stubborn fire that began on the sixth floor of one of Denver's original "skyscrapers," the Kittredge Building at Sixteenth and Glenarm Place. The home of the Denver Press Club was located on the second floor. Newspaper references to the previous homes of the press club indicated the walls of the club were adorned with caricatures and photographs of famous individuals of newspaper fame. Those images have never re-surfaced in the modern years of the press club and may have suffered water damage during the fire and lost from the club's history.

The blaze in the Kittredge Building in 1913 was caused by faulty electrical wiring in the lavatory on the sixth floor, spread through wire conduits between the floors, and rapidly blazed to the four upper stories. Stripping the plaster to get to the fire caused more damage than the actual fire, resulting in $22,000 in repairs. The fire was discovered just before midnight by Denver Press Club members who detected smoke and alerted night watchman Frederick Herron who found the actual fire.

It was fortuitous that the Pioneer Motion Picture Advertising Company of Denver, under the supervision of Denver Director Field Carmichael, was on the scene to film the fire. The Denver Press Club seized the opportunity to use the film footage as the foundation of an educational silent-film photoplay *and* a promotional opportunity to "boost" the upcoming April public ball at the Auditorium. James R. Noland of the *Denver Post* wrote a screenplay that combined the actual fire footage, embellished with a staged rescue, and created an instructional film describing how newspapermen cover a story.

Unannounced at 1:30 in the afternoon, a series of fire gongs, staged for the film crew, sent Denver's hook-and-ladder and hose trucks racing to a three-story structure "fire" on Champa Street between Fourteenth and Fifteenth streets where flames and thick black clouds of smoke were recreated. Downtown Denver's lunch-time crowd surged against the fire lines that were quickly established by a squad of police. An overflow crowd squeezed into the open windows of the houses opposite the burning building. Suddenly the shriek of a "frightened" actress screamed from a third-story window — "My child! Save my child!"[131]

According to the script a pretty brown-eyed girl, selling newspapers on Champa Street, saw a thin curl of smoke emanating from one of the two "old-timer" wooden buildings next to the Gas Company building. She dropped her papers, ran to the nearest fire call-box and broke the glass, dramatically cutting her hands. She then madly ran back into the house where she knew an invalid woman resided on the third floor. The alarm was also transmitted to the newspaper office where the police reporter received the information and raced to the scene just in time to see the torn skirt of the newspaper girl flap against the door jamb as she ran into the burning building. The reporter quickly followed her into the building while the crowd cheered upwind from the billowing clouds of smoke that poured from the building. Soon the reporter, struggling against the eye-stinging smoke, appeared with the pale, limp form of the young newspaper girl in his arms as the crowd renewed their cheers. A fireman, reaching the third floor, found the sick woman and carried her down the ladder. As the *Denver Post* reported, "Although the woman was sick, she was not emaciated, and the fireman showed a remarkable amount of skill and strength when he carried her to safety on the sidewalk."[132]

Few people knew what a motion-picture company looked like. The wooden camera-box with a crank handle and poised on the apex of a tripod, must have looked odd, but the excitement of the fire and rescue distracted people from the man who was cranking away on the box. It was 1913 and Hollywood only became synonymous with the motion picture industry that year, and the Pioneer Motion Picture Company of Denver was on the cutting edge of the industry.

Back at the reenacted and scripted news room when the call came in, "The city editor received the call over the phone," the *Denver Post* reported, "gave the 'tip' in one sentence, terse and dramatic, to the reporters and photographers, who were out of the office in a whirl so vehement as to defy all chance of seeing their faces except in a blur. The office which had been busy with reporters bringing copy to the city editor's desk was changed in an instant to what seemed to be a madhouse, although I could see that there was a system somewhere which kept the rushing, shouting reporters and editors from actually killing each other. Twice I was swept off my feet, and at last found safety on top of some old newspaper files piled up in a corner on a desk."[133]

A rich banker (in the screenplay) learned of the young newspaper girl's heroism and showed great interest in her welfare. The police reporter located the young news seller and took her to the banker. He proceeded to adopt her, providing her with a beautiful home and an enviable position in Denver's social world. In place of newspapers, her collection of German and French dolls with real hair and blue silk dresses complemented the girl's nails that were polished by the city's leading manicurists. In the last reel of the film, the girl is "grown up" and on her way to participate in the Denver Press Club's Twentieth Century Ball where everyone was expected to "rag a little now and then." She appeared with the police reporter "who will shower glances of such dulcet tenderness that it will be easy to detect the 'happiness ever after' which is the true end of every story."[134]

When the film was presented at the Empress Theatre, the audience craned their necks to identify the adult-version of the newspaper heroine who caught the attention of the cinematically heroic police reporter. The camera intentionally framed the dance scenes that prevented the audience from ever knowing the identity of mysterious dancer on the screen in a manner who was portrayed as being at the upcoming Denver Press Club Twentieth Century Ball. What began as news-reel footage, changed to an educational film about newspaper reporting, and ended as a shameless advertisement for the upcoming press club fund-raising ball.

A century later, Colorado film historian Howie Movshovitz enlisted his fellow silent-film enthusiasts to search the Library of Congress and other archives to search for the 1912-1913 film shot on highly combustible nitrate film stock. Like many silent films of the era, the earliest film record of the Denver Press Club deteriorated into history.

Harry Lee Wilber was elected as the 1913 president of the Denver Press Club and proposed reorganizing the club as "a force in all civic affairs." Copies of the "Colorado Creed" were adopted at the club's annual meeting on March 9, 1913 and distributed to newspapers, commercial organizations, members of the legislature and the Citizens' Protective League (an organization formed to combat "Yellow Journalism" in newspapers and magazines). The League was seeking to regulate newspapers and the press club's "Colorado Credo" was an attempt to satisfy the League's concerns while chastising the League's misguided intentions. In the verbiage of the resolution that preceded the Creed, the press club stated,

> Whereas, a recently formed organization known as the Citizens' Protective League is pretending to censor the morals of the Denver newspapers, and in so doing is reflecting on the character, integrity and work of the editorial and reportorial staffs of the various Denver newspapers; and
>
> Whereas, some of the leading members of the so-called Citizens' Protective League are persons who have succeeded in keeping out of the newspapers stories of a discreditable nature by which they themselves might have been held up to public scorn; and,
>
> Whereas, the so-called Citizens' Protective League has mistakenly caused to be circulated the false statement that Denver is losing many good citizens because of its newspapers; and,
>
> Whereas, the Denver Press Club always has stood and does now stand for that which is clean, that which is right, that which is ethical and that which is honorable; and,
>
> Whereas, the Denver Press Club, from its birth, has sought only to destroy the germs of wrong and to plant seeds of right thinking and right living; therefore, now, be it
>
> Resolved, that, in protesting against the acts of any organization that casts discredit on the newspaper profession, and in protesting against the acts of any organization that pretends to attempt to exercise control over another man's business, the Denver Press Club adopts and calls upon other optimistic organizations to adopt the Colorado Creed.[135]

Denver readers, tired of the sensationalized Yellow Journalism, called for a stop to the muckraking press stories that infiltrated many newspapers, including those throughout Colorado.

The Denver Times, February 1, 1913

COLORADO CREDO[136]

We believe in the commonwealth of Colorado and the municipality of every city and town within its borders.

We believe in the land of Colorado, whence spring the world-famed products of the farm and whence comes the metal wealth that moves the marts of the universe.

We believe in the water of Colorado that, flowing from the virgin snows of the majestic crest of the continent, cools the parched lips of man and beast and gives new life to the thirsting plain.

We believe in the air of Colorado that rejuvenates the old, keeps the young youthful and drives away scourge and plague.

We believe in the commercial interests of Colorado and the men who guide and control them, each in his own sphere, and we believe it is our duty to aid and foster them, to consider each man an expert in his own field, to encourage industry, to criticize honesty, to crush that which is dishonest and unfair.

We believe in the laws of Colorado and will endeavor to uphold them and increase respect for them and try to drive into outer darkness any who seek to evade or defy those laws.

We believe in the manhood of Colorado and we will try to stamp out cowardice and unmanliness and anything that tends to bring disgrace on the commonwealth, in order that all good impulses may be quickened, that the sacred ideals of the state may be held in reverence and that we may stand forth among all these United States now and forevermore as Colorado the Clean.

For the first time, not every Colorado newspaper agreed with the press club's stand. *The Denver Times* devoted several editorial pages and display-advertisement space to the cause of the Citizens' Protective League. A *Colorado Springs Gazette* editorial noted the Denver newspapers "have kept the capital city in a turmoil for years with their petty rivalries, their wholesale vilifications, and the grafting and black-mailing for which at least one of their number is notorious."[137] The *Gazette* suggested that opposition to the Citizens' Protective League would benefit neither Colorado's capitol city nor its newspapers; the Colorado Springs newspaper claiming their Denver counterparts were responsible for already giving Colorado a bad reputation abroad. "They magnify every crime and scandal, every political upheaval, every accident, every unpleasant and undesirable thing of all kinds, and spread it before the world in a fashion calculated to make outsiders believe that Colorado is the very fountainhead of every conceivable sort of trouble."[138]

Nevertheless, the Colorado Credo was introduced into the minutes of the Colorado State Senate. Senator Hayden moved it be read a second time, but the request was rebuked by Lieutenant Governor Fitzgarrald who stated "The motion is out of order. It is bad enough to read it the first time."[139]

Club president Harry Lee Wilbur was still in his first month of leadership of the press club when another scandal struck the newspapermen organization. The Twentieth Century Ball, a fund-raising event under the auspices of the Denver Press Club, proposed to include demonstrations of popular dances that were "ragging" the East-Coast rag-time dance floors in 1913. This included the sinfully controversial "tango" and the "bunny hug," a dance that protectors of public decency likened to the mating of rabbits.

Mrs. Crawford Hill, acknowledged leader of Denver's most exclusive "Sacred 36" social set, and several other "stars of society" volunteered to be "patronesses" for the press club ball. "I should just love to officiate as patroness," explained Mrs. Hill with a gay little laugh. "Dancing is the most innocent amusement in the world. Vulgarity dwells only in the mind of a perverted dancer, and even the so-called 'rag' depends for its vulgarity on the dancers. Dancing has expressed joy, youth, and happiness since the world began. All the emotions of the race, time-old and ever new have found expression therein, and it is only the narrow-minded individual who prates of its vulgarity."[140]

CHIEF O'NEILL O. K.S BUNNY HUG
FOR PRESS CLUB BALL TUESDAY

Gail Wallack and Miss May Kurtz demonstrating the Bunny Hug, as it will be danced at the Denver Press Club ball, before Chief of Police O'Neill. The chief and Officer Picard (at the left) carefully watched the dance.

Courtesy of the *Denver Post*

Sermons and official orders throughout the country were attempting to regulate or suppress the modern rag dances. To pave the way for the "bunny hug," the "grizzly bear," and other animal dances, the Denver Press Club arranged for a committee headed by Mayor Arnold, Chief-of-Police O'Neill, and Thomas Anneal to pre-approve the dance steps for the press club ball on April 8. Other members of the committee included members of the recently appointed commission on vice: Miss Josephine Roach (official censor of dance halls), various representatives of "private societies devoted to the oral welfare of the community," several state officials, and Governor Elias M. Ammons.[141]

*****

As President Wilson's personal representative to the coal mine disputes, Secretary William B. Wilson of the Department of Labor arrived in late-1913. Secretary Wilson was scheduled to address the Economics students at the University of Colorado in Boulder, but also found time to spend relaxing with the Denver Press Club members at the Kittredge Building.[142] A month later, President Woodrow Wilson arrived and returned and found familiar hospitality in the rooms of the Denver Press Club a week before Christmas 1913.

Sometime during December 1913, several of the press club boys were holed-up in the club, unable reach home due to a bad snow storm. Among the distraught newspapermen, protected only by knowing they just received their paychecks, had little to while-away the time. They were about to discover the poker artistry of Colonel Gideon B. McFall, a friend of the newspapermen. His unsuspecting compatriots were Lee Taylor Casey, Gene Fowler and Jack Carberry. When the heat in the club failed, the quartet headed to McFall's nearby home. For four days and five nights the poker game continued while four feet of snow piled up outside, tearing down power lines and clogging the city. The editorial room of the *Rocky Mountain News* needed their boys back. By the time a rescue team with shovels and a replacement bottle of bourbon arrived, Casey was out two-weeks' pay.[143]

Press club activities, even when removed from the club premises, were rarely outside the view of Jimmy Wong. The poker players assigned him to carefully monitor Colonel McFall's dealership and notify the other players if there were shenanigans. Night-Steward Wong, a pillar of ethics and a Denver newspaper legend, was often more than inscrutable. "Colonel McFall plain good poker player. Casey and Fowler plain nuts."[144]

When House Manager Lester J. Barkhausen, in the guise of Santa Claus, made his annual appearance at the press club to entertain seventy-five press club families at the club rooms, he bore packages containing complete cowboy and cowgirl costumes to enable each young buckeroos in the family to blend into any modern cattle-camp on the range. A well-decorated and illuminated tree with branches adorned with gifts of every kind and larger boxes strewn around the base was on display in the main room of the club. Each child in line became more excited as gifts were received, opened, and compared with their starry-eyed peers. The party, decorations, and gifts were all drawn from the club coffers for the members and their families.[145]

The Denver Press Club put 1913 to bed and welcomed 1914 with a three-hour open-house that began at 2 p.m. on the last day of the year for the business men of the city. The club rooms were beautifully decorated with palms, potted plants, and flowers as a courtesy by the Daniels & Fisher Stores Co.[146] There was some suspicion that the party may have gone well beyond the club's five-o'clock closing hour.[147]

Lester Barkhausen was a long-time member of the Denver Press Club and manager from 1913 to 1915. At a celebration of the club's history held in 1980, he related some of his opinions about the club. "I joined in hard times," the 89-year old told of his 68-year association with the press club. "There was a depression of sorts going on, and Prohibition came to the state in 1914. Since the club was basically a place to drink, play cards, and shoot pool, we thought its end was near."[148] Barkhausen contacted the Camel Music Company and purchased a player piano for $550 and then invited every member to bring their favorite records (piano rolls). To the tune of "Tea for Two" endlessly repeated, the club lived through those difficult years. Did the club serve alcohol during prohibition, Dolores Eyler of the *Rocky Mountain News* inquired? "We weren't allowed to serve liquor during Prohibition," Barkhausen said with a smirk, "but of course, we did."[149]

Jay G. Hilliard, a member of the Denver Press Club and considered a "finished musician," provided a concert in front of the offices of *The Denver Post*. The street-side performance included "Vocalino or Sweet Voiced Siren" as part of the promotion for a club fund-raising smoker to be given at the Auditorium Theater by the press club. The Vocalino was one of the upcoming features of the combined Sells-Floto and Buffalo Bill shows that would begin their season later in 1914.[150] While the definition of "vocalino" has been lost, it may have been somewhat like jazz scat-singing or some other form of musical voice manipulation.

The actual smoker entertainment was arranged through the Denver Athletic Club. Newsboys (affectionately known as Newsies) were invited to the Auditorium Theater to watch the entertainment portion of the smoker. Inside, three six-round bouts of pugilistic expertise, including a ten-round bout between Spider Roach of San Francisco and Young Abe Attell of Denver for lightweight honors was added to a bout between Morris Burke and Johnny Murphy in the 115-pound category, and an additional heavy-weight bout between Young Hector and Fireman Harris. Following the boxing exhibition, a vaudeville program provided stunts, and a wrestling match between the 250-pound Indian wrestler Chief War Eagle and Denver Patrolman Peterson. Chief War Eagle unceremoniously "dumped" the patrol officer within fifteen-and-a-half minutes of mat work.[151] Additional acts from the Empress and Pantages theaters, performance by the Tajoe family, Indian acrobats and gymnasts, were also included on the bill.[152]

When some of the guests wandered back to the rooms of the Denver Press Club, they were treated to a "wireless" party where messages were exchanged and verified among wireless radio operators transmitting from Arlington, Virginia and other wireless stations throughout the country. A transmitting apparatus was installed in the press club for the participation and entertainment of the guests of the club.[153]

After four years on the second floor of the Kittredge Building, the Denver Press Club moved into ten rooms on the second floor of the Denham Theatre building at Eighteenth and California Streets.[154] A special open house was provided on 5 March with musical entertainment by Leo Gibbons, Matt Walters, Charles Marshall and Al Kempter as the club "choir" tested the fine acoustics of the new club rooms. A cartoon room was proposed; filled with caricatures from the pens of every leading cartoonist from newspapers throughout the country.[155]

Caretakers of the new press club were newly elected officers Frank C. Farrar (president), news editor of the *Rocky Mountain News;* Robert G. Seymour (vice president), news editor of the *Denver Post;* Russell Forbes (secretary), staff of the *Denver Post;* and Charles McAllister Willcox (treasurer). Directors included Eugene Parrott Fowler, Howard D. Sullivan, Dowell Livesay, A. P. Johnson and Robert S. Courtney.[156]

"The Denver Press Club is one of very few organizations in the United States that is distinctively a newspaperman's club," reported the *Denver Post* in 1914. "Only those members who are actively engaged in newspaper work are eligible to the presidency and vice presidency, and the membership is limited strictly to actual newspaper workers, or those who have followed this calling for a number of years. The only exception to the rule in the matter of active newspapermen belonging to the organization is in regard to associate and honorary members. The list for the former is limited to twenty-five and the only honorary members are Presidents Roosevelt, Taft and Wilson. These three chief executives always include the press club in their list of reception engagements when in Denver in recognition of its being a strictly newspaperman's organization and free from political tendencies."[157]

1   *Contemporary Review,* "Government by Journalism," William Thomas Stead, May 1866

2   "Receptions and Parties . . ." *Denver Post,* January 2, 1910, p. 2

3   "Col. Irby Chosen President Press Club of Denver," *Denver Post,* March 14, 1910, p. 9

4   "Press Club Has 'House Warming' Next Thursday," *Denver Post,* March 28, 1910, p. 5

5   "Press Club Feed By New Officers," *Denver Post,* April 10, 1910, p. 8

6   "No Superstition in Oldfield," *Trenton Evening Times,* April 17, 1910

7   "Press Club Plans Electric Auto Race," *Denver Times,* April 19, 1910, p. 14

8   "Oldfield Will Drive in Race Meet at Overland," *Denver Post,* March 27, 1910, p. 29

9   "Grandstand at Overland Burns, Loss is $8,000," *Denver Post,* April 21, 1910, p. 2

10 "New Grandstand at Overland Will be of Concrete," *Denver Post,* April 22, 1910, p. 16

11 "Airship Tournament in Denver May 13 and 14," *Weekly Courier* (Fort Collins, CO), May 5, 1910, p. 14

12 "Oldfield Is Going After One and Two Mile Marks," *Denver Post,* May 12, 1910, p. 12

13 Daniels & Fisher store advertisement, *Denver Post,* May 13, 1910, p. 5

14 "Denver Press Club Members are Coming," *Colorado Springs Gazette,* May 14, 1910, p. 6

15 "'A Scramble' Up Mount Morrison," *Denver Post* June 19, 1910, p. 10

16 www.mountainproject.com

17 "John Brisben Walker, the Man and Mt. Morrison," *Historically Jeffco,* Vol. 18, Issue 26, 2005, pp. 4-8

18 "Newspaper Folk Have Delightful Day at Morrison," *Denver Post,* June 27, 1910, p. 5

19 "Press Club Picnics in Shadows of the Pines," *Denver Times,* July 25, 1910, p. 8

20 Ibid

21 "Press Club Shot to Greeley in D., L. & N. Steel Projectile," *Denver Post,* December 12, 1910, p. 5

22 "Newspapermen to Christen D., L. & N. New Power Coach," *Denver Post,* December 11, 1910, p. 10

23 "Press Club Invites Roosevelt to Denver," *Denver Post,* June 17, 1910, p. 6

24 "Cowboy Breakfast to Roosevelt in Denver," *Denver Times,* July 12, 1910, p. 8

25 "Press Club Will Give Roosevelt Cowboy Breakfast," *Denver Post,* July 13, 1910, p. 11

26 "Press Club Will Give Roosevelt Cowboy Breakfast," *Denver Post,* July 13, 1910, p. 11

27 "Ted to Denver," *Rockford (Illinois) Republic,* July 15, 1910, p. 1

28 "Pinchot Declares He Has Faith in the Insurgents," *Denver Post,* July 27, 1910, p. 8

29 "Pinchot Declares He Has Faith in the Insurgents," *Denver Post,* July 27, 1910, p. 8

30 "Ye Scribles Will Put Ye King T. R. to Ye Real Test," *Denver Post,* July 31, 1910, p. 17

31 "Newspapermen Will Come With Roosevelt," *Denver Times,* August 4, 1910, p. 6

32 "Here Are 'His' Doin's Monday," *Denver Times,* August 27, 1910, p. 1

33 "Famous Western Characters Assemble Here to Greet Theodore Roosevelt," *Denver Post,* August 28, 1910, p. 30

34 "Famous Western Characters Assemble Here to Greet Theodore Roosevelt," *Denver Post,* August 28, 1910, p. 30

35 "Roundup Luncheon for T. R." *Beaumont Enterprise and Journal,* August 29, 1910

36 "Famous Western Characters Assemble Here to Greet Theodore Roosevelt," *Denver Post,* August 28, 1910, p. 30

37 "Does He Like Denver? Sure!" *Denver Times,* August 29, 1910, p. 7

38 "Press Club Chuck Wagon Eat an Affair That Puts Teddy in Condition to Fear Nothing," *Denver Post,* August 29, 1910, p. 1

39 "'Bully,' He Says At Chuck Feed," *Denver Times,* August 29, 1910, p. 5

40 101.9 King website, kingfm.com, 2017

41 "Press Club Prepares to Build Club House," *Denver Post,* August 4, 1910, p. 2

42 Papers of Hamlet J. "Chips" Barry, III; Colorado State University Water Resources Archive, Colorado State University, Fort Collins

43 "Press Club Sues for Clear Title," *Denver Post,* October 15, 1910, p. 2

44 "Real Estate Transfers," *Denver Post,* September 17, 1910, p. 8

45 "Press Club Buys Realty," *Denver Times,* September 17, 1910, p. 3

46 "Press club Buys Property for $7,500," *Denver Post,* September 18, 1910, p. 7

47 "A bomb explodes in the Los Angeles Times Building," www.history.com

48 "Press Club to Aid Times Victims," *Denver Post,* October 3, 1910, p. 6

49 *Denver Post,* December 23, 1910, p. 5

50 "Press Club Will Remember Kiddies," *Denver Post,* December 25, 1910, p. 8

51 Ibid

52 "Sidelights On Sporting Stage," *Evening Times [Grand Forks, ND],* March 9, 1911, p. 3

53 "Good Program Arranged for Press Club Entertainment," *Denver Post,* March 18, 1911, p. 7

54 "Injunction to Stop Boxing Bout Denied," *Albuquerque Journal,* March 19, 1911, p. 3

55   "Clean Boxing Will Be the Feature at Press Club Show," *Denver Post*, March 20, 1911, p. 9

56   "Press Club Entertainment at the Auditorium Tonight," *Denver Post*, March 21, 1911, p. 8

57   boxrec.com, Fight 147646, March 21, 1911

58   "Two Boxers Arrested On Warrant at Denver," *Duluth News-Tribune*, March 22, 1911

59   "Fighters Arrested; to Appear Before Gavin Today," *Rocky Mountain News*, March 23, 1911, p. 11

60   *Law Notes*, Volume 15, E. Thompson Company, Northport, New York; January 1912, p. 197

61   *Denver Post*, April 13, 1911, p. 7

62   "Great Aviation Meet Planned for Denver; Noted Men Coming," *Denver Post*, April 16, 1911, p. 11

63   "Most Daring aviators in World to Fly at Overland at a Three Days' Meeting," *Denver Post*, April 19, 1911, p. 1

64   "Airship and Auto to Race During Meet at Overland," *Denver Post*, April 20, 1911, p. 1

65   "One Ten-Minute Flight in 2 Days Disgusts Public," *Denver Post*, 23 April 1911, p. 11

66   "Denver Professors Decline to Address Wilson in Homerian," *Colorado Springs Gazette*, May 9, 1911, p. 3

67   "Wilson's Trip to Denver Fifth Presidential Visit," Albert W. Stone, *Denver Post*, September 7, 1919, p 5

68   "800 Men Cheer Until Hoarse for Governor Wilson," *Denver Times*, May 9, 1911, p. 5

69   "Record-Breaking Reception Planned for Governor Wilson," *Denver Post*, October 6, 1912, p. 4

70   "Wilson Says He's No 'Stiff Old Ass;' He's Human and Has Temper of Own," Oliver P. Newman, *Cincinnati* (Ohio) *Post*, November 6, 1912, p. 4

71   "Wilson Fancy Billiard Shot," *Tulsa World*, April 30, 1915, p. 6

72   "Pres. Wilson Made Honorary Member Denver Press Club," *Colorado Springs Gazette*, December 15, 1913, p. 1

73   "Press Club to Give to President Gold Card of Membership," *Denver Post*, March 15, 1914, p. 26

74   "Press Club Asks President to Pay Visit to Denver," *Denver Post*, January 2, 1915, p. 1

75   "President Will Stop in Denver if He Goes to the Fair in Frisco," *Denver Post*, January 4, 1915, p. 1

76   "Visiting Editors Are Welcomed at Denver Press Club," *Denver Post*, October 16, 1912, p. 3

77 "Tuileries Track to be Opened Next Sunday," *Denver Post,* May 14, 1911, p. 30

78 http://archivemoto.com/thearchive/2017/5/16/erle-armstrong-and-cort-edwards-tuileries-motordrome-denver-summer-1911; Chris Price, May 16, 2017

79 "Newspaper People to See Stock Show," *Denver Post,* May 26, 1911, p. 12

80 "Park Entertains Newspaper Folk," *Denver Post,* May 27, 1911, p. 9

81 "Press Club Will Give Reception," *Denver Post,* June 8, 1911, p. 5

82 Form letter to Denver Press Club members from James R. Noland, president of the Denver Press Club, circa June 1911

83 "Press Club Camp Wins Approval of all Visitors," *Denver Post,* June 25, 1911, p. 4

84 "Gunnison is Freed of 'Gun Toters,'" *Denver Post,* June 26, 1911, p. 4

85 "Trout Make Rainbow Effects for Wolfe Londoner's Birthday," *Denver Post,* July 9, 1911, p. 9

86 Ibid

87 "Railroad Makes a Fishy Claim," *San Francisco Call,* September 12, 1911

88 "Corn-Fed Tourt Are Menaced," *Oregonian,* September 19, 1911, p. 10

89 "Lineup Announced for Salida-Gunnison Game," *Denver Post,* August 13, 1911, p. 26

90 "University Men Perfect Vender of Newspapers," *Denver Times,* August 13, 1911, p. 5

91 "Press Club to Have Picnic at Ft. Collins," *Denver Post,* August 30, 1911, p. 6

92 "Press Club Takes Day Off On Union Pacific," *Denver Post,* September 4, 1911, p. 5

93 "Denver Press Club Picnics Near Fort Collins Sunday," *Denver Times,* August 29, 1911, p. 5

94 "Press Club Has Jolly Picnic at Lindenmeier Lake," *Denver Times,* September 4, 1911, p. 5

95 "Members of the Denver Press Club Enjoy Picnic," *Weekly Courier* (Fort Collins, Colorado), September 8, 1911, p 6

96 "President In a Storm," *Times-Picayune* (New Orleans), October 5, 1911, p. 1, 8

97 "Taft's Train is Late," *The Flint Daily Journal,* October 3, 1911

98 "Noted 'Scribes' in Taft's Party 'Kidnaped' [sic] Here," *Denver Times,* October 3, 1911, p. 4

99 "Newspapermen As Press Club Guests Eat in D&F Tower," *Denver Post,* October 3, 1911, p. 4

100 "Mr. Taft's Route in City Includes Residence Part," *Denver Times,* September 28, 1911, p. 12

101 "No Parade, Plan of Committee on Mr. Taft's Coming," *Denver Times,* September 26, 1911, p. 4

102 "Taft's Schedule While in Denver is Now Complete," *Denver Post,* September

23, 1911, p. 2

103 "Taft to be Received in Denver Press Club," *Rocky Mountain News,* October 3, 1911, p. 3

104 "'Bill' Taft Now Member of Denver's Press Club," *Rocky Mountain News,* October 5, 1911, p. 5

105 "'Bill' Taft Now Member of Denver's Press Club," *Rocky Mountain News,* October 4, 1911, p. 1

106 "Denver to Keep Taft on the Jump," *Denver Post,* October 2, 1911, p 1

107 "Queen of Apple Carnival Race Led by Miss Alberta Smith," *Denver Post,* November 15, 1911, p. 1

108 "Acrimony Develops in Contest for Apple Queen," *Rocky Mountain News,* November 16, 1911, p. 3

109 "Host's Christmas Treat Pleases 1,000 Children Visiting 'Bright Eyes' Today," *Denver Post,* December 25, 1911, p. 3

110 "T. H. Mackall, Denver Newspaperman, Dead," *Denver Post,* January 22, 1912

111 "Maturo Retains Title by Defeating Endicott," *Denver Post,* January 26, 1912, p.14

112 "Judges Who Will Award Gold Watch and Diamond Ring," *Denver Post,* January 28, 1912, p. 3

113 "Lincoln Essay Contest Closes Today With Host of Entrants," *Denver Post,* February 9, 1912, p. 9

114 "Both Lincoln Essay Contest Winners Are High School Pupils," *Denver Post,* February 15, 1912, p. 2

115 "Press Club Children to Have Easter Party," *Denver Post,* April 6, 1912, p. 2

116 "Roped Arena," *Salt Lake Telegram,* April 8, 1912, p. 7

117 "Ardourel is Matched for Go With Ritchie," *Rocky Mountain News,* January 23, 1913, p. 1

118 Ibid.

119 "Press Club Goes to Mt. Morrison," *Denver Post,* July 29,1912, p. 4

120 *The First Hundred Years: An Informal History of Denver and the Rocky Mountain News,* Robert L. Perkin; Doubleday & Company, Inc., Garden City, New York, 1959, pp 433

121 *The Wildest of the West,* Forbes Parkhill, Sage Books, Denver, 1957, p. 199

122 Ibid

123 Ibid. p. 433

124 *The 1967 Denver Westerners Brand Book,* "The Denver Press Club," Cecil R. Conner, The Westerners, Denver, 1968, p. 138-139

125 "Famous Bill Nye Banquet," John E. Leet, *Denver Times,* February 16, 1902; published in *Newspaper Career of E. D. Cowen,* authors Edwin David Cowen, Charles Arthur Murray, Slason Thompson, Robert Emmett Monaghan

Strickland, Charles Elwood Arney, and others; Western Co., publishers; Seattle, Washington, 1930

126 "Londoner's Body to Lie in State," *Denver Times,* November 28, 1912, p. 7

127 "Five Hundred Picnic Held by Coloradoans," *San Diego Union,* January 26, 1913, p. 16

128 "History—Panama-Pacific International Exposition," www.ppie100.org

129 "San Diego Will Boost Denver's 1915 Pageant," *Denver Post,* January 28, 1913, p. 11

130 Ibid

131 "Thrilling Rescue Witnessed at Fire on Champa Street," *Denver Post,* March 27, 1913, p. 8

132 Ibid.

133 Ibid.

134 Ibid

135 "Press Club Adopts Ringing Creed for Greater Colorado," *Denver Post,* March 10, 1913, p. 12

136 Ibid

137 "Denver and its Papers," *Colorado Springs Gazette,* March 11, 1913, p. 4

138 Ibid.

139 "Road Commission Bill On Its Last Reading in Senate," *Denver Post,* March 11, 1913, p. 15

140 "Leaders of Denver Society Approve Placing of Tango on Program of Press Club," *Denver Post,* March 16, 1913, p. 8

141 "Latest Rag Steps to be Danced at Press Club Ball," *Denver Post,* March 2, 1913, p. 5

142 "Wilson to Address State University: Secretary Will Be Guest of the Denver Press Club Thursday Afternoon," *Denver Post,* November 25, 1913, p. 13

143 "Rekindling the Press Club Spirit," Pasquale Marranzino, *Rocky Mountain News,* February 24, 1971, p. 43

144 *The First Hundred Years: An Informal History of Denver and the Rocky Mountain News,* Robert L. Perkin; Double & Company, Inc., Garden City, New York, 1959; p 433

145 "Press Club Kiddies Yell Their Joy as Santa Bestows Gifts," *Denver Post,* December 25, 1913, p. 6

146 "A Courtesy Appreciated," *Denver Post* advertisement, January 3, 1914, p. 3

147 "City Revels Is New Year Makes Bow," *Denver Post,* January 1, 1914, p. 1, 3

148 "Press Club All Set for Diamond Jubilee Bash," Dolores Eyler, *Rocky Mountain News,* October 31, 1980, p. 35

149 Ibid

150 "Come to the Post Tonight Hear Vocalino Concert," *Denver Post,* January 23, 1914, p. 15

151 "Boxers Feature On Press Club Smoker Card," *Denver Post*, January 24, 1914, p. 6

152 "Stockmen's Smoker tonight at Auditorium Winds Up Festivities," *Denver Times*, January 23, 1914, p. 13

153 "Denver Press Club Gives 'Wireless' Entertainment," *Colorado Springs Gazette*, January 26, 1914, p. 3

154 "Press Club Moves to Fine New Home," *Denver Post*, March 1, 1914, p. 9

155 "Press Club Host in New Quarters; Election Sunday," *Denver Times*, March 6, 1914, p. 7

156 "Frank C. Farrar New President of Denver Press Club," *Denver Post*, March 9, 1914, p. 10

157 Ibid

CHAPTER 7

Now comes the Denver Press Club brandishing its pens and solemnly swearing that it will bring to Denver the biggest crowd that has ever been seen in this bright 'City of Lights' in mid-winter. In fact, it will be surprising if the attendance is not a record breaker in every way.[1]

Round-Up Week! Somethin' doin' every minute of the day and evening.[2]

This was the claim made by the Denver Press Club, the National Western Stockmen's Association, and the Denver Chamber of Commerce in preparation for the Ninth Annual National Western Stock Show. With a carnival and novelty program to hype what they claimed would be "the biggest thing of its kind in the history of the state,"[3] the press club and stockmen's association expected to bring quality exhibitions to the stockyards and the best entertainment for the guests staying in hotels downtown. The press club appointed nine committees to work on entertainment[4] and served as a consolidated press agency on behalf of the stock show.[5]

Support from the Denver Motor Club, the Denver Shriners,[6] Elks, and the Denver Athletic Club[7] were last-minute additions to make the events surrounding the stock show both exciting and successful. Nearly 900 newspapers in Colorado, Montana, Utah, Wyoming, and New Mexico lent their publications to the press-club publicity campaign.[8] The press club further extended an invitation to all newspaper editors in Colorado, Utah, New Mexico, and Wyoming to "attend a novelty banquet tendered free."

This feast would complement a Masked Ball at the Auditorium Theatre to reinstate the old days of the cattlemen's masked balls. Even the Sons and Daughters of Colorado society group offered to forego their annual grand ball to provide greater attention to the Denver Press Club's foray into the world of masked balls.[9]

The old-fashioned Stockmen's Masquerade Ball, also under the auspices of the Denver Press Club, opened with a packed audience in the Auditorium Theater. The city closed a block of streets from Fourteenth Street to Eighteenth and from Curtis to Champa and turned them over to the overflow crowd of masked revelers.[10] The streets were illuminated with a blaze of colored lights extending from the Auditorium and down the entire length of Champa Street all the way to the stockyards. Motivating the promotion of the focus on the stock show was an agricultural report that indicated that Colorado's agriculture produced $125,000,000 worth of crops during the previous year.[11] Entertainment was on every corner between Fourteenth and Eighteenth Streets, providing music for several thousand revelers to dance the tango or turkey trot.[12]

The Denver Times had fun with an article written in the vernacular of the cow camp:

> "It's this-a-way—"
> The Old Cattleman leaned back against the wall, with a faraway look in his eyes.
> "You-all hear what Denver is aimin' to pull off?" . . .
> "Over in Denver, which same is what the trooth, none whatever, there is a bunch of intellectooal coyotes which dubs themselves the Press Club. Shore, they're all of them plum lit'ry. They aims to elevate public opinyun through the medium of the press.
> "At the same time—simultanoos, as you all might say—these lit'ry gents is hot sports. They aims to fly high, an' as a general rool they do that—when they have the dinero. . .
> "Yes, of course, my remarks has reference to this yere Press Club. They ain't bashful, none whatever. They horns right in an' to no time whatever they has most of the chaps slacked their side o' the table. . .

"Startin' in that-a-way, an' it havin' come aroun' to fifth drink time, nach'ly they figgers the fust thing is to feed the crowd. So they arranges what they calls a 'Brand-Iron' dinner, the same being in name sort of free an' easy an' suggestive o' cattle an' critters an' roundups. . .

"To resoom—as I was sayin', the next thing is a smoker. No, don't go a-gallopin' off that-away with the idee this is just a plain smoker.

"Those yere Press Club galoots, bein' as I tell you-all, plum full of ambishun, aims for to trim it up till it's what you-all could term some maverick of a smoker. They aim to pull so many stunts an' so vareg'ated that you-all lets your cig'root into the discard. What stunts? Son, I can't tell you-all none. There is times when only seein' is believin'. You-all has to go and see.

"No, the Press Club ain't playin' no lone hand. The Livestock Exchange, the Denver Convention League, the Shriners, the Elks, the Motor Club, the Athletic Club, the Chamber of Commerce, the Sons of Colorado, the Rot'ry Club—they all sits in the game with stacks of bloos an' the roof for a limit.

"Jes' the same, these Press Club litterchoors, they rings in the joker, aimin' for to-run it wild an'figgering that-away they holds the edge on ev'rything . . .

The Old Cattleman rose, wiped his mustache again and walked down the street.

A few steps away he stopped and called back over his shoulder:

"Son, you be THAR!"[13]

A "smoker" with a "stockmen's stuff" theme was scheduled in addition to a "Gridiron" stunt banquet for the Rocky Mountain editors. Vaudeville acts, singers, dancers, acrobatic and gymnastic features, wrestling, sparring, and other lines of amusement were provided from the Denver theaters and connections maintained by the Denver Athletic Club patrons.[14] Three nights of entertainment were already "on tap," and each event was going to be "a hum-dinger in the real 'Press Club way.'"[15]

Miss Bessie Ammons, daughter of Governor Ammons, was elected to officiate at the stock show as "Queen Bess." A special honor was bestowed upon the young lady crowned "Queen of the Roundup" as part of the press club festivities. She rode onto the Auditorium floor astride an Arabian horse, stopping in front of Colonel William F. "Buffalo Bill" Cody who placed the crown on her head during the Roundup-Week festivities.[16] Another account claimed the queen was crowned with a sombrero[17] and presented a gold branding iron by President Harry Wilbur of the Denver Press Club. Her father then led Bessie and her horse during the grand march at the masquerade ball.[18] Behind the governor/daughter duo marched Mayor and Mrs. Perkins, Harry Lee Wilber (president of the press club) and his wife, visiting editors, the Elks' drill team, the Shriners' rube band, the Motor Club, fifty members of the Sons of Colorado, visiting stockmen, and numerous masked attendees.[19] Following the ceremony, entertainment was provided by the Elks drill team, an Indian dance by Ryley Cooper, and the Sons of Colorado performing patriotic maneuvers.[20] When the dance music began, the visiting newspapermen and stockmen "loped the lariat," "ragged the range," and "stampeded the stunner" from nine in the evening until two the next morning.[21]

The 1913 attendance was more than 25,000 people; the press club proposed to nearly double the previous attendance record with 45,000 visitors in 1914. The railroads serving Denver proposed a one-fare rate for travelers traveling from anywhere among the Rocky Mountain states, an offer that was never extended to any other convention in Denver. For guests from outside the Rocky Mountain area, rail tickets were offered at two-cents per mile.[22] From Rifle, Colorado, a Pullman on the Rio Grande was already reserved for stockmen and their families heading to Denver. Additional train reservations were made from Chicago, Kansas City, Omaha, St. Joseph, and other stations.[23]

During the week before the official start of Round-up Week, the press club began to reveal the special events they prepared for the stockmen and the public. At Inspiration Point, Norwegian skier Carl Howelsen provided a side-show of "How to fly without an aeroplane" with a "special ski exhibition of high and daring jumping." Howelsen arrived in Colorado in 1913 and brought ski jumping and Nordic cross-country competitions to Steamboat Springs. Early in 1914, he organized the Steamboat Springs Winter Sports Club training program for children. His appearance as part of the 1914 Western Stock Show was a mutual opportunity for both the press club and Howelsen's contribution to Colorado's expanding participation in national events.[24]

In addition to the professional demonstration, amateur ski jumpers had an opportunity to win prizes based on the distance of their ski-jumps, providing the contestant remained on his feet upon landing. C. Anderson, the organizer of the Denver Ski Club, was an expert ski jumper and offered daily training sessions at Inspiration Point. As his contribution to the Denver Press Club event, he pledged to give free instructions to anyone who wished to participate in the competition.[25]

More than one-thousand people headed to Inspiration Point, near the Lakeside Amusement Park, to watch a dozen or more contestants vie for the prize of being the most successful amateur ski-jumper.[26] Anderson believed ski jumping had developed sufficiently to create a national event that could be held the following year in Colorado.[27] The Denver Press Club exhibition was the first ski tournament ever held in Denver. "I am going to give as good an exhibition as I can tomorrow," Carl Howelsen told the *Denver Post*. "I want to get the people of Denver interested in the sport, so that we can have better tournaments in the future. Then we can have some of the best jumpers in the world come here and compete. With plenty of snow, it affords great sport."[28]

Only one-in-every-2,000 spectators ever saw ski jumping. The top four contestants with the best points received silver loving cups for their efforts. As a result of the success of the Denver Press Club exhibition, a new organization of ski-jump enthusiasts was formed, and B. Gordon Chaney was elected president. Another contest for Mt. Morrison was proposed to commence before winter's end.[29]

The Brand-Iron dinner, attended by Governor Ammons, drew prominent members of the community and newspapermen from throughout the country. President Wilson's views on Mexico, currency and tariff policies, the coal-miners' strikes, and other current events were lampooned during the press-club dinner. The president had yet to receive the accolades of being the club's third honorary president, due to scheduling conflicts. Early in the evening of the Brand-Iron dinner, a "messenger" rushed into the banquet hall to announce that President Wilson finally accepted the press club's honor. The bogus messenger claimed the president was able to accept the accolade in person and awaited outside the banquet room, prepared to make a personal address to the group. The doors were flung open and an actor dressed as President Woodrow Wilson entered the room to present a message chastising the press of the country for "the continued misquoting of my attitude on all the preponderating questions and puzzling problems of the day."[30]

The "president" continued to declare that he never opposed the annexation of Mexico, with the exception that such a move would "flood the United States with hot tamales and frijoles."[31] The evening continued with actors portraying various local and national news events.

The March 1914 annual meeting provided the third attempt to amend the press club's constitution (to allow former newspapermen who have changed professions to hold executive office in the Denver Press Club). After a spirited debate and a close vote, the measure was turned down. The Denver Press Club was the only newspapermen's club in the country led by an active newspaperman, and only active newspapermen qualified for *active* membership.[32] This created an uncomfortable situation when Governor Ammons submitted his application for active membership despite his lack of newspaper experience.[33]

During the next month's board meeting, the earliest surviving copy of the Denver Press Club board minutes described a special meeting where Governor Ammons was invited to deliver a short talk to the sixty-four club members in attendance. He clarified that "the members of the club can be of material assistance in building up and further developing the state."[34] Three days later, a regular board meeting included instructions that the governor's dues and application be returned to him, citing the club's constitutional requirement that active membership ". . . include such men as are actually employed upon or who have been employed upon daily, weekly or monthly newspapers or magazines devoted to the recording current events, and not issued in the interest of a particular trade, business or profession."[35]

In another administrative clarification made at the April 8th board meeting, the men ruled that any time there were ladies present at any function given in the club rooms, "that the bar-room should be closed and that nothing intoxicating should be served in the way of a punch, etc."[36] The new ruling was carried. Other board minutes indicated that even in 1914, some club members were delinquent in the buffet accounts; House Manager Barkhausen was instructed to consult with members about their over-due tabs.[37] Within a few weeks, Jay Hilliard, Hugh Taylor, Clarence E. Hagar, and J. Hooper Caffee were expelled from the club for unpaid buffet accounts and were refused admittance to the club rooms as a member or guest, until the tabs were paid in full.[38]

A new sports challenge developed as the Denver Motor Club challenged the Denver Press Club in a weekly billiards competition that alternated on a daily event schedule between the two clubs.[39] When the spring weather returned to the Rockies, the first of a series of outings began with a May 31, 1914, "picnic-basket" at Lookout Mountain near Golden for the press-club members, wives, children, and sweethearts. The tramway company provided the special train to Golden where John M. Kuykendall of the Denver Omnibus & Cab Company provided a motor line to the foot of the mountain. Rees C. Vidler then transported the picnickers up Lookout Mountain to the park via the funicular cars. In the afternoon, the crowd was returned to Golden where C. F. Quaintance loaded the group onto another funicular up Castle Rock.[40]

Back in town, the Elks Club members gathered at their fraternal home at 14th and California Streets, preparing for the upcoming Grand Lodge Golden Jubilee session in July. The Denver Press Club pledged to keep their club doors open to accommodate the visiting newspapermen covering the event at their new club rooms in the Denham Block.[41] The Denham digs were described as the most commodious rooms that the press club had enjoyed to-date. Likewise, officials of the Denver Fair and Racing Association were guests of the press club to develop closer working relations for future events.[42]

When the press club board met in June, they ruled to sell the building they owned at 1330 Glenarm Place. If they sold it for $5,000 net, the club would assume no indebtedness to taxes, repair bills, etc.—and earn a profit of $1,000 on the investment.[43] But by August, the tenant residing on the property provided $80 worth of repairs and upgrades to the property and the press club board agreed to deduct the amount from the next month's rent.[44] The board chose to hold onto the modest rental property.

After the great success of the relationship with Western Stock Show, the Denver Press Club sought a more ambitious promotional event. Lincoln Beachey was bringing his aviator-tricks to thrill audiences throughout the country; often his exhibition was sponsored by local press clubs to maximize attention. Accompanying the aerialist was Barney Oldfield who proposed breaking several land-speed records at Overland Park. Oldfield planned to bring his best racing cars and Beachey would fly in his own aeroplane—billed as the smallest exhibition machine in the world.[45]

DENVER, COLORADO, THURSDAY, APRIL 20, 1911. —14 PAGES. 3

WHY NOT DECIDE THE SENATORIAL RACE, AT THE PRESS CLUB SHOW AT OVERLAND.

Courtesy of the *Denver Post*

Noting the popularity of the Beachey-Oldfield race exhibition, the *Denver Post's* editorial cartoonist (above) satirized how a political senatorial race could be conducted. The real race-car stunt-plane race was sponsored by the Denver Press Club (below).

Courtesy of the Library of Congress, "Race between Lincoln Beachey in airplane and Barney Oldfield in automobile, going around race track," 1912, https:www.loc.gov/item/2003656134/

In the September 15, 1914 board minutes, the house manager was instructed to pay Harry B. Curtis, promoter of the Beachey-Oldfield exhibition, twenty-five percent of the gross proceeds of the receipts from the Denver Press Club Aviation Program, that was scheduled for October 8 in Denver.

Aerial acrobatics were fraught with danger in Colorado's rarified air. In mid-September, Mr. Beachey lost his flying partner during a similar exhibition in Pueblo. In November 1910, 24-year-old Ralph Johnstone died in Colorado while attempting a spiral glide in front of 15,000 cheering spectators in Pueblo, Colorado who didn't initially realize the rapid descent wasn't part of the show until his plane hit the ground. Mr. Johnstone was a member of the Wright Brothers' Exhibition Team and was the holder of the World's Altitude Record of 9,714 feet. The *Dayton Daily News* reported that as soon as the plane hit the ground, "morbid men and women" swarmed to the crash site, fighting over souvenirs of the crash—including the flyer's gloves and a broken wooden stay from the wing that impaled the flyer. "Before doctors or police could reach the scene one man had torn this splinter from the body and run away, carrying his trophy with the aviator's blood dripping from its ends."[46]

The Denver Press Club event's star flyer, Lincoln Beachey, was a "world-renowned aerial navigator and thriller of souls, [who] will baffle science by flying upside down, looping-the-loop, and other hazardous feats in mile-high atmosphere."[47] In speaking of the death of his partner, Weldon B. Cooke, the previous week in Pueblo, Beachey explained to the *Denver Post*, "I shall fulfill my date in Denver for the Denver Press Club at any hazard. It is sad indeed to lose one of our best men, such as Cooke, but I shall undertake to disprove the statements that one cannot fly upside down or loop-the-loop in such a high altitude. My life is to be wagered on the result, but if I win, I will have done that which no other aviator can say he has accomplished."[48]

In addition to being an entertainment spectacular, the Press Club exhibition aerobatics was also a propaganda demonstration of the potential use of airplanes in military engagements. Beachey's exhibition included the simulation of how his bi-plane could drop bombs on warships and cities. "The aeroplane is one of the most potent factors in modern warfare," explained Beachey. "The fight of inhabitants from Paris was due more to bomb dropping skill of aviators than to fear of siege guns of the enemy.[49] . . . In my exhibition for the press club and people of Denver will be shown the importance of an aviator being skilled in judgment of distance and sureness of flying."[50] Despite the outbreak of war throughout Europe, President Woodrow Wilson declared a policy of U.S. neutrality on August 4, 1914, which held for two-and-a-half more years.

Event-day arrived, and a crowd gathered at Overland Park. "The unseen fingers seemed to be clutching at his throat, grasping relentlessly thru the very breath of his whirring engine," wrote the *Denver Post* reporter. "He had swept to the sky with a sputtering rush. He poised birdlike, immovable but alert, startling calm. His features through the field glasses were those of a professional gamester who holds winning cards in his hand. The purr of the engine, half muffled by the distance and the clouds, sang a strange song, a weird chant of space. Then came a downward glide, a complete loop, and Lincoln Beachey, aviator and more, shook hands with the Silent Reaper of Souls yesterday while 30,000 awed persons looked on."[51]

The initial flight was not without problems. According to Beachey, the engine misfired the entire time and needed to be disassembled to find the problem. Instead of promising a series of flights, the star attraction suspected that the crowd had seen his only appearance. To keep the crowd entertained, Barney Oldfield stepped up his race-car exhibition on the one-mile track, trying to break his 52.5-second record four years ago at the same track; his first trial beat the old record by three-tenths of a second. The next run beat the old record by a full two seconds. The crowd would have to be satisfied with the one flight, because the advertised race between the two daredevils had to be benched while the airplane's engines were repaired.

*****

By October 1914, the press club board of directors was also keeping busy. The three-year mortgage on their present club house rooms at the Denham Theatre was due for renewal.[52] At the next meeting, the board voted to extend the mortgage.[53] Also on the agenda, a Halloween party was scheduled for the members, ladies, and "kiddies of the Press Club." The following month, the board began planning for another collaboration with the Western Stock Show to prepare for the next Brand-Iron Banquet[54] as long as the event was cost-free to the club. In addition to the no-cost arrangement, the club noted that $300 was still owed the club from last year's banquet.[55] There was a question whether a stock show could even be held that year. The upcoming Panama-Pacific Exposition in San Francisco would draw the best livestock for that international event, and some livestock operators were unsure of transporting their best stock to Denver because of an outbreak of hoof-and-mouth disease.[56] In case the full stock show was canceled, the board of directors suggested the Brand-Iron Dinner at the Auditorium may be given during a session of the Colorado State legislature.[57]

The November 1914 board meeting shed light on the non-public aspects of the club. The board ruled that after November 16, "for the best interest of the club that there shall be no poker played in the club rooms . . . The attendants were instructed that in the future they were not to play any card game when there was any one [sic] in club rooms outside of those playing in game."[58] Among the line items for the next meeting's financials, the house manager was instructed to purchase two barrels of whiskey for $176.40. He was also instructed to determine the costs to repair the pool table to return it to first-class condition.[59]

At the end of 1914, the board of the directors had little to worry about than to authorize $10 checks be drawn for each of the club stewards—Joseph Diner and Jim Wong; and for the House Manager L. J. Barkhausen. An additional $40 was spent for presents for the three gentlemen who kept the club operating day and evening. One other rule was passed by the board—in the best interest of the club, the playing of "Black-Jack" would henceforth also be prohibited at the club.[60]

Livestock-related diseases and an effort to preserve the best stock for exhibition at the Pan Pacific International Exposition deflated interest in scheduling the 1915 Western Stock Show in Denver. In a letter from Thorndike Deland, secretary of the Denver Chamber of Commerce to Russell Forbes, secretary of the Denver Press Club, "Owing to the scarce and differences of opinion at the Stock Yards, the Association has called off the Show, but it is the belief of the business men of the city that we should at least hold the Horse Show, the Poultry Show and other departments from which there will be no danger."[61]

The revised National Horse Show and Mid-Winter Fair was scheduled for January 18-25 at the Union Stockyards under the auspices of the Gentlemen's Driving-and-Riding Club and commercial organizations; the Brand Iron Dinner and Grand Ball was planned by the Denver Press Club in the style of the Washington, D.C. "Gridiron" banquet. The finesse of the previous stock show was temporarily lost as the event became more like a country fair. "A unique feature will be a 'Milk' show," reported the *Journal of Douglas County*, "although it will not be possible to have on exhibition the prize winning milch cows; the modern hygienic processes of handling milk and manufacturing products and by-products will be exhibited. There will be demonstrations of the proper methods of sterilization, pasteurization, separating, measuring butter content, butter making, and the like."[62]

Added to the schedule was an ad hoc sportsmen's show promised to be of interest to the motorist, hunter, fisherman, prospector, and others who loved the outdoor life and to mimic the Madison Square Garden sportsmen's show in New York.

For various reasons, several key members of the Denver Press Club Brand-Iron committee resigned at the end of January 1915 and the board voted to indefinitely postpone the dinner and ball. Because of the lack of interest for the Brand-Iron dinner, Harry Lee Wilber's resignation letter explained "the Brand Iron stunt itself was originated for the strict purpose of progression, that is, improvement with each succeeding year; and I believe our outline at present does not reach that standard."[63] Never a group to pass up a chance to party, the board voted to give a keg party within the club rooms on February 10.[64]

The mid-March annual board meeting elected a new board to represent the club. George Emmet Lewis was elected president—the youngest man at the time to preside over the club.[65] When an attempt was made to conduct statehouse business without the purview of a statehouse reporter, the press club became politically active and protested the closed-door activities under the state-house dome. The same month, the membership unanimously voted to send a resolution condemning the lower house of the 20th General Assembly of the State of Colorado:[66]

> Whereas, the lower house of the Twentieth General assembly of Colorado has seen fit to exclude from its deliberations the reporters of one of the leading newspapers of the state; and
>
> Whereas, such action is absolutely unprecedented in the history of Colorado, and unparalleled in the records of the English-speaking people since the time of the heptarchy, and is plainly an effort on the part of the legislature to stifle the liberty of the public press; and

> Whereas, such action is calculated to hold the fair name of Colorado up to scorn and contempt among her sister states of the union; therefore, be it.
>
> Resolved, by the Denver Press Club, in annual meeting assembled, that we condemn the action taken by the legislature and declare to the public at large that we are opposed to, and shall unceasingly denounce any action by any body of men that shall tend to take away those rights of the liberty of the press and the freedom of speech which are granted by the federal constitution to a liberty-loving people.[67]

When the annual breakfast meeting was held (as an extension of the annual board meeting), former president Frank C. Farrar received a diamond stick pin from the club in appreciation for his service. He then approached the podium to announce that during the past year, the club was nearly self-sustaining, aside from the cost of the initiation feed of new associate members and the aviation exhibition.[68] When the club was reorganized in 1892, one of the purposes was to create a home for aged and invalid newspapermen who "have broken down in the work."[69] During the 1915 annual breakfast, a resolution was passed to fulfill that promise. Mr. John Brisbane Walker of Morrison, Colorado, offered to donate a parcel of land for the construction of a National Home for Aged Newspapermen, near Morrison.[70] Senator Simon Guggenheim once offered $2,000 of seed money for such a facility, but there is no record of that pledge being applied to a retirement home for journalists.

At the May 28, 1915 meeting of the board of directors, members were reminded of a club rule that was still in effect. After buffet items were consumed or games of pool or billiard were played, the members were requested to tear off the stub on tabs. Attendants were instructed to collect those tabs so that the individual members could be billed for activities. Apparently, too many members were avoiding the dunning procedure with free meals and games while at the club. The board asked members to inform the attendants of any members who neglected to follow-through with this gentlemanly system of billing members for goods and services consumed.[71]

The Great Depression was still fourteen years away, but members of the Denver Press Club were beginning to resign from membership in 1915, citing great financial indebtedness that needed to be addressed before they were able to continue as members in good standing.

*****

Hot weather in Denver provided press club members with excursions to several of the mineral springs in the foothills of the Colorado Rocky Mountains. The Idaho Springs "Splash" brought press-club member families and the Writers' Club to the hot-springs thermal pools.

Courtesy of the Denver Public Library, Western History Collection, Harry Mellon Rhoads Photographic Collection, Image # ZZR700186414

The summer heat of June 1915 provided the ideal conditions to schedule the Denver Press Club's annual "Splash" for members, families, and friends at the hot springs in Idaho Springs. Leaving Union Station in Denver on a special Colorado & Southern train, the group divided the day into "Splashes." Splash No. 1 was the "thrilling trip by train through the famous Newhouse tunnel, replete with scenic sensations and guaranteed to produce in each and every member a satisfactory yearning . . ." Splash No. 2 was a superb "chicken tango luncheon"[72] served in the Hot Springs Hotel. Splash No. 3 and 4 included dancing at the Trocadero casino[73] preceded by swimming in the "radium charged waters of the pool which is fed from the hot caves,"[74] followed by Splash No. 5—a reception hosted by the mayor and council of Idaho Springs, and members of the Elks Club. The intent was to top previous excursions to Cripple Creek, Colorado Springs, and the previous year's "Splash" at Eldorado Springs.[75] As a pre-luncheon bonus, the boys were challenged to use the hand-cart through the Big Five Tunnel to get to the 9,000-ft. level. At the end of the tracks, each weary newspaperman was presented with a miniature sack of gold ore from a recent strike on the Lincoln group.[76]

The *Denver Post* was gracious in pointing out that "On all of these occasions the towns visited have been enlivened and much edified—so highly edified. In fact, that the fame of the club has gone broadcast and other envious towns beg and clamor each year for the privilege of being host to the newspapermen on the annual 'splash' which they open each summer social season."[77]

The mid-summer-month board meetings began planning for a female minstrel show with Colonel C. B. McFall serving as chairman of the seven-member Minstrel Show Committee.[78] By the end of August, the newspapers began to boost the September 11, 1915 "Frivol" sponsored by the Denver Press Club. "With the fairies of Newport and other advanced Eastern resorts setting the pace in uncovered-ah'm, well-uncovered nether limbs," reported the *Denver Post,* "Denver society is agog with the excitement of a bizarre attraction, and some have declared in confidence that they, too, would don rolltop or ankle-high stockings if—well, if someone would just start the fad here."[79]

The Denver Press Club Frivol was promoted as "fun, music, dancing and other exquisite entertainment." Signor Cavallo and his orchestra would accompany the all-female white-face minstrel show with a chorus of "dainty Denver maids." George Wells, Denver's "Charlie Chaplin" and a reporter for one of the local newspapers, served as the interlocutor (the master of ceremonies and pitch-man) for the various stunts of the troupe. Several dances were performed throughout the three-hour show that was staged without an intermission.[80]

The Christmas press club party was another gallant celebration for the families of the members, and sweethearts of the club. Toys, candy and "suitable gifts for the older people,"[81] were all donated by the club.

It was common for the Denver Press Club to visit with the managers of Denver's stage theaters and glean their interest in providing a "Denver

Press Club Night" as a fund-raising opportunity for the club and to showcase one of the theatrical season's performances.[82] A touch of class came to the Denver Press Club as the three Cherniavsky Brothers were scheduled to come to Denver. Before the war broke out; Leo, Jan, and Mischel Cherniavsky entertained European royal families respectively on violin, piano and cello for the past fourteen years. They were among the last entertainers to accept an invitation to leave Europe and come to America where they resumed entertaining the more common folk.

Through arrangements made by the Denver Press Club, the dulcet baritone voice of Charles W. Clarke was able to leave the Eastern symphonies and orchestras to perform solo and in concert with the Cherniavsky Brothers.[83] The United Workers for the Blind held their annual meeting in Denver and accepted the invitation by the Denver Press Club, to attend the concert December 29, 1917.[84]

For a simpler fare, the March 1917 board of directors instructed the club's Music Committee to purchase seventy-five player-piano rolls at the cost of ten-cents each.[85]

The Denver Press Club moved their headquarters once again in 1917 from the Denham Building to the Aspen Building because of an increase in rent to $115 a month (exclusive of janitorial service). Past-president George E. Lewis appeared before the new press-club board to explain the necessity of the move. The club had approximately $1,800 in the treasury and the rent on the new quarters was only $53 a month. The quarters needed some "fix-up," and the board requested a committee of three to spruce up the place and to lease the adjoining room at a reasonable rate.[86]

The Denver Press Club was hardly settled into their new quarters in the Aspen Building when complaints were being made to the landlord about the noise created by the club members. Likewise, some club members found the quarters "undesirable and inconvenient on account of the complaints of tenants"[87] and the restrictions placed by the landlord. Representatives of the Theatrical Mechanics Association offered an alternative choice of four rooms in the Hamburger Building for $80 a month, another four rooms for $70, five rooms for $90 and the privilege of using the reception hall for entertainment for an additional $8. The board recognized the problems with the Aspen Building, chose not to renew the lease, and considered returning to the Denham Building or move on to the Hamburger Building. After the board made a visitation to the Hamburger Building with F. N. Gaudy of the Theatrical Mechanics Association, the club was able to negotiate the five-rooms down to $80 a month beginning May 1, 1917. At the April 15th annual breakfast meeting, the membership voted to authorize the board to sign the papers with the new landlords.

With the saving on the club's monthly lease, the board was able to pay down the $3,500 mortgage on the club's income property at 1330 Glenarm Place and renew the loan on $3,000. The house manager was instructed to repair and renovate the Glenarm property and rent it for a year at $22.50 a month.[88]

A relationship with the theatrical producer Robert Slack began to pay off when he proposed to bring the San Carlo Grand Opera Company to Denver under the auspices of the Denver Press Club.[89] This was the theater group's third appearance in the city and would present "La Traviata" and "Tales of Hoffman" at the Auditorium Theater.[90] By the end of the year, Slack was instructed not to select any opera of German name or origin for presentation in Denver.[91] When the curtain fell on the Denver Press Club's "opera season," the club enjoyed a profit of $2,079.98.

"I would like to underline right here the subtle fact that our operatic offering to entertain the Denver public with the San Carlo Opera Company has shed a halo of unfrazzled glory upon our efforts," reported Lute Wilcox during his press-club presidential message in 1918. "It was by long odds the greatest piece of show business ever essayed by this institution and brought us the money at a time when we needed it the most. The details of the enterprise were turned over to our clever impresario Mr. George Lewis who knows how to do something without grunting over it. During this engagement, the club extended the courtesies to eighty-seven members of the United Workers for the Blind of Colorado who occupied the stage gallery during the performance of Il Trovatore and to the most of them it proved a rare experience for which they were duly thankful."

Despite the outward trappings of success in the eyes of the community, it was House Manager D. F. Stackelbeck that brought the stark reality of Prohibition's constraints on serving alcohol when the board met in October 1917. The house records indicated a deficit when combined with the buffet receipts, dues, entrance fees, and real-estate rent. "If anything," reported Mr. Stackelbeck, "the buffet receipts will grow less during the next six months because the club will not have the income from the sale of certain refreshments which it enjoyed during the greater part of the first six months of the present club year. With a monthly deficit of anywhere from $75 to $100 to face you, you will see the present cash balance exhausted before long unless you succeed in compelling the membership to pay their dues promptly."[92]

Stackelbeck continued, "I regret to report that despite all my efforts to collect dues, a great portion of the membership absolutely declines to pay dues. They simply ignore the bills sent to them at the beginning of every month or refuse point blank to pay when approached in person . . . If no steps are taken to compel these members to fulfill their duty towards the club, we might just as well close the club rooms. . . I also might mention that some of the very members who have not contributed a cent are the very men who constantly criticize and find fault with the rooms you provide for them, the buffet service and other matters. They also make a habit of running up buffet bills and not paying for them."[93]

In keeping with war-time efforts, the board instructed the club manager and attendants to observe meatless, wheat-less and pork-less days, as requested by the federal food administration. Mr. Stackelbeck also reported to the board that "police officers in citizens clothes" paid a visit to the clubrooms on the morning of February 3, 1918 and made a search for liquor on the premises. The club's president formed a committee to call upon Chief of Police Armstrong to inquire into the reasons for the raid.[94]

*****

Colonel Theodore Roosevelt was preparing for his fifth visit to Colorado and extolled the hospitality of the people and the quality of the state's rare and beautiful climate. When he reached Denver on October 25, 1916, he reminded everyone that he predicted Colorado would become a vacation destination for the world. He challenged the state to develop accessible means of seeing the scenic areas that could make Colorado "the best-loved and most frequented of the great playgrounds of the world."[95] He explained that the war in Europe was building to become a world war, turning a tremendous number of tourists away from the battlefields around the Swiss Alps, and redirected the European tourists back toward the Rocky Mountains.

"For the first time they are 'seeing America,'" explained Colonel Roosevelt. "With but little effort this can be made a permanent . . . These people will come back in increasing numbers each year, until this area and the great West will become centers of an enormous annual movement of tourists and travelers. Your national parks constitute a tremendous asset that should be thoroughly capitalized, without destruction of any of the natural features that make for beauty in their wonderful territory."[96]

World War I (1914-1918) brought a new role of compassion and benevolence for the Denver Press Club during Frank C. Farrar's tenure as club president. In 1915, a new constitution and bylaws were written for the Denver Press Club Relief Association. The benefits of the new organization enabled "any member who becomes so sick or disabled that he is incapacitated for work (not the result of his own indiscretions) and whose dues in the Press Club are fully paid for the quarter shall receive from the association the sum of $5 for the first week and $5 per week for the next five weeks or any part thereof he is incapacitated for work."[97]

The accounts of press club activities during the war were rare in the Denver newspapers—Lieutenant Max D. Melville, a young Denver attorney, former newspaperman, and member of the Denver Press Club as well as other societies and associations, was at Camp Funston, Kansas, where he was training soldiers for the 355th infantry.[98] The club also obtained a service flag in honor of current and past members of the press club who were serving in the military and naval services. A complete list of press club servicemen was posted along with the flag that contained one star for each member currently in the military[99] and was flown from one of the windows of the club's quarters. All members of the press club currently in the service of the United States were carried on the books as paid active members for the duration of the war.[100]

The annual spring meeting for 1918 was conducted and the membership elected Robert G. Seymour of the editorial staff of the *Denver Post* as president. During the meeting, the membership voted to purchase $500 worth of the forthcoming Liberty Bonds to help the war effort.[101] The State of Colorado raised $6,175,250 in 1918, more than half of their quota; Denver banks included 3,889 subscribers who took out $1,191,450 in bonds; a woman's committee announced $104,100 in subscriptions; and the stockyards committee added another $13,450. Private individuals contributed in the four-to-five-digit categories.[102] One blind member of the United Workers for the Blind began planting and cultivating six war-gardens in vacant lots; a partial supply of seed was provided by the Denver Press Club.[103]

Belts were tightened within the club and the board agreed that any member whose dues were more than six-dollars in arrears, would have to pay off their debts or be dropped from membership.[104] As indicative of the entertainment era, the board voted to spend $25 for a cabinet to hold the player-piano records [rolls] and an additional $10 for graphophone records.[105] [Volta Graphophone Company was the original name that eventually became Columbia Records. The graphophone "records" were cylinders played by a phonography-type needle and transmitted via a cone]. By July, the board authorized the purchase of an electric fan for $15.[106]

The income property at 1330 Glenarm Place was not meeting the expectations of the club since the newspaper boys purchased it in 1910. By 1917, building expenses increased as the club needed to put the two-story house into "fairly decent shape to make it habitable," according to House Manager D. F. Stackelbeck. "Sometime in April, just after you [the current board of directors] had taken charge of the club's affairs, the tenant decamped in the night, leaving the house in almost unbelievable shape. Dead chickens and dead rabbits were rotting in the cellar, the rooms were filled with refuse of every description, the paper had been torn off some of the walls and the woodwork had been ruined by spikes and nails being driven into it. Paperhangers and decorators refused to go to work in the house until the cause of the stench and the refuse had been removed."

Even with the mortgage balance of $3,000. Mr. Stackelbeck considered the property to be a poor investment with a liability that did not expect being beneficial to the club's finances. With a six-percent interest rate on the mortgage ($180 per annum), $90 city property taxes, water rent $25.50, and fire insurance $6 — the club was renting at $25 a month, when a tenant could be found.

Denver Press Club President Wilcox also served as the president of the United Workers for the Blind. Wilcox reiterated, "When we came to make personal inspection of our real estate possession at 1330 Glenarm Street—that *bête noir* of all former administrations—we found the premises in deplorable condition with everything in the most disgusting state of dilapidation imaginable. The former tenant had evaporated with two charming daughters, leaving an unpaid rental bill of $80 which has never been collected for the reason that we could not locate the missing tenant."[107] If the club president wasn't blind of sight, his assessment of the building would be based on more than his olfactory assessment.

After three days of work, the house was clean enough to discover that some of the plumbing was removed, the house keys were missing, the walls required repapering, and the plumbing had to be returned to being functional. When winter set in, the press club discovered the roof was badly leaking and the water threatened to destroy the furnishings in the upper rooms.

Stackelbeck explained that work on the building should have been done years ago, and the previous tenant helped speed the deterioration of the building after paying only $15 in rent before skipping town. Repairs cost the club $616.70 and total rental revenue was $140.00; a net loss of $476.70 for one year. President Wilcox's presidential message described the building as "the shack" and the "incubus" during his presentation at the annual meeting.

"I submit these figures to your board for your serious consideration," wrote Stackelbeck. "In my judgment, the club should not hesitate to sell the property at once and invest the proceeds in certificates of deposit or some good bonds, even if the sale meant the sacrifice of part of the investment."[108] When the board invited their house manager to present his findings during the next board meeting three days later, it only took one motion to recommend the sale of the club's equity in real estate for no less than $6,000.

The 1917-1918 press club activities included the annual picnic which offered a 200-mile auto-car excursion to Estes Park for eighty-seven of the members and "women folks" through the courtesy of Harry Behrens of the Tourist Bureau and the Estes Park Transportation Company. The value of the donated excursion for the Denver Press Club was valued to be close to $900 in 1917 prices.

At a special meeting of the Board of Directors, past president Lute Wilcox was granted active life membership in the Denver Press Club because of his "faithful and efficient management of the club in that capacity and his long and faithful devotion to the interests of the organization."[109] The following month, the board voted to amend the club's constitution to allow voting rights to previously non-voting active members of the club — there was no explanation for the category "non-voting active members" versus "voting active members." Additional agenda items included a $25 donation to the Red Cross, and instructions to deny all privileges to club members who failed to pay their buffet tab. Once the buffet chits were cleared, previously deficient diners were be allowed a maximum of $3.00 in buffet credits.[110] By September, Denver Press Club President Seymour tendered his resignation as president for unspecified reasons, but was outvoted by the remainder of the board; President Seymour resumed his presidency.[111] At the November 11 meeting of the board of directors, it was decided that "because of its present financial difficulties, at once sell at market price the five $100 Liberty Bonds of the Third Issue held by the club."[112]

The beginning of 1919 spawned the usual festivities; Spencer Penrose, president of the Broadmoor Hotel, invited the forty-to-fifty[113] members of the Denver Press Club to come to Colorado Springs as his guests.[114] The purpose of the trip was seen as a fence-building effort of getting the newsmen from both cities to drop the rivalry that developed during the past few years.[115]

The March annual board meeting of the Denver Press Club was held with many members absent. President Robert G. Seymour addressed the remaining members. "War conditions have been a source of difficulty in conducting the affairs of the club thru-out the last press club year. Nevertheless, the war has added to the glory of the club history. It is enough merely to point to the service flag flying from the window and tell its history to convince you of that . . . There are thirty-three stars on that flag, one of them of gold, for [the death of] Harvey Setchel. Here is the list of the other members and former members who offered themselves to the country's cause but whose lives, thank God, were spared."

John S. Barrows	Karl W. Davey	Jerome M. Strauss
Lester Barkhausen	Deane H. Dickason	John C. Vivian
Russell Chellgard	Charles E. Lounsbury	Delos Walker
Harry B. Curtis	Marty O'Toole	E. J. Welch
Victor Friar	James Grafton Rogers	F. H. Ricketson
Milton Dunn	Frank McKnight	Philip S. Van Cise
Charles Gray	George Minot	W. R. Fawcett
Lloyd Hamilton	Stanley Mitchell	Alexander B. Cuscaden
Joseph Hosmer	Ray M. Humphreys	Frank E. White
E. M. Hoover	Ray T. Morgan	Fred M. Pettit
Charles Mace	John F. O'Brian	Albert Gardner
Arthur McLennan	William A. Robinson	John M. Steele
Byron L. Akers	Joseph Satterthwaite	Richard Milton

"And while we glory in this record," continued the club president, "we must consider seriously the materiality of this incident in our affairs as it affects the club. For the absence of a few men from the club rooms each day means all the difference between meeting expenses and not meeting them."[116] The operating expenses of approximately $5,500 fell short of the $5,000 in revenue for the year. Even with the addition of three associate members, the club was losing $100 a month during the war. The club attempted to sell the building at 1330 Glenarm Place, but the war conditions created in a slack business-property market. Buffet tabs, unpaid dues, and a decrease in membership due to the war effort was putting the club's finances into jeopardy.

President Seymour noted that a provision in the club's constitution prohibited indebted members of the club from voting at regular meetings, albeit they must pay dues. Mr. Seymour noted that provision was completely illegal under the laws of Colorado. "It is perfectly legal to restrict the officers of the club to members actually employed on newspapers," the club president explained. "If the club wished, it might provide that only members with red hair might be president of the club. But once a man is member of the club, he acquires a voting interest and the property interest in the holdings of the club which is removed by depriving him of his right to a voice in the control of the club holdings." President Seymour described this situation as "practically killing the spirit of a great number of members and in keeping them from taking any interest in the club's affairs." With the privilege restored, the club resumed monthly meetings to rejuvenate the spirit of the club and refresh the income stream. "You will readily see that if you get half a dozen more members of the club coming to the rooms regularly and spending only twenty or thirty cents, the club receipts would more nearly approach the $10 a day needed to meet expenses,"[117] said Mr. Seymour.

Additional problems were cited, including a federal tax of ten-percent on dues; the club could reduce the annual dues to $11 and provide each member an additional month of free dues, or increase the dues to $1.25 a month to pay the tax.

The influenza epidemic closed many public performances and canceled the 1918 press club fund-raising show. Nevertheless, the club president proposed "an amateur theatrical stunt that should prove a 'scream,' and another that the club alone, without the intervention of any so-called impresarios of local infamy, bring some great artist like [operatic German contralto Ernestine] Schumann-Heink or [operatic Irish tenor John Francis] McCormack to the Auditorium at popular prices."[118]

The return of overseas servicemen after the war rekindled the press club. John S. Barrows returned to newspaper work after spending a year overseas as a lieutenant in the American Expeditionary Forces. Two other ex-service men, Jerome Strauss and Ford M. Pettit, were honored with places on the board of directors.[119]

*****

Maud Powell became a featured entertainer at the Auditorium Theatre under the auspices of the Denver Press Club. She performed in Denver often enough to gain a following of admirers. As the *Denver Post* reported, "With her playing and the Press Club's plugging, the concert will be an assured success in both an artistic and a social way."[120] The newspaper later reported in the purest "plugging" sense, "Maud Powell is one of the few in artistic life who is possessed with common sense. She takes no liberties because she is an artist. She does not presume that the public is willing to overlook eccentricities. She is too much American to insist upon privileges because of her talents. She is also one of the few artists who project themselves over the foot-lights, who take their audience into their confidence and lay their heart's impulses bare in their interpretations of the masters, who feel, and make their hearts feel joy, sorrow, pathos and victory triumphant."[121]

Proceeds from the concert were $1,650 from the Auditorium ticket sales, minus $160 for the war tax. After paying for the entertainment, the net profit for the performance was approximately $500 in 1919 dollars.[122] The performance was one of her last; she collapsed on stage in St. Louis later that year with a non-fatal heart-attack and passed away of a second heart attack during the warm-up for a concert in Uniontown, Pennsylvania.[123]

Salary increases were on tap following the October 1919 board meeting. The salary of the board secretary was doubled from $5 a week to $10, and the weekly pay for Jimmy Wong and Joe Diner (evening and daytime club stewards) was increased $3 a week, providing them each with a weekly salary of $20.[124] The club property at 1330 Glenarm Place was once again put on the market for $7,500.[125] Another small committee was established to begin searching for new club quarters for the newspapermen.[126]

The renewed financial stability of the Denver Press Club apparently improved to enable Santa Claus to visit the club and leave presents for the children of Denver's newspapermen. This was his first visit to the club since the war, and the celebrants were entertained with a jazz orchestra, a brilliantly illuminated Christmas tree, and refreshments. The annual custom to give each child his most urgent request written in a letter to

Santa Claus was reinstituted.[127] According to the board minutes, the Christmas party to entertain the fifty children cost $150.[128]

Before the end of the year, the press-club board accepted an invitation from the Colorado Editorial Association to attend their annual banquet at the Albany Hotel on January 19. The club performed three or four skits in the "Gridiron" style and provided music and dance after the supper. The three-day conference covered various aspects of the newspaper profession.[129] According to press club secretary Jerome M. Strauss, "It is safe to say that the benefits to the club in general, recognition, and goodwill; will remain for years to come. The dinner and entertainment were attended by the governor, mayor, and prominent state and city officials. The occasion served to bring the Press Club into the spotlight of publicity, a paradoxical position for its members, who are more accustomed to give this than receive."[130] Members were encouraged to re-develop publicity for the press club within their own newspaper offices. The club recognized that the amount and quality of press coverage for the work the Denver newspapermen provided to the community, were dwindling. Members believed their profession should be raised back to the same level as lawyers and physicians. "The dissemination of knowledge thru the medium of the press is no mean task," reported the club president. "The Press Club should lay claim to its share of influence and prestige in the community."[131]

Several months later at the annual meeting, the members noted that the future of the club resided in the organization paying more attention to the families of members. It was recommended that social events be scheduled once a month to be of interest to both men and women.

During 1919-1920, the Denver Press Club held a Christmas tree party for nearly two hundred people, including seventy-three children; and a memorable New Year celebration. The Press Club Frolic and a Cowboy Stampede, given jointly with the Colorado Editorial Association, also featured appearances by Miss Colorado and Miss Wyoming. The annual picnic and Splash were held at Eldorado Springs and a barbecue at W. N. W. Blayney's ranch was attended by an odd conglomeration of more than five-hundred people, including visiting theatrical folks as well as officials from Denver packing houses. Two pool tournaments, the entertainment of Poet Edgar A. Guest of Detroit, and a visitation by Senator Warren G. Harding were among the other activities of the year.[132]

The annual meeting on March 1, 1920, was better attended than the previous year; the servicemen were back in town and working, and the Denver

Press Club was regaining its social luster of the pre-war days. The previous eleven months generated $8,724.39 in receipts and $7,568.87 in disbursements, leaving a positive cash flow of $1,155.52 to add to the bank balance of $450.09. The total cash balance on hand and in the bank was $1,605.61, according to the annual report.[133] During that time, forty-six new members were enrolled and only sixteen names were stricken for various reasons.

The club's real-estate investment property at 1330 Glenarm Place remained unsold. Attempts to keep the building rented for $30 a month nearly offset the interest and taxes, leaving nothing in the return on the investment. The greatest economic concern for the club was the property and the $3,000 mortgage; the three-year note covering the property loan was due in July 1920.[134] At that time, the board could retire the remaining debt and the building would become a debt-free asset to the club. The club's present rooms at 1715 California Street cost $90 a month to rent (including janitorial services), but the lease expired on April 1, and the owner refused to renew the lease. The club could continue the rent for $127.50 a month without a long-term lease or move on. "The Press Club was seriously affected by the war," reported Secretary Jerome M. Strauss. "Many of its members were in the nation's services. Its social activities were almost wiped out. The natural results were a depleted treasury and a general lessening of interest in the affairs of the club."[135]

Members at the annual meeting thought this was an appropriate time for the club to move into their own building and another search committee was formed. The club was unable to negotiate a long-term lease for the present club rooms and engaged in a month-to-month rental, prohibiting the club from budgeting funds for improvements. Committees were appointed to seek suitable quarters, but nothing was found. The nearby Ramona Hotel was being rehabilitated, but even the smallest number of rooms required by the club would cost the press club $200 a month with only a five-year lease. Club president John S. Barrows appealed to the members during the 1920 annual meeting.

"We have a ten-room house on Glenarm street [Place] opposite the Denver Athletic Club," stated Barrows. "The only value the property has at present is a location value; the house itself being in very poor condition. The first and chief objection in the past to this house as a possible club house has been its distance from newspaper center."[136] The press club property was located five blocks from the *Denver Post* which is approximately the same as their present meeting rooms. It was closer to the *Denver Express* and to the State House, but a longer walk for members from the *Rocky Mountain News* and *Denver Times*. Money spent on rehabilitating the building would be in the interest of the club and would enhance any future price when the building was sold.

With approximately $3,000 of capital improvements, the club could add a stucco facade, a porch could extend the width of the building, and a partition removed to make a large reading room and a pool/billiard room on the second floor. Wood fireplaces could be installed on the first and second floors, a kitchen, dining, card room, and other rooms could also be added. Steam heat could be conducted across Glenarm from the Denver Athletic Club at a reasonable cost. Outgoing President Barrows encouraged the next administration to give this proposal some consideration.[137] Each "could" carried its own substantial price tag.

The club's finances had to be rebuilt, membership and activities rekindled, and the club had to re-establish its position of influence in the community and service to its members. "What has been accomplished by the present administration may be attributed in large part to the support and co-operation of the general membership," continued the club secretary. "The success of the club necessarily must come thru the efforts of all, rather than of the few chosen as officials. Continuation of the spirit already shown cannot fail to place the Press Club in the front rank of the organizations of the city."[138]

A discussion was held about raising the membership dues, but the club treasurer believed that was ill-advised. "The purpose of the Press Club is to be of service to members of the newspaper profession at the least possible cost to them," Treasurer Charles McAllister Willcox reported. "The expense attaching to membership should be so low as to work no degree of hardship upon any member."[139] Others believed that revenues should be raised through other means other than assessing the members. Club members were encouraged to solicit new members and to actively participate in the club buffet as a means of strengthening the club's financial condition. As a further enhancement to encourage new members, the club's library was being enlarged with new books and periodicals for the popular use of the members.

The Entertainment Committee was instructed to consult with Abe Pollock and Rick Ricketson, Jr. to see if the club could schedule a smoker at the Elks Club to raise funds for the general operating fund.[140]

The Denver Press Club hosted a reception on behalf of Senator Warren G. Harding of Ohio on March 10, 1920. Senator Harding, a former newspaper editor, visited the club on several previous occasions and the attendance at the reception was extremely gratifying. "The club," president Jerome M. Strauss explained, "whenever possible, should have as guests the most important men of the nation on their visits to Denver. Its members are by the nature of their work in close touch with the leaders of business, professional and political affairs. The club should maintain itself on the same high place of importance."[141]

Future presidential candidates may promise a "chicken in every pot," but the Denver Press Club followed Senator Warren Harding's visit with a chicken fry at Troutdale in Bear Creek Cañon but prepared by the chefs from Denver's ten leading hotels. Automobile transportation was provided by the Union Motor and the Martin-Sweet Motor companies and supported by state and city officials, and prominent business men.[142] Before the event, the *Denver Post* reported additional details: "They will make the trip in two large motor buses, one a Hawkeye truck donated for the occasion by the Union Motor company, local Hawkeye truck and Templar car distributors."[143]

To continue raising funds to help repair the coffers of the Denver Press Club after the war, the mid-spring "frolic" was scheduled for May 19 in the Auditorium Theater. Among the "stunts" scheduled was a Denver Press Club minstrel show; performances by the Denver University Glee Club, the Little Theater players, and the Junior League.[144] Dancing was provided by nearly two dozen Denver society girls appeared in four of the performances, tumblers from the YMCA, and a variety of singing groups from various community organizations.[145]

Mrs. Grover Coors (wife of one of Adolf Coors' sons) pitched in with a lofty promotional stunt that seemed odd for one of Denver society's grand dames. Three thousand feet above the emerging skyline of Denver, Mrs. Coors and I. B. Humphreys steered an Oriole plane over the noontime lunch crowd and maneuvered the craft through a series of acrobatic paces before littering the streets with Denver Press Club Frolics leaflets thrown from the open cockpit of the stunt airplane.[146] Newspaper advertisements promoting the Frolic had better page-placement than the theater-section advertisements for the "Four Marx Brothers" who were appearing the following week at the Orpheum Theatre in Denver.[147]

When the curtain rose for the Denver Press Club Frolics, eleven vaudeville acts with local and professional talent delighted the local audience. As the *Denver Post* reported, Mlle. Domina Marini, late of the

Pavlova Imperial Russian ballet, and her troop provided a series of classical dances. Ned Connors, Floyd Spencer, and Mlle. Marini "presented a sketch entitled 'Pulling Caesar's Nose,' a burlesque-style interpretive dance the reviews described as screamingly funny and brought forth plenty of applause. One of the outstanding specialties of the evening's bill was the presentation of a brief comedy skit, 'The Very Naked Boy,' by a trio of Junior Leaguers." After a series of skits, songs, and dances, the Denver Press Club minstrels provided "local jokes and sallies," and minstrel interlocutor George T. Wells served as a "ouija-board medium of note."[148]

The success of the Frolics provided the Denver Press Club with sufficient funds to pay off the $3,000 mortgage on the club's property at 1330 Glenarm Place and release the title to the club with no further encumbrances.[149]

Governor James M. Cox of Ohio, Democratic presidential candidate, arrived in Denver through the auspices of former press-club president James R. Noland (and current Secretary of State) and was chauffeured to the Auditorium Theater by Mrs. Noland. Immediately after his speech to his supporters, the press club welcomed the candidate for a half-hour, private, meet-and-greet with the newspapermen.[150] Governor Cox was the publisher of a newspaper in his home town of Marion, Ohio, and earned the respect of the newspaper fraternity.[151]

Throughout the city, clubs and organizations found their niche in helping less fortunate in the community. The Denver Press Club held its annual Christmas party at the club rooms at 1715 California Street where seventy-five sons-and-daughters of newspapermen were entertained by local artists who provided dance music for the celebrants.[152] Songs were sung by the Denver Optimists' Club Quartet; interpretative dances exhibited by Mattie Lu Thomas, the eight-year-old daughter of one of the press club members; a short story was read by Janet Jersome of the Denver Public Library's staff of children's story tellers; and a solo was performed by Mrs. Horace Wilcox. Santa Claus bore an uncanny resemblance to press-club member Harry N. Burnhams of the Denver Tourist and Publicity Bureau.[153] A few days before Christmas, Santa Claus paid a visit to Denver—via the wireless radio. The press club board approved $10 gifts to C. E. Stout of Crestone, Colorado and Hugh O'Neill; Mr. Stout had a leg amputated while in the service overseas, and Mr. O'Neill was blind.[154]

Several packing companies and the Denver Livestock Exchange invited the Denver Press Club and their families to a September barbecue at the W.

N. W. Blayney Ranch in Lakewood.[155] The continuing relationship with the livestock component of Denver and the Rocky Mountain region was rekindled as the Colorado Editorial Association joined with the Denver Press Club in the production of a show for Stock Show Week. The January 22 presentation, "Cowboy Stampede," was held at the Auditorium and included a series of stunts.[156]

The Denver Press Club invited members of the Cheyenne Frontier Days to attend the final night of the Denver livestock show on January 22, 1921. Dr. B. F. Davis, chairman of the Frontier committee and the Wyoming Press Club, provided the services of several fancy-trick-rope twirlers, the appearance of Miss Wyoming, and other dignitaries.[157]

During the March 1921 Annual Meeting, the secretary reported a balance of $1,831.87 in the club's treasury, an increase of $347.88 over the previous year. During the year, thirty-five members were enrolled and sixteen were stricken from the membership rolls for various reasons, resulting in a net increase of nineteen new members.[158]

The May 1921 board of directors continued to look for new accommodations. While commercial property-broker T. B. Stearns was solicited by the club for one of his properties, the board also negotiated with the current landlord, Mr. Hamburger, for an extended lease agreement at $90 a month with improvements to be made to the entrance to the club's quarters.[159]

The stock-show entertainment collaboration with the Colorado Editorial Association proposed to outdo the previous entertainment and fill the Auditorium Theater. Booked for the event were five headliner numbers, a twelve-piece orchestra, and "a big bunch of singers—you know the kind—they sing the air while the orchestra wails and moans and groans in the throes of modern jazz and the Methodists in the audience have to sit on their feet to keep 'em still."[160]

To warm up the near sell-out crowd in the Auditorium Theater the Denver Press Club and the Colorado Editorial Association staged a "stampede" on stage in the form of an amateur variety show. A grand march formed behind Lieutenant Governor and Mrs. Cooley, and the Mayor and Mrs. Bailey.[161]

The 1921 event was a blend of the old and new. Miss Colorado was scheduled to ride into the Auditorium on horseback and participate in a staged hold-up to kick-off the tribute to the Old West. It "made the red blood of westerners tingle with old-time realism,"[162] according to a newspaper account. The governor, mayor, and their entourage led the grand march, but with air-borne music piped from the live radio station at Fitzsimons Hospital. It was the first time a large dance event was held in Denver with radio-transmitted music. Attired in appropriate western garb, noted western story-teller William MacLeod Raine escorted the newly crowned Miss Colorado, sixteen-year-old[163] Myrtle Pratt.[164] Helen Bonham, the reigning Miss Wyoming, was also in attendance at the western-themed editorial event.[165] She arrived a week early and was treated with great hospitality by the governor of Colorado and the press club.

To reciprocate, the Wyoming Frontier committee extended an invitation for Miss Colorado and her mother to be guests of the Cheyenne Frontier Days celebration July 26-29, 1921.[166] In a staged press event Miss Wyoming rode her horse to the Colorado statehouse, dismounted and walked into Governor Shoup's office to extend the formal invitations of the Cheyenne Frontier Days Committee and the Chamber of Commerce. Speaking directly to the governor, Helen Bonham declared her invitation to the Cheyenne Frontier Days, "This is the real thing in invitations. This is no bunk. We want you to be there."[167] Miss Wyoming then remounted and crossed the park to the Denver City and County Building to extend the same invitation to the mayor. A reception was scheduled for 10 a.m. in the governor's office—without the horse.[168]

Miss Colorado Myrtle Pratt and Miss Wyoming Helen Bonham made appearances together throughout 1921 until a controversy developed in October. The state delegation of the American Legion was preparing to attend their national convention in Kansas City at the end of the month and proposed to hold a beauty contest to select their own "Miss Colorado" to attend the event. The Denver Press Club filed a complaint with the American Legion that choosing a competing "Miss Colorado" was "in bad taste and 'ill advised.'"[169]

"The American Legion challenges the right of the Denver Press Club or any other organization to question the American Legion in its proposed selection of a Miss Colorado,"[170] declared William S. Rathbun, chairman of the Denver central-committee. "The American Legion announced a short time ago that it purposed the selection of Colorado's 100 percent girl. This was to be a statewide campaign, and the final selection was to be made among candidates representing every section of the state. The selection was to be made on merit alone . . . The American Legion has no wish to interfere with the Denver Press Club in any of its activities, nor does it dispute its right to make a selection of that character, but it does call upon the Press Club to show how and why Miss Pratt comes by her title, and, if the title really is her's [sic], whether she can show to the satisfaction of the legion and the people of Colorado that she really is qualified to be designated as 'Colorado's 100 percent girl' . . . There is no intention on the part of the legion to question the desirability of Miss Myrtle Pratt. She is undoubtedly a representative Colorado girl, wholesome, pretty and of a winning personality, but is she superior to all other Colorado girls? . . . It is up to the Denver Press Club to prove its point."[171]

Despite the assertion that the Denver Press Club's Miss Colorado was supported by the governor, the Colorado Springs members of the American Legion continued to protest the newspapermen's representative of Colorado feminine wholesomeness. Victor W. Hungerford, the commander of the Colorado American Legion, saw no reason a single organization should take it upon themselves to appoint Miss Colorado without a fair competition among all of Colorado's young women.[172] President Griffin of the Colorado Editorial Association countered with a plea "in deference to the proclamation of Governor Shoup and the wish of the Denver Press Club,"[173] that Miss Pratt should maintain the honor of representing the state.

By mid-October, the 16-year-old representative of Colorado was tired of the controversy. In a letter to the governor, Miss Pratt wrote, "I have been reading the pieces in the papers from the legion and the Press Club, and I don't know what to do. Of course, I would consider it an esteemed honor to go to Kansas City with the legion boys, but if there is any question about me going as 'Miss Colorado,' why I would rather not go . . . I think the best thing for me to do is to tender my resignation as 'Miss Colorado,' for I am terribly mixed up over the whole affair . . . and while I do not like to annoy you with this matter, I think it would probably be better for me to drop quietly out of the whole affair and thereby stop further debate."[174]

Not wanting to harm a teenage girl's dreams, the Denver American Legionnaries stepped forward, refused Miss Pratt's resignation, and requested that the governor renew her appointment to the coveted honor. They also "begged" her to represent the legion as Miss Colorado at their national convention in Kansas City. W. S. Rathbun of the American Legion committee acknowledged that "her refusal to allow a conflict to rage between two friendly organizations shows that she has their interests at heart, and it would be a most unchivalrous attitude for the legion to take if it permitted her to resign at this time."[175]

To show there was no ill-will between the two organizations, the Denver Press Club provided a "royal send-off" as the American Legionnaires prepared for their national convention in Kansas City. Speeches by the governor, mayor and other public-spirited citizens enlivened interesting stories, music and stunts quickly prepared for presentation at the Auditorium theatre party. With no admission charged, the press club expected a packed house on behalf of the Legionnaires.[176]

The Colorado Springs Legionnaires had one final word—Miss Rowena Dashwood was officially designated "Miss Pikes Peak" and would join Miss Colorado and Miss Wyoming at the national convention.[177]

During the October 6, 1921, regular board meeting; book-publisher Joseph Landers met to discuss "a biographical work of prominent men and women in the Rocky Mountain region."[178] The proposition was appealing enough to be fully offered at a special meeting four days later. At that time, the board agreed to enter into an agreement for the publication and delivery of the book on a 60-40 basis with Landers assuming all expenses and receive the sixty-percent share. The Denver National Bank held the escrow fund.[179] *Who's Who in the Rockies* provided a compendium of "the leaders in every line of endeavor—industry, letters, statecraft, education, social progress . . . It is with a view to diffusing the knowledge of their works, and of rousing in the hearts of those who shall come to citizenship after them a desire for similar patriotic service that this book is brought before the public."[180]

By September 1922, Landers reported approximately $22,500 was collected and he requested an extension of the solicitation period to January 1923. The proposed book included the name of each subscriber in gilt lettering on the back cover; this was later repositioned to appear on the front cover at the bottom. It was decided by the club's publications committee, that neither the former presidents of the club, the incumbent, the book committee nor any other names should appear in the book.[181] *Who's Who in the* Rockies was an effective fund-raising gimmick that enabled the new wave of young Denver businessmen to help fatten the press club's building fund by paying for their photograph and biographical sketch published in the impressive leather-bound book. Press club members McEniry, White and Bartlett were designated to ghost-write the biographies appearing in the book.[182]

The board assigned Robert G. Seymour to write a brief sketch for the Denver Press Club's page. Seymour was appointed as the press club's second historian. For the book project, the board asked him to compile data on the organization.[183] His response appeared as "The Denver Press Club Creed." that referenced the more recent incorporation of the club instead of the 19th Century origins.[184]

> Ever since its birth in 1905, the Denver Press Club has been a vital force in the Rocky Mountain region.
>
> Never in politics, it always has fought against anything that tended to bring disgrace to Colorado and striven for everything that would maintain the sacred ideals of the Commonwealth. Never in business, it nevertheless has sought to encourage commerce and industry, to criticize honestly, and to stamp out unmanliness and cowardice, to quicken good impulses, and crush that which is dishonest and unfair.
>
> Its charities, though limited, are discriminating, heartfelt and unheralded.
>
> The Denver Press Club stands for that which is clean, that which is right, that which is ethical, and that which is honorable. It seeks to destroy the germs of wrong and to plant the seeds of right thinking and right living.
>
> It represents a profession whose breadth and power is limited only by the confines of the world itself. Its basic membership is composed exclusively of newspapermen in Denver and throughout the state.[185]

The October board chose to recognize the valuable services being rendered to the club by awarding a complimentary active membership and a key to club to Mr. Landers, valid until the new board was elected in April 1923.

1   "Stage Set for Grand Round-Up Week Jan. 19-24," *Denver Post,* December 28, 1913, p. 66
2   "Roundup Week! It's Comin' Folks Biggest, Best Denver's Ever Seen: Press Club Prepares to Stage Greatest Entertainment In City's History to Tickle Fancies of Visitors When Annual Stock Show Is On," *Denver Post,* November

16, 1913, p. 5

3   Ibid

4   "Social Doings in Stock Show Week to be a Feature," *Denver Post*, December 7, 1913, p. 19

5   "Press Club Plans Grandest Boost West Ever Had," *Denver Post*, December 21, 1913, p. 10

6   "Western Stock Show: Denver Press Club Plans Succession of Entertainments and Surprises for Forty Thousand Visitors," *Journal of Douglas County* (Castle Rock, Colorado), December 26, 1913, p. 6

7   "One Lively Week Assured Guests of City, Jan. 19-24," *Denver Post*, January 4, 1914, p. 11

8   "All Denver Clubs Unite in Boosting Roundup Festival," *Denver Post*, December 28, 1913, p. 15

9   "Other Events Give Way to Press Dance," *Denver Times*, December 11, 1913, p. 12

10   "400 Editors Coming for Round-Up Week," *Denver Times*, December 29, 1913, p. 12

11   Ibid

12   "To Tango on Streets," *Greensboro* (North Carolina) *Record*, January 21, 1914, p. 2

13   "Roundup Week? Shore! Them Lit'ry Guys Sets In On Stacks O' Bloos!, *Denver Times*, January 9, 1914, p. 7

14   "Press Club Plans Big Smoker for Entertainment of Stockmen," *Denver Post*, January 7, 1914, p. 12

15   "Press Club Doin's to be Humdinger Stockmen's Week," *Denver Post*, November 30, 1913, p. 29

16   "Honor in Store for Some Girl as 'Round-Up Queen'," *Denver Post*, December 14, 1913, p. 17

17   "Roundup Queen to be Crowned Tonight," *Denver times*, January 21, 1914, p. 5

18   "Queen Bess to Ride in State at Press Club Round-Up Fete," *Denver Post*, January 15, 1914, p. 14

19   "Roundup Queen to be Crowned Tonight," *Denver Times*, January 21, 1914, p. 5

20   "Stockmen Lope 'The Lariat' at Press Club Hop," *Denver Times*, January 22, 1914, p. 5

21   Ibid

22   "40,000 Persons to Visit Denver and Stock Show," *Denver Post*, December 14, 1913, p. 31

23   "New Features for Stock Show Expected to Attract 40,000 Outside Visitors to Stadium," *Rocky Mountain News*, December 18, 1913, p. 9

24 "Howelsen Hill Area, ColoradoSkiHistory.com; www.coloradoskihistory.com/history/open/howelsen.html

25 "Ski Jumping Is Opener of Roundup Week," *Denver Post*, January 11, 1914, p. 30

26 "Throngs Flock to Ski Run for Roundup Jumps," *Denver Post*, January 15, 1914, p. 10

27 "Amateur Bird Men Ready for Big Ski Jumps," *Denver Post*, January 16, 1914, p. 10

28 "Norway's Champion Ski Jumper to Thrill Denver Folk Today," *Denver Post*, January 18, 1914, p. 6

29 "International Ski tournament to Be Staged in Denver," *Denver Post*, January 19, 1914, p. 5

30 "Denver Press Club Applies the 'Brand-Iron' to Celebrities of State and Nation in Burlesque," *Gazette-Telegraph*, January 20, 1914

31 Ibid

32 "F. C. Farrar Heads Denver Press Club," *Denver Times*, March 9, 1914, p. 5

33 Minutes, Denver Press Club Board of Directors, April 8, 1914

34 Minutes, Special meeting of the Denver Press Club, Adams Hotel, Sunday, April 5, 1914

35 Minutes, Board of Directors meeting, April 8, 1914

36 Ibid

37 Minutes, Board of Directors meeting, April 12, 1914

38 Minutes, Board of Directors, Sunday May 3, 1914

39 "Press Club Calls Motor Cue Tourney," *Denver Post*, March 19, 1914, p. 10

40 "Press Club Plans Frolic in Hills," *Denver Post*, May 24, 1914, p. 10

41 "Week Bulging With Good Things to Come With Reunion of Elks," *Denver Post*, June 7, 1914, p. 4

42 "Race Officers Guests of Denver Press Club," *Denver Post*, June 13, 1914, p. 9

43 Minutes, Board of Directors, June 14, 1914

44 Minutes, Board of Directors, August 10, 1914

45 "Beachey Will Loop Loop in Denver Under Auspices of the Press Club," *Denver Post*, September 6, 1914, p. 8

46 "Spectacular Flight Ends in Grim Death," Dr. Richard Stimson, *Wright Contemporaries*, www.wrightstories.com

47 "Air King Beachey Wagers Life He'll Loop the Loop in Denver," *Denver Post*, September 20, 1914, p. 24

48 Ibid

49 Ibid

50 "Navy Secretary Considers Aviator Beachey's Plan to Improve Nation's Air Fleet," *Denver Post*, September 27, 1914, p. 12

51 "Beachey Dares Death to Keep Contract with Denver People," *Denver Post*,

October 9, 1914, p. 6

52 Minutes, Board of Directors, October 11, 1914

53 Minutes, Denver Press Club Board of Directors, October 18, 1914

54 Minutes, Board of Directors, November 8, 1914

55 Minutes, Denver Press Club Board of Directors, November 15, 1914

56 Correspondence from Frank Farrar, President, Denver Press Club to an unknown recipient; November 21, 1914

57 Minutes, Denver Press Club Board of Directors, November 22, 1914

58 Minutes, Denver Press Club Board of Directors, November 15, 1914

59 Minutes, Denver Press club Board of Directors, November 19, 1914

60 Minutes, Denver Press Club Board of Directors, December 20, 1914

61 Minutes, Denver Press Club Board of Directors, January 3, 1915

62 "Stock Show Week in Denver," *Journal of Douglas County,* January 8, 1915, p. 1

63 Letter, Harry Lee Wilber, Denver Post; to Harry N. Burnhams, Chairman Brand-Iron Dinner Comte, Denver Press Club; January 31, 1915

64 Minutes, Denver Press Club Board of Directors, January 24, 1915

65 Minutes, Annual Meeting of the Denver Press Club, 14 March 1915; "Press Club Elects Lewis President," *Denver Post,* March 15, 1915, p. 10

66 Minutes, Annual Meeting of the Denver Press Club, March 14, 1915

67 "Press Club Denounces House for Excluding Post Reporters," *Denver Post,* March 15, 1915, p. 3

68 Minutes, Annual Breakfast Meeting of the Denver Press Club, Metropole Hotel, April 11, 1915

69 "Delegates Home from Press Club Convention," *Wilkes-Barre Times,* July 24, 1905

70 Minutes, Annual Breakfast Meeting of the Denver Press Club, Metropole Hotel, April 11, 1915

71 Minutes, Denver Press Club Board of Directors, May 28, 1915

72 "Idaho Springs Host at Press Club Fete," *Rocky Mountain News,* June 21, 1915

73 "Press Club Visits Idaho Springs, Members Splash in the Radium Pool," *Denver Times,* June 21, 1915

74 "Press Club to Go On Outing; to be Guests of Idaho Springs," *Denver Times,* June 17, 1915

75 "Press Club to Make Annual Splash of Season Sunday at Idaho Springs," *Denver Post,* June 17, 1915, p. 6

76 "Idaho Springs Host at Press Club Fete, *Rocky Mountain News,* June 21, 1915

77 "Press Club to Make Annual Splash of Season Sunday at Idaho Springs," *Denver Post,* June 17, 1915, p. 6

78 Minutes, Board of Directors of the Denver Press Club, June 24, 1915

79 "Press Club Fairy Going for Stroll in Low-Cut Socks," *Denver Post,* August 29, 1915, p. 22

80 Ibid

81 "Best and Most Glorious Christmas Leaves Glow in Every Denver Heart," *Denver Post,* December 26, 1915, p. 3

82 Minutes, Denver Press Club Board of Directors, May 19, 1916

83 "Proteges of Czar Play in Denver at Press Club Show," *Denver Post,* November 19, 1916, p. 14

84 "Directors Elected by Blind Workers," *Denver Post,* December 21, 1917, p. 23

85 Minutes, Denver Press Club Board of Directors, March 22, 1917

86 Minutes, Denver Press Club Board of Directors, April 1, 1917

87 Minutes, Denver Press Club Board of Directors, April 8, 1917

88 Minutes, Denver Press Club Board of Directors, June 15, 1917

89 Minutes, Denver Press Club Board of Directors, September 10, 1917

90 "Marcella Craft Shines in role of 'Violetta' in 'La Traviata'," *Denver Post,* December 29, 1917, p. 4

91 Minutes, Denver Press Club Board of Directors, December 3, 1917

92 Letter, D. F. Stackelbeck, House Manager, Denver Press Club; to the Board of Directors of the Denver Press Club; October 1, 1917

93 Ibid

94 Minutes, Denver Press Club Board of Directors, February 4, 1918

95 "Roosevelt Predicts State Will Be Playground of the Entire World," *Rocky Mountain News,* October 26, 1916, p. 1

96 "Roosevelt Predicts State Will be Playground of the Entire World," *Rocky Mountain News,* October 26, 1916, p. 1

97 Ibid

98 "Lieut. Melville Training Soldiers" *Denver Post,* February 17, 1918, p. 36

99 Minutes, Special Meeting fo the Denver Press Club Board of Directors, June 14, 1918

100 Minutes, Denver Press Club Board of Directors, March 4, 1918

101 "Denver Press Club Selects as President Robert G. Seymour," *Denver Post,* March 18, 1918, p. 5

102 "Whole City Responds on First Day of Great Liberty Loan Drive," *Denver Post,* April 16, 1918, p. 8

103 "Blind Workers of City Planting and Cultivating War Gardens," *Denver Post,* April 21, 1918, p. 18

104 Minutes, Denver Press Club Board of Directors, April 1, 1918

105 Minutes, Denver Press Club Board of Directors, April 15, 1918

106 Minutes, Denver Press Club Board of Directors, July 9, 1918

107 The President's Annual Report, Lute Wilcox, March 1918

108 Letter, D. F. Stackelbeck, House Manager, Denver Press Club; to the Board of Directors, Denver Press Club; March 7, 1918

109 Minutes, Denver Press Club Special Meeting of the Board of Directors, April

23, 1918

110 Minutes, Denver Press Club Board of Directors, May 20, 1918

111 Minutes, Denver Press Club Board of Directors, September 9, 1918

112 Minutes, Denver Press Club Board of Directors, November 11, 1918

113 "Turner Makes Plans for Press Banquet," *Colorado Springs Gazette-Telegraph,* March 11, 1919

114 "Denver Press Club Invited to Springs, *Colorado Springs Gazette,* January 18, 1919, p. 1

115 "The Denver Press Club's Visit," *Colorado Springs Gazette,* January 22, 1919

116 Annual Report of the President of the Denver Press Club, Robert G. Seymour; March 9, 1919

117 Annual Report of the President of the Denver Press Club, Robert G. Seymour; March 9, 1919

118 Ibid

119 "Barrows Elected Press Club Head," *Denver Post,* March 10, 1919, p. 3

120 "Maud Powell Plays in Auditorium Under Press Club Auspices," *Denver Post,* May 18, 1919, p. 49

121 "Maud Powell is One Artist Who Confides in Audience," *Denver Post,* May 25, 1919, p. 44

122 Minutes, Denver Press Club Board of Directors, June 6, 1919

123 www.maudpowell.org

124 Minutes, Denver Press Club Board of Directors, October 1, 1919

125 Ibid

126 Minutes, Denver Press Club Board of Directors, December 29, 1919

127 "Santa Visits Denver Press Club Party," *Pueblo Chieftain,* December 25, 1919

128 Minutes, Denver Press Club Board of Directors, December 29, 1919

129 "Colorado Editors Open Convention Monday Morning," *Denver Post,* January 19, 1920, p. 3

130 Annual Report of the President of the Denver Press Club, March 14, 1920

131 Ibid.

132 Presidential message, 1920 Annual Report, March 1920

133 Report of the Secretary of the Denver Press Club for the Eleven Months Ending March 1, 1920

134 Ibid.

135 Ibid

136 Message from the President, John S. Barrows; Denver Press Club Annual Meeting, March 1920

137 Message from the President, John S. Barrows; Denver Press Club Annual Meeting, March 1920

138 Message from the President, John S. Barrows; Denver Press Club Annual Meeting, March 1920

139 Message from the President, John S. Barrows; Denver Press Club Annual Meeting, March 1920

140 Minutes, Denver Press Club Board of Directors, March 14, 1920

141 Ibid.

142 "Hotels to Entertain Denver Press Club With Chicken Dinner," *Denver Post*, April 18, 1920, p. 70

143 "Denver Press Club Members to Go to Boulder in Autos," *Denver Post*, May 2, 1920, p. 39

144 *Denver Post*, May 1, 1920, p. 6

145 "Pretty Society Girls to Dance at Press Club Frolic May 19," *Denver Post*, May 13, 1920, p. 22

146 "Society Woman to Press Agent Frolic From Sky," *Denver Post*, May 16, 1920, p. 5

147 Advertisement, *Denver Post*, May 17, 1920, p. 9

148 "Press Club Makes Decided Hit with its Annual Frolic," *Denver Post*, May 20, 1920, p. 9

149 Minutes, Denver Press Club Board of Directors, July 28, 1920

150 "Cox Will Go Directly From His Train to the Auditorium to Speak," *Denver Post*, September 24, 1920, p. 16

151 "Governor Cox Pays Respects to Oligarchy Ruling Senate," *Colorado Springs Gazette*, September 25, 1920, p. 1, 3

152 "Jolliest Christmas Ever is Provided by Denver People," *Denver Post*, December 22, 1920, p. 6

153 "Press Club Gives Out Program for Christmas Party," *Denver Post*, December 29, 1920

154 Minutes, Denver Press Club Board of Directors, December 29, 1920

155 "Denver Press Club to Attend Big Feed at Blayney Ranch," *Denver Post*, September 5, 1920, p. 59

156 "Editors Will Disport in 'Cowboy Stampede' Week of Stock Show," *Denver Post*, December 12, 1920, p. 10

157 "Frontier Day Events at Denver on Final Night Stock Show," *Wyoming State Tribune*, December 31, 1920, p. 2

158 Report of the Secretary of the Denver Press Club for the Eleven Months Ended March 1, 1921

159 Minutes, Denver Press Club Board of Directors, May 6, 1921

160 "Cowboy Stampede Big Feature Stock Show," *Eaton Herald*, January 7, 1921, p. 1

161 "Stampede Draws Big Attendance to Auditorium," *Denver Post*, January 23, 1921, p. 47

162 "Expresses Thanks for Help on Show," *Wyoming State Tribune-Cheyenne State Leader*, January 31, 1921, p. 2

163 "Miss Colorado is Invited to Attend Frontier Roundup," *Rocky Mountain News,* July 8, 1921, p. 5

164 "'Cowboy Stampede' at the Auditorium Offered by Writers," *Denver Post,* January 16, 1921, p. 41

165 "Miss Wyoming May Meet Miss Colorado," *Wyoming State Tribune* (Cheyenne, Wyoming), January 20, 1921, p. 1

166 "Miss Colorado Invited to Come to Celebration," *Wyoming State Tribune-Cheyenne State Leader,* July 7, 1921

167 "'This is No Bunk,' Says Miss Wyoming to Governor Shoup; Latter Will Attend Frontier," *Wyoming State Tribune-Cheyenne State Leader,* July 16, 1921

168 "Miss Wyoming to Invite Miss Colorado Here," *Wyoming State Tribune,* July 14, 1921, p. 10

169 "Press Club Protests Selection of Miss Colorado by Legion," *Denver Post,* October 9, 1921, p. 66

170 "Legion Challenges Right of Press Club to Dictate Choice of 'Miss Colorado'", *Denver Post,* October 11, 1921, p. 2

171 Ibid.

172 "Says No One Has Mortgage on Name of 'Miss Colorado'", *Gazette-Telegraph,* October 14, 1921

173 "Editorial Association Protests Selection of a 'Miss Colorado' as Proposed by American Legion," *Denver Post,* October 14, 1921, p. 20

174 "Miss Myrtle E. Pratt Resigns as Miss Colorado to Conclude Press Club-Legion Dispute," *Denver Post,* October 16, 1921, p. 5

175 "Quarrel Over 'Miss Colorado' Ended When Legion Requests Miss Pratt to Represent It," *Denver Post,* October 17, 1921, p. 11

176 "Busy Week Ahead for Theatergoers," *Denver Post,* October 23, 1921, p. 40

177 "Miss Pikes Peak Introduced Denver at Rally Last Night," *Colorado Springs Gazette,* October 28, 1921, p. 5

178 Minutes, Denver Press Club Board of Directors, October 6, 1921

179 Minutes, Denver Press Club Board of Directors, October 10, 1921

180 "Who's Who in Rockies to be Great Biographical Work," *Colorado Springs Gazette,* August 14, 1922, p. 7

181 Board Minutes, Denver Press Club Board of Directors, September 8, 1922

182 Minutes, Denver Press Club Board of Directors, July 6, 1922

183 "Press Club Names Historian, Plans Entertainment," *Rocky Mountain News,* May 1, 1922, p. 3

184 Minutes, Denver Press Club Board of Directors, September 8, 1922

185 "The Denver Press Club Creed," *Who's Who in the Rockies,* The Denver Press Club, Denver, Colorado; Compiled by Joseph Landers, circa 1925

CHAPTER 8

Cherish those who seek the truth but beware of those who find it.
- Voltaire

A special meeting with thirty members of the Denver Press Club in attendance was held on January 15, 1922. In two weeks, the monthly rent on the present rooms of the club rooms at 1715 California Street was scheduled to increase by $22.50. Chairman of the House Committee John Steele reported that the new $150 monthly rental did not include $300 needed to redecorate the present rooms. He explained that two rooms were available in the Tabor Grand building for $100 a month (including heat and janitorial service). Repairs to the property at 1330 Glenarm Place were estimated to cost $600, but $600-to-$800 a year could be saved if the press club moved back into their own building. A lively discussion ensued about how the press club could raise the ongoing expenses for a new home.

Finally, George Lewis and Tim Davis moved to accept the report of the Building Committee to consider the plan for a new building on the lot at 1330 Glenarm Street. A reputable architect expressed his opinion to the board that the existing building at that location was "impossible of remodeling or saving for any length of time, and that the Committee was of the opinion that a bond issue of $15,000-to-$20,000 should be floated and a new building erected."[1]

The new board of directors of the 1922 press club had a challenge to address. To drive home the point about the quality of the club's rental property, President Frank E. White of the *Denver Post* held the annual election of officers at the club's "new" quarters—the rental property that wasn't supposed to be used as the home of the Denver Press Club. The

1330 Glenarm Place property was supposed to be investment property
and not adapted as the headquarters for the Denver Press Club. One of
the items discussed at that annual meeting was the plan for a new club
building that could be built on the grounds of the building where they
were meeting.[2]

Indecision from among the ranks of the membership forced the board
to put a new coat of paint on the infamous rental property.

The April 20, 1922[3] housewarming party at the 1330 Glenarm
Place rental property brought the usual characters from local theaters to
complement the comic talents of members of the Denver Press Club at
the refurbished club rooms across from the Denver Athletic Club.[4] The
anticipated move into their own headquarters prompted an increase in
new membership with the objective to sign-up all writers and artists from
the Denver daily newspapers.[5] Members of the Colorado Springs Press
Club were invited to what they described as "a sort of baptismal house
warming."[6] Among the entertainment were Joe Moorhead, John Steele
and George Lewis—members of the "Mirth and Laughter" committee.[7]
The wives of the press club members were treated to their own reception
at the new club rooms.[8]

It didn't take long for the members to recognize the old rental property
was still unfit to occupy. Fund-raising efforts were renewed for a building
fund for a permanent club house. Within months, the newspapermen
prepared for a combination vaudeville and Press Club Gridiron Show for
a winter production.[9] The Denver Press Club was faced with additional
challenges to bring luster back to the organization as a major component
of Denver's civic community. The construction of a new club house was
important to White's mission to the membership. "There can be no doubt
that any member of this club who is interested enough to pay dues is
desirous of making the organization one that will be a source of pride
and pleasure to the newspapermen of Denver. All of us . . . are as one in
making the club attractive to every member. That this be brought about
will require several changes and additions more than new quarters. The
club should be a meeting place where men who 'speak the same language'
may congregate to mutual advantage. There is cause for the criticism that,
at present, the club's attractiveness is limited to those of us who care only
for the limited means of entertainment. A better library, a better lounge
where members may foregather for discussion; a better cafe where members
can find a greater variety of food and to which we will be glad to invite

outside friends; a greater number of entertainments for members and their families and occasional functions in honor of our own and visiting men of prominence in the writing profession and activities that will be of importance to the community are some of the improvements that should and can be brought about if the club wants them and is willing to back their officers by sufficient encouragement and willingness to help when called upon. None of these improvements can be expected until we have adequate quarters. How to get these quarters is the big problem your board of directors submits to you and for consideration and the action of the incoming administration to which we extend our best wishes for success."[10]

The memo continued with an observation made during previous club meetings. Anecdotal insistence from the members conclusively indicated that the club must not change or modify the membership requirements to let "down the bars to a host of business men, professional men and others at present excluded by the rigid rules in force since the inception of this institution" just to try and raise the membership revenues of the club by broadening the specific objectives of a newspapermen's club. Only forty-percent of the eligible newspapermen in Denver were members of the Denver Press Club. Making a greater effort to encourage their support and membership would enable the club to grow as a press club, while maintaining the unique characteristics afforded by a dedicated coalition of newspapermen supporting the Denver community.

Expanding the role of writers, the Denver Press Club offered a series of awards to bolster the development of writers in the community. First place in the theatrical-play competition went to Mrs. L. A. Miller for her fantasy, "Dreamland." She also won first place in the poetry category for "Will You Tell Me, Mistress April?" and a second-place award for her short-story "Unto a Far Country." The competition was highlighted by Lillian White Spencer's offer of a special prize for literary excellence in honor of her late father; it was awarded to Mrs. Miller for her short story.[11]

The annual Denver Press Club breakfast at the Metropole Hotel included state legislators and visiting newspapermen from other states. One of the highlights of the entertainment was the broadcast of a radio concert made possible through the wireless station at Fitzsimons General Hospital.[12] The *Denver Post* radio editor, Captain W. L. Winner, Jr. began reporting on other public demonstrations of national radio broadcasts from Denver's KLZ Reynolds broadcasting station, and from listening stations outside the *Denver Post* on the W. D. Pyle station. "Radio Magnavox's and loud-speaking horns will sprout the wireless music to the crowds on the streets [during] Music week," reported the *Denver Post*.[13] Frank E. White, president of the press club and drama editor of the *Denver Post* provided a wireless address on behalf of the Colorado newspapermen temporarily working in the Black Hills, expanding the live outreach of the Denver club.[14]

Heading outdoors once again for a series of events, "members of the typewriter pecking organization," their wives and sweethearts, and special guests turned "a deaf ear to the news events of the day"[15] and headed to the hills for the annual spring picnic basket event at Red Rocks near Morrison. The newspapermen were the guests of the Yellowstone Park Transportation Company, and former magazine editor and Morrison resident John Brisben Walker.[16] The hardier members of the party hiked more than three miles of trails among the hills while the others engaged in dancing in the pavilion to the music of accordion player Joe Perito.[17] Trail guide was Police Reporter Blondy Lebfrom.[18]

Past-president Lute Wilcox and fellow press-club member Abe Pollock, former boxing promoter and state representative from Denver, joined together for the organization's seventh annual picnic in Washington Park on Colorado Day (August 1). "Ringmaster" Pollock provided six hours of entertainment for the 400 attendees who included Slater's famous jazz orchestra, Olinger's senior band under the baton of Major Bert Lake, a policeman's quartet, a humorous stunt, blind-folded running races (aided by bells to guide the runners in obvious deference to the sightless co-director Wilcox), a tug-of-war, and other stunts that were adapted for the blind. An immense Magnavox loudspeaker provided sound to all areas of the picnic center. Twenty-five cases of soft drinks and fifty gallons of ice cream were doled out by members of the press club.[19]

Members of the Denver Press Club, their families and friends, were also the guests at Rose Acre gardens, 6320 W. 26th Avenue near Edgewater in August 1922. According to horticulturists, the display of flowers was "one of the largest and most artistic in the West."[20] Goldfish ponds among the lilies complemented the show gardens, owned by the Liebhart estate,[21] that attracted domestic and foreign visitors.

*****

250

Bill Stapleton, one-time managing editor of the *Denver Republican,* was on a round-the-world trip with Lute Johnson, drama editor for the same paper. As day-steward Joe Diner at the Denver Press Club explained, the *Republican* scribes were sailing on the Mediterranean Sea in the early 1920s and reached a point where Stapleton turned to Johnson and said, "Lute, this is where I want to be buried. I want you to scatter my ashes over this very spot." Lute consulted with the ship's captain, determined the longitude and latitude, and wrote down the coordinates. Stapleton's Last Will and Testament named Johnson as his executor of the estate and $25,000 was set aside for carrying out the agreement which Johnson fulfilled several years later.

When Lute Johnson returned, he dropped into the press club bubbling to share his experience. "When he walked in," related Joe Diner, "Johnson saw the same fellows playing a game of poker who were playing when he left. He greeted everyone and dragged up a chair expecting to go over his trip. One of the players looked up and said 'Oh, hello there, Lute. Been out of town?'" Johnson never did get to tell his story.[22]

According to another published press-club legend, the early newspaper days of Denver journalistic roommates Hamish McLaurin and Damon Runyon claimed there were four Chinamen in the kitchen of the Denver Press Club who chipped in so that Runyon could pay his fare to take his first job in New York City. National correspondent and columnist Westbrook Pegler in his "Fair Enough" column disproved that legend when he explained to readers that it was actually Hamish McLaurin who staked Mr. Runyon's travel expenses.[23]

Another version of the story was published by L. H. Gregory in his Sunday *Oregonian* sports column. The story claimed former club president Damon Runyon heeded the call of the Hearst newspaper chain in New York but couldn't afford to make the trip. He apparently told Jimmy Wong of his tale of economic woe. The night manager told him to "wait a minute" and returned with a $250 gold coin that he pressed into Runyon's hand as a personal loan for the trip.[24]

Jimmy Wong was a magnanimous benefactor to many members of the club, but unfortunately an accurate history of the sagacious sage of the Denver Press Club is as mysterious as their night manager. Club members were often the beneficiary of Wong's economic frugality that helped him provide loans to financially inept journalists. While membership dues and bar/restaurant tabs were often left unpaid, the newspapermen always found a way to pay back the night manager.

Rarely did the night manager leave the press club to visit his wife and family in China. Accurate information about Wong's family is muddled with anecdotes without documentation. One story described his attempt to propagate a male child. When one of his return visits to the Wong household in China produced success, the economic constraints of the Depression years prevented the proud father from watching his newborn son grow into his teen years. For two weeks, the Denver Press Club tapped their political connections to bring father and son together.

Abraham Thomas "Abe" Pollock, state representative and member of the board of directors of the Denver Press Club mustered the politically well-connected members of the club to pool their source-connections to expedite reunite father and son together. "A year or more ago Jim [Wong] saved enough money to bring his son, whom he has not seen for sixteen years, to the United States," reported the *Denver Post*. "He didn't bring him to Denver, for Chinatown here was dwindling and there was nothing for the 'boy' to do to earn his living." Wong Don Way Kai, was now 37 years-old and Jimmy Wong had not seen his son since his last visit to China twenty years earlier. His son was married and sired several of his own children that his father never met.

On Christmas Day 1922, members of the club gave their night manager a Christmas present in the form of a round-trip ticket to Seattle and expense money to visit his son. With funds earned by his father, Jimmy Wong's son was educated as a lawyer and became a member of the provincial assembly of Canton after the Chinese revolution; he served as a leader of the judicial bar in his city and province for several years. Honorary press-club members Senators Lawrence C. Phillips and Samuel D. Nicholson worked with two consuls general in China and immigration officials in the United States to cut through the bureaucratic red tape to enable Wong Don Way Kai to come to Seattle where he embarked on a program teaching young Chinese students the path of enlightenment as taught by Confucius.

When club members told sixty-five-year-old Jimmy Wong that the club members pooled their contributions to buy a round-trip Pullman train ticket to Seattle plus spending money, tears poured down his cheeks. He said (or tried to say) a simple "Thank you," before the club members hoisted him onto their shoulders and paraded him through the club rooms that were decked for the holidays.

A large contingent of Denver Press Club members gathered at the Denver Union Terminal to bid their night manager a safe journey. John Keating, manager of the terminal company, dictated a telegram to the Burlington railroad agent in Billings, Montana, providing Wong's itinerary and requested a confirmation when Wong made his connection in Billings.[25] When the Denver train reached Billings, another group of well-wishers was waiting to greet for their celebrated traveler. Jimmy Wong was not aware of his Montana welcoming because he was soundly sleeping. When Keating received confirmation from Billings, the telegram from Billings Station Agent W. E. Scott read, "Account train not passing here until midnight. Jim Wong was not disturbed. A fellow Chinese Pullman porter reported, 'Jim he likee trip and sleep velly well, but anxious to see his son.' Connection made."[26]

While the Denver Press club's night manager was on his first holiday, the newspapermen held their annual Christmas Tree party at their headquarters at 1330 Glenarm Place. In the role of Santa; Harry Burhans, manager of the Denver tourists' bureau, greeted the children and distributed the gifts.[27] As the *Rocky Mountain News* reported, Burhans' "natural physical proportions fitted him well for the part he played in the afternoon's entertainment."[28] Jim Wong's daytime counterpart since 1907, Joe Diner, served ice cream and cake while long stockings of candy, nuts, apples, bananas, and oranges topped off with a tin horn, were distributed to the ninety-five sons and daughters of the newspaper fraternity under the auspices of Abe Pollock. Pollock once again stepped up to manage the annual year-end open house at the press club.[29]

*****

Upon the motions of George Lewis and Pollock, it was moved that the club proceed with architectural drawings and specifications drawn to remodel the present building at Glenarm Place as the permanent headquarters of the Denver Press Club.[30] According to Cecil R. Conner, "The crowded card room was at the foot of the stairs (there was no basement); the improvised kitchen contained few facilities; eating and drinking space was extremely limited; and upstairs rooms were sometimes rented to wayfaring newsmen and other transients."[31]

A month later, the board members reversed their decision to remodel the old two-story derelict building. During the December 1922 meeting of the Denver Press Club board of directors, it was decided that a $25,000 building would replace the infamous rental property. The design provided a two-story building with a basement and constructed to permit an adjoining building or additional stories when the need arose. The new club meeting room plans included a large grill room and lounge, a library, billiard room, card room, five sleeping rooms, kitchen and heating plant for a building large enough to accommodate 150 members.[32]

D. F. Stackelbeck proposed a resolution to raze the present clubhouse on January 1, 1923, erect the new clubhouse in its place be built within a budget of $18,500, borrow no more than $10,000 to pay for the construction, and move to temporary rent-free quarters at the Navarre Hotel across from The Brown Palace. Other club members made last-minute suggestions to consider other available properties—two lots at 1430 Tremont street, a building at 1436 Stout Street, Marble Hall at 14th and Stout, the Sadler Furniture Building on Welton Street, and a property at 1532 Court Place.

Visitations from Santa Claus became a feature of the Denver Press Club's holiday celebration. Today, the club is the final stop for the Parade of Lights night-time parade.

Courtesy of the Denver Press Club

The membership rose to 159 members in 1923 and maintained a bank balance of $1,200 with all current bills paid, but the overhead of operating the club was still approximately $3,700 a year. The club's biographical book *Who's Who in the Rockies* generated $35,000 in gross earnings which helped defray some[33] of the club's expenses while serving as a $12,000 nest-egg established by the board of directors for a new building.[34]

In a memo distributed to the members of the Denver Press Club, Frank E. White, chairman of the board of directors, explained the club needed better quarters. "The advice of the club at special meetings has deterred the board in taking any definite action toward acquiring better quarters," wrote White, "but we are convinced that this can and should be done in the near future." He acknowledged the club had a trust fund of $12,000 for building purposes and that the present property at 1330 Glenarm Place was worth somewhere between $5,000 and $10,000; a nucleus of approximately $18,000 without indebtedness that could be supplemented with additional fund-raising efforts.

Chairman White's missive continued with the admonition that every member wanted to make the organization a source of pride and pleasure to the newspapermen of Denver. Having a building that was attractive, appealing, and owned by the club always was a goal, but White wanted much more.

At the 1923 annual meeting, Secretary Warren E. Boyer called for an unofficial expression of opinion with a standing vote on three propositions. For those in favor of building a new clubhouse for $18,600, eleven club members rose with their approval. To remodel the present quarters, the assembly remained seated. For the effort to remodel the building for $10,000 or less—only Secretary Boyer and one other member rose. Mr. Seymour, of the original building committee, repeated their conclusion that the old building was not worth saving. New city ordinances required foundation side walls to be poured 10.5 feet into the ground; a point of stability not found in the old building.

*****

The June 1923 annual Denver Press Club Frolic and picnic at Eldorado Springs was where "reporting, copy-reading, editorial writing and all the why-fores and where-fores of newspapers were forgotten by the city's newspaper workers for a while,"[35] reported the *Rocky Mountain*

News. Approximately 300 newspapermen, their wives or sweethearts, and children boarded the Denver & Interurban railroad under the personal charge of C. W. Richards, general agent of the Kite route. Frank Fowler, manager of the picturesque mountain resort and father of noted scribe Gene Fowler, opened their doors to the press club gathering. The day's events included field-and-track events for twenty-five prizes donated by business friends of the club. This was merely a warmup for the arrival of another distinguished guest from Washington, D. C.

On June 24, 1923, President Warren Harding and his wife arrived in Denver via the Santa Fe Railroad. Awaiting the president at Union Station were Governor Sweet, Mayor Stapleton, U.S. Senators Phipps and Adams, and Chairman Thomas B. Stearns of the presidential executive committee. This was the first visit to Denver as *President* Harding; he previously visited Denver as *candidate* Harding on March 11, 1920.[36] Among the statewide activities, President Harding's long years as an active newspaperman at *The Daily Marion Star* made a visit to the Denver Press Club a required stop.[37]

Local newspapermen planned to entertain the thirty-five visiting news writers, correspondents and moving-picture press-service representatives[38] accompanying the president with an informal drive through the mountain parks on the afternoon of the president's arrival.[39] The newspapermen were taken by motorcar from Denver to the top of Lookout Mountain, a visit to Buffalo Bill's grave, and then a stop at Pahaska Tepee for a fresh-trout luncheon.[40] Afterwards, the party began their return to trip via Genesee Mountain, Bergen Park, Evergreen, Bear Creek Canyon, and Morrison.[41]

Thomas F. Dawson, director of the historical department of the state historical and natural history society and the Denver Press Club's first official historian, was with the Associated Press until 1913 and made many similar trips with public men throughout his career. He explained the newspaper contingent that accompanied the president was important in conveying the message a president may make to a gathering of several hundred people, and then repeat it to millions of potential voters throughout the country who read the newspaper columns. "There are some twenty or more newspaper correspondents in the Harding party and the party is comparatively small," explained Mr. Dawson. "I have seen the time when there would be forty or fifty newspapermen on the trail of men of great distinction who might be called upon to tour the country, that was when free railroad passes were to be had."[42]

A crowd gathered along the impromptu parade route where President Harding traveled from Union Station to The Brown Palace Hotel. The shop-talk among the newsreel photographers worried the Denver policemen on duty in front of the Boston Building on 17th Street, "You get set right by the door of the hotel and shoot him the minute he got out of the automobile," instructed the cameraman's director. "You shoot close up and I'll be on top of the building across the street and take a long shot from there."

"We're movie camera men, officer," they explained to a nervous policeman detailed to the presidential route. "To shoot is, in photographers' lingo, to point the lens of the celluloid hand organ and turn the hand crank."

"Aw, talk United States," growled the officer in blue and turned away amid the chuckling from the other spectators who were more familiar with the parlance of the new film industry.[43]

Past presidents with journalistic backgrounds traditionally met with the Denver Press Club. However as economic times were becoming difficult, the club replaced the solid-gold honorary membership cards adorned with semi-precious stones. Awaiting President Harding was a token of remembrance from the Denver newspapermen—a large, blue editing pencil.[44]

The first afternoon of the president's visit to Denver turned tragic. During the press club's sojourn into the Denver mountain parks, one of the ten press cars went over a cliff in Bear Creek Canyon, dropping seventy-five feet into the creek bed. Tommie French, thirty-year-old statistician for the Great Western Sugar Company of Denver, died while driving the car that also killed fifty-four-year-old Sumner Curtis, representative of the Republican National Committee; and injured forty-year-old Donald A. Craig, manager of the Washington bureau of the New York Herald, and forty-year-old Thomas F. Dawson of the Denver Press Club.

The cars were in a caravan behind a motorcycle escort. As they drove around what was known as the Upper Looking-Glass Turn, Mr. French's car started down the straight-away, suddenly and sharply darted over the embankment, and fell a sheer fifty feet before tumbling the remainder of the way. Mr. Craig was almost immediately ejected upon the initial impact and Mr. Dawson lay three-quarters of the way down with French lying only a few feet away. Mr. Curtis was pinned under the car.[45] When word reached President Harding, he canceled all further appointments scheduled for his Denver trip. "I am unutterably distressed that such an accident should have occurred," the president's official statement read. "It intrudes a sorrow upon what has been a happy trip. Only this morning Mr. Curtis was telling of the joy he was experiencing. He was always a gentleman and a very able newspaperman. My regret is beyond expression, but there is some consolation in the hope that the injured men may recover."[46] The next day, Dawson passed away as a result of his injuries. An examination of the wrecked car discovered that a broken steering knuckle rendered the vehicle impossible to steer, sending the vehicle over the cliff.[47]

The luster of the Denver Press Club's national attention of lively camaraderie and hospitality was dulled by such a public tragedy. Journalists are often toughened by their daily reportage of tragic events and with time, the members of the press club moved on to more-optimistic visions for the Denver Press Club.

*****

A special meeting of the resident members of the Denver Press Club was held on December 7, 1924 to formalize the decision to build a new clubhouse on the site owned by the club on Glenarm Place. President E. C. Day explained that additional funds were necessary to supplement the building fund. With a gambling sense of high expectation that the additional funds could be quickly raised from club members who were encouraged to attend the next meeting with checkbooks in hand, the board unanimously decided to release $12,000 of the $27,000 of cash-on-hand and building-fund pledges. The partial funds made it possible to pay for the initial construction costs.

The board secretary wrote, "The general plan of the building was outlined by President Day, saying it would contain a lounge, auditorium, card room, buffet, and library, and the expression of the members generally was that the Club should not go into debt, if possible."[48]

An undated newspaper clipping indicated the 1330 Glenarm Place property was originally purchased by the Denver Press Club for $3,000 from realtor Victor Olmstead who "learned that the Club had amassed about $2,000 in cash from a gift or other sources." Cecil R. Conner recalled, "At that time, an adjoining lot to the east could have been bought for not to exceed $2,500, making a two-lot parcel, but for some reason no effort was made to go out and get the additional amount."[49] At the time, the membership was grumbling about the lot price and turned down the extra expense of the adjacent lot.

President Day attempted to negotiate a donation from the estate of George W. Linger, which owned the neighboring 1336 Glenarm Place residence, southwest of the press club's 1330 Glenarm Place property, in order to expand the property footprint. A. F. Linger, administrator of the estate, explained that family debt required them to list the property at $13,500.[50] The Denver Press Club chose not to further the debt owed by the club by adding the adjacent property to double the existing club's real estate holdings. The $13,500 for downtown city property was approximately half the club's entire building fund. The lot was later offered to the press club for $25,000 and again turned down by the members.[51]

The widow of Verner Z. Reed did subscribe $2,000 to the Denver Press Club's building fund with the request that no announcement of the donation be made public. President Day enthusiastically responded, "I cannot find words to express the great joy which the newspapermen have felt over your most generous gift. It certainly is wonderful of you and you can be assured that the members of our club will never forget your great kindness . . . Recalling what you said about helping the boys would be pleased with your action, I want to say that they are more than pleased. They are wildly enthusiastic and profoundly grateful. Your donation practically assures the newspapermen of a new home, so you can see what it means to them."[52] U. S. Senator Lawrence C. Phipps also contributed $1,000 once actual construction began on the new building.[53]

Despite a pledge to begin demolition more than a year earlier, the board finally approved the acquisition of bids to raze the house at 1330 Glenarm Place, dismantle the brick, and acquire separate bids on furnishings from the old building.[54] The West Side Wrecking Company was awarded the first bid and the Girvin Furniture and Auction Company was awarded the contract to remove the furniture and fixtures from the old house.[55] Some of the old trappings of the press club needed to be cleaned up for installation in the new club building—cleaning and adding a felt border to the club's bear rug added $34 to the expense ledger.[56] Lee Casey was appointed to solicit caricatures and editorial cartoons for the card room.[57]

While the building was being demolished and a new club house erected, the newspapermen maintained temporary residence in a room on the first floor of the Navarre Hotel, offered without charge by hotel manager Andrew Dillon.[58]

In December 1924, Walter A. Boyer, secretary of the Denver Press Club received a letter from the Red Feather Mountain Lakes Association. Club members J. E. Moorhead and Greenawalt thought the newspapermen also needed a retreat at Red Feather Lakes and began unauthorized negotiations with Dr. Norton of the Red Feather Lakes Company to acquire two free lots for the Denver Press Club on the condition that they build a summer clubhouse on the property.

Since the club was about to commence with the construction of the new Denver Press Club home, Boyer explained they could not entertain building a summer home until the "town house" was financed and built. "Right here I want to say that some of the members of the club have learned that at least one of your salesmen has used the Press Club gift as a talking point in selling lots, and for some reason he asserted that the building was in process of construction. He happened to have tackled a member of the board with that selling talk and of course, some explanations will have to be made."[59]

Club records indicated someone was ominously crunching the operational numbers prior to the construction of the new club house. The operational deficit of the Denver Press Club during 1923-1924 was $1,500; and another $2,000 for 1924-1925;[60] and a further deficit of $1,500 expected for 1925-1926. E. C. Day's administration raised $24,000 for the construction of the building that actually cost $23,900 and additional furnishings cost $5,819. Despite the cost of the new facility, the new club building was generating approximately $600 in revenues. "Here is the danger," the unsigned report relates. "Take February operation, the Club just about broke even although the dining room showed a gain of $100, not including salaries and heating . . . Last three months have been first time in history of organization that Club has been self-sustaining, or at least in many years, not since the town went dry."[61] No one raised the concern that the club's history of questionable business practices would be difficult to sustain the operation of the new club building.

Throughout the history of the club, members were often dropped from the membership rolls for not staying current on their dues or "buffet" tabs and for behavioral issues. The earliest recorded termination of a member for "conduct unbecoming a member," was bestowed upon J. Harry Carson of 2019 Stout Street. No explanation of the infraction was recorded in the board minutes.[62] On the positive side of member-rewards, the board voted President Edward C. Day a Life Active Membership, recognized with a silver membership card and case awarded during a special session of the board on August 24, 1925."[63] On the reverse side of the card was the inscription "In recognition of the loyal services of Edward C. Day as President of the Denver Press Club during the planning and construction of the New Club House."

The soft opening of the club was scheduled for November 1, 1925 for members and their invited guests; a formal opening a week later for public officials, and then a week later a celebration for regular- and associate members and their families. Furnishings for the club, at discounted prices or as a donation, were negotiated with the Daniels & Fisher executives for $3,868.50. Rugs were priced at $635, stair carpeting $125, lamps $240, draperies $400, furniture $1,968.50, and upholstering $500.[64]

The exterior of the 1330 Glenarm Place home of
the Denver Press Club opened in 1925.

Courtesy of the Denver Press Club, Harry Rhoads photographer

As guests enter the 1925 Denver Press Club building, a living room atmosphere welcomes them. The fireplace wall (left) was taken over by a long bar in the later years of the 20th Century. When the building was later restored, the bar was moved, and the fireplace returned to a functional amenity.

Courtesy of the Denver Press Club, Harry Rhoads photographer

The original dining room had a picture window at the far end that had an unobstructed view of the Colorado State Capitol building. As Denver's downtown continued to grow, the view was blocked by additional buildings, enabling the Denver Press Club to add an addition to the building to accommodate the expanded kitchen. The original kitchen was located on the other side of the wall on the left side of the photograph.

Courtesy of the Denver Press Club, Harry Rhoads, photographer

The original 1925 kitchen of the Denver Press Club
was adjacent to the main floor dining room. It was
later moved when the building was expanded.

Courtesy of the Denver Press Club. Harry Rhoads, photographer

The original basement of the Denver Press Club accommodated
three pool tables. The room was reduced by two-thirds when
women were admitted to club membership; a ladies room was
added to the far left corner of the room and a manager's office
was created in the space behind where the photographer stood.

Courtesy of the Denver Press Club. Harry Rhoads, photographer

A second-floor meeting room with a small stage and a
library (behind where the photographer stood) continues
to be used for Denver Press Club functions.

Courtesy of the Denver Press Club. Harry Rhoads, photographer

The new building, designed as an old English tavern, was built for $50,000 (nearly double the existing building fund) but opened debt-free in November 1925[65] thanks to additional one-time donations to the building fund. The guest register of nearly 500 visitors read like a "who's who" of city, state, and federal officials and Denver's leading business, professional and educational men.

Floral arrangements filled the club's new rooms as members of the Optimist Club, Denver Lodge No. 41, Knights of Pythias, the Denver Athletic Club (located across the street), Philip P. Friederich (general manager of the Lakeside Park and Amusement company), H. Brown Cannon and the Crown Hill Floral Company, George W. Olinger, and W. M. Wright celebrated the opening of the permanent location of the Denver Press Club.

The musical fanfare for the press club event was provided by the senior band of the Olinger Highlanders who marched to the club after concluding their afternoon concert at the Municipal Auditorium. Additional vocal selections were provided by the Civitan trio of Martin

Dougherty, Harry Morton and Don Wilson; and the Olinger quartet of Frank Farmer, Royden S. Massey, Everett E. Foster and Charles H. Reid. George Morrison's orchestra provided instrumental entertainment during the three-hour reception that began mid-afternoon.

Harry Rhoads, photographer

Courtesy of the Denver Press Club

Harry Rhoads was a cherubic and impish master of the flash powder and one of the noteworthy photographers of Denver's newspaper heritage. Never one to pass up a good party, Harry provided the refreshments for the grand opening of the Denver Press Club building despite the opening being in the middle of Prohibition (1920-1933). A large seizure of illicit liquor was stored at the West Side Court building. Officers, who initiated the coup of boot-leg liquor, were eager to have the Denver press corps arrive to photograph them posed with the seized booty. "Harry computed how much flash powder would be required to blind his subjects temporarily without burning the building down," wrote Robert L. Perkin in *The First Hundred Years: An Informal History of Denver and the Rocky Mountain News.* "While the officers groped around in the smoke 'Red' Feeney carried several cases of choice [liquor] bonded out to Harry's Model T coupe."[66]

Some of the key members of the raid were late to be included in the initial photo-op, so Harry re-grouped the officers for a second photo, and repeated the blinding flash. Feeney was able to make two more trips to the curb with the bootleg liquor. "Red got so much liquor into that Ford I could hardly drive away," explained Harry Rhoads. "The back end was full, and the seat propped up so high I couldn't reach the pedals. I took it all out to Eddie Day's house, handed it in through a side bedroom window and it was stashed under his bed. Everyone at the Press Club opening seemed to have a very nice time."[67]

The building was architecturally designed by M. H. and Burnham Hoyt, built by Francis J Kirchhof, manager of the Kirchhof Construction company; and decorated by James A. MacLellan, interior decorator for the Daniels & Fisher's store. As reported by the *Denver Post*, "The joy of the club member in the mere existence of the building is enhanced by pride of possession."[68] The blueprints of the building included a small bar stashed in the middle of the main floor, far from the front windows and the prying eyes of the revenuers.

The Denver Press Club finally had their own "club rooms" that were fully functional by the end of 1925. During the December 6 general meeting of the club, President Day was already soliciting advice from the membership regarding sources of revenue to maintain the building, dues structure, and dining room service; and asked for advice on ways to improve service to the members. Action on those questions was deferred for sixty days until the club could report on the actual costs of maintaining the new press club.

Jimmy Wong returned to Denver and was re-hired by club president Eddie Day when the new club opened in 1925. He was the same affable protector of the gentlemen of the quill, who now claimed to be "75 years old, China Count." Many years ago, Mr. Wong buried glass bottles containing his life savings. It was just a few years before the economic crash known as the Great Depression, but Wong maintained his distrust of banks. The night steward opened an account in one of the Denver banks, but through an error, claimed the bank cheated him out of $10. He immediately withdrew all his money and gathered five of his Chinese friends. They acquired a large steamer trunk, bolted it to the floor and wall of Wong's room, secured it with six padlocks, and placed their life savings in it. All six keyholders had to be present before anyone would get into the trunk.[69]

The 1924-25 fiscal year prior to the opening of the club building ended with a deficit of $2,000 in operating expenses. But the first fiscal quarter in the new club broke all financial records for revenue since 1916 and directed the future of the Denver Press Club as a financially self-sustaining organization. However, the cost of running their own club building also rose from approximately $4,000 a year to $6,500. Club house manager and secretary of the board of directors, Warren E. Boyer, issued a stern warning to the membership. "It should be remembered, however, that the receipts of the Club, other than for dues, and games, in February, for example, were $400 less than in the opening month, and $200 less than in the second month. While the Club should be kept exclusively for members and their guests, the receipts indicate clearly that the fullest cooperation and patronage possible is necessary in order to maintain the pace that has been set."[70]

During the next three years, active memberships jumped from ninety-five members to an average of one-hundred-forty-five—an increase of fifty members. Approximately half of the building fund of $24,000 was raised through new associate memberships. To accommodate the financial and membership needs of the club, the board held more free outings, picnics, entertainments and theater parties to encourage new memberships.

The Denver Press Club's new building provided enough optimism to assure they had recovered from the economic problems incurred by many of their members going off to war. But in just a few years, the newspapermen would be busy reporting on the fall in stock prices, the Dust Bowl, and eventually another world war—and an ultimate national shift away from fraternal-type organizations.

The railroad industry found it necessary to consolidate the routes used by many of the short-line trains; the popularity of the touring cars replaced the demand for narrow gauge railroads frequented by press club excursions to mountain resorts. Budget-pinching households found the impromptu excursion to the mountain resorts may have been an economical way to beat the summer city heat, but still an extravagance that was not necessary. Resorts fell on hard times like the rest of the country and expense-paid invitations to the Denver Press Club newspapermen to curry a few inches of free advertising in the local newspaper columns ceased to be offered.

Lavish-and-costly live-theater stage productions which served as the main staple for Denver Press Club fund-raising were rapidly replaced by motion picture theaters. Often the movie palaces were smaller theaters and the stages were inexpensively covered by a white screen. The theater organ replaced stage orchestras, providing musical accompaniment for the silent movies. Abe Pollock—ring promoter, sporting-news reporter, and active member of the Denver Press Club—was showing his influence upon the club during the years prior to- and during the Great Depression. Mr. Pollock's familiarity with the popularity of pugilistic talents of the ring recognized that exhibitions could accompany large crowds at a very low production cost.

Quickly, national newspapers included Denver bouts alongside similar fighting news from Chicago, Houston, and Los Angeles. "Sammy Mandell, world lightweight champion, will meet Eddie Mack, Rock mountain [sic] lightweight champion, in a 10-round bout Aug 26, under auspices of the Denver Press Club. Mandell's title will not be at stake"[71] reported the *Oshkosh Daily Northwestern* in Wisconsin, the *Sterling Daily Gazette* in Illinois, and the *Portsmouth Daily Times* in Ohio.

World heavyweight boxing champion Jack Dempsey, former heavyweight boxer and restauranteur Eddie W. Bohn, and Denver Press Club president and boxing writer Abe Pollock enjoy a game of cards at the Denver Press Club. Both Dempsey and Bohn were Denver residents.

Courtesy of the author

When the state high-school football 1929 championship game occurred between Cañon City and Greeley, Denver promoters and the chamber of commerce tried to host the game midway in Denver. To farmland high-school sports enthusiasts, this was tantamount to having professional sports champions from opposite sides of the country hold their championship in Denver where the event had no relevance to the local population. "Our opinion," wrote the editor of the Greeley *Tribune-Republican,* "is that the financial inducement to go to Denver, on a percentage basis, was rather illusory."

The local newspapers believed the championship game would be a financial success and should be underwritten by the football fans through early purchases of tickets. They saw no value to splitting the profits with the Denver Press Club who was promoting the championship game to be played in Denver. As the Greeley editor wrote, "The proposition of the Denver Press Club is not a new one. It has irked the Denver sport writers to see the state football classic played outside the state's principal city. They have bemoaned this state of affairs for years. The Denver sport writers and the Denver Press Club have lacked the influence necessary to bring the Denver high-school football teams into state league competition. If that is done Denver will secure a championship game when it earns one, just as Eaton, La Junta, Cañon City, Greeley, Longmont and Fort Collins have earned them."[72]

By 1930, the newspaper industry journalism was ripe for self-examination. Edward T. Leech, editor of the *Rocky Mountain News,* told delegates at the second annual Newspaper Week at the University of Colorado. "The Modern Newspaper, a Sentinel and a Champion" was Editor Leech's topic on the role of the press in uncovering corruption; correcting political, social and economic abuses. "This is a period of unprecedented perplexity," Mr. Leech explained. "Our whole economic and social structure is undergoing not one, but a dozen major changes at the same time. None of us knows what the outcome will be."[73]

New business mergers, and new methods of group and trust financing were gradually eliminating small businesses and making "millions of white-collar workers cogs in a machine just as their brothers in the auto industry first became cogs in the great production line," reported the *Rocky Mountain News.* The corresponding changes in the social fabric created a growing "technological unemployment that develops from improved machinery, business consolidation, and other economic efficiencies and economies. . . A very serious factor of this problem has been a lowering of the so-called age limit of usefulness, throwing out of work thousands of men not yet in their prime and bringing an uncertainty and dread that sits to some degree on almost every household."[74] Mr. Leech explained the newspapermen were not exempt from the problems of the new business model.

Addressing the advent of radio entertainment, Dr. R. Sommer, professor of psychiatry at the University of Giessen, Germany, warned that radio listeners may be exposed to too many impressions. During the First International Congress on Mental Hygiene in Washington, D.C., Dr. Sommer elaborated, "Just as too much food is harmful, the modern invention of radio allows the individual to expose himself to a great number of impressions. People must be temperate in listening to lectures and music and not try to take in in a short time an international mixture from all sorts of cities."[75] The *Rocky Mountain News* article doubted whether the average American will "weigh the calories of music before tuning in. As long as he likes it he will absorb it, be it food, sport or entertainment." The newspaper noted that youngsters reading the latest "yellow back" novels about the exploits of Jesse James, Diamond Dick, or ghost stories will experience the same long, lonesome, sleepless nights rehashing the exciting stories in their minds after listening to the latest adventures on the radio. "With an infinite variety of radio entertainment literally on the shelves of our living rooms," the newspaper continued, "must we weigh the entertainment carefully, choose just so much and not 'eat' a particle more? Nope, it ain't American."[76]

In 1930, a Berlin electrical engineer developed a top hat that he converted into a radio receiver. The music came from the loudspeaker horn mounted at the front. The tuning dial replaced the customary bow on the left side of the hat. Two masts arose from opposite sides of the crown to support the antenna. The coil was mounted on top of the hat and wires led to small batteries carried in coat pockets.[77]

RADIO RECEIVING SET IN GARTER LATEST ACCESSORY OF HOSETTE

Girls, have you a radio garter?

It's absolutely the latest thing in hosiery supporters, and it will be very nifty with the colorful new spring hosettes, my dears.

Miss Julia Elmendorf of Seattle is here shown wearing the fancy radio garter receiving set, invented by Walter E. Miller of the same city. Miss Elmendorf is able to pick up a lot of intersting gossip with her attractive radio set fastened just below her knee—Photo by International.

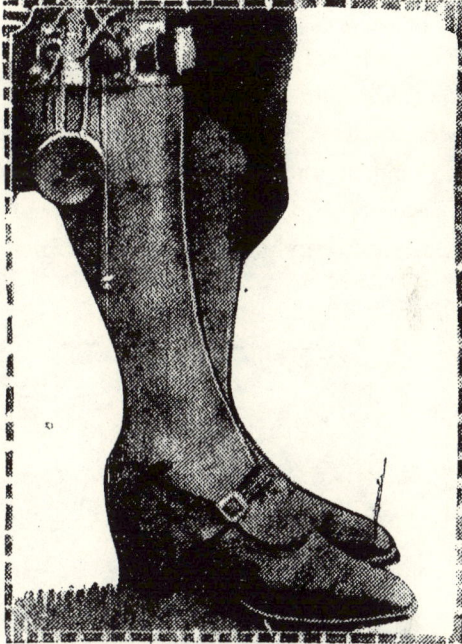

Other creative ways of receiving radio broadcasts were developed to conceal the cumbersome contraptions while still making the radio portable.

Courtesy of the *Denver Post*

Likewise, conference attendees in 1930 were warned of the development of television. "Consider what can be done in the field of news reels alone!" explained William S. Paley, president of the Columbia Broadcasting System in a chapter "Radio and Entertainment" published that year in Martin Codel's book, *Radio and Its Future*. "Imagine seeing, flashed upon the screen in simultaneous sight and sound, a news event of major importance as it is taking place! Visualize world-series baseball games, football games, automobile and horse races, transported the instant they occur on super-sized, natural-color stereoscopic screens! Perfections in the projection of motion pictures will play a large part in making television applicable to theater rather than home presentation."[78]

During the early 1930s there were very few articles published in the newspapers about the Denver Press Club, and most of the board minutes are missing. A single-paragraph 1932-story from the Associated Press noted the Colorado Supreme Court ruled that the Denver Press Club would have to pay back taxes. The position written by Justice Alter determined the Denver Press Club was primarily a social organization and not a charity organization as the club attorneys contended.[79]

Another "noteworthy" story described Lee Taylor Casey's success in having eight kings in a pinochle game during a game at the Denver Press Club. The accomplishment made the front page of the *Rocky Mountain News* and was picked up by Associated Press newspapers throughout the country.[80]

Lee Taylor Casey in the 1925 Denver Press Club
library on the second floor of the building.

Courtesy of the author

When Mr. Casey was a young reporter, his city editor sent Casey his first assignment with the instructions, "I want a story that is brief, to the point, with no words wasted." A short time later, the reporter returned with his copy: "At the wedding reception, the jilted suitor complained of feeling ill, took a glass of punch, his hat, his coat, his departure, a taxi, a pistol, and his life."[81]

Despite his reputation as "Denver's most beloved newspaper writer,"[82] Lee Casey was first to admit that he wasn't letter-perfect at pinochle, enjoyed poker, but preferred bridge as a better-mannered game. "Poker is a game of deception," he explained, "bridge a game of information. There is no code of behavior for poker, whereas a bridge table is one of the few remaining examples of good manners."[83] His record of poker playing earned him a self-imposed ban from the Denver Press Club tables but relaxed that restriction when actress Ginger Rogers appeared at the press club poker tables on a press junket.

One of the life-members of the club, Rollie Bradford of the Bradford-Robinson Printing Co., enjoyed telling his story about being solicited for a contribution of $50 for a membership in the Denver Press Club. "What are your club's benefits?" Rollie asked the solicitor. "Why, just think, Mr. Bradford, you'll be able to eat there with all the famous newspapermen. You can watch such great columnists as Lee Casey playing pinochle. . ." "Did you say Casey?" Mr. Bradford interrupted. "Good Lord, man, I'll double the bet and give you $100 if you can guarantee I'll never see Lee Casey again."

The only other documented news took place a few months later when another light heavyweight boxing clash in 1935 was scheduled in a "gigantic Denver Press Club smoker"[84] and again at the end of the year.[85]

The 1936-report of the house-manager during the Annual Meeting painted a dire economic picture during the Great Depression in the United States. Between 1935 and 1936, a marked deficiency in receipts exceeded the previous financial report. E. P. Lyons reported 1935-1936 ended the fiscal year with a total intake of $7,557.78 and expenditures rose to $7,891.75. Dues collection totaled $1,057, boxing and wrestling exhibitions accounted for $1,081.80, and slot-machine returns amount to $46.40 (between 1933 and 1934, the slot machine returns earned $800 for the club). Additional gaming returns dropped $200 to $' compared to the previous year, "… but these sums are periodical d largely on the men who love play, have time, and, generally families to please," continued Secretary Lyons. The "buffet" receipts totaled $2,072.60, noting the included "liquids fared quite well."

Membership dropped to sixty-nine members. "It is a fact that is cause for much regret that so many eligible men on the *Post*, the United Press, the Associated Press, and the *News* have not been convinced of the pleasure they should have in their craft to join the club that stands so high not only in Denver but all over the world where it has become known,"[86] reported E. P. Lyons. "Concerted work by the incoming list of officers may adjust all these difficulties. They are not at all difficult to solve, merely demanding team work as our best citizens are not only willing, but in many cases willing to give aid to the Denver Press Club, not as a charity, but as a duty to their city and to the members of the craft they know so well and esteem so highly."[87]

The May 10, 1936 Gridiron Breakfast rounded up the usual local participants; Clyde Tingley, governor of New Mexico was invited, but had to turn the offer down because of a conflict with the Governor's Day party at Carlsbad Caverns the next day. New Mexico's good-natured rivalry with Colorado became apparent in Governor Tingley's letter of regrets: "I am not sure that I would be able to enter the state of Colorado, although diplomatic relations have been resumed between the two states and hostilities have ceased. However, peace negotiations are under way and New Mexico is interested in obtaining some very important sanctions which are as important to us as the adoption of the Versailles Treaty was to all nations of the world. You may tell Governor Johnson for me that I shall be happy to enter into a secret conference with him at any time he sees fit. If he deems it advisable, I shall be happy to send Colonel House of the administration to confer with him prior to our meeting."[88]

The poker games of the Denver Press Club were legendary—and long. Joe Diner remembered the longest game during his thirty-eight years of his day-time stewardship at the club lasted three days with six players only breaking for a brief meal and occasionally checking in with their newspaper offices.

Unknown man, Lee Casey, and actress Ginger Rogers enjoy
a wager-less hand of cards in the basement poker room of the
1925 Denver Press Club building. The mural composite of
a Denver newspaper editorial room was painted in 1945 by
Herndon Davis, allegedly to pay off a bar debt at the press club.

Courtesy of the Denver Press Club

"However, the funniest game I remember," related Mr. Diner, "was one in 1908. The club was located in the Mining Exchange Building. We had two rooms there and were given notice to vacate temporarily so some remodeling could be done to the building. We acquired clubrooms in the old Navarre Hotel, and the day the movers came there was a big poker game in session. The players refused to stop the game. A special trip was made in the moving van, with the players still sitting around the table as the furniture was moved to the new quarters."[89] Room in the van was more spacious than at the Navarre. There was room on the second floor for a pool table, a few chairs, card tables, and little else.[90]

During the 1937 Annual Meeting members were asked to accept the offer from the Press Benevolent Association (a separate nonprofit corporation that shared the identical board with the Denver Press Club) to purchase and take over the twelve-year-old club building at 1330 Glenarm Place, all furniture and fixtures, and assume all liabilities of the Denver Press Club. This was in apparent response to the 1932 ruling against the club's claim as a charitable corporation. Memberships in the Press Benevolent Association would be issued to all members of the Denver Press

Club. The Press Benevolent Association, which was incorporated in 1936-1937, would also have the right to use the name "Denver Press Club."[91]/[92]

"Financial problems were always plaguing the club," reflected Chet Nelson, former sports editor of the *Rocky Mountain News* and president of the Denver Press Club in 1937 and again twenty years later. To fulfill the club's charitable qualifications as a 501(c)(3) nonprofit corporation, funds were raised for a scholarship to a worthy University of Colorado journalism student. "The Internal Revenue Service removed that status [again] in the '50s" continued Nelson, "deciding we were more of a social organization."[93]

Sports writers of the Denver Press Club included *Rocky Mountain* News sports writer Chester Nelson and Denver Press Club president Abe Pollock interview World Heavyweight boxing champion Jess Willard.

Courtesy of the author

While the club kept shifting between the "Denver Press Club" and the "Press Benevolent Association," board member N. V. Gabbert was canvassing local jewelers where he found a craftsman who could make 100 gold pins for $4.50 or silver pins for $3.00. The pins bore the insignia of the Denver Press Club and were sold to club members for $5.[94]

Some aspects of the press club were considered hallowed grounds to many of the members. No matter what the admirable objectives were for the actual organization, preservation of the liquor storage was as sacred as it was in Wolfe Londoner's 1867 Cyclone Cellar. Tragedy struck the press club two weeks before Christmas 1942; the nails were removed from a back window of the club and the window was broken open by an insensitive robber or robbers.

"They took all the o-o-old whiskey," explained veteran club president A. Thomas Pollock as he choked back tears during the telephone interview with the *Rocky Mountain News*. "All the O-o-old Taylor, all the O-o-old Grandad, all the O-o-old Crow, all that Gordon Distilled Gin, all that Teachers Cream. There was cigars and cigarettes and silverware, and $50, $60 hid away, but they didn't take any of them — all they took was the o-o-old whisky. And out there in the parking lot, they took a bottle of that O-o-old Taylor and they dropped it there and it broke, and that O-o-old Taylor ran all over the parking lot."[95]

World War II was a gut-punch to any organization like the Denver Press Club, struggling to re-stabilize itself after World War I, Prohibition, and the Great Depression. The call-to-arms emptied the membership and the remaining newspapermen spent more time in the newsroom. The club became a sanctuary to hide from the world.

As James Briggs of the *Rocky Mountain News* described the once-vibrant club, "Located at 1330 Glenarm Place in the afternoon shadow of the Denver Athletic Club, the Press Club brings to members of the newspaper fraternity and scribes the fulfillment of a 'home' to relax in. Unpretentious but artistic, plain and yet comfortable, compact but of ample proportions, the Press Club is the sanctuary of scores of this town's Fourth Estaters. A place where the clack of typewriters is forgotten; the busy teletypes; the paste pots and the jangling of telephones are put aside as the scribes take it easy in comfort in the lounge room. Or perhaps a poker game or a game of bridge. And there's always someone trying to get up a pinochle session. Or maybe the tired news editor prefers to close his fist around a long, tall, cool one and sit around and swap yarns of the old days with whoever happens to be around. And what fabulous and fantastic yarns are spun around the massive fireplace in the lounge room set apart as a place of tranquility and rest."[96]

The kitchen, located along the north wall of the dining area, was presided over by Joe Diner whose "Diner Special" was a concoction of scrambled eggs and cheese. He was assisted by Mrs. Myrtle Schwartz and Millie Mallard who provided their expertise to steaks and hamburgers, when those meats were available. The club manager was Philo (Phil) Hewitt while Ray Broussard replaced Jim Wong as night steward.

In 1948, the press club interior design migrated from an olde English tavern to the eccentric decor that reflected the idiosyncratic nature of the members. The small bar boasted having old street car straps hanging above, lending support for the imbibers. They were the gift of Howard Robertson of the Denver Tramway Company. For additional revenue, a row of illegal one-armed bandits was located at one end of the bar area; there was some concern whether the proceeds were actually going to the club or to the pockets of any one of the managers during that era.

A wall of autographed presidential portraits included Presidents McKinley, Teddy Roosevelt, Harding, Wilson, Taft, Hoover, and Franklin D. Roosevelt; a *Rocky Mountain News* story previously claimed all were honorary members of the club, but only four of them actually received the distinguished honorary designation. Pictures of past press-club presidents were displayed in the dining room including Frank E. White, Poss Parsons, Lee Casey, Chet Nelson, Jim Hale, Gene Cervi, Curley Grieve, Eddie Day, John Polly, Ed Keating, Jim Kelley and Tom Hunter. Other likenesses included Leonard Cahn, *Rocky Mountain News* sports writer; Abe Pollock, eleven-term president of the Denver Press Club; W. C. Shepherd, retired publisher of the *Denver Post*; and Elsie Ward, tireless switchboard operator for the *Rocky Mountain News*. Today most of those pictures are missing. A few individual portraits that may have been among those paintings have survived and were painted by Herndon Davis. The paintings were replaced by several walls of more recent caricatures of past presidents, managers, and individual club members who made significant contributions to the club.

The *Rocky Mountain News* continued the story of the daytime steward in the form of his obituary in 1946—Joseph E. Diner, steward of the Denver Press Club for more than forty years, was buried at Mount Nebo Cemetery at the age of sixty-six. He was born in Austria and emigrated to America where he began as a baker's apprentice in Newark, N.J. and later became interested in club management and catering. In 1905 he came to Denver for his health and within hours of his arrival, was working at the Denver Press Club. He was known for being readily available to assist any "down-and-outer." Friends recalled that when he loaned money to someone, they were known by their first name; when the loan was paid, Mr. Diner would revert to addressing the person with a customary formal address of "Mister."[97]

Despite more women entering the newspaper city rooms, the 1948 Annual Meeting "reaffirmed the club as a sanctuary for men,"[98] and a proposal to admit active newspaperwomen as members was rejected by a large majority. Several exceptions were made to the men-only rule. Life memberships were bestowed on Helen Bonfils, secretary-treasurer of the *Denver Post;* Elsie Ward, the veteran switchboard operator at the *Rocky Mountain News* and is featured in the Herndon Davis mural in the basement poker room; and Betty Craig and Frances "Pinky" Wayne, *Denver Post* reporters.[99]

The board approved a motion to hold a Christmas party for pre-teen children of members; toys and candy, but no money was given as presents. An adult Christmas party for members was eliminated, but a Thanksgiving-eve party was scheduled.[100] The board also voted to create a committee to increase the benevolent activities of the club.[101]

Most notable of the magicians behind the bar was the eccentric Jimmy Fillas, the resident Greek Sheik. He was born in Athens Greece in 1913 with the birth name of Demetrius Lefteddy Phillapkis, but emigrated to America with his mother when he was only 18 months of age. They settled in Lafayette, Colorado where his stepfather worked in coal mines. Eventually, Demetrius anglicized his full name to James T. "Jimmy" Fillas. He played American Legion baseball in the late 1920s and was able to shout out signals to other Greek ballplayers by speaking in their native language. According to his 1990 obituary, Fillas worked in a variety of occupations — most notably as a bootlegger, fry cook, hot-dog vendor, carnival games operator, and dice-and-card shark.[102]

After serving his time at Wade's Keg (located next to the old Denham Theatre on 18th Street) he moved to the Denver Press Club in the late 1940s and he remained a fixture at the club for two decades. Fillas endeared himself to the newspapermen by providing cheese and crackers when they were low on their food budgets. His repartee was a little Don Rickles and a little as Irish priest in the confessional. Guests traveled long distances just to be the brunt of Jimmy's sharp tongue. "The Gracious Greek" was also known for his creativity with the English language. When skeptically listening to a dubious story, "Likee de Hell" expressed his doubt. When anxious wives of spouses, who overstayed their time at the press club bar, telephoned Fillas, his response was usually "No husbands here."

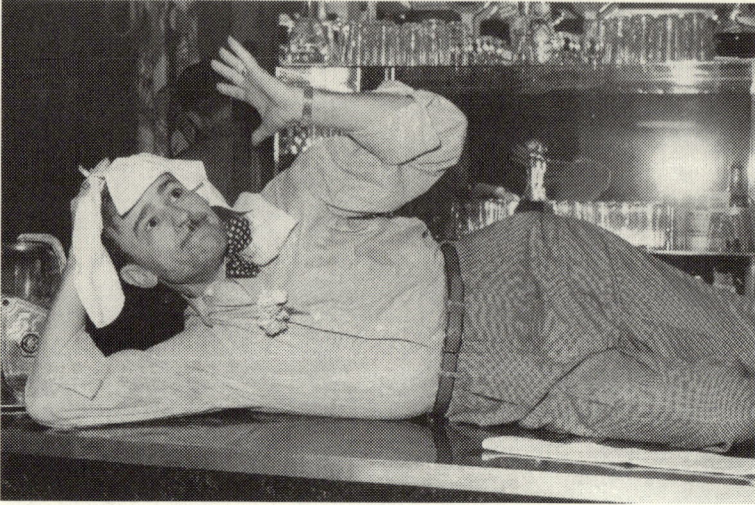

One of the most colorful Denver Press Club managers
was Jimmy "the Gracious Greek" Fillas.

Courtesy of the *Denver Post*

"If Fillas had ever heard the maxim, 'familiarity breeds contempt,' he must not have believed it," wrote Gene Amole on one of his columns for the *Rocky Mountain News*. "Arnold Toynbee, the distinguished British historian once found his way into the Press Club. He hadn't even finished his first drink before Fillas was calling him 'Arnie.'"[103]

When Fillas left the club in 1966 as "maître'd, bookkeeper, bartender, chief referee and arbitrator, and occasionally a cook," as *Rocky Mountain News* columnist Bob Collins described him, he became the proprietor of the Gracious Greek restaurant in South Denver for another ten years. The nickname was supposedly bestowed upon him by a disgruntled, thin-skinned press-club patron. Denver advertising man and club patron Sam Lusky explained "Calling Jimmy gracious was like calling Attila a fairy."[104]

Cecil R. Conner, former news editor of the *Daily Mining Record*, assistant city editor for the *Denver Post* and the *Rocky Mountain News*, had the honor for attending almost fifty years of Denver Press Club annual meetings. His insight into the press club activities included a variety of card games: "Cribbage, hearts, bridge, mahjong, pitch, pinochle, panguingue (the crazy Mexican game played with parts of seven decks), to different forms of poker—draw, stud, 'Kansas City Liz,' and stripped deck draw, to increase the excitement. Until legally banished, a slot machine furnished manual exercise for a few optimists, the lucrative 'take' going into the Club's benevolent fund for worthy newspaper folk in distress."[105] In 1946, the board agreed to purchase a new nickel slot machine for $290 and turn the old one in for $110 credit.[106]

Pool, straight and "pay ball," took up much of the recreational time within the club rooms to the point where the tables needed to be resurfaced from the excessive use. In more modern times, the soft felt was irresistible to a more sporting version of the Mile-High Club, as press club legends claim.

In 1952, the Denver Press Club had $24,739.98 as cash-on-hand and in the bank.[107] Between 1951 and 1953, 374 prospective names were submitted for approval for membership in the Denver Press Club—none was a member of the press.[108] Chet Nelson was appointed to a committee to examine the feasibility of the press club sponsoring sport and entertainment events as a revenue producer for the club.[109]

A resurgence in club interest during post-World War II times prompted the board to finance an addition to the club building. The general membership voted on a $30,000 club expansion program to extend the club's two stories twenty feet east to accommodate a new kitchen and a room with a seating capacity of sixty people on the ground floor; the extended second floor accommodated the club's banquet facilities.[110] Approximately six months later, the sixty members of the Denver Press Club in 1954 agreed that the now *$45,000*-building expansion needed to go forth under the leadership of the newly elected club president, Willard C. Haselbush, *Denver Post* city editor.[111] When Hollywood starlets Rita Moreno and Mary Murphy were photographed, posed on the shovel end of a power shovel with Mayor Quigg Newton and press club president Willard Haselbush a month later, the *Denver Post* stated the new *$50,000*, 25-ft.-addition to the club was underway. The starlets were in Denver to attend the opening of the new Fox Centre theater and were escorted from The Brown Palace to the Denver Press Club in two Jaguars furnished by Denver Imported Motors.

The old kitchen was converted into additional dining space, the second-floor banquet area serviced by a dumb-waiter, and the bar on the first floor was moved back and new restrooms were added to the basement and second floors.[112]

Adlai Stevenson was confident that he would win the 1956 presidential elections but decided to sit for a presidential portrait at the Denver Press

Club. "It's an old superstition among Denver newsmen," an Associated Press report circulated, "that no candidate for president can win unless his picture has been taken in the club. If he is elected, the picture will hang alongside those of all other U.S. presidents since 1900. Every one of them visited the club and sat for the photographer. There's only one hitch: Dwight Eisenhower's photograph was taken in the club during the 1952 campaign. He beat Stevenson to the punch."[113]

Bob Perkins, chairman of the 1957 scholarship committee, proposed a grant for a journalism student at the University of Colorado. In 1962, the Denver Press Club added to their support of journalism students by presenting a memorial scholarship in honor of the late Gene Fowler. The scholarship provided full tuition and fees for a senior journalism student from the Denver area. Mr. Fowler originally planned to study medicine, but a chance encounter with the journalism professor on an interurban car from Denver to Boulder pushed him toward his celebrated newspaper career. After a year in college, Fowler quit school and became a cub reporter on the *Denver Republican* and later worked for *The Rocky Mountain News* and the *Denver Post* before moving on the *New York Daily Mirror, New York American, New York Morning Telegraph,* and as a press agent and manager for fighters and wrestlers.[114]

The club membership rose to 1,225 in 1957 and board members decided it was time to revive the Thanksgiving club party with punch, turkey and other buffet items provided by the club and a cash bar available for adult beverages. A Christmas party was planned at the Bonfils Memorial Theater, and a New Year's party was proposed for the club building but was later rescinded.

The large membership meant that some delinquencies also occurred. By January 1958, twenty-nine members were dropped—twenty-three for non-payment of dues, three for delinquent buffet accounts, and three for both. Occasionally, club member behavior was brought to the attention of the board. Gene Cervi was cited for "incidents of bad conduct" including throwing glassware and sandwiches, spattering guests of the club with broken glassware, abuse of the stewards and use of profanity in the presence of women. The board designated him as "persona non grata" at the club until his behavior was in accord as a gentleman, and until he apologized to Club Steward Karl Wade.[115] The letter of reprimand was never sent, and the board unanimously decided to table the matter.[116]

Another complaint was filed with the board that year. George Kelly criticized the club for "allowing unescorted women to monopolize the bar during the cocktail hour."[117] Board member Tangney explained the details of the situation, but the details were not recorded in the minutes of the meeting. Mr. Kelly's letter was received, filed, and a nondescript motion passed by the board.

Following the war, the move to the suburbs meant fewer newsmen hanging out at the press club after their newsroom shifts. Providing an oasis for journalists while looking for lucrative revenue streams from visiting entertainers and sporting opportunities became less viable with the advent of television in Denver.

A tentative offer from entertainer and humanitarian Danny Thomas indicated a possible interest in performing a show in Denver under the auspices of the Denver Press Club. Thompson R. Watt of the *Denver Post* and Walter "Dusty" Saunders of the *Rocky Mountain News* were selected to investigate the offer.[118] Sam Lusky approached the board to suggest the club consider sponsoring an annual spring revue for charity. The revue could be staged on two consecutive nights and tickets for the premiere sell for $10 and press-club members could attend the second night for $5. First-night profits would go to charity and second-night profits to benefit the press club. Bradford Hatton, director of the Civic Theater and Bob Stapp agreed to help produce the revue and the Bonfils theater was solicited for the venue. As Lusky explained, "It would tend to arouse interest among members of the Press Club, that it would lend prestige to the Club and give the city a good show, in addition to raising money for charity and the Club."[119] The board unanimously voted to approve the project in principle and to study the idea in greater detail, but no record of the event was found.

An annual picnic was discussed to be held at Peaceful Valley. President Bob Pattridge proposed having a cocktail party or dinner as a means of stimulating interest in the club. The guests of honor would be ex-presidents and possibly ex-directors of the club; the decision was postponed until the next meeting.[120] Reading through the minutes of the press club, it seemed that the 1960s were full of postponed decisions for issues that came before the board and minimal upkeep on the building maintenance.

At the 1962 annual meeting of the Press Benevolent Association, Robert Collins cited all the activities from the previous year: "In general it was a good year from an economic standpoint, although down a little from the year before. There were no big problems. Delinquent accounts had been reduced to a manageable form. There were a number of improvements made in the club; painting, new lighting, and other small property improvements which were all paid for from current income. Also, Blue Cross health insurance was extended to employees of the club who were/are considered permanent help."[121] Secretary Dick Davis concluded the minutes with "Meeting ended, and drinking started."

In July, invitations from the Flamingo Club in Las Vegas to participate in the Press Christmas party and from the Aviation Club for special privileges were discussed, but the board took no action on either invitation.[122] The September board highlights included an application for a bulk-mailing permit that was rejected by the post office, and the purchase of four Denver Broncos season tickets to be distributed to members by a drawing. A spaghetti dinner was tentatively set for the following month and a "smoker" was tentatively set up for the following month with entertainment, and a trip for two to the Desert Inn in Las Vegas. Steward Jimmy Fillas was unanimously authorized to solicit bids for an awning at the front door,[123] but difficulties with the awning company and the cold weather prevented that project from being fulfilled.

Highlights of 1963 included a July 14 picnic and a golf tournament the next day. Other events included a spaghetti dinner on November 11 and a Follies event on December 3. The board minutes of the club do not mention a profit or loss for the events.

"Walter Winchell's America" nationally syndicated column made a passing reference to a bar companion drinking a beer on the rocks. Winchell commented the drink is no novelty to the Denver Press Club— "out thar (where reporters are men) they call it 'a Texas beer.'"[124] *Rocky Mountain News* writer, Pasquale Marranzino also remembered that era's club steward, Jimmy Fillas and his economic resourcefulness. When a large fire burned across the street at the Denver Athletic Club, Fillas increased the prices of his drinks and food, opened the doors to spectators. Marranzino states that Fillas cashed in big and "put the club in the black for the year."[125]

1   Minutes, Denver Press Club Board of Directors, Special Meeting, January 15, 1922

2   "Denver Press Club Elects Officers for the Coming Year," *Denver Post,* March 13, 1922, p. 6

3   Minutes, Denver Press Club Board of Directors, April 9, 1922

4 "Press Club to Give Housewarming in new Home Saturday," *Denver Post*, April 3, 1922, p. 5

5 "Press Club Opens New Denver Home," *Denver Post*, April 9, 1922, p. 22

6 "Springs Newspapermen Invited to the Denver Press Club," *Colorado Springs Gazette*, April 7, 1922, p. 5

7 Ibid

8 "Denver Press Club to Hold Reception for Members' Wives," *Denver Post*, April 18, 1922, p. 10

9 Minutes, Denver Press Club Board of Directors, June 22, 1922

10 Ibid

11 "Mrs. L. A. Miller Winner of Press Club Sweepstakes," *Gazette-Telegraph*, March 22, 1922

12 "Press Club to Hear Radio Concert at Annual Breakfast," *Denver Post*, April 21, 1922, p. 5

13 "Post Radiograms," Capt. W. L. Winner, Jr., *Denver Post* Radio Editor; Denver Post, May 12,1922, p. 10

14 *Denver Post*, May 12, 1922, p. 10

15 "Press Club Plans Annual Outing in Red Rocks Park," *Rocky Mountain News*, June 2, 1922, p. 3

16 "Surprise 'Stunts' to Feature Big Press Club Picnic," *Rocky Mountain News*, June 3, 1922, p. 3

17 "Denver Press Club Holds Annual Outing in Red Rocks Park," *Denver Post*, June 5, 1922, p. 11

18 "Press Club Holds Annual Picnic at Red Rocks Park," *Rocky Mountain News*, June 5, 1922, p. 4

19 "Denver's Blind to Hold Monster Picnic at Washington Park on Colorado Day," *Rocky Mountain News*, July 30, 1922, p. 3

20 "Members of Press Club Guests of Noted Gardens," *Rocky Mountain News*, August 13, 1922, p. 13

21 "Members of Press Club to be Rose Acre Guests," *Rocky Mountain News*, August 10, 1922, p. 5

22 Ibid

23 "Fair Enough," Westbrook Pegler, *State Times Advocate* (Baton Rouge, Louisiana), 27 April 27, 1953, p. 6

24 "Greg's Gossip," L. H. Gregory, *Sunday Oregonian*, September 30, 1956, p. 1, Sec. 2

25 "Newspaper Writers' Mentor Leaves to Visit Son," *Rocky Mountain News*, December 19, 1922, p. 16

26 "Jim Wong Sleeps Soundly, Misses Billings Sendoff," *Rocky Mountain News*, December 21, 1922, p. 3

27 "Big-Hearted People of Denver to Observe Glorius Yuletide," *Denver Post*,

December 24, 1922, p. 38

28 "Press Club Plays Santa to Children," *Rocky Mountain News,* December 25, 1922, p. 13

29 "Gayety to Usher in New Year as All Denver Celebrates," *Rocky Mountain News,* December 31, 1922, p. 2

30 Board Minutes, Denver Press Club Board of Directors, October 18, 1922

31 *The 1967 Denver Westerners Brand Book,* "The Denver Press Club," Cecil R. Conner, The Westerners, Denver, 1968, p. 137

32 "$25,000 Building Will be Built by the Press Club," *Denver Post,* December 11, 1922, p. 13

33 Typed draft report to "Members of the Denver Press Club" from Frank E. White, chairman, board of directors, circa 1923

34 Report of the Secretary and House Manager for an Approximate Eleven Months of the Fiscal Year Ending March 31, 1923

35 "Newspaper Staffs Meet at Eldorado Springs for Outing," *Rocky Mountain News,* June 18, 1923, p. 3

36 "Harding on Second Visit to Denver," *Rocky Mountain News,* June 24, 1923, p. 2, Sec. 1

37 "Notables Will Welcome Harding Upon Arrival in Denver Sunday Morning," *Denver Post,* June 22, 1923, p. 9

38 "Local Press Club to Entertain Men in Harding Party," *Rocky Mountain News,* June 24, 1923, p. 5, Sec. 1

39 "Harding to Reach Denver at 10 Tomorrow Morning," *Denver Times,* June 23, 1923, p. 1

40 "Local Press Club to Entertain Men in Harding Party," *Rocky Mountain News,* June 24, 1923, p. 5, Sec. 1

41 "Two Killed, 2 Hurt in Bear Creek Crash," *Rocky Mountain News,* June 25, 1923, p. 5

42 "Arrival of Harding's Party Reminds Denver Resident of Days When He, as Journalist, Knew All Presidents," *Rocky Mountain News,* June 24, 1923, p. 5, Sec. 1

43 "Cop Sees Plot as Camera Men Talk of 'Shooting' Harding," *Denver Times,* June 25, 1923, p. 8

44 "Harding Will Get Blue Pencil from Newspapermen," *Denver Post,* June 24, 1923, p. 4

45 "Two Die as Auto Plunges Into Bear Creek," *Rocky Mountain News,* June 25, 1923, p. 1

46 "3 Die in Auto Smash in Hills: Adviser of President Dead as Crash Halts Writers' Mountain Trip," *Denver Times,* June 25, 1923, p. 1

47 "3 Died in Auto Smash in Hills," *Denver Times,* June 25, 1923, p. 1

48 Minutes, Denver Press Club Board of Directors, Special Meeting, December

7, 1924

49 *The 1967 Denver Westerners Brand Book,* "The Denver Press Club," Cecil R. Conner, The Westerners, Denver, 1968, p. 137

50 Letter from A. F. Linger, administrator of the estate of George W. Linger, to E. C. Day; March 29, 1924

51 "Denver Press Club Can Boast of Colorful Past," unknown newspaper clipping

52 Letter from E. C. Day to Mrs. Verner Z. Reed, October 15, 1924

53 Letter from Lawrence C. Phipps to E. C. Day, February 4, 1924

54 Minutes, Denver Press Club Board of Directors, March 10, 1925

55 Minutes, Denver Press Club Board of Directors, March 18, 1925

56 Minutes, Denver Press Club Board of Directors, Special Meeting, August 24, 1925

57 Minutes, Denver Press Club Board of Directors, September 9, 1925

58 Resolution, D. F. Stackelbeck, circa 1924

59 Letter from J. E. Moorhead to B. H. Princell, Red Feather Mountain Lakes Association, January 8, 1925

60 Typewritten draft notes, "Report of the Secretary and House Manager [Warren E. Boyer] of the Denver Press Club Covering a Three-year Period (1923-1926) but More Specifically for the Two-Year Period April 1, 1924 to April 1, 1926 (Actually to March 1, 1926)"

61 Typed and handwritten undated and unsigned financial notes, circa first quarter 1926

62 Minutes, Denver Press Club Board of Directors, August 13, 1925

63 Minutes, Denver Press Club Board of Directors, Special Meeting, August 24, 1925

64 Minutes, Denver Press Club Board of Directors, October 8, 1925

65 "Denver Press Club Opens New Home With Due Ceremony," *The Inter-Mountain Press,* November 1925, p. 11

66 *The First Hundred Years: An Informal History of Denver and the Rocky Mountain News,"* Robert L. Perkin; Doubleday & Company, Inc., Garden City, New York, 1959, p. 451

67 Ibid

68 "Denver Press Club Opens New Home," *Denver Post,* November 22, 1925, p. 18, Sec. 2

69 Ibid

70 Typewritten notes, "Report of the Secretary and House Manager of The Denver Press Club Covering a Three-year Period (1923-1926) but More Specifically for the Two-Year Period, April 1, 1924 to April 1, 1926 (Actually to March 1st, 1926," March 7, 1926

71 "Sports Briefs," *Oshkosh Daiy Northwestern,* August 18, 1927, p. 13

72 "Denver Fails to Seize Title Game," (editorial), *The (Greeley) Tribune-Republican*, December 3, 1929, p. 10

73 "Hope of Solving U. S. Problems is in Newspapers, Editor Says," *Rocky Mountain News*, May 3, 1930, p. 3

74 Ibid

75 "Mental Hygiene Expert Warns on 'Radio Indigestion,'" *Rocky Mountain News*, May 9, 1930, p. 4

76 Ibid

77 "Radio Set in a Hat," *Denver Post*, May 18, 1930

78 "Television Will Help Operate Theaters," *Rocky Mountain News*, May 9, 1930, p. 4

79 "Press Club Must Pay Taxes," *Greeley Daily Tribune*, December 27, 1932, p. 1

80 "Editorial Writer Crashes Page One," *Evening Independent* (Massillon, Ohio), November 27, 1933, p. 1

81 "So This Is Greeley," Jim Briggs, *Greeley Daily Tribune*, February 2, 1976, p. 4

82 *The First Hundred Years: An Informal History of Denver and the Rocky Mountain News*, Robert L. Perkin; Doubleday & Company, Inc., Garden City, New York, 1959, p. 433

83 Ibid

84 "Lenhart Meets Patrick Tonight in Tacoma Bout," *Seattle Daily Times*, October 10, 1935, p. 20

85 "Martinez to Defend Light-heavy Boxing Title Against Lenhart," *Greeley Daily Tribune*, December 27, 1935, p. 5

86 Report of Secretary-House Manager Annual Meeting, Denver Press Club, March 8, 1936

87 Ibid

88 Letter from Clyde Tingley, Governor of the State of New Mexico to John C. Feeney, President of the Denver Press Club, May 2, 1936

89 Ibid

90 *The 1967 Denver Westerns Brand Book*, "The Denver Press Club," Cecil R. Conner, The Westerners, Denver, 1968, p. 138

91 Minutes, Annual Meeting of the Denver Press Club, March 14, 1937

92 Minutes of the Organization meeting of the Press Benevolent Association, March 15, 1937

93 "Press Club All Set for Diamond Jubilee Bash," Dolores Eyler, *Rocky Mountain News*, October 31, 1980, p. 35c

94 Minutes, Denver Press Club Board of Directors, April 8, 1946

95 "Liquor Theft Bitter Blow to Press Club," *Rocky Mountain News*, December 12, 1942

96 "Tired Newsmen Revive at Denver Press Club," *Rocky Mountain News*,

October 20, 1946, p. 7B

97 "Rites Today for Diner, Press Club Steward," *Rocky Mountain News,* January 16, 1947, p. 9

98 "Press Club Votes to Continue Ban Against Women," *Denver Post,* March 15, 1948, p. 18

99 "Denver Press Club Can Boast of Colorful Past," unidentified press clipping

100 Minutes, Denver Press Club Board of Directors, October 7, 1952

101 Minutes, Denver Press Club Board of Directors, October 16, 1951

102 "Mr. James T. or Jimmy or Demetrius Lefteddy Phillapkis or Fillas, 77; *Rocky Mountain News,* June 12

103 "Diamond in Rough," Gene Amole (Amole's Corner); *Rocky Mountain News,* August 14, 1980, p. 6

104 "Mr. James T. or Jimmy or Demetrius Lefteddy Phillapkis or Fillas, 77; *Rocky Mountain News,* June 12, 1990

105 *The 1967 Denver Westerns Brand Book,* "The Denver Press Club," Cecil R. Conner, The Westerners, Denver, 1968

106 Minutes, Denver Press Cub Board of Directors, July 8, 1946

107 Income Statement, June 1952

108 Joe Landers to Don Davis, secretary of the Denver Press Club, November 8, 1951; December 10, 1951, January 7, 1952, February 4, 1952, March 11, 1952, June 10, 1952, July 7, 1952, August 5, 1952, September 8, 1952, November 18, 1952, February 18, 1953, March 13, 1953

109 Minutes, Denver Press Club Board of Directors, February 12, 1952

110 "Addition Voted for Press Club," *Rocky Mountain News,* October 26, 1953, p. 8

111 "Press Club Okays $45,000 Expansion," *Denver Post,* March 29, 1954, p. 8

112 "Starlets Give Assist in Press Club Rites," *Denver Post,* April 30, 1954, p. 25

113 "Adlai Sits for Press Club Photo," *Advocate* (Baton Rouge, Louisiana), September 24, 1956, p. 9

114 "Fowler Scholarship Given by Press Club," *Rocky Mountain News,* March 25, 1962, p. 16

115 Minutes, Denver Press Club Board of Directors, January 17, 1958

116 Minutes, Denver Press Benevolent Association Board of Directors, February 19, 1958

117 Minutes, Denver Press Benevolent Association Board of Directors, May 13, 1958

118 Minutes, Denver Press Club Board of Directors, August 22, 1958

119 Minutes, Denver Press Club Board of Directors, December 12, 1958

120 Minutes, Denver Press Club Board of Directors, April 5, 1962

121 Minutes, Press Benevolent Association Board of Directors, Annual Meeting, March 18, 1962

122 Minutes, Denver Press Club Board of Directors, July 23, 1962

123 Minutes, Denver Press Club Board of Directors, September 10, 1962

124 "Winchell's America," *San Diego Union*, February 18, 1964, p. 10

125 "Rekindling the Press Club Spirit," Pasquale Marranzino, *Rocky Mountain News*, February 24, 1971, p. 43

CHAPTER 9

The newspaper editor is the most misunderstood and generally the most abused man in every community. Other men have unbiased opinions—honest thoughts, but the newspaper man, [sic] never. If he takes the right side of a moral question he is "playing to the churches," or is "afraid he will lose a subscriber." If he is on the other side, he is in league with criminals or is being paid for his views. If he is conducting a partisan paper, it is for "the graft there is in it." If his paper is independent, he is trying to "shake down the politicians." No matter what stand he may take on any public question he may expect to be criticized for it. He is either biased or "has been seen."[1]

During the 1960s, the press club attempted to renew theme-dinners, activities, and other events, but there is no record of whether the programs were profitable for the club. The board minutes reflect frequent tabling of ideas or long delays in reestablishing programs that were successful during earlier years of the club. Board minutes also reveal concerns about the negative financial status of the club, indicating that some problems remained unresolved. Committees were created for any issue, and members were frequently being reprimanded for bad behavior. The club's infrastructure was showing wear and the boards of directors were reluctant to address the overall problems of the aging building. The board minutes were written with vague references to problems: "Discussion held with Jim Fillas on prices and situation in kitchen. Fillas said steps had been taken to correct situation. Price increases also were explained by Fillas. He reported no portions had been increased."[2]

Mort Margolin, chairman of the House Committee noted the club faced economic difficulties because of increased food costs. He praised the club steward for offsetting the increased costs by making changes to the menu and revision of some prices. Members praised the manager's frugality when specialty-dinners with prime steaks occurred whenever a case of prime beef "fell off a truck" near the stockyards. Charles Garrity of the Social Committee reported the picnic, annual stag and spaghetti nights were popular, but did not document the financial matters of holding those events. Gene Mullins reported the annual golf tournament—the 1965 event made a profit of $34 with promises to hold a more profitable tournament in 1966.[3] Regrettably, the subsequent tournament experienced an $85 loss.[4] Accountant Fred Brown explained that the buffet and bar reported a decrease of $2,282.51 but other revenues provided an increase in the club's overall operating balance of $453.25 compared to a net increase of $844.12 the previous year.

The club fulfilled other pledges to the membership through the Press Benevolent Association under the aegis of the Denver Press Club. Hundreds of dollars were distributed to members who were ill and/or to the widows of deceased members of the club. In 1964 the Welfare Committee wrote $1,798 in checks and $2,031.80 the following year.[5]

Mr. Buchanan, reporting for the Social and Special Events Committee, told the 1967 Annual Meeting that new family and three-drinks-for-a-dollar nights were "successful, but not very profitable." Since their purpose was to stimulate interest in the club, board member David Brofman noted those events stimulated some spending that was not necessarily noticeable on the paper books and that "the financial picture couldn't be that dark."[6] At the time of the March 1967 Annual Meeting, the club now had 418 members,[7] a drop from the high of 1,225 ten years earlier.

When steward Jimmy Fillas tendered his resignation to the board of directors, he proposed a report of written recommendations for improvement of the club's management and facilities. The document was not included in the surviving club minutes, but subsequent board minutes indicated what may have been in Mr. Fillas' report. Max Morton of Petry Construction Co. attended the May 1966 board meeting to offer advice for remodeling the club. He said the club building was sound, but the heating should be addressed first. The total cost of remodeling was $33,600.[8] Guest membership cards, valid only during sessions of the 46th General Assembly would also be issued to male members of the state legislature.

Financial matters continued to get worse as additional building repairs became necessary and fund-raising efforts were paltry. President Tom Gavin reported that 1968 would be a "make or break" year for the club and that some "belt-tightening" and a "modest" increase in menu prices may be necessary. The board was also informed that board meetings would become more frequent while current economic problems were resolved. All the books would be audited by an outside accounting firm.[9]

One of the most contentious aspects of the Denver Press Club's history innocently occurred during the club presidency of Walter "Dusty" Saunders. During an economic period when board members struggled to reverse a dangerously rapid decline of club revenues and deterioration of the barely fifty-year-old club building, President Saunders shook the blokeish core of the club. Board members Saunders, David Brofman, Cal Queal, Hal Heffron, Harley Key, John Snyder, Ernie Azlein, George Franco, Past President Gene Mullins, and Bill Kostka, Sr. (invited by President Saunders) joined the discussion on February 12, 1969, to expand the economic diversity and opportunities for the club. Simply noted by Secretary Franco in the board minutes, "The board offered, with no recommendation, a change in Club by-laws to provide for female membership, same to be published 30 days in advance of the March 23 annual meeting and to be voted on by the full active membership."[10]

With slightly more than a month to contemplate the change in what the newspapermen called their "club house," President Saunders brought the board's proposed by-law change to the March 23, 1969 annual membership meeting, with one caveat. The admission of qualified female members would be made on "a guest basis." Secretary Franco's minutes reflect the contentiousness of the proposal: "Sanders called for discussion from the floor on the proposal . . . and there was plenty. After about two hours and followed a call for vote on the motion of Barron Beshoar and a second by Bernard Kelly, the proposal was defeated 19-17 on a ballot vote. Three ballots were submitted in blank form and one ballot was ruled illegal for lack of member signature."[11]

Board Secretary Hal Heffron's notes on the 1970 Annual Meeting reported: "A letter was read from Carol McMurrough, *Post* reporter, asking that consideration be given to the admission of newspaperwomen to the club membership. After some lively discussion, Pat Coffey moved, Paul Lilly seconded, that a special general membership meeting be called not later than June 1, 1970 . . . to resolve the proposition that ladies of the press, radio, and television in news gathering capacities be admitted to full membership in the club with voting rights, and not as associate members. Motion passed."[12]

The issue of female members to the nearly century-old male club-house rooms was contentious on several levels. Certainly, the Denver Press Club was a men-only club, but likewise the Writers' Club and the Denver Woman's Press Club morphed into the latter organization that also enjoys their own club house and successful contributions to Colorado's press legacy and longevity. On November 7, 1893, Colorado was the first state to pass women's suffrage into law. The following year, Clara Cressingham, Carrie Clyde Holly, and Frances Klock were the first women in any legislature when they were elected into the Colorado House of Representatives.

From a historical record of the state's contribution to equality among the genders, welcoming the women of the press in the club should have been uncontentious. The men-only role of the Denver Press Club was more likely attributed to behavioral issues and not on gender bias. Certainly, newspapermen maintained a high level of respect for Nellie Bly, Ida B. Wells, Ethel L. Payne, Ida Tarbell, Dorothy Dix, Wendela Hebbe and many more who wrote as well as their male contemporaries. The "boys only" stigma held on when club members had to dodge the occasional stag parties, 8mm silent nudie film exhibitions, and the women in various stages of undress who entertained an occasional party at the club, hosted by normally sedate members of Denver's judiciary and corporate elite. They were not proud moments in the Denver Press Club's post-World War II history, but those events did help stimulate and arouse the bar-and-buffet profits on those party nights. As recently as the November 30, 1966 monthly board meeting, the decision to prohibit "stag shows" on the club premises was rescinded by a five-to-two vote.[13]

The February 16, 1967 board minutes indicate that bad checks were being written by a member who previously was suspended "for poor conduct."[14] Cases of bad behavior among the 418 active members, 219 associate members, and 479 life members were not common, but they did create a stir when brought before the boards of directors of that era.[15] And likewise, club members may have wanted to spare their female counterparts from the periodic fierce arguments that sometimes resulted in guns being drawn and members being threatened to be thrown through closed windows.

To tighten the financial belt of the press club, President Gavin questioned if the night bartender should be let go and the manager work a shift at the bar. Club Manager Fred Mangino complained he was already working 12-14-hour days and that a night bartender was necessary to manage the four-banquet-a-week business. No decision was made on Gavin's inquiry.[16]

By July, Mangino resigned as manager of the club. The board was unsure if the resignation was serious or just tendered as a moment of anger, and appointed a committee of Saunders, Franco and Heffron to meet with the club manager. President Gavin then submitted his own resignation, stating it was apparent the board wanted the club manager back and he hoped his own sacrifice would restore harmony within the club. As Acting Secretary Hal Heffron reported in the board minutes, "He [President Gavin] said he knew his action would be criticized in some quarters and he might be accused of running out at a time the club was facing a crisis. But he said he felt his decision was in the best interests of the club."[17] Mr. Mangino's position as club manager was restored.

Relationships between members and the club steward were addressed by the board. On the night of January 26, 1970, Fred Mangino and members John McLaughlin and Rich Maes were engaged in a "disturbance" at the club. While Mangino was suspended with pay for two weeks, the board summoned participants and witnesses to the events that night to relate their stories. Fred Mangino was allowed to offer his side of the story before the board voted whether or not to accept his "resignation" from the club.[18]

The special meeting of the Board of Directors was called on February 8, 1970 to address the kerfuffle. Testifying in order of appearance were Rich Maes, participant; John McLaughlin, participant; John Rogers, John Deasy, Bill Symons, Barbara Schellhorn, witnesses; and Fred Mangino, participant. As Hal Heffron wrote in the board minutes, "At the conclusion of the testimony and extended discussion, Snyder moved, Azlein seconded that 'Fred Mangino's resignation as club manager be rejected; that Fred Mangino be severely reprimanded, in writing and verbally, for his conduct of that night; that the board work closely with Fred Mangino on delinquent account problems.'"[19] The notion was passed unanimously, ten to none.

Temperaments flared once again as the board received several complaints about "one specific luncheon donnybrook" pertaining to bad food and service, and Club Steward Mangino's mishandling of the situation. As the extremely vague board minutes reflected, "Mangino remembered the occasion well and, after discussion, it was generally agreed that what happened shouldn't have, that it was a day when all went to pot—and, God willing, it won't happen again. It was brought out, however, that complaints of this type should be presented immediately, when a board member hears of them, to the house committee. The house committee, then, will discuss the problem, go to Mangino if necessary, then report to the board."[20]

Members considered leaving the club house at 1330 Glenarm Place and look for finer quarters (despite the ongoing financial straits). One recommendation was to acquire the YWCA building at 1545 Tremont Place which was for sale at $1.1 million. The building's facilities, potential rental office space plus club rooms, swimming pool, gym and auditorium caught the interest of many of the members during the May 22, 1970 board meeting.[21] The next month, a proposal was considered to move the Denver Press Club to the Chamber of Commerce Building (ironically, the home of the club when the building was first constructed). Board-member Berger noted "the club was growing, and there were comments that the club should be actively engaged in a search for better, larger quarters—possibly involving use of the DAC [Denver Athletic Club] (across Glenarm Place) for special facilities—swimming, other sporting room, etc.).[22] During the August 1971 board meeting, Dick Fenton reported on the feasibility of purchasing the 21-year-old Eagles Building as a replacement for the present press club building. It was possible to add four additional floors, the furnace and other equipment were in good condition, there was a 500-seat auditorium, and parking for twenty cars.[23] The source of the funding for such extravagances nor the extra staffing was never revealed in the records of the club.

The resurgence of women in business and politics continued to help fuel the reconsideration of Dusty Saunders' call for inclusion into the Denver Press Club on an equal footing with the men. At the April 17, 1970 monthly board meeting, "the board approved the wording of a proposed by-law change which would permit the club to accept women as active members."[24] The proposal was offered by Queal and Brofman and unanimously approved by the board. During the same meeting, an application from Marjorie Barrett, religion reporter for the *Rocky Mountain News* was received but tabled, pending a vote of the membership to accept the by-laws change and admit women as members.

The May 22, 1970 monthly board meeting continued the discussion of women members. A special meeting was already scheduled, but concern was circulating among board members when a letter from Sheldon Steinhauser, director of the Anti-Defamation League in Denver, threatened to resign from the club if women weren't admitted. The letter was passed among the board members with little comment.[25]

The much-anticipated special Membership Meeting of May 24, 1970, was gaveled open by President George Franco. Absent that Sunday afternoon were Mel Schieltz, Dave Scher and Cal Queal. With a quorum, the president explained the purpose of the special meeting was to allow club membership to women. "It was emphasized during the discussion that the proposed change dealt only with active memberships, not associate memberships," Secretary John Snyder, secretary to the board, wrote. "There also was discussion about the legality of the club barring women members of the press—with no clear opinion rendered—and that the decision to change or not to change the section would be made at the present assembly."[26]

After considerable discussion by both active and associate members; only one active member, Doug Bradley, spoke against the change. Those speaking in favor of the change included Bill Kostka, Jr., Pat Coffey and John Rogers. After additional discussion, President Franco called for a voice vote, but John Rogers moved for a standing vote to challenge the rules to allow women. President Franco called for the standing vote; those who rose in favor totaled seventeen. Only two unnamed members stood in opposition.

The Special Meeting was gaveled closed and a regular monthly meeting was gaveled open to approve two new members. The applications of Virginia Culver, religion editor of the *Denver Post* was received and her $40 in dues were paid. The application for Marjorie Barrett, reporter for the *Rocky Mountain News* for active membership was likewise approved—once her $40 in dues were paid.[27] In the race between the two arch-rival newspapers, this time the *Denver Post* beat out the *Rocky Mountain News* in having the first woman represented as an active member of the Denver Press Club.

By the June board meeting, it was decided to give Helen G. Bonfils, president of the *Denver Post*, an official club card as an honorary member. Previously, Miss Bonfils and two other women were granted unofficial honorary memberships, but Miss Bonfils was the only survivor when women were officially granted membership in 1970.[28] The following month, four more women joined the press club—Lois Barr, Joan White and Jane Earle, all of the *Denver Post;* and Barbara Browne of the *Rocky Mountain News.* The application for active membership submitted by Mrs. Helen Corey of the *Rocky Mountain News* was tabled while the board contemplated whether Mrs. Corey's position as an executive secretary at the *News* qualified her as a full-time employee in the newspaper business.

The mid-1970s marked the fiftieth anniversary of the press club in their own building, but it was also a matter of survival as a press club, benevolent association, and physically as a building. In 1971, club profits for the year were $356.[29] Accountant Bob Truitt told the Annual Meeting that the club was moving in the correct direction, a little profit was a positive step forward, but the club had a long way to go before regaining solvency. Collection of delinquent accounts had been a problem for at least the past decade and prompted the contemplation of a "straight cash operation."[30] Upon John Buchanan's resolution, the club voted to develop a "get tough policy" when addressing delinquent accounts. By August 1971, twenty-four delinquent accounts were turned over to the attorney for collection and forty-five members were suspended.[31] A few months later, Zeke Scher reported his Delinquent Accounts Committee recouped $324.09 above legal costs by taking eighteen accounts to court; all but two were collected without needing to actually step into the courtroom.[32]

Despite the delinquency of the club's accounts, Past President Dusty Saunders had a sense of the club's legacy when he found an old bar available for $490 in an antique shop. He believed the bar may have been the second bar used by press club. Current President Franco appointed Starr Yelland and Al Pocius to check the bar for authenticity and to determine if the club should purchase it. The antique now occupies the former "library" at the head of the stairs on the second floor of the Denver Press Club.

Starr Yelland proposed a "Hall of Fame corner" be established in the club to recognize "members who receive recognition for out-standing service to their respective fields."[33] Among the members of the club, Yelland proposed Pulitzer Prize winners Paul Conrad and Pat Oliphant; plus Jack Foster and Palmer Hoyt, retired editors of the *Rocky Mountain News* and *Denver Post.*[34]

One of the few club events held at the club in 1971 was a Cheese Night sponsored by the Wisconsin Dairy Association.[35] Some consideration for dances held prior to football trips was introduced by President Hal Heffron in 1971, but it was noted that attendance had been "fair" and "mostly old-type folks."[36] Club losses continued to plague the press club to a point when the national fraternity of journalists, Sigma Delta Chi,[37] wanted to use the club when visiting the city, the Denver Press Club turned down their request.

The 1972 Annual Meeting brought thirty-seven people to the press club. Financially, bar revenues showed a profit, but the food operation continued to operate in the red. Delinquent accounts continued to bring down the economic stability of the club. Several members suggested adding a three-percent surcharge to meals or add a $10 surcharge to dues that could be re-directed to a new building fund; other members questioned whether the management of the club was working as efficiently as possible.

The meeting was full of challenges to the board management as a means of fine-tuning the operations of the club. Some of the conflict came from within the membership. Several accounts of club steward vs. member conflicts were brought to the board of directors. At the annual meeting Doug Bradley introduced a resolution "to put teeth in the authority of the manager to handle any out-of-line members while in the club or at any of the club's outside functions." The board moved that resolution of those conflicts would be made by the board.[38]

Conversation pertaining to finding a new home for the press club continued to rumble through the membership. Dick Wanek suggested looking into space at some of the newer hotels where the hotel and the club could share space.

When John Snyder took the presidential seat in 1972, his goals included keeping the club on a paying basis, maintaining nonprofit organization status, but "to build up a sinking fund toward building replacement." While Bob Rolander thought moving into a hotel would ease the club financial problems, Mel Schieltz thought that action would "lose the club for good." Others believed that owning their own building provided something to preserve as the legacy of the club. Chuck Green proposed the idea of assessments that could be used to return the focus of the press club to benevolent projects.[39]

Delinquent funds were not being efficiently resolved; by April 1972 twenty-seven members were on the suspended list with the total money owed topping $1,944.00. One member owed $415.[40] By July, a special meeting was held to discuss the president's resignation due to advice from his doctors pertaining to the stress levels that the club problems were causing for the president.[41] In September, the club was burglarized and the contents from the unlocked safe were ransacked.[42]

By the end of the year, Mel Schieltz reported on the condition of the press club building and described it as "falling to pieces" with an immediate need to repair the boiler room and storage room at a cost of between $2,000 and $8,000. To help reactivate the club traffic, a "happy hour" was initiated with bar-drinks sold at a 20-cent discount between four and six in the afternoon.[43] Various assessments brought in over $8,000 in needed funding, but Mr. Truitt stressed the club had to look to outside sources for income to take care of forthcoming large maintenance expenses.[44] Mel Schieltz's report to the membership noted that $10,000 to $12,000 worth of updates and upkeep were necessary to keep the press club operational. Bob Rolander reviewed an IRS ruling with regard to outside income of private clubs and noted that the press club banquet income could indicate a violation of that ruling.

To answer the question, "What is the future of the club?," the board pushed harder on the findings of the previous building committee. There were two big alternatives—staying in the present building or move to new quarters. The board gave themselves a year to come up with a "nuts-and-bolts figure" to answer the question.

The annual Denver Press Club golf tournament moved from a decade-long relationship with Highland Hills without showing any profit, to Park Hill where the better course helped bring $1,000 profit to the club. Of the 179 golfers entered, only 44 of them were actually press club members. Other excursions included an "Evening With Gershwin" at Central City, football tours, and a bus-trip to Cloverland Kennel Club.[45] But most of the club's focus was on economic survival.

President Mel Schieltz and the 1973 board began to explore the synergy of working with the Denver Athletic Club and the next-door Colorado Press Association. The following year, Bill Lindsey of the Colorado Press Association withdrew their interest in pooling property interests with the Denver Press Club.[46] John Deasy suggested using the second-floor bar and dining area, possibly for specialty events that included a new-member night, *Denver Post* night, *Rocky Mountain News* night, an associate-member night, etc. Deasy proposed that "special occasion" nights would attract a new collection of newspaper people who may not be familiar with the club.[47] Starr Yelland proposed studying the potential for benevolent gifts, donations, and other sources of income.[48]

In an announcement for the February 28, 1974 meeting, President Mel Schieltz proposed "More in '74" as the slogan for the upcoming year.

"Our records now show 771 members," wrote the president. "If this club is to prosper and grow we should have a drive for another 200 members both active and associate. If each board member would bring in one new member each month we could reach that goal."[49] He urged that the club "move forward in its present building" and that it would be a "big mistake to lose this building."[50]

Pulitzer-winning cartoonist Jim Conrad took the challenge laid down by the club president. Despite skepticism from the rest of the board, Conrad presented a plan to raise a minimum of $30,000 on a voluntary basis to help with the club infrastructure by renovating the bar area and remodel the kitchen.[51] For the next few years, club activities involved raising money to pay for repairs, or another discussion about purchasing the adjacent parking lot for the third time.

In the late 1970s, the lunch crowd became so large that the bar served as a secondary excuse to swap stories, have lunch among outspoken members of the press, and wash it all down with an adult beverage. A long-standing unwritten press club rule was "anything overheard at the press club stayed at the press club." It was an era when the press club luncheons provided a good opportunity to interview sources for a story or for newspapermen to talk to fellow journalists about stories they were developing. The close proximity of the tables and bar stools made it extremely easy to scoop a competing newspaper by listening to their reporters. Likewise, the front-room location of the bar was observable to any patron entering the front door and moving to the dining room located near the center of the main floor of the club.

A rare gathering of presidents of the Denver Press Club include those who served over a forty-year period. Included in the first row (left to right) are Ernie Azlin (1977), Dusty Saunders (1969), Dan Gibson (1983), Hal Hefron (1971), Tom Pade (1999), Brian Weber (1993), Lee Olson (1958), Kevin Flynn (1991), and Lou Kilzer (a two-time Pulitzer Prize winning journalist). The back row includes John Ensslin (1995), Andrew Cohen (1994), Denny Dressman (1988), Carl Miller (1989), Don Kinney (1990) and Chuck Green (1978).

Courtesy of the Denver Press Club

When Joseph Rutkofsky, better known in Denver as Joe "Awful" Coffee's Ringside Restaurant and Lounge closed at 1120 - 17th Street in the late 1970s, the diminutive 5-ft. 1.5-in. boxer brought his cordiality to the Denver Press Club. Standing somewhere behind a lectern that was placed at the entrance to the dining room, "Little Joe" welcomed patrons to the press club lunch hour with the warmth of a long-lost uncle at a family dinner.

A Colorado State law prohibited the sale of liquor on election day between 7 a.m. and 7 p.m. while the polls were open. The purpose was to prevent unscrupulous politicians from plying prospective voters to loosen up their vote. At 11:30 a.m. Herbert Porter, a former press club member and current investigator for the Liquor Control Division, received word that booze was flowing at the Denver Press Club on election day.

He sat the bar, ordered a bourbon and water, and noticed the alcoholic drink was being served in a coffee mug. The press club tradition began in 1906 and was never questioned, despite the large number of lawyers and judges who were members. The state law provided a maximum penalty of a year in jail, a $5,000 fine, or both. Porter cited Press Club Manager Ernest Azlein and an unidentified waitress, and the incident sent the club's liquor license for administrative action.[52] The Press Club appeared before State Revenue Director Alan Charnes who determined the incident was "a transgression" and suspended the club's license for one Saturday,[53] the least-active day the club was open.

By 1981 it appeared that the press club finances were heading in a favorable direction. In 1976 the club reported a net loss of $9,842. In 1980 the club's books showed a net profit of $18,000 with no long-term debts. Auditor Truitt expressed concern that conducting business by cash instead of checks (which frequently bounced) was a potential safety hazard for the club employees. He also noted that the use of a poker machine to generate "donations" to the club was still a possible source of problems with the IRS.[54] However, a new threat was blowing in from the North.

With new economic development riding the energy wave, a Canadian developer bid more than $2.2 million for two press-related Denver landmarks in 1981—the Colorado Press Association building at 1336 Glenarm Place and the adjacent Denver Press Club. This was the third offer Canadians made for the properties and the first one given serious consideration by the boards of directors. Alan Cunningham of the *Rocky Mountain News* reported, "The club has been remodeled countless times, has experienced its share of turmoil and often seemed on the brink of disaster. It also has seen some timeworn traditions collapse: its ban against women members and the illegal practice of serving liquor in coffee cups on election day."[55]

Bill Lindsey, manager of the Colorado Press Association, explained that Norcal Corporation of Calgary, Alberta wanted to break ground on a Denver Athletic Club parking lot and "they were afraid they were going to shake our building down. Sort of a veiled threat there, I guess."[56] Norcal attempted to play one press organization against the other, but instead, the two groups began to compare notes about Norcal's intent for the block.

The developer offered a 21st-floor penthouse suite in the glass-and-steel giant that would replace the historic buildings. When the press club turned down the offer, the developer presented plans of a building wrapping around two tiny historic buildings. Another proposal from the Colorado Press Association created a consolidated Press Building, a medium-sized building able to rent space to Associated Press, United Press International news wire services, and various public relation firms. The bottom line was that the press club would end up paying rent to the developer, at rates that would have quickly depleted the $780,000 being offered for the historic building.[57]

Bob Threlkeld, board member and chairman of the building committee, recognized that a $1 million renovation of the first and second floors of the Denver Press Club building would be necessary within the next two decades. Club president and veteran newsman Bob Palmer explained in reference to a new club facility and a more stable financial condition, "I have no feel of the membership pulse. If you asked twenty different members, you would get twenty different responses. Some love the club the way it is. I love the club; but if I can put it in a mink coat, I would do it,"

James Briggs described the club's ambience in 1946, "Unpretentious but artistic, plain and yet comfortable, compact but of ample proportions, the Press Club is the sanctuary of scores of this town's Fourth Estaters."[58] But in 1981, Club Steward Jimmy Fillas updated the description. "Now, it's like a beer joint. There are no more newspaper people, just a bunch of flags. There are different people in there each time you show up."[59]

An agreement was signed by the Denver Press Club to move the club, from their home of more than fifty-five years, to a 21-story building to be erected on the same block. The club's historic two-story brownstone would become part of the building's parking garage. The club's rent was $1 a year for fifty years (renewable for another fifty years) from Norcal and the developer could rent space for the parking garage for an identical lease agreement. The building was expected to be completed within eighteen months.[60] The deal was too good to be true and fell through; the Denver Press Club doors remained open.

The Norcal situation in 1982 caused city officials to dust off old records and made an interesting discovery. The oldest press club in the country had been serving meals for fifty-seven years without a city-issued restaurant license. The city's Excise and Licenses Division administrative assistant Joyce Mullan only replied, "All I can say is that we issue 22,000 licenses a year, in ninety-four different categories. There may be businesses we miss. We try the best we can."[61] She acknowledged the club's liquor license went as far back as historic records go, but the club should have had an annual $225 restaurant license, too. Obviously, she didn't recognize that many newspapermen of the era thrived on liquid luncheons.

Rocky Mountain News columnist Gene Amole said the press club membership was "shocked to learn food is served there at all" because the restaurant area "is tucked away at the rear of the building, where it is likely to go unnoticed."[62] The bar was near the front door along the southwest wall where the fireplace was located.

In 1985, revenuers from the Colorado Liquor Division and the Secretary of State's office began a two-week investigation into the press club's fundraising staple, the one-armed bandit. In jeopardy, once again, was the club's liquor license. The club believed that the device was no more devious than bars all over town who had "pickle" jars with cards that matched numbers that netted the card owner a modest financial prize and pushed the matter to get a definitive ruling on the slot machine revenue. Nonprofit organizations could sponsor bingo games, raffles and other games of chance; the club considered the one-armed novelty to be in the same category.

Three months of revenue from the machine grossed $9,140 according to records from the State; $3,616 was paid to the winners and the remaining $5,324 was split by the club and its supplier, the Modern Music Company. Club President Fred Brown explained, "We applied for and received a license making it perfectly clear what we intended to do with it. We have been told there are hundreds of these things around the state. Our feeling was we were the only place in the state that was trying to do it legally."[63]

The state's liquor division initially offered the club a fifteen-day suspension of their liquor license; the normal first-violation was forty-five days. The newspapermen maintained the club was operating within the law. Members of the board believed the law was vague and liquor-licensed establishments throughout the state were doing the same thing but without attempting to legalize it with a bingo-raffle license. The liquor officials were swayed to the argument and reduced the fine to a suspension of nine days (January 26 to February 3) when the club was operating with minimal patrons.[64]

In an effort to provide some protection against surrounding development, Brown submitted an application to Denver's Landmark Preservation Commission in 1985 for the club to be approved as a local historical landmark. The stipulations stated that no exterior alterations can be made without advance approval from the landmark commission. If the building was slated for demolition, a 90-day waiting period was required to seek a new use or buyer.[65]

In the late 1980s, the press club began to follow the old adage that good journalists do not necessarily make good managers. The club accountant noted that in 1987 there were ten different methods of collecting dues and members involved with communication didn't necessarily do well in explaining the criterion for each level. A membership assessment to pay off bills only raised $14,000 while $27,000 of current and overdue bills were still on the books. Fingers were pointed, employees threatened, delinquent dues dunned, and recommendations were made to replace the entire board. It got to a point where board member Carl Miller proposed a motion "that no board member may take any unilateral action on behalf of the club unless such authority first has been conferred by the board. [Irv] Moss moved a friendly amendment to add the declaration that the business of the Denver Press Club is to be conducted by the board of directors operating as a committee of the whole."[66] The motion passed unanimously.

Club overhead averaged $375,000 over the past four years. The food/bar revenue continued to decline during the same period with revenue for the most recent fiscal year floundering at $235,000. The deficit of $140,000 would have to be covered by dues and a special membership assessment, but only $105,000 to $115,000 was realistically expected. In a letter to the membership, the board challenged, "This Club belongs to the members. Use it a lot, and it will survive and possibly even prosper. Stay away, and it will disappear in a very short time."[67] During an October 1987 board meeting, Dennis Dressman reported, "We're not only in trouble, but we're behind last year's trend which also was troublesome."[68] In addressing the most serious board problem, Dressman explained "I couldn't find any evidence that any previous board tried to operate the club with an annual budget. Had we been doing that we would have known of the problem."[69]

In one of the first newspaper articles about the Denver Press in many years, Steven Wilmsen, *Denver Post* business writer, reported "Unless the Press club can get a shot in the arm in the form of about 200 new members, it will close in the next several weeks." Wilmsen's article concluded "The club still wears the image of hard-drinking, card-in-the-hat reporters. Reporters in this new era of smoke-free newsrooms and health consciousness, have shied away."[70]

Most business organizations and fraternal organizations began to lose membership as Denver's work force changed and a greater number of former members were drifting to the suburbs where family time was spent with their children's sports teams and other community activities; Wilmsen's conclusions were gaining traction as city-club memberships declined. A 1991 quaint review of downtown Denver's "social clubs" included the Denver Press Club with a slight tone of desperation compared to the club's once-lustrous image: "Not one of the city's more glamorous institutions, the Press Club still gets high marks for color and venerability. The Press Club doesn't require you be a member of the Fourth Estate to join. It has two categories, one for active working journalists, and the other for everyone else. When it comes to augmenting its 275-dues-paying members roster, club officials aren't playing hard to get."[71]

For the next few years, the only mention of the Denver Press Club in the local newspapers was when it was included in the obituaries of the many members who died during the 1990s. Despite the nonprofit status that would have provided a home for contributions from once-loyal advocates of the club membership, the Denver Press Club was rarely (if ever) included as a beneficiary. It was time for the Denver Press Club to re-invent themselves once again.

"Generation X" poets under the age of thirty actually turned to the staid Denver Press Club and other venues as a means of expanding the club's diversity and to look for something other than a pre-packaged opportunity to express their poetic art form. After all, one of the club's most celebrated members was Thomas Hornsby Ferril, the late poet laureate for Colorado.[72] Praised by Carl Sandburg, Robert Frost and H. L. Mencken, the then-eighty-seven-year-old poet laureate of Colorado received the Denver Press Club's 1983 Outstanding Colorado Communicator Award. Ferril, a former *Rocky Mountain News* journalist published at least six volumes of poetry about Colorado and the West.

Thomas Hornsby Ferril
Courtesy of the *Denver Post,* Ed Maker photographer

"There is no other communicator of Ferril's talent and stature," remarked master-of-ceremonies Gene Amole. "He stands alone. While most of us chronicle today's events, Tom Ferril writes for generations yet unborn. His stage is our mountains and our plains, but the subject of his poetry is man. These expressions are the essence of us."[73] A bronze plaque commemorating Ferril's achievements was enshrined in the public plaza of Daniels & Associates headquarters at 2930 E. Third Avenue in Denver. Bill Daniels, sponsor of the honorary luncheon for forty of Ferril's friends at Craig Morton's Restaurant in Cherry Creek, also donated $2,500 to the Denver Press Club's scholarship fund.

The Denver Press Club, in concert with the late-*Rocky Mountain News* and the University of Colorado School of Journalism and Mass Communications re-activated the club's support of today's journalism students. Named after the late press-club member and police reporter Al Nakkula of the *Rocky Mountain News,* the award goes to a reporter for outstanding accomplishments in police reporting from entrees submitted from throughout the country.

In 1908, seventeen of the one-hundred members of the Washington, D.C. Gridiron Club came to Denver and encouraged the Denver Press Club to create their own version of the show. The locally written lampooning of current events of the day and the leaders of the community gradually died out until the *Rocky Mountain News'* city editor, Sam Lusky, and columnist Pasquale "Pocky" Marranzino decided to resurrect the comedy event to re-invigorate post World War II newspaper guild members. "We played the idea back, and back again, and with each liquid stimulant visions of theatrical sugarplums danced through our heads,"[74] Marranzino explained in 1984. The production continued annually until 1979. Tom Murray and Tom Pade resurrected the Gridiron event in 1984, with 800 movers-and-shakers of the Denver political, social and media communities that showed up to lampoon themselves and raise $5,000 for the Denver Press Club's renewed scholarship program.

At the 1984 Gridiron, then-Governor Dick Lamm "urge[d] everyone attending the dinner to roast, grill, insult, slander and revile everyone attending or not attending the Gridiron Dinner with artistry, affection and zeal, in honor of their dedication and devotion to their profession and community." Lamm appeared in that show as the Statue of Liberty, wearing a tinfoil crown and carrying a tinfoil torch. Long-time press club president, Bruce Goldberg, revived the Gridiron in 1990 by convincing the horribly tone-deaf governor John Hickenlooper to "sing" a selection at various productions.

Since 1996, three-to-six club members (living and posthumously) are recognized for their contributions to the club with a dinner and induction into the club's Hall of Fame. "Friends of the Club" include the Public Relations Society of America, the Colorado Association of Black Journalists and other groups have been welcomed to unite with the Denver Press Club in maintaining a vibrant history of journalism and media-relations in the state. Other club members are recognized with a "hanging" in the dining area; reviving the old Denver Press Club tradition of recognizing members, past-presidents, and club managers, and members who have made significant contributions to the welfare of the club with a caricature of questionably exaggerated accuracy often drawn by Pulitzer-winning or leading local editorial cartoonists.

During the turbulent days of the 1980s (give or take a decade), the club was patched together to keep the doors open. Visitors were warned not to touch the wall sconces because none of them was grounded. Anecdotal stories describe the club's records being maintained in the same room as the aging furnace and age-weakened water heater. One weekend, the water heater was said to have given up and flooded the room, turning many of the club records and historic photographs into an archival swampy ooze. Leaking second-floor plumbing bubbled many of the historic caricatures in the dining room below. The entire building reeked of decades of beer, whiskey and layers of cigar and cigarette smoke. Even after the club welcomed women, most spouses wanted nothing to do with the unkempt decor and man-cave residue. Even club manager Carmen Green's eccentric collection of snow globes that lined the rafters above the bar had to eventually be boxed and removed. Late-night bartenders welcomed their fellow bartenders, taxi-drivers, horse-drawn carriage drivers, and even the occasional exotic dancer from the Diamond Cabaret a block away—all found the press club to be a sanctuary after their shifts and helped fill the bar's late-night coffers in a hassle-free eccentric club. Their cash-paid bar-tabs helped keep the club afloat, one crisp garter-belt dollar bill at a time. For a while the classy strip club down the block from the press club was jokingly referred to as the Denver Breast Club.

New management, new board members, and a new drive to keep the club alive survived another attempt to demolish the historic press club house to be replaced by another steel-and-glass nondescript high-rise building on Denver's skyline. As Joe Sebastian Sinisi of the *Denver Post* wrote, "The old club was down at the heels and not a place to impress out-of-town visitors. Nor had it aged or fared well in an era when bottled water and a trip to the gym have replaced an after-work beer with colleagues."[75] Something had to change, and club president Mike McPhee of the *Denver Post* led his board of directors to make some necessary changes to years of neglect. His objective was to take the oldest press club in the country and bring it back to the glory days when "you'd find federal judges and lawyers, along with journalists for stimulating conversation."[76]

Impetus for the remodeling occurred when board vice-president and *Rocky Mountain* News reporter Peggy Lowe and Mike McPhee discovered the front-room fireplace and press club shield shown in 1925 photographs could still be hiding behind the tacky wall paneling behind the bar. A portion of the old fireplace was now being occupied by the beer cooler. The old fireplace was replaced with a more efficient gas fireplace during the remodel, but the club shield remained a bit of a mystery. The initials DPC were intertwined with a sword placed behind a feather pen—the pen is mightier than the sword. However, above the club shield was the mystery—a profile of bird, a wall that looked like the spine of a book, and profile of a horse's head.

The crest of the Denver Press Club is located on the wall over the fireplace in the 1925 Denver Press Club building. The initials DPC (Denver Press Club) are entwined with a representation that the "pen is mightier than the sword." The symbolism of the horse, book, and bird remain a mystery.

Courtesy of the author

When the puckish librarians of the Denver Public Library Western History Department were asked if they had any clue about the meaning of the bird and horse on the press club shield, they responded with several communication-centric suggestions, "It's quite clear that it refers to 'A little bird told me that I got the information straight from the horse's mouth.'" Another librarian explained the bird as the earliest reference to "tweeting" information.

Stripping the walls down to the basic infrastructure, the club utilized professional and volunteer club help to rebuild the rooms to a close resemblance of the 1925 club look with a very clean and modern feel. Instead of walking through the front door to view the backs of local newspapermen at the bar, visitors now walked into a living room where journalism students gathered around the restored gas fireplace for a "fireside chat" with visiting experts in modern journalism. Past board president and former *Rocky Mountain News* reporter John Ensslin explained "the future of the club is found in its past. And by returning to its 1925 design, the club actually seems more modern."[77]

Club president McPhee pitted *Denver Post* publisher William Dean Singleton against *Rocky Mountain News* executive editor John Temple to out-donate the other. The initial contribution was $25,000 each, and an anonymous donor kicked-in an additional $100,000. Dues were raised to $200 a year for regular-membership and a new-membership drive brought new blood to the club. The club was closed down for three months while Denver architect Guy Thornton brought the old club alive again. As Joe Sebastian Sinisi reported, the ratty carpets were torn up, revealing oak floors on the main and second floor; garish lighting was torn out, and the dining area reopened in appetizing style. "Gone is the old paneling and false ceilings that masked cross-beams and architectural details," reported Sinisi. "Warm colors have replaced the previous paint job that oozed all the charm of a warehouse."

The front living room is warm and inviting in the style of the original club. The walls are now lined with replicas of the Pulitzer Prizes, mostly earned by club members. The caricatures fill several walls of the Fourth Estate dining room, and its wall of signed presidential portraits began when it was considered good election-luck for a presidential candidate to be photographed in the Denver Press Club. The 1943 Herndon Davis mural in the basement poker room that was caked with cigar smoke was carefully restored through a grant from the State Historical Society. Legend claims that Davis painted the mural to pay-off a bar tab at the club.

Former *Rocky Mountain News* reporter John Head told Sinisi, "It's a great combination of old and new with the feel of a lot more space. The cartoon wall is reminiscent of the celebrity-wall at Sardi's restaurant in

New York's theater district. But our people have an average IQ about eighty points higher."

But by the fall of 2005, the club was still facing a stack of unpaid vendor bills, late tax payments, and a temporary loss of insurance. A contentious board meeting called for the removal of eleven board members and hire an outside auditor to examine the club's financial books. Mark Stutz had been appointed president just a few months earlier was also ready to resign. "I wasn't thrilled to run a meeting of seventy-five people, many of whom were angry last night, but by the same token it showed they cared," Stutz told *Denver Post* reporter Tom McGhee.[78]

Carmen Green

Popular Denver Press Club manager Carmen Green was honored with a public hanging of his caricature, drawn by cartoonist Jean Tool.

Courtesy of Dick Nosbisch

The 2006 board of directors under Bruce Goldberg brought a new approach to managing the club. Income-generating fund-raising projects like the annual Damon Runyon Award dinner and Hall of Fame banquet would continue; club membership staples like Dusty Saunders' "Wild Turkey" toast at the bar just before Thanksgiving continued to draw a crowd, and the club's location at the finish line of Denver's Parade of Lights holiday event provided a warm viewing post from the club's windows for the large group of members that attend each year. Club Manager Carmen Green initiated a land-locked clambake, guest-bartenders who brought their co-workers to the club for their introduction to the club, and an annual "Frank Sinatra Night" continued to support the eccentric nature of the club—as long as they turned a profit for the club. On weekends when the club was rarely used, wedding parties rented the historic quarters, and Denver's community television network as well as C-Span and other media outlets now record events from the Denver Press Club.

One of the Denver Press Club's "friends" included the Denver Press Club as a "Historic Site in Journalism" in 2008. The Society of Professional Journalists bestowed the award when the club's origins were thought to be in 1877 under the presidential leadership of William Byers, the first editor of the *Rocky Mountain News* and the first president of the Denver Press Club. Subsequent research showed that the origins of the press club began at least a decade earlier with Wolfe Londoner being the club's first informal president.

In 2017, the 1330 Glenarm Place club house was added to the National Registry of Historic Places by the United States Park Service.

1   "The Newspaper Editor," *The Denver Republican,* February 14, 1914, p. 1
2   Minutes, Denver Press Club Board of Directors, June 16, 1965
3   Ibid
4   Minutes, Denver Press Club Annual Meeting, March 19, 1967
5   Minutes, Denver Press Club Annual Meeting, March 20, 1966
6   Ibid
7   Ibid
8   Minutes, Denver Press Club Annual Meeting, March 19, 1967
9   Minutes, Denver Press Club Board of Directors, April 11, 1968
10   Minutes, Denver Press Club Board of Directors, George Franco, secretary; February 12, 1969
11   Ibid.
12   Minutes, Denver Press Club Annual Meeting, Hal Heffron, secretary, March 15, 1970
13   Minutes, Denver Press Club Board of Directors, Tom Gavin, Secretary;

January 11, 1967
14 Minutes, Denver Press Club Board of Directors, Tom Gavin, Secretary; February 16, 1967
15 Minutes, Denver Press Club Board of Directors, Tom Gavin, Secretary; March 20, 1967
16 Minutes, Denver Press Club Board of Directors, Mark Bearwald, Secretary; May 23, 1968
17 Minutes, Denver Press Club Board of Directors, Hal Heffron, acting secretary; July 19, 1968
18 Minutes, Denver Press Club Board of Directors, Hal Heffron, secretary; February 2, 1970
19 Minutes, Special Meeting of the Denver Press Club Board of Directors, Hal Heffron, secretary; February 8, 1970
20 Minutes, Denver Press Club Board of Directors, John Snyder, Secretary; December 18, 1970
21 Minutes, Denver Press Club Board of Directors, John Snyder, Secretary; May 22, 1970
22 Minutes, Denver Press Club Board of Directors, John Snyder, Secretary; June 19 1970
23 Minutes, Denver Press Club Board of Directors, August 20, 1971
24 Minutes, Denver Press Club Board of Directors' Meeting, Cal Queal, Secretary Pro-Tem; April 17, 1970
25 Ibid
26 Minutes, Special Membership Meeting of the Denver Press Club; John Snyder, secretary; May 24, 1970
27 Minutes, Denver Press Club Board of Directors, John Snyder, Secretary; May 24, 1970
28 Minutes, Denver Press Club Board of Directors, John Snyder, Secretary; June 19, 1970
29 Minutes, Denver Press Club Annual Meeting; March 21, 1971
30 Ibid
31 Minutes, Denver Press Club Board of Directors; August 20, 1971
32 Minutes, Denver Press Club Board of Directors; January 21, 1972
33 Minutes, Denver Press Club Board of Directors; May 21, 1971
34 Minutes, Denver Press Club Board of Directors; May 21, 1971
35 Minutes, Denver Press Club Board of Directors; September 24, 1971
36 Minutes, Denver Press Club Board of Directors; October 27, 1971
37 Minutes, Denver Press Club Board of Directors; December 17, 1971
38 Minutes, Denver Press Club Annual Meeting; March 26, 1972
39 Minutes, Denver Press Club Board of Directors; March 26, 1972
40 Minutes, Denver Press Club Board of Directors; April 21, 1972

41 Minutes, Denver Press Club Board of Directors, Special Meeting; July 7, 1972

42 Minutes, Denver Press Club Board of Directors; September 29, 1972

43 Minutes, Denver Press Club Board of Directors; December 1, 1972

44 Minutes, Denver Press Club Board of Directors; March 25, 1973

45 Minutes, Denver Press Club Board of Directors; June 28, 1973

46 Minutes, Denver Press Club Board of Directors; January 25, 1974

47 Minutes, Denver Press Club Board of Directors; September 28, 1973

48 Minutes, Denver Press Club Board of Directors; January 25, 1974

49 Monthly Meeting Notice, Mel Schieltz, circa February 1974

50 Minutes, Denver Press Club Board of Directors—Annual Meeting; March 26, 1974

51 House Committee Meeting, Denver Press Club; May 14, 1974

52 "Revenuers hit Press Club Well, Lou Kilzer, *Rocky Mountain News;* September 13, 1978, p. 10

53 "Illegal Drink Closes Press Club for Day," *Denver Post;* November 25, 1978, p. 3

54 Minutes, Denver Press Club Board of Directors, March 22, 1981

55 "Firm Offers $2.2 Million for Press Buildings," Alan Cunningham, *Rocky Mountain News;* August 31, 1981

56 Ibid

57 Ibid

58 "Press Club Members to Decide Fate of Buildings," Mark Lusky, *Denver Downtowner;* October 28, 1981, p. 19

59 Ibid

60 "Press Club Signs Pact for New Building," *Rocky Mountain News;* March 29, 1982, p. 8

61 "Press Club 77 Years Late," *Rocky Mountain News,* September 3, 1982, p. 7

62 "Easily Overlooked," *Omaha (Nebraska) World Herald;* October 6, 1982, p. 2

63 "Gambling Probe Unplugs Press Club Poker Device," Kevin Flynn, *Rocky Mountain News;* August 8, 1985, p. 10, 11

64 "Press Club's License for Liquor Suspended," Kevin Flynn, *Rocky Mountain News;* January 16, 1986, p. 27

65 "Press Club Seeking Status as Landmark," Kevin Flynn, *Rocky Mountain News;* August 14, 1986, p. 56

66 Minutes, Denver Press Club Board of Directors; October 21, 1987

67 Undated report to the membership by the Board of Directors and the Past Presidents Committee, circa October 1987

68 Minutes, Denver Press Club Board of Directors; October 28, 1987

69 Ibid

70 "Dwindling Membership May Spell End to Denver Press Club," Steven

Wilmsen, *Denver Post;* July 21, 1989

71 "A Casual Tour Through Downtown's Social Clubs," James B. Meadow, *Rocky Mountain News,* October 1, 1991, p. 36

72 Untitled article by Molly Hall, Associated Press; *St. Albans (Vermont) Daily Messenger;* August 5, 1994, p. 12

73 "Press Club Names Ferril Outstanding Communicator," Bob Diddlebock, *Rocky Mountain News,* July 14, 1983, p. 16

74 "Denver Press Club Gridiron Show," DenverPressClub.org

75 "Denver's Revived Press Club Debuts," Sebastian Sinisi, *Denver Post Knight Ridder/Tribune Business News,* December 11, 2002

76 Ibid

77 Ibid

78 "Press Club Finances in Distress," *Denver Post,* October 5, 2005, p. 3C

CHAPTER 10 – EPILOGUE

An editor should have a pimp for a brother, so he'd have someone to look up to.
- Eugene (Gene) Fowler, Denver Press Club member

In theatrical worlds, there is a ritual of leaving a lamp illuminated on stage after the actors and crew have left after the evening's performance. The purpose was to make sure no one walks off the stage and into the open orchestra pit ten feet (or more) below the stage. "The superstition around it is that theaters tend to be inhabited by ghosts," says Broadway stage manager Matt Stern. "Whether it's the ghost of old actors or people who used to work in the building . . . ghost lights are supposed to keep those ghosts away so that they don't get mischievous while everyone else is gone."[1]

Whether it was the Denver Press Club's close alliances with Denver's theater crowd, or whether the spirits of Denver's departed newspapermen in Riverside Cemetery may still be trying to pad their bar tabs with the contemporary club, but many believe the 1925 press-club building is haunted. The origins of the press club ghost are as varied as the tellers of the tales of the hauntings. Journalists are never supposed to interject themselves into a news story, but I hope you'll indulge me for this one opportunity to tell of my own experiences. Many of my hours at the Denver Press Club were spent in the wee hours of club, and that's when I first experienced a visitation from "Charlie," the euphemism for a benign introduction to the club's phantasmic non-dues-paying member. The fictional personage of a very real spirit was so-named by Club Manager Patty Brown. Anecdotes portrayed the ghost in almost playful terms.

When the club patrons would go home for the night, I found it an ideal time to wander the quiet hallways of the press club. At key places throughout the club, I'd experience a chill-like sensation on the back of my neck that was surprising, but not uncomfortable. This provided an opportunity to engage in conversations with Club Manager Carmen Green and various barkeepers at the time. They all had similar experiences—but were also glad to share additional stories.

In earlier days of the press club, the kitchen was a maze of hanging utensils above the work area. One day when Green was alone in the club, he entered the kitchen and found all the pots and pans swinging wildly from their hooks as if someone had playfully pushed them. Bartender Brian Perry described looking in the mirror that once hung over the bar, and saw a figure come down the stairs. He spun around only to find the stairway empty.

"Have you experienced the ghost tonight?" became a frequent greeting of those of us who hung out at the club late at night. One night after the official city hour for closing the bar, several of us ventured upstairs to continue our general chit-chat. As we sat in a semi-circle between the two sections of the club's second story, a sense of surprise crossed the faces of each of us in the order of our seating. Sometimes the unseen experience stopped one of our conversations in mid-sentence. When the last person felt the hair on the back of their neck return to normal, the room fell silent. Finally, someone asked, "Did anyone else feel something strange?" Everyone confessed experiencing the same sensation. There were no drafts, no open windows—just "Charlie".

Club manager Patty Brown often commented that she didn't enjoy working in the office on the second floor above the kitchen added to the rear of the building in 1954. "I would sit there for hours, feeling increasingly depressed, but never knowing why," explained Brown during a taping of a documentary about three psychics who came to bring light to the haunting of the press club. "The psychics kept describing to me that when they went into my office, they said a very sad and traumatic experience happened in that area."[2] Brown explained that a burned woman's body was allegedly found in the dumpster behind the press club before the addition was built; Brown's office would have been directly above where that dumpster was located. This story added to the speculation that "Charlie" was not alone in the press club.

"The most powerful incidence was the time that me and Alan Kania were sitting at the bar," Bartender Brian Perry reflected for the video. "I was behind the bar and Alan was sitting there drinking a Glenlivet on the rocks, I believe—he only had one. We were talking and during the whole conversation, we were being interrupted by noises that sounded like people walking around. Alan kept looking at me and said, 'Did you hear that?' Yeah, I heard that, it sounded like someone was downstairs, then, all of a sudden it sounded like someone was upstairs."[3]

We were the only people in the building and the upstairs noises were unmistakable deliberate stomping sounds on the floor above us. There are only two stairways that lead to the upstairs area of the press club. Brian ran up one and I headed for the other. We met in the middle of the second floor and acknowledged that neither of us found an intruder. Brian merely said, "The club — is closed. I'm going home!"

Perry continued to express the same experience that many of us who have met "Charlie" have felt. "I get this feeling that there is this presence. It was kind of like when you're in a crowded room, and someone is right behind you. You don't see them, but you feel them. You feel their magnetism or whatever."

My most powerful experience with the ghost was during the visit by the three psychics for the video documentary. During the walk-through of the club where Cleo Briggs, and psychics Eshaya and Vija repeatedly supported each other's paranormal incantations. "Oh yes, I feel the ghost here. Do you feel the ghost? Oh yes, I feel it, too." At one point early in the evening, the three ladies asked club manager (and staunch believer in the existence of "Charlie") Carmen Green to leave his own club building because he was emitting too many uncomfortable vibes that interfered with the psychics' attempt to reach the ghost. "It's the only time I've ever been thrown out of my own club!" bemoaned Green.

Eshaya stood at the top of the second-floor stairway near the front of the building and raised her hands to hauntingly announce that "Ooooh yes! I feel the presence of a spirit here." Dutifully Vija and Cleo confirmed the presence of the spirit. I was attending a board meeting that evening and several of my fellow board members were there to watch the "cleansing" by the psychics. I looked up from the main-level bottom of the stairway and clearly saw a semi-transparent figure staring blankly past Eshaya, no more than a foot away from her.

"I use a rod, and I came up the stairway and I visualized this man, standing at that window, looking out," explained Eshaya on the video. "He did not like me standing there in his space. I definitely got that impression. He basically went through me; I had a sensation like he went through me. And I saw an image of him; he gave me an image. And I turned around and the man down the stairway said, 'Did you see him?' Yeah, I did."[4]

I was "the man" at the bottom of the stairway but had already turned and grabbed a napkin from the bar directly behind me. Quickly, I wrote a detailed description of what I saw at the top of the stairs. After a repetitive exchange of "what did you see?" "No, you tell me first;" I told Eshaya, "No, we're not going to play this game. I've written what I saw. You tell me what you saw." Eshaya proceeded to provide a detailed description of a tall man in dark clothing and a mustache, wearing a cape that was reminiscent of the late 19th Century. When she finished, I unfolded my description written on the bar napkin. The details were nearly exact.

Denver Press Club ghost stories abound. KIMN-radio talk-show host Peter Boyle even hosted a call-in talk show from the upstairs meeting area. His live program on Halloween evening may have hoped for an exclusive interview with "Charlie," but the ghost never made himself available. KUSA-TV's Ward Lucas presented an entertaining demonstration of the tricks of con-men who prey on the gullible during another "waiting for Charlie to appear" party. An oft-repeated press-club factoid is that a poker game continued from one location to another as the table, cards, chips, and players were loaded onto the moving van. For years, that true story was geographically misrepresented as a move to the 1330 Glenarm Place location. With that erroneous story known, many of the psychics who have visited the club provided affirmations that the ghost(s) of the press club were those original poker players who refused to end their game during the move to the press club.

While early press-club members have committed suicide in the club, it was never within the historic property on Glenarm Place. A careful review of deaths and suicides in the early years of Denver failed to produce anything that would connect a death with the property. Besides, the late-1800s attire of the figure at the top of the stairs was not wearing clothing appropriate of that era. The press club building was constructed in 1925 when fashion was considerably different. An infrared photograph taken by Jeffrey Ravage showed a shadowy figure of a person standing in the second-floor meeting room—wearing the same style of clothing seen by both the psychic and myself.

When the Colorado Press Association occupied the building to the north of the club, they also felt a ghost on days that employees at the press club did not (and vice versa). The ghost was apparently haunting the site and not the specific buildings. Behind the bar, new, fashionable t-shirts began appearing with the unofficial press-club logo and the lettering, "We serve spirits."

Other spirits are easier to document. The Denver Press Club turned to national role-models of excellence in journalism as a fund-raising effort to reward scholarships to students in regional schools of journalism. The recipients of the Denver Press Club's signature Damon Runyon Award are known for their excellence in quality journalism and preservation of the First Amendment.

The first Damon Runyon Award was presented to the most appropriately Runyonesque character, Jimmy Breslin. Club president John Ensslin, growing up outside of New York City, looked upon Breslin as a personal journalistic hero. Breslin showed how "the heart of journalism is found not just in the big events, but in the small details."[5] Ensslin went on to explain that while other reporters were covering the funeral procession of John F. Kennedy in the early 1960s, Breslin spent time to write an extremely moving column from the grave-digger's point of view.

That first Runyon dinner had a humble beginning with a hundred people filling the second floor of the press club building. The crowd had gathered, but the honoree was nowhere to be found.

Breslin flew out to Denver and *Denver Post's* Steve Lipsher was dispatched to retrieve the New York columnist at the airport. Breslin's wife already left a phone message to Ensslin, delivered in a strong New York accent, "Make shore, he gits, a haircut." The honoree was left in the good hands of The Brown Palace Hotel barber while Lipsher promised to return to escort Breslin to the press club. When the appointed hour arrived, Breslin was nowhere to be found. Eventually, the concierge handed Lipsher a note, "I'm at the Y."

Lipsher raced in a panic to the nearby YMCA, searched the bowels of the building, and as Ensslin related, "there he finds a rather large New York City columnist doing laps, face down, slowly going back and forth in the swimming pool. . .. And just as Jimmy touched the tiles at one end of the pool, Steve gently put his shoe down on Jimmy's wet knuckles. THAT got his attention! That, and twelve insane minutes later, got him to the Denver Press Club. The two of them walked through the door . . . Jimmy had a very nice haircut. His hair was still wet. It smelled like — chlorine. Things settled down after that, and Jimmy gave one helluva speech about the importance of putting one's passion into journalism every day."[6]

Jimmy Breslin who was presented with a pocket watch and a dinner attended by enthusiastic journalistic peers in the audience. "It used to be if they gave you a watch, you wouldn't have to keep it," expressed Breslin before the event. "You could turn it in later for $25," he told the press club. "The watch didn't have any works in it. It was worthless, and they could give it away over and over again. I bet there's going to be works in this one. You know, that's where the term 'Give him the works,' came from. It's even worse when they engrave your name in the watch. Then you're really stuck with it."

The journalistic curmudgeon appropriately addressed the same changes to journalism that the Denver Press Club was facing with the decline of quality in newspaper writing. "It's because of the computer terminals," Breslin told *Rocky Mountain News* reporter Alan Dumas. "The writing is twenty-percent of what it once was. People sit in front of those terminals as if they were writing a situation comedy. The screens are all that they see, and it's like TV, they start to use a passive voice. Journalism is not contemplative. It's nervous energy. Words should be the product of nervous energy. Writers should get out there and be moved by what they see, get excited by it, and then maybe their language will get more exciting. Newspapers will last forever if they get back to the basics, and that's writing the news. But there's no news in buildings. There's no news in city hall or police headquarters. News is on the street, where the people live. If newspapers are just giving people the kind of news they see in the morning on TV, and then again on TV before they go to sleep, what good are they?"[7]

The following year, Damon Runyon Award recipient Mike Royko continued to beat the drum for journalism by lamenting the loss of street-savvy reporters. The Chicago journalist eulogized those reporters: "They'd been around and had done things other than go straight from prep schools to college to the newspapers. They tended to have more fun and were less judgmental than today's crop of journalists. If you were in a foxhole and saw a guy next to you get his head blown off, you tended not to take the day's problems as seriously as people who led more sheltered lives."[8]

Molly Ivins, who once worked in Denver as the *New York Times'* western correspondent, provided one of the "funniest, rip-snorting" Damon Runyon banquet speeches, according to Ensslin. It was the third annual presentation and Ivins shared the stage with equally celebrated columnist for the *San Francisco Chronicle,* Herb Caen. Unknown to the club, both recipients were fond admirers of each other, and that night it was evident. The event was held at the old Shriners' Temple on 19th Street with somewhat challenging acoustics. "Undeterred," Ensslin reminisced, "Molly grabbed the microphone, plunged into the crowd, and gave a memorable speech on the importance of journalism and upending the status quo. 'I am here,' she said that night, 'to speak on behalf of irreverence, improper behavior, and the occasional imbibing of far too much liquor. I am here to speak on behalf of mischief, upset and roiling the waters.' She went on to say, 'As long as we are raising Hell, and having fun, we'll be doing our jobs.'"[9]

Sharing the stage was Herb Caen who was enjoying one of his last public appearances. Of all the recipients of the award, he was the only one who actually met Damon Runyon when the award's namesake was dying of cancer. As Ensslin explained, despite his own approaching last deadline, Caen maintained a remarkable spirit, prankster wit, powers of observation, and a love for god-awful puns.

"I remember watching him walk so-o-o-o slowly up the stairs at the Shriner's Temple, leaning so heavy on this elaborate walking stick he had," reminisced Ensslin about Herb Caen. "At the top of the stairs, he looked right at me, pointed at the stick and said, 'Look! It's Herb's cane!'"[10]

For 150 years, the Denver Press Club and its members made the transitions from newspapers that were printed on whatever type of paper was available to the frontier town, to the realm of scores of pages that were printed from huge rolls of newsprint. Journalism made further transitions to newsreels shown in theaters, to radio, and on to television and computer screens. Each form of communication brought its own method of telling a story, but each was presented in a way that strove to present the information as fairly and as accurately as possible.

However, journalists have struggled to make sense between what the public needs to know and what the public wants to know. For journalists to place their lives and reputations on the line to bring fair and accurate stories to the public, only to discover that the newspaper is still at the end of the driveway were the paperboy last dropped it, is a disheartening observation to any hard-working journalist. At some point, accepting a newspaper's employee buy-out to a publication that may cease to exist, becomes a realistic face-slap that conflicts with a reporter's reasons for becoming a journalist.

When Eugene Fowler wrote his last book, *Skyline*, which was published the year after his death in 1960, he was able to look back to the 1920s in ways that are still relevant a century later.

> Forty years ago, the newspaper was the world's information booth, the most immediate agency of public reference. This should be kept in mind when one thinks of the newspaper's place in the scheme of the 1920s. The great change in the character of the news reflected the change in men's thoughts and deeds and recorded their growing worship of the machine.
>
> The newspaper lost its spark of immediacy when radio and television pre-empted the headlines. Now the spot news comes piecemeal every hour or less over the air or through pocket computers. It is like eating between meals; by the time the newspaper arrives at the table your appetite has been spoiled.
>
> Other problems harass the newspaper, some of them self-induced. A newspaper must stay free of obligation to anyone other than the public, but it also must be solvent to survive. With rising costs, as well as the intrusions by other media, the wonder is not that the press sometimes falters in its mission, or that daily papers fail, or merge to keep in business, but that the Fourth Estate still has a voice.
>
> It has become more and more a publisher's voice, however. In other days the editor was in command. Editors, for the most part, were one-purpose men. They tried to reflect the public interest, to defend the public's right to know. The old-time editor had an austere disdain for the complaints of the business office. This independence is still obtained in the outstanding newspapers, but the besetting evils of the haywire economy, as well as the reprisals exacted by ferocious minorities against anyone

who prints unpleasant truths, has taken much of the do-and-dare spirit out of the makers of newspaper policies. When appeasement supplants editorial enterprise, and silences the outspoken criticism of evil men, the newspaper forfeits its character, loses its influence—and eventually its life. Public servants become public masters. All freedoms are endangered when that of the press is assailed.[11]

When visitors come to the Denver Press Club, a frequent question is "Why is there still a press club? Isn't your purpose out-of-date in today's digital communications world, where anyone can Tweet, blog, and express their own version of freedom of speech in any form they wish?" Certainly, but with the quantity of information available, few people are apt to sift through all the oysters in the mud to find the rare one that contains a pearl of wisdom.

Press clubs existed in major cities around the country and even in the mountain communities throughout Colorado. The University of Denver established the first college press club in Colorado for campus publications in the new commerce building. "I believe that proper publicity is one of the greatest stepping stones to progress that civilization has developed," said Chancellor Heber Reece Harper (1922-1927). "Publicity had a direct bearing upon the winning of the war. It was not used solely for the benefit of welfare organizations. It did great service in the floating of the liberty loans and in increasing the morale of the people."[12] Sometimes the creative fund-raising and benevolence from the club members and the stewards were destined to privately help individual members of the club.

Journalism students at what was called Metro State College at the time in Denver, engaged in a discussion of what constitutes "quality news." It was like trying to define "quality music." People hear music on popular radio stations, in grocery stores, in elevators, fitness classes and office buildings — it's everywhere, and usually it's pleasant and satisfying. But if you want quality music (like jazz or classical), a person needs to search for it because quality music is not readily available. It's helpful to have a background to understand the subtle nuances that make it special. But once you find it, the listener knows they're richly rewarded by the effort. Quality news is the same concept.

Talking-heads on cable "news" networks, "conspiracy commerce" (coined by former President Bill Clinton), blogs, and talk shows are everywhere and too frequently spread their information without the slightest effort to fact-check or verify. People with little interest in challenging their own preconceived views of current events will lash out at the journalistic "messengers". After all, writing is easy; thinking is hard.

The role of press clubs is more important, today, than it has ever been in the past. The public has failed to keep up with the contradictions among what is increasingly becoming pop-culture news, and often falsely contrived information, versus the more-difficult-to-find remaining bastions of quality news. Quality news is still available, but despite the public demands for it, the community will rarely support it. Again, thinking is hard.

The International Communications Forum in England believed that journalism needs to change from "If it bleeds, it leads" to "If it answers needs, then it leads." When the organization held one of its international conferences in Denver, ICF Founder Bill Porter reiterated the claim made by the *Financial Times*—the communications industry has become the largest industry in the world. As a major international publisher, Porter pondered the dilemma—if the communications industry was the largest, was it also the most responsible in providing quality news and information?

Porter began to ask himself and his peers in the publishing industry, "What is the effect of your products for good or ill on the people who read, listen to and watch them? If we did something which had a good social effect I was happy to take some praise, but if it had a bad effect I washed my hands of it, saying that those problems were a matter for politicians, religious leaders, and sociologists, but not for me. I had freedom to publish. There was freedom of information and the consequences were not my affair."[13]

Malik Faisal Moonzajer, an Afghan journalist once told me, "When the doctor is not well-known (poorly trained), he will kill the patient. But when the journalist is not well-known, he will kill the society." The Preamble to the Code of Ethics for the Society of Professional Journalists explains, "Ethical journalism strives to ensure the free exchange of information that is accurate, fair, and thorough. An ethical journalist acts with integrity."

Andy Rooney, CBS News resident curmudgeon and one of the [Edward R.] "Morrow Boys," was in Denver during the early 1980s. He was brought to the Denver Press Club where Rooney felt like he was among journalists from anywhere in the world, gathered for camaraderie and support at a time when the industry was experiencing drastic changes. "The men and women in newsrooms across the country all know the same things I know," Rooney wrote of the Denver Press Club in his syndicated newspaper column. "We share common problems and we have common goals. We can start our conversations further along than you can normally start a conversation with someone you've never met because of this feeling of common knowingness. . . If the time comes when the newspaper itself is not a paper at all but an image that can be called up on the screen of a computer in a person's home, a lot of what they love about the business will be gone. There won't be much reason to hold out against switching over to television, where the journalism may be worse but the pay better. Newspapermen wouldn't sit around the Denver Press Club eating, drinking and arguing about a product that doesn't really exist anywhere but in the brain cells of a computer."[14]

Past president of both the Denver Press Club and the Society of Professional Journalists, John Ensslin, reflected on the club in a video documentary. "I had an editor who was showing me Denver. I'm just some kid from New Jersey, I didn't know the town. I noticed the facade that said 'Denver Press Club' ... I asked, 'What's that place?' He just said, "Oh just skip it, it's a place for old wheezers.' . . . But when I did get to go one night, what I saw was a guy at the bar with an oxygen tank, plugged into his nose and everything. I'm thinking, 'Oh, maybe he was right.' Turns out that guy was Thomas Hornsby Ferril whom I very much regret not having met, having seen him — the great Poet Laureate of this state at that time and a long-time member of this club. So, I wish I got to know the old wheezer."[15]

"Walking into this place always makes me feel like you're part of something bigger than your own little life," continued Ensslin, "that you're a part of a continuum of people who want to keep this place alive and healthy and fun over the years."[16]

Over the next several decades, a cavalcade of old-guard journalists and graduates of regional journalism classes will continue to have an opportunity to gather at the press club to help resurrect the art-and-craft of journalism for new generations of reporters, viewers, listeners, and readers. The Denver Press Club will always be a place where people who have a healthy respect for the First Amendment and enjoy good civil discourse, can gather for a respectable exchange of ideas. While the spirit of 150 years of journalism is heralded within the walls of the oldest press club in the United States, the only ghost light necessary would merely be for the benefit of "Charlie".　　　—30—

1   "The Story Behind the Ritual that Still Haunts Broadway," Andy Wright, *Atlas Obscura*, October 1; http://www.atlasobscura.com/articles/the-story-behind-the-ritual-that-still-haunts-broadway

2   "Members and Ghosts Only: An examination of paranormal experiences at the Denver Press Club, Jeffrey Ravage and Denver Press Club, 1996

3   Ibid

4   Ibid

5   Ibid.

6   Ibid.

7   "There Are No 'Guys' and 'Dolls' Anymore," Alan Dumas, *Rocky Mountain News;* October 13, 1994, p. 13D, 14D

8   "Journalist Yearns for Old Days," *Augusta Chronicle;* October 11, 1995

9   "Legends of the Press," a video production of Denver 8, City and County of Denver; May 6, 2005

10 Ibid.

11 *Skyline*, Gene Fowler, Viking Press, New York, 1961; pp. 247-248

12 "Publicity Boosts World, Says Harper," *Rocky Mountain News*, November 24, 1922, p. 2

13 *Do Something About It!: A Media Man's Story*, Bill Porter, Caux Books, Switzerland, 2005, p. 129

14 "Black, White and Read—For Now," Andy Rooney, *Trenton Evening Times*, March 28, 1982

15 "The Denver Press Club: Back Then and Now," Tom Pade documentary, 1995

16 Ibid

INDEX

Author's note: The names of some organizations were not consistently represented in newspaper accounts and other publications. As a result, some organizations will be listed as separate organizations when they *may* have been the same organization. Some names were misspelled in the various newspapers; I have done the best that I could to correct the spelling of all proper names. Please be creative when searching key words from this book.

A

Abbott, Emma (Operatic soprano and impresario), 56

Abbott English Opera Company, 56

Adams, James Barton (Cowboy poet), 142

Albany Hotel, 84, 87, 88, 90, 98, 101, 109, 125, 133, 136, 140, 147, 148, 156, 167, 173, 179, 230

Alexander, S. H. (Manager, Savoy Hotel), 98

Allen, R. S. (*Reveille*), 38,

Alter, Justice Wilbur M., 272

Amalgamated Order of Mavericks, 107, 108, 109,

American DeForest Wireless Telegraph Company, 93

American Federation of Labor, 139

American Furniture, 90

American House (hotel), 42, 50, 109

American Press Humorists Association, 142, 143

Amole, Gene, ix, 280, 305, 308

Anti-Defamation League, 297

Arapaho (Indians), 13

Archer, Colonel James, 42

Armstrong, Police Chief Hamilton, 126, 223

Armstrong, S. T., 43

Associated Press, 102, 183, 256, 272, 274, 304

Auditorium Hotel, 55, 156

Auditorium Theater, 81, 94, 144, 146, 162, 167, 168, 180, 182, 188, 197, 207, 209, 216, 222, 228, 229, 233, 234, 235, 238, 264

Auraria, 3

Autobiography of a Curmudgeon, ix

Aviation Club, 284

Avril, Charles, 129

D

Dailey, John, xvi

Damon Runyon Award, 314, 322, 323, 324

Daniels & Fisher (also Daniels & Associates), 90, 159, 179, 197, 261, 266, 308

Daniels, Bill, 308

Dashwood, Rowena (Miss Pike's Peak), 238

Davidson, Mrs. Eva, 32

Davis, Dr. B. F., 114, 235

Davis, Burt (Denver City Clerk), 169

Davis, Dick, 284

Davis, Herndon, 275, 278, 279, 312

Davis, Tim, 247

Davis, Walter Juan, 85, 88

Dawson, Thomas F. (Denver Press Club historian), Dedication page, 31, 42, 47, 256, 257, 258

Day, Eddie C., 266

DeForest, Dr. Lee, 93

Deasy, John, 295, 300

Debs, Eugene V., 128

Deland, Thorndike, 216

Dellenbaugh, "Professor", 31

Democratic National Convention, 139, 143, 144, 145, 146

Dempsey, Jack, 127, 268

Denham Block, 212, 221

Denham Theatre, 198, 215, 279

Denver Ad Club, 94

Denver Athletic Club, 149, 150, 166, 197, 206, 208, 231, 232, 248, 264, 277, 284, 296, 300, 303

Denver Brewery, 42

Denver Broncos, 284

Denver Chamber of Commerce (also see Board of Trade), 20, 59, 87, 93, 103, 136, 146, 178, 188, 206, 208, 216, 236, 296

Denver Chamber of Commerce Building, 296

Denver Christian Blue Ribbon Union, 72

Denver Civic Theater, 283

Denver Convention League, 140, 208

Denver Country Club, 179, 180

Denver Dry Goods, 90

Denver Elks BPOE, 93, 104, 106, 107, 121, 124, 135, 206, 208, 209, 212, 220, 232

Denver Fair and Racing Association, 158, 212

Denver Fire Department, 42, 43, 158

Denver Gas & Electric Company, 125, 189

Denver Hotel Men's Association, 100

Denver Imported Motors, 281

Denver Landmark Preservation Commission, 55, 303, 305, 306

Denver Livestock Exchange, 208, 234

Denver Motion Picture Theater (17th Street between Curtis and Arapahoe)

Denver Motor Club, 206, 208, 209, 212

Denver Moving Picture Theater (17th Street between Curtis and Arapahoe), 165

Denver National Bank, 238

Denver & Northwestern Mining Company, 96

Denver Omnibus & Cab Company, 212

Denver Optimists' Club Quartet, 234, 264

Denver Post Boys' Band, 109

Denver Press Benevolent Association, 74, 292, 298

Denver Press Club Aviation Program, 214, 284

Denver Press Club Creed, 239

Denver Press Club Frivol, 220

Elks, BPOE, 93, 104, 106, 107, 124, 135, 206, 208, 209, 212, 220, 232
Ellis, Edward S., xi
Empress Theater, 190, 198
Emrich, Detective, 54
Endicott, Arthur (billiards), 183
Ensslin, John, 302, 312, 322, 324, 328
Erlenborn, Bedt (boxer), 135, 168
Eshaya (psychic), 320, 321
Estes Park Transportation Company, 226
Evans, Governor John, 160, 166
Evening with Gershwin, 300
Exchange Bank, 31
Eyler, Dolores, 197

F

Farmer, Frank, 265
Farmer, Joseph P., 40
Farrar, Frank C., 85, 198, 205, 218, 224
Feeney, "Red", 265, 266
Feldwisch, Henry L., 64, 67, 73
Fenton, Dick, 296
Ferril, Thomas Hornsby (Colorado Poet Laureate), 135, 307, 308, 328
Field, Al G. Minstrels, 129, 131, 142, 156
Field, Eugene "Gene", 22, 55, 56, 57, 58, 62, 63, 65, 114, 142
15th Universal Congress of Peace, 112
Fillas, Jimmy, Dedication page, 279, 280, 284, 291, 292, 304
Finch, "Doc Bird", 125
1st Amendment to the U. S. Constitution, 41, 83, 322, 328
First Hundred Years: An Informal History of Denver and the Rocky Mountain News, 38, 185, 265

1st International Congress on Mental Hygiene (Washington, D. C.), 270
Fisher, Colonel C. W. (South Park railroad), 41
Fisher, T. E. (passenger agent, Colorado & Southern railroad), 160
Fitzgarrald, Lieutenant Governor Stephen R., 19
Fitzsimons Hospital, 236, 249
Flamingo Club, Las Vegas, 284
Flynn, E. J., 150
Flynn, Kevin, 302, 316
Foley's Breakfast
Foley, J. T. (concessionaire at Denver City Park), 99, 104, 105, 128
Folk, Governor Joseph F., 89
Foltz, Dr. J. F. , 48
Fontaine qui Bouille, xxii
Forbes, Russell, 198, 216
Forrester Opera House, 31, 72
Foster, Everett E., 265
Foster, Jack, 298
Fort Kearney, xvi, xxi
Fort Laramie, xviii
Fort St. Vrain, xvi, xviii
Fowler, Eugene Parrott, 186, 196, 198, 256, 282, 318, 325
Fowler, Frank (Manager, Eldorado Springs), 134, 256
Fox Centre Theater, 281
Franco, George, 293, 295, 297, 298
Franklin Mine, 105
French, Tommie (Great Western Sugar Co.), 257
Frick's Shoe Store, 33
Friederich, Philip P. (General Manager, Lakeside Park & Amusement Co.), 264
Friedman, Mayer (president, Denver Chamber of Commerce), 136

Frost, Robert, 307
Fuller, Royal Kent (*New York Herald*), 178

G

Gabbert, N. V., 276
Gahan, Johnny (saloon owner), 185
Garden of the Gods, 109
Gardner, Jimmy (boxer), 168, 183
Garland, Hamlin (author), 100
Garrity, Charles, 292
Gaudy, F. N., 221
Gavin, Justice of the Peace C. J., 169, 183
Gavin, Tom, 293, 295
Gavisk, Michael J., 22, 43, 48, 67, 68, 69
Generation X (poetry), 307
Genesee Mountain, 256
Gentlemen's Driving-and-Riding Club, 216
Georgetown Loop, 109, 140-141
Gibbons, Leo, 198
Gibson, Dan, 302
Gibson, Thomas, xv, xvii, xix, xx
Gideon, Melville (vaudeville stars with Orpheum circuit), 167
Giffen, Larry, 107
Gilpin, Governor William, 17, 18
Girvin Furniture and Auction Co., 259
Goddard, Justice L. M. (Colorado Supreme Court), 88
Goldberg, Bruce, 309, 313
Goldfield mining camps (Nevada), 128
Goldrick, Clara A., 70
Goldrick, Owen Joseph, x, 2, 3, 6, 7, 67, 69, 70
Goldrick, William, 70
Goodman, Kid (boxer), 168
Gove, "Professor" Aaron, 48
Golvin, Representative B. R., 17

Granite Block, 81
Grant, Harry, 163
Graphite propelling, 165
Graves, Bandmaster, 134
Gray, David (aka Theodore Roosevelt, Jr.), 109
Great American Desert, xix, 2
Great Depression, 74, 218, 266, 268, 273, 277
Green, Carmen, Dedication page, 310, 319, 320
Green, Chuck, 299, 302
Gregory, L. N. (sports columnist), 251
Gregory Mines, xix
Greeley, Horace, xix, 66, 113, 114, 141
Greenawalt, Mr., 260
Gridiron Breakfast, 147, 274
Gridiron Club and Foundation (Washington, D. C.), 102, 145, 147, 309
Grieve, Curley, 278
Griffin, President (Colorado Editorial Association), 237
Grimes, Captain (Englewood Volunteer Fire Department), 158
Guest, Edgar A. (poet), 230
Guggenheim, Senator Simon, 218
Guys and Dolls (by Damon Runyon), 126

H

Hager, Clarence E., 183
Hale, Jim, 278
Hall, Captain Frank, 20, 31
Hall, P. J. (Denver agent for Chicago Film Exchange), 147
Hallet, Louis (manager, Curtis Theater), 89
Hamburger Building, 221
Hamlin, C. C., 142
Hanging (caricatures), 136, 188, 198, 259, 278, 309-310, 312, 313

Printed in the United States
By Bookmasters